ENVIRONMENT AND
CULTURAL BEHAVIOR

Andrew P. Vayda,
as a Fulbright scholar, did research in New Zealand after
receiving his A.B. from Columbia in 1952. He was awarded his
Ph.D. from that university in 1956 and has since taught at the
University of British Columbia, the University of Hawaii, and
Columbia University. He is presently professor of anthropology
at Cook College, Rutgers University.

Dr. Vayda has studied cultural change in Polynesian atolls,
and in New Guinea he investigated the human ecology of the
Bismarck Mountain region. He is the author of *Maori Warfare*
and numerous articles. He is also the editor of *Peoples and
Cultures of the Pacific* and, with Anthony Leeds, *Man, Culture,
and Animals.*

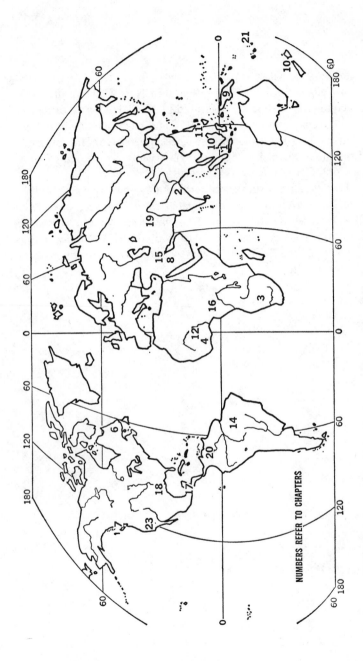

NUMBERS REFER TO CHAPTERS

Texas Press Sourcebooks in Anthropology
were originally published by the Natural History Press, a division of Doubleday and Company, Inc. Responsibility for the series now resides with the University of Texas Press, Box 7819, Austin, Texas 78712. Whereas the series has been a joint effort between the American Museum of Natural History and the Natural History Press, future volumes in the series will be selected through the auspices of the editorial offices of the University of Texas Press.

The purpose of the series will remain unchanged in its effort to make available inexpensive, up-to-date, and authoritative volumes for the student and the general reader in the field of anthropology.

Environment
and
Cultural Behavior

Ecological Studies in Cultural Anthropology

Edited by Andrew P. Vayda

University of Texas Press

Austin and London

Library of Congress Cataloging in Publication Data

Vayda, Andrew Peter, comp.
    Environment and cultural behavior.

    (Texas Press sourcebooks in anthropology; 8)
    Reprint of the ed. published for the American Museum of
Natural History by the Natural History Press. Garden City, N.Y.,
in series: American Museum sourcebooks in anthropology.
Includes bibliographies and index.
1. Human ecology—Addresses, essays, lectures. 2. Man—Influence
of environment—Addresses, essays, lectures. 3. Ethnology—
Addresses, essays, lectures. I. Title. II. Series. III. Series: American
Museum sourcebooks in anthropology.
[GF31.V38 1976]   301.31   75-43928
ISBN 0-292-72019-X

Published by arrangement with Doubleday & Company, Inc.
Previously published by the Natural History Press in cooperation
with Doubleday & Company, Inc.

CONTENTS

PART II   ORIGINS AND DEVELOPMENT

Andrew P. Vayda

INTERACTIONS BETWEEN living organisms and their environments are the subject matter of ecological studies. In the case of man, much of the behavior involved in interactions with the environment is learned behavior that has become part of the repertoire of responses of particular human groups. It is, in other words, cultural behavior. The main focus of the twenty-three studies collected in this volume is on the relation between cultural behavior and environmental phenomena. More specifically, these studies by anthropologists and other scientists are, for the most part, concerned with making cultural behavior intelligible by relating it to the material world in which it develops or occurs. The material world is of course not the only source of influences upon cultural behavior. However, it is a basic source and accordingly deserves at least as much attention as the ideologies, human valuations, antecedent cultural practices, linguistic categories, motivational patterns, personality structures, and similar factors which anthropologists and other social scientists have tended to emphasize in their attempts to make items of cultural behavior intelligible.

Two main ways of relating cultural behavior to environmental phenomena may conveniently be distinguished: either showing that items of cultural behavior function as part of systems that also include environmental phenomena or else showing that the environmental phenomena are responsible in some manner for the origin or development of the cultural behavior under investigation. By means of the first approach, we help to make cultural practices intelligible by showing something about how they work, but we are not necessarily trying to answer the quesns about their evolution to which the second approach is directed. Although a single study may utilize both approaches, I have nevertheless found it convenient to divide the studies collected here into two groups or parts, the first being primarily concerned with systemic description or analysis and the second being more focused on problems of origins or development. In only a few cases—the articles by Lee, Dumond, Leeds, and Duncan—was it difficult to decide to which of the two groups an article should be assigned.

Within Part I, the studies concerned not so much with any specific cultural practices as with more comprehensive treatments of particular ecosystems are presented first: Geertz' comparison of the swidden and wet-rice ecosystems to be found in Indonesia; Parrack's description of the flow of energy through a square mile of land in rural West Bengal; and Lee's analysis of the energy relations of a population of hunters and gatherers in Africa's Kalahari Desert. These studies are followed by ones focused upon particular items or types of cultural behavior. Alland presents an outline for the investigation of practices affecting exposure to disease organisms and illustrates this with observations made among a West African people. Stott, using data on various societies, examines cultural behavior (as well as physiological mechanisms) operating in response to pressure on food resources and serving to reduce that pressure through population limitation. Other authors offer analyses dealing with particular peoples and with how their cultural practices function within ecosystems or in relation to environmental phenomena: Moore is concerned with the divinatory rituals of the caribou-hunting Naskapi Indians of Labrador; Piddocke with the potlatch ceremonies of the Kwakiutl Indians of the northwest coast of North America; Sweet with the institutionalized camel-raiding and certain other activities of north Arabian Bedouins; Rappaport with a cycle of rituals among the Maring, a primitive agricultural people in New Guinea; Vayda with the warfare of two other agricultural peoples, the Maoris of New Zealand and the Ibans of Borneo; and Conklin with the farming techniques of the Hanunóo, shifting cultivators on Mindoro Island in the Philippines. Two authors, in their articles, are dealing not necessarily with what people actually do but rather with what they might do, i.e., with how they might optimize the yield or profits from given resources:

Gould is concerned with various possibilities in growing crops and trading cattle in Ghana and adjacent parts of West Africa, while Watt's problem is the assessment of alternative means of managing renewable natural resources under modern world conditions. The game theoretic and computer simulation techniques discussed by these two authors may of course be used not only for evaluating proposed or possible strategies for obtaining subsistence or managing resources but also for comparing the effectiveness of proposed strategies and such controversial extant ones as those used for cattle husbandry in India (Parrack in this volume and Harris 1966) and pig husbandry in the New Guinea interior (Rappaport in this volume and Vayda, Leeds, and Smith 1961).

In the final article in Part I, Wagley examines infanticide among the Tapirapé Indians of central Brazil and finds that it cannot be made intelligible by reference to contemporaneous environmental phenomena. Indeed, the trait does not seem at all suited to the people's material world. Anthropologists are often confronted with such traits. When this happens, the first analytic task, if cultural behavior is what is to be accounted for, is to investigate further to see whether the apparently maladaptive or dysfunctional trait might not actually fulfill some important but not readily discernible adaptive functions in relation to extant environmental phenomena. Sometimes, as in the cases of cattle husbandry in India (Parrack in this volume) and primitive warfare in New Zealand and Borneo (Vayda in this volume), some evidence of such functions will be found, but, at other times, it will not. In the latter event, the further analytic task is to look to the past to see whether the trait in question might not have been functional in an environment or ecosystem that no longer exists. The fact that Wagley has performed this task enables him to suggest that Tapirapé infanticide formerly contributed to the population stability which was required for the operation of various social units important in food production and distribution as well as in ceremonies. As for the persistence of infanticide in an environment significantly altered by the arrival of Europeans and their decimating diseases, this may be regarded as an example of lag in adaptation, such lag being an important and often noted aspect of cultural evolution (see the discussions in

Hawley 1950:27–28; Campbell 1965:35; Vayda 1969:117) but one with which the present volume is not primarily concerned.

Within Part II, several articles concerning, among other things, the origin, development, or spread of types of subsistence are presented first: Flannery relates the beginnings of food production in Mesopotamia to the characteristics of a variety of southwest Asian environments; Wiesenfeld explores interactions of genes, cultural practices, and environmental conditions in the development of root- and tree-crop cultivation in sub-Saharan Africa; and Dumond, as part of his argument that shifting cultivation could have provided a sufficient economic base for Maya civilization, presents data from various societies on the conditions (particularly with regard to land availability) under which a transition from extensive to intensive agriculture takes place. Kroeber and Barth also deal with the influence of environmental factors on the development or spread of subsistence patterns—maize cultivation in native North America in the case of Kroeber's study and systems of single-cropping, double-cropping, and two kinds of herding in Swat, North Pakistan in the case of Barth's article. These two articles are of special interest as illustrations of the uses and limitations of the culture-area approach in studying environmental influences on cultural phenomena.

The authors of the remaining articles are concerned with the origin or development of a variety of cultural practices. Leeds' objective is to identify the conditions that foster and those that inhibit the development of chiefly authority and its exercise, and, to this end, he examines in detail a South American Indian case of ineffective chieftainship. Sahlins uses Fijian materials to explore the hypothesis that the possession and use of concentrated rather than scattered resources is conducive to living in independent rather than extended family households. Whiting presents a hypothesis of a long causal chain leading from climatic factors in the rainy tropics to the practice of circumcision and uses data from a large sample of societies to test the hypothesis. And, finally, Duncan, in addition to arguing for the greater use of the concept of ecosystem by social scientists, examines some of the cultural behavior that is developing in response to air pollution in modern Los Angeles. His discussion, with which the book ends, serves to indicate that the study of environment and cultural behavior, illustrated in this volume mainly with cases concerning the disappearing world of primitive man, will have a place—perhaps a very important one—in the world of the future.

A Note on Diversity. The first criterion applied in selecting articles for inclusion in this volume has already been indicated: that the articles should be concerned, at least to some extent, with making cultural behavior intelligible by relating it to the material world in which it develops or occurs. Ecological studies that limit themselves to other concerns—for example, to showing the influence of cultural values or ideas on the use of resources —could not be included. The goal in selecting among the large number of valuable studies meeting this first criterion was that the volume as a whole should be characterized by diversity in the geographical areas, types or levels of economy, and categories of cultural behavior dealt with and in the methods of investigation and analysis used. I think it can be fairly claimed that this diversity has been achieved. The populations whose cultural behavior is examined include ones from most of the major world areas: North America (Moore, Piddocke, Duncan), South America (Wagley, Leeds), Africa (Lee, Alland, Gould, Wiesenfeld), mainland Asia (Parrack, Sweet, Flannery, Barth), and Oceania (Geertz, Rappaport, Vayda, Conklin, Sahlins). The majority of the populations are, as in the world today, agriculturalists, but also included are hunters and gatherers (Lee, Moore), fishing populations (Piddocke), and pastoralists (Sweet, Barth). The cultural behavior dealt with includes practices assignable to various traditional categories of cultural anthropology, e.g., economics (Lee, Piddocke, Gould, and others), social organization (especially Wagley and Sahlins), government (Leeds), and religion (Moore, Rappaport). And, although no attempt was made to include articles representative of all approaches that have been historically important in the development of ecological research in cultural anthropology and such related fields as geography and sociology (see Vayda and Rappaport 1968 for discussion of some of these approaches), the methods used in the studies included in the volume do range from intensive system-specific analyses (e.g., Rappaport) to extensive cross-cultural surveys (e.g., Whiting); from detailed historical reconstruction (e.g., Flannery) to essentially non-historical approaches (many of the articles in Part

I); and from traditional ethnographic ordering of data to data-processing by computers (Watt).

Acknowledgments. All but two of the articles—those by Parrack and Alland—have been previously published. The original place of publication is given in a footnote on the first page of each article. Two of the studies—those by Geertz and Kroeber—are sections of published monographs, and Duncan's article, as it first appeared, had some additional discussion not included here. All of the other previously published articles and their bibliographies are reprinted here in their entirety.

BIBLIOGRAPHY

Campbell, Donald T.
   1965 "Variation and Selective Retention in Socio-Cultural Evolution,"
   in Herbert R. Barringer et al. (eds.), *Social Change in Developing
   Areas: A Reinterpretation of Evolutionary Theory*. Cambridge, Mass.:
   Schenkman.
Harris, Marvin
   1966 "The Cultural Ecology of India's Sacred Cattle." *Current An-
   thropology*, 7:51–66.
Hawley, Amos H.
   1950 *Human Ecology*. New York: Ronald Press.
Vayda, Andrew P.
   1969 "An Ecological Approach in Cultural Anthropology." *Bucknell Review*, 17 (1): 112–19.
Vayda, Andrew P., Anthony Leeds, and David B. Smith
   1961 "The Place of Pigs in Melanesian Subsistence," in Viola E.
   Garfield (ed.), *Proceedings of the 1961 Annual Spring Meeting of the
   American Ethnological Society*. Seattle: University of Washington Press.
Vayda, Andrew P., and Roy A. Rappaport
   1968 "Ecology, Cultural and Noncultural," in James A. Clifton (ed.),
   *Introduction to Cultural Anthropology: Essays in the Scope and Meth-
   ods of the Science of Man*. Boston: Houghton Mifflin.

Part I / SYSTEMS IN OPERATION

1 TWO TYPES OF ECOSYSTEMS

Clifford Geertz

INNER VS. OUTER INDONESIA

A HANDFUL OF mere statistics of the most routine, humdrum sort can sketch a picture of the basic characteristics of the Indonesian archipelago as a human habitat with more immediacy than pages of vivid prose about steaming volcanoes, serpentine river basins, and still, dark jungles. The land area of the country amounts to about one and one-half million square kilometers, or about that of Alaska. Of this only about one hundred and thirty-two thousand square kilometers are in Java, the rest making up what are usually called "the Outer Islands"—Sumatra, Borneo (Kalimantan), Celebes (Sulawesi), the Moluccas, and the Lesser Sundas (Nusa Tenggara). But the country's total population (1961) is around ninety-seven million, while Java's population alone is about sixty-three million. That is to say, about 9 percent of the land area supports nearly two-thirds of the population; or, reciprocally, more than 90 percent of the land area supports approximately one-third of the population. Put in density terms, Indonesia as a whole has about 60 persons per square kilometer; Java has 480, and the more crowded areas of the central and east-central parts of the island more than a thousand. On the other hand, the whole of Indonesia minus Java (i.e., the Outer Islands) has a density of around twenty-four per square kilometer. To summarize: all over, 60; the Outer Islands, 24; Java,

Chapter 2 of Clifford Geertz, *Agricultural Involution*, Berkeley: University of California Press, 1963. Reprinted by permission of the author and publisher.

480: if ever there was a tail which wagged a dog, Java is the tail, Indonesia the dog (Sumaniwata 1962).[1]

The same plenum and vacuum pattern of contrast between Java and the Outer Islands appears in land utilization. Almost 70 percent of Java is cultivated yearly—one of the highest proportions of cropland to total area of any extensive region in the world—but only about 4 percent of the Outer Islands. Estate agriculture aside, of the minute part of the Outer Islands which is cultivated, about 90 percent is farmed by what is variously known as swidden agriculture, shifting cultivation, or slash-and-burn farming, in which fields are cleared, farmed for one or more years, and then allowed to return to bush for fallowing, usually eventually to be recultivated. On Java, where nearly half the smallholder's crop area is under irrigation, virtually no swidden agriculture remains. In the irrigated regions, field land is in wet-rice terraces, about half of them double-cropped, either with more wet rice or with one or several secondary dry crops. In the unirrigated regions, these dry crops (maize, cassava, sweet potatoes, peanuts, dry rice, vegetables, and others) are grown in a crop-and-fallow regime. Production statistics present, of course, the same picture: in 1956 approximately 63 percent of Indonesia's rice, 74 percent of her maize, 70 percent of her cassava, 60 percent of her sweet potatoes, 86 percent of her peanuts, and 90 percent of her soya beans were produced in Java (Metcalf 1952; Central Bureau of Statistics of Indonesia 1957:51).[2]

Actually, this fundamental axis of ecological contrast in Indonesia is not altogether accurately demarcated when one phrases it, following the received practice of the census takers, simply in terms of Java (and Madura) versus the Outer Islands, because in fact the "Javanese" pattern is found in southern Bali and western Lombok as well, and is but weakly represented in the southwestern corner of Java (South Bantam and South Priangan) where a pattern more like that of the Outer Islands, including a certain amount of swidden, is found. Thus, we might better refer to the contrast as one between "Inner Indonesia"—north-

---

[1] Madura is included with Java in the calculations but the transitional area of West New Guinea (Irian) is not included. For a useful general summary of Indonesian demographic realities, see Mochtar et al. 1956.
[2] Commercial crop cultivation shows, however, a sharply contrasting pattern.

west, central, and east Java, south Bali, and west Lombok; and "Outer Indonesia"—the rest of the Outer Islands plus southwest Java, which do in fact form more or less of an arc pivoted on central Java. (See Map.) Such a division is, in any case, a gross one which needs modification in detail: patches of relatively intensive irrigation agriculture are found at either tip,

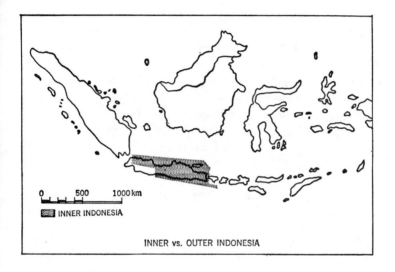

INNER INDONESIA

INNER vs. OUTER INDONESIA

around Lake Toba, and in the western highlands in Sumatra as well as in the southwest arm of the Celebes, for example, and eastern Madura deviates somewhat from the Javanese norm (Terra 1958). But it does lead, in a broad and general way, to a fruitful discrimination of two different sorts of ecosystems with two different sorts of dynamics—one centering on swidden agriculture, one on wet-rice agriculture—in terms of which the striking differences in population density, modes of land use, and agricultural productivity can be understood.

SWIDDEN

As Conklin (1957:149) has pointed out, much of the inadequate treatment swidden agriculture has received in the literature is a result of the fact that characterizations of it have tended to be negatively phrased. Thus, Gourou (1956) outlines as its four most distinctive features: (1) it is practiced on very poor tropical soils; (2) it represents an elementary agricultural technique which utilizes no tool except the axe; (3) it is marked by a low density of population; and (4) it involves a low level of consumption. Similarly, Pelzer (1945:16ff.) says that it is marked by a lack of tillage, less labor input than other methods of cultivation, the nonutilization of draft animals and manuring, and the absence of a concept of private landownership. For Dobby (1954:347–79), it represents "a special stage in the evolution from hunting and food gathering to sedentary farming," this specialness evidently consisting of such null traits as nonrelation to pastoral pursuits and the production of very little which is of trading or commercial significance. And for many, by far its most outstanding feature is that singled out by Spate—namely, that its practice is "attended by serious deforestation and soil erosion" (Spate 1945:27, quoted in Leach 1954:22). Aside from the fact that most of these depreciatory statements are dubious as unqualified generalizations (and a few are simply incorrect), they are not of much help in understanding how swidden farming systems work.

In ecological terms, the most distinctive positive characteristic of swidden agriculture (and the characteristic most in contrast to wet-rice agriculture) is that it is integrated into and, when genuinely adaptive, maintains the general structure of the pre-existing natural ecosystem into which it is projected, rather than creating and sustaining one organized along novel lines and displaying novel dynamics. In the tropics, to which, for reasons we may postpone considering, this form of cultivation is today largely confined, the systemic congruity between the biotic community man artificially establishes on his swidden plot and that which exists there in stable climax independent of his interference (in the main, some variety of tropical forest) is striking. Any form of agriculture represents an effort to alter a given ecosystem in such a way as to increase the flow of energy to man: but a wet-rice terrace accomplishes this through a bold reworking of the natural landscape; a swidden through a canny imitation of it.

The first systemic characteristic in which a swidden plot simulates a tropical forest is in degree of generalization. By a generalized ecosystem is meant one in which a great variety of species exists, so that the energy produced by the system is distributed among a relatively large number of different species, each of which is represented by a relatively small number of individuals. If, on the contrary, the system is one with a relatively small number of species, each of which is represented by a relatively large number of individuals, it is said to be specialized. Put somewhat more technically, if the ratio between number of species and number of organisms in a biotic community is called its *diversity index,* then a generalized ecosystem is one characterized by a community with a high diversity index, a specialized one by a community with a low diversity index. Natural communities tend to vary widely in their degree of generalization, or the size of their diversity index: a tropical forest, and in particular a rain forest, is a very generalized, very diverse community, with an enormous variety of plant and animal species sporadically represented; a tundra is characterized by a very specialized, uniform community, with relatively few species but, at least in the subarctic, a large number of clustered individuals.[3]

Much of the most effective human utilization of the natural habitat consists of changing generalized communities into more specialized ones, as when natural ponds containing a wide variety of green plants, aquatic animals, and fishes are transformed into managed ones in which the number of types of primary plant producers is sharply reduced to those which will support a few select types of fish edible by man. The rice terrace, which can, in these terms, be viewed as a sort of slowly drained, managed pond focused on an edible plant, is an outstanding example of artificially created specialization. The reverse process, increased generalization, also occurs, of course, as when man introduces into a temperate grassland area (for example, the American prairie) a wide variety of interrelated domestic plants and animals, which, though they constitute a much more diverse community than that indigenous to the area, nonetheless prove to be viable within it.

Still other human adaptations, however, attempt to utilize the habitat not through altering its diversity index, but through more

---

[3] These concepts are taken from Odum 1959:ii, 50–51, 77, 281–83, 316, and 435–37.

or less maintaining its over-all pattern of composition while changing selected items of its content; that is, by substituting certain humanly preferred species for others in functional roles ("niches") within the pre-existing biotic community. This is not to say that such adaptations do not seriously alter the indigenous ecosystem (as, in a gross sense, most hunting and gathering adaptations do not), or that their general effect on the balance of nature may not sometimes be a radical one; but merely that they alter the indigenous ecosystem by seeking to replace it with a system which, although some of its concrete elements are different, is similar to it in form, rather than by a system significantly more specialized or more generalized. Large-scale cattle herding during the nineteenth century on the previously buffalo-dominated southern and western plains is an example of this type of adaptation within a specialized system. Swidden agriculture is certainly an example of it within a generalized one.

The extraordinarily high diversity index of the tropical forest, the kind of natural climax community which still characterizes the bulk of Outer Indonesia, has already been mentioned. Though there are probably more floral species in this region than any other of comparable size in the world (van Steenis has estimated that between twenty and thirty thousand species of flowering plants, belonging to about 2,500 families, can be found in the archipelago), continuous stands of trees or other plants are rare, and the occurrence of as many as thirty different species of trees within a hundred square yards is not at all uncommon (van Steenis 1935; Dobby 1954:61).[4] Similarly, on about a three-acre swidden plot in the Philippines (detailed field studies are lacking for Indonesia as such) Conklin (1954) has seen as many as forty different sorts of crops growing simultaneously, and one informant drew an ideal plot containing at one time forty-eight basic kinds

---

[4] This floral diversity is paralleled by an equally great wealth of fauna: the industrious as well as famous naturalist A. R. Wallace found 200 species of beetles in a square mile of Singapore forest and brought back a total of more than 125,000 animal specimens from the general Malaysian region (Robequain 1954:38–59). For a general ecological analysis of tropical forest plant diversity, see Richards 1952:231–68. More popular accounts, but which include some discussion of fauna as well, are Bates 1952:175–211; and Collins 1959.

of plants. The people of the area, the Hanunóo of Mindoro, distinguish more than sixteen hundred different plant types (which is a finer classification than that employed by systematic botanists), including the astounding number of four hundred thirty cultivates.[5] Conklin's vivid description of what a Hanunóo swidden in full swing looks like gives an excellent picture of the degree to which this agriculture apes the generalized diversity of the jungle which it temporarily replaces:

> Hanunóo agriculture emphasizes the intercropping of many types of domesticated plants. During the late rice-growing seasons, a cross section view of a new [plot] illustrates the complexity of this type of swidden cropping (which contrasts remarkably with the type of field cropping more familiar to temperate zone farmers). At the sides and against the swidden fences there is found an association dominated by low, climbing or sprawling legumes (asparagus beans, sieva beans, hyacinth beans, string beans, and cowpeas). As one goes out into the center of the swidden, one passes through an association dominated by ripening grain but also including numerous maturing root crops, shrub legumes and tree crops. Pole-climbing yam vines, heart-shaped taro leaves, ground-hugging sweet potato vines, and shrublike manioc stems are the only visible signs of the large store of starch staples which is building up underground, while the grain crops fruit a meter or so above the swidden floor before giving way to the more widely spaced and less rapidly-maturing tree crops. Over the first two years a new swidden produces a steady stream of harvestable food in the form of seed grains, pulses, sturdy tubers, and underground stems, and bananas, from a meter below to more than 2 meters above the ground level. And many other vegetable, spice and nonfood crops are grown simultaneously.[6]

The second formal characteristic common to the tropical-forest and swidden-agriculture ecosystems is the ratio of the quantity of nutrients locked up in living forms (that is, the biotic com-

---

[5] Conklin 1954. Other valuable field studies of swidden in Malaysia include: Freeman 1955 (on diversity, pp. 51–54); and Geddes 1954 (on diversity, pp. 64–65). A brief description of swidden-making in East Indonesia can be found in Goethals 1961:25–29.

[6] Conklin 1957:147. Conklin estimates that in the first and most active year of the swidden cycle up to 150 specific crop types may be planted at one time or another.

munity) to that stored in the soil (that is, the physical substratum): in both it is extremely high. Though, as with the
tropical forest itself, much variation is found, tropical soils are
in general extensively laterized. As precipitation in most of the
humid, rain-heavy tropics greatly exceeds evaporation, there is
a significant downward percolation through the soil of relatively
pure, lukewarm water, a type of leaching process whose main
effect is to carry away the more highly soluble silicates and
bases, while leaving behind a dreary mixture of iron oxides and
stable clays. Carried to an extreme, this produces ferralite, a
porous, crumbly, bright-red, acidic soil which, however excellent
the Indonesians find it for making bricks without straw, is of much
less value from the point of view of the support of plant life.
Protected to a certain extent by the shielding effects of the thick
vegetation cover, most tropical soils have not developed such a
serious case of what Gourou (1953b:21) has called pedological
leprosy. But the great majority of them, having been exposed to
these ultrastable climatic conditions over very long periods of
time, are markedly leached, and thus seriously impoverished in
minerals requisite to the sustenance of life.[7]

This apparent and oft-remarked paradox of a rich plant and
animal life supported on a thin soil is resolved by the fact that
the cycling of material and energy among the various components
of a tropical forest is both so rapid and so nearly closed that only
the uppermost layers of the soil are directly and significantly involved in it, and they but momentarily. The intense humidity and
more or less even distribution of rainfall, the equable, moderately
elevated temperatures, the small month-to-month variations in
day length and amount of sunlight—all the monotonous con-
stancies of the tropics—are conducive to a high rate of both decomposition and regeneration of animal and vegetable material.
Speedy decomposition is insured by the multiplication of bacteria, fungi and other decomposers and transformers which the
humid conditions favor, as well as by the multitude of herbiver-
ous animals and insects who are so ravenous that, as Bates
(1952:209) remarks, virtually "every fruit and every leaf [in

---

[7] This paragraph and those immediately following are based mainly on
Richards 1952:203–26; Dobby 1954:74–84; and Gourou 1953b:13–24.
However, much remains to be learned about soil factors in the tropics.

the tropical forest] has been eaten by something." An enormous amount of dead matter is thus always accumulating on the forest floor—leaves, branches, vines, whole plants, faunal remains and wastes; but their rapid decay and the high absorptive capacity of the luxuriant vegetation means that the nutrients in this dead organic matter are reutilized almost immediately, rather than remaining stored to any great extent or for any great length of time in the soil where they are prey to the leaching process.

The role of humus in creating a topsoil storehouse of nutrient materials in colloidal form to be drawn upon gradually as needed, which looms so prominently in ecosystems at higher latitudes, is here minimized; organic materials rarely extend in significant quantity more than a few inches beneath the forest floor, because the nutrients set free by the rapid decay of dead matter are quickly taken up again by the shallow, splayed root systems of the intensely competitive plants. Thus, despite the heavy rains, loss of nutrients due to runoff in this process of transfer is very slight, so that quite marginal additions of energy from outside the system through nitrogen fixing in leguminous trees and adsorption of minerals released by rock decomposition are themselves enough to compensate for it. The climax community, once established, through still imperfectly understood processes of ecological succession, is thus virtually self-perpetuating. By maintaining most of its energy in the form of living things most of the time, the tropical-forest ecosystem is able to prevent any significant escape of energy across its boundaries and to circumvent the problem of impoverished soil conditions by feeding largely upon itself.

Swidden agriculture operates in essentially this same supernatant, plant-to-plant, direct cycling manner. The burning of the slashed plot is at base a means both of accelerating the process of decay and of directing that process in such a fashion that the nutrients it releases are channeled as fully as possible into certain selected food-producing plants. A significant proportion of the mineral energy upon which swidden cultivates, and especially the grains, draw for their growth comes from the ash remains of the fired forest, rather than from the soil as such, so that the completeness with which a plot is burnt is a crucial factor in determining its yield, a fact of which probably all swidden cultivators are aware.[8] A good burn, in turn, is dependent on the one hand upon the care and thoroughness with which the vegetation has been cut, and on the other upon the dryness of the weather during the cutting-planting period. Over the thoroughness of the cutting the cultivators have a high degree of control and, though different groups of swidden agriculturalists, as any other type of farmers, vary widely in their skills, yet their felling, slashing, trimming techniques, as well as their actual firing methods, are commonly well developed. Over the weather they have, of course, no control (though they are usually adept at estimating it), and intense ritual activity is commonly directed toward preventing rain, or at least maintaining confidence, during the anxious, all-important few weeks between cutting and sowing. At any rate, the primary function of "slash and burn" activities is not mere clearing of the land (the use of the term "clearing," with respect to swiddens is actually somewhat misleading) but rather the transfer of the rich store of nutrients locked up in the prolific vegetation of the tropical forest to a botanical complex whose general ecological productivity, in the sense of the total energy flow in the system, may be substantially smaller but whose yield to man is a great deal larger.[9]

General ecological productivity is lower because this transfer is less efficient than that which takes place under natural conditions of decay and regeneration. Here, a large amount of energy does escape across the boundaries of the system. Gourou (1953b:26) estimates that between six and nine hundred pounds of nitrogen alone go up in smoke in the burning of a single acre of forest; and, despite the utmost shrewdness in judging the weather and the greatest speed in firing and planting, much ash is inevitably

---

[8] For example, among the Mandaya of eastern Mindanao, those cultivating over 1,700 feet where burning is impossible because of the absence of a dry period harvest about 10 to 15 cavans of rice per hectare, while those cultivating in lower areas where burning is possible average 30–35 (Aram A. Yengoyan, personal communication). In general, however, the precise effect of firing as a fertilizing mechanism remains to be investigated experimentally, like so much else about swidden.

[9] This analysis is based on the descriptions of swidden techniques given in Conklin 1957:49–72; Freeman 1955:40–48; and Hose and MacDougal 1912. For the distinction between ecological productivity and yield to man, see Clarke 1954:482–500.

washed away by the rains before it can be utilized by the cultivates, fast growing as they tend to be. Further, as the cultivates are less woody in substance than those indigenous to the forest, they do not form a very appropriate material for the technique of accelerating and channeling nutrient transfer through the deliberate production of ash, and so the firing process is not continuously repeatable. The result is, of course, the well-known drop in fertility on swidden plots (rice output of south Sumatran plots is known to drop as much as 80 percent between a first and second cropping), and the surrender of the plot to natural regeneration (Pelzer 1945:16).

But, despite the fact that secondary forest growth is, at least in the earlier phases of regeneration, notably less luxuriant than primary, if the period of cultivation is not too long and the period of fallow long enough, an equilibrated, nondeteriorating and reasonably productive farming regime (productive in the sense of yield to man) can be sustained, again to a significant degree irrespective of the rather impoverished soil base on which it rests (Conklin 1957:152; Leach 1954:24; and Geddes 1954:65–68). The burned forest provides most of the resources for the cultivates; the decaying cultivates (nothing but the edible portions of plants is removed from the plot) and the natural processes of secondary succession, including invasions from the surrounding forest within which plots are usually broadly dispersed rather than tightly clustered, provide most of the resources for the rapidly recuperating forest. As in the undisturbed forest, "what happens" in an adapted swidden ecosystem happens predominantly in the biotic community rather than in the physical substratum.

Finally, a third systemic property in which the tropical forest and the swidden plot tend to converge is general architecture: both are "closed-cover" structures. The tropical forest has often been compared to a parasol, because of the effectiveness with which the tall, closely packed, large-crowned, evergreen trees both deflect the rain and shut out the sun so as to protect the soil against the worst effects of the leaching process, against baking, and against erosion. Photosynthesis takes place almost entirely at the very top of the forest, from a hundred to a hundred and fifty feet up, and so most of the growing things (as well as

much of the faunal life) reach desperately toward this upper
canopy seeking their small place in the sun, either by climbing,
as the thousands of woody lianas and other vines, by finding an
epiphytic perch, as the orchids and ferns, or by mere giantism, as
the dominant trees and the bamboos, leaving the darkened floor
relatively free of living plants (Bates 1952:200–3). In a swidden,
this canopy is, of course, radically lowered, but much of its
umbrella-like continuity is maintained, in part by planting cultigens not in an open field, crop-row manner, but helter-skelter in a
tightly woven, dense botanical fabric, in part by planting shrub
and tree crops of various sorts (coconuts, areca, jakfruit, banana,
papaya, and today in more commercial areas rubber, pepper,
abaca, and coffee), and in part by leaving some trees standing.
In such a way, excessive exposure of the soil to rain and sun
is minimized and weeding, exhausting task in any case, is brought
within reasonable proportions because light penetration to the
floor is kept down to a much lower level than in an open-field
system.[10]

In sum, a description of swidden farming as a system in which
"a natural forest is transformed into a harvestable forest" seems
a rather apt one (Kampto Utomo 1957:129). With respect to
degree of generalization (diversity), to proportion of total system
resources stored in living forms, and to closed-cover protection
of an already weakened soil against the direct impact of rain
and sun, the swidden plot is not a "field" at all in the proper
sense, but a miniaturized tropical forest, composed mainly of
food-producing and other useful cultivates. Yet, as is well known,
though less well understood, the equilibrium of this domesticated
form of forest system is a great deal more delicate than that of
the natural form. Given less than ideal conditions, it is highly

---

[10] For an excellent description of the concurrent employment by recent
immigrant Javanese farmers of an open-field system and by indigenous
farmers of a closed-field one in the Lampong area of south Sumatra,
and of the essential defeat of the former by the weeding problem, see
Kampto Utomo 1957:127–32. Some forms of partial swidden-farming—
i.e., where swidden is auxiliary to other forms of cultivation—are, however,
open-field systems; while integral systems—i.e., where swidden is the sole
form of cultivation—commonly are not. I owe this point to Harold Conklin.

susceptible to breakdown into an irreversible process of ecological deterioration; that is, a pattern of change leading not to repeated forest recuperation but to a replacement of tree cover altogether by the notorious *imperata* savannah grass which has turned so much of Southeast Asia into a green desert.[11]

Swidden cultivation may turn thus maladaptive in at least three ways: by an increase in population which causes old plots to be recultivated too soon; by prodigal or inept agricultural practices which sacrifice future prospects to present convenience; and by an extension into an insufficiently humid environment in which the more deciduous forests have a much slower recovery rate and in which clearing fires are likely to burn off accidentally great stands of timber.[12] The population problem has been much discussed, though exact figures are difficult to obtain. Van Beukering (1947) has put the population ceiling for swidden in Indonesia over-all at about 50 per square kilometer, Conklin (1957:146–47) estimates that the Hanunóo area can carry 48 per square kilometer without deterioration, and Freeman (1955: 134–35) calculates 20–25 as the maximum in his central Sarawak region; but it is not known to what degree the various local population densities in Outer Indonesia now exceed critical limits and are producing grassland climaxes as a result of the need for more rapid recultivation.[13] With the population of the region now increasing at 2 percent or more annually, however, the problem seems likely to become overtly pressing in the not too distant future; glib references to Outer Indonesia as "grossly under-populated" constitute a simplistically quantitative and ecologically naive view of demography.

The fact that wasteful or inept methods may be destructive to the long-run equilibrium of swidden agriculture not only under-

---

[11] Gourou (1953a:288) estimates that about 40 percent of the Philippines and 30 percent of Indonesia are covered with *imperata,* presumably nearly all of it caused by man. These figures may be somewhat high, however: Pelzer (1945:19) estimates the Philippine grassland percentage at 18.

[12] A full consideration of the factors relating to the breakdown of the swidden cycle into a deflected grassland succession would need, of course, to consider topographical and edaphic variables, the role of animal husbandry, associated hunting practices, and so on. For such a micro-analysis, see Conklin 1959.

[13] These various figures are all somewhat differently calculated.

scores the wide variation in proficiency with which different groups of shifting cultivators operate, but, even more important, demonstrates that cultural, social, and psychological variables are at least as crucial as environmental ones in determining the stability of human modes of adaptation. An example of such a thriftless use of resources by swidden farmers is provided by Freeman (1955:135–41), who says that the Iban have been less shifting cultivators than *mangeurs de bois*. Located in a primary forest area into which they have fairly recently expanded at the expense of indigenous tribes, the Iban are well below maximum population densities. But they nevertheless seriously overcultivate, often using a single plot three years in succession or returning to a fallowed one within five years, and thereby causing widespread deforestation. The reasons for this overcultivation are various, including an historically rooted conviction that there are always other forests to conquer, a warrior's view of natural resources as plunder to be exploited, a large village settlement pattern which makes shifting between plots a more than usually onerous task, and, perhaps, a superior indifference toward agricultural proficiency. But, again, to what degree such prodigality exists among the swidden agriculturalists of Outer Indonesia is virtually unknown.

As for the climatic factor, the most highly generalized, evergreen, closed-cover tropical forest, commonly specified as "rain forest" is chiefly characteristic of equatorial lowland areas where a marked dry season is absent; as one moves toward higher-latitude areas with a marked dry season, it shades off, more or less gradually, into a shorter, more open, less diverse, and at least partly deciduous variety of tropical forest, usually called "monsoon forest" (Dobby 1954:62, 65–70).[14] The delicacy of swidden equilibrium increases at equal pace with this transition toward a more subtropical environment because of the steadily diminishing power of the natural community rapidly to reconstitute itself after human interference. The greater ease, and uncontrollability, with which such drier woodlands burn, fanned often by stronger winds than are common in the rain forest areas, only increases the danger of deterioration to grassland or scrub savannah and,

---

[14] Variation in tropical forest composition is also affected by altitude, soil, and local land mass configurations. For a full discussion, see Richards 1952:315–74.

in time, by erosion to an almost desert-like state. The southeast portion of the Indonesian archipelago, the Lesser Sundas, where the parching Australian monsoon blows for several months a year, has been particularly exposed to this general process of ecological decline, and in some places devastation is widespread (see Ormeling 1956). All in all, the critical limits within which swidden cultivation is an adaptive agricultural regime in Outer Indonesia are fairly narrow.

SAWAH

The micro-ecology of the flooded paddy field has yet to be written. Though extensive and detailed researches into the botanical characteristics of wet rice, its natural requirements, the techniques of its cultivation, the methods by means of which it is processed into food, and its nutritional value have been made, the fundamental dynamics of the individual terrace as an integrated ecosystem remain unclear. (For an encylopedic summary of such researches, see Grist 1959.) The contrast between such a terrace—an artificial, maximally specialized, continuous-cultivation, open-field structure to a swidden plot could hardly be more extreme; yet how it operates as an organized unit is far from being understood. Knowledge remains on the one hand specialized and technical, with developed, even experimental, analyses of breeding and selection, water supply and control, manuring and weeding, and so on, and, on the other, commonsensical, resting on a vast, unexamined accumulation of proverbial, rice-roots wisdom concerning similar matters. But a coherent description of the manner in which the various ecological components of a terrace interrelate to form a functioning productive system remains noticeable by its absence. So far as I am aware, a genuinely detailed and circumstantial analysis of any actual wet-rice field (or group of fields) as a set of "living organisms and nonliving substances interacting to produce an exchange of material between the living and the non-living parts" does not exist in the literature.[15]

---

[15] The quotation is the formal definition of an ecosystem given in Odum 1959:10.

The most striking feature of the terrace as an ecosystem, and the one most in need of explanation, is its extraordinary stability or durability, the degree to which it can continue to produce, year after year, and often twice in one year, a virtually undiminished yield (Gourou 1953b:100 and 1953a:74). "Rice grown under irrigation is a unique crop," the geographer Murphey has written,

> . . . soil fertility does affect its yield, as does fertilization, but it does not appear to exhaust the soil even over long periods without fertilization, and in many cases it may actually improve the soil. On virgin soils a rapid decline in yield usually takes place, in the absence of fertilization, within the first two or three years, but after ten or twenty years the yield tends to remain stable more or less indefinitely. This has been borne out by experiments in various parts of tropical Asia, by increased knowledge of the processes involved, and by accumulated experience. On infertile soils and with inadequate fertilization the field stabilizes at a very low level, as is the case now in Ceylon and most of South Asia, but it does stabilize. Why this should be so is not yet entirely understood (Murphey 1957).

The answer to this puzzle almost certainly lies in the paramount role played by water in the dynamics of the rice terrace. Here, the characteristic thinness of tropical soils is circumvented through the bringing of nutrients onto the terrace by the irrigation water to replace those drawn from the soil; through the fixation of nitrogen by the blue-green algae which proliferate in the warm water; through the chemical and bacterial decomposition of organic material, including the remains of harvested crops in that water; through the aeration of the soil by the gentle movement of the water in the terrace; and, no doubt, through other ecological functions performed by irrigation which are as yet unknown.[16] Thus, although, contrary to appearances, the paddy plant actually requires no more water than dry-land crops for simple transpirational purposes, "the supply and control of water . . . is the most important aspect of irrigated paddy culti-

---

[16] In addition to the mentioned Grist (esp. pp. 28–49), Gourou, and Murphey references, useful, if unsystematic, material on the micro-ecology of irrigated rice can be found in Pelzer 1945:47–51, and especially in Matsuo 1955:109–12.

vation; given an adequate and well-controlled water supply the crop will grow in a wide range of soils and in many climates. It is therefore more important than the type of soil" (Grist 1959: 28, 29).

This primary reliance on the material which envelops the biotic community (the "medium") for nourishment rather than on the solid surface in which it is rooted (the "substratum"), makes possible the same maintenance of an effective agricultural regime on indifferent soils that the direct cycling pattern of energy exchange makes possible on swiddens.[17] Even that soil quality which is of clearest positive value for paddy growing, heavy consistency which irrigation water will not readily percolate away, is more clearly related to the semiaquatic nature of the cultivation process than to its nutritional demands, and paddy can be effectively grown on soils which are "unbelievably poor in plant nutrients" (Pendleton 1947, quoted in Grist 1959:11). This is not to say that natural soil fertility has no effect on wet-rice yields, but merely that, as "paddy soils tend to acquire their own special properties after long use," a low natural fertility is not in itself a prohibitive factor if adequate water resources are available (Murphey 1957). Like swidden, wet-rice cultivation is essentially an ingenious device for the agricultural exploitation of a habitat in which heavy reliance on soil processes is impossible and where other means for converting natural energy into food are therefore necessary. Only here we have not the imitation of a tropical forest, but the fabrication of an aquarium.

The supply and control of water is therefore the key factor in wet-rice growing—a seemingly self-evident proposition which conceals some complexities because the regulation of water in a terrace is a matter of some delicacy. Excessive flooding is often as great a threat as insufficient inundation; drainage is frequently a more intractable problem than irrigation. Not merely the gross quantity of water, but its quality, in terms of the fertilizing substances it contains (and thus the source from which it comes) is a crucial variable in determining productivity. Timing is also important: paddy should be planted in a well-soaked field with little standing water and then the depth of the water increased

[17] For the distinction between "medium" and "substratum," see Clarke 1954:23–58, 59–89.

gradually up to six to twelve inches as the plant grows and flowers, after which it should be gradually drawn off until at harvest the field is dry. Further, the water should not be allowed to stagnate but, as much as possible, kept gently flowing, and periodic drainings are generally advisable for purposes of weeding and fertilizing (Grist 1959: 28–32).[18] Although with traditional (and in some landscapes, even modern) methods of water control the degree to which these various optimal conditions can be met is limited, even at its simplest, least productive, and most primitive this form of cultivation tends to be technically intricate.

And this is true not only for the terrace itself, but for the system of auxiliary water works within which it is set. We need not accept Karl Wittfogel's theories about "hydraulic societies" and "oriental despotisms" to agree that while the mobility of water makes it "the natural variable *par excellence*" in those landscapes where its manipulation is agriculturally profitable, its bulkiness makes such manipulation difficult, and manageable only with significant inputs of "preparatory" labor and at least a certain amount of engineering skill (Wittfogel 1957:15). The construction and maintenance of even the simplest water-control system, as in rainfall farms, requires such ancillary efforts: ditches must be dug and kept clean, sluices constructed and repaired, terraces leveled and dyked; and in more developed true irrigation systems dams, reservoirs, aqueducts, tunnels, wells and the like become necessary. Even such larger works can be built up slowly, piece by piece, over extended periods and kept in repair by continuous, routine care. But, small or large, waterworks represent a level and kind of investment in "capital equipment" foreign not only to shifting cultivation but to virtually all unirrigated forms of premodern agriculture.

This complex of systemic characteristics—settled stability, "medium" rather than "substratum" nutrition, technical complexity and significant overhead labor investment—produce in turn what is perhaps the sociologically most critical feature of wet-rice agriculture: its marked tendency (and ability) to respond to a rising

---

[18] One of the primary functions, aside from nutrition, of irrigation water is, in fact, the inhibition of weed growth.

population through intensification; that is, through absorbing increased numbers of cultivators on a unit of cultivated land. Such a course is largely precluded to swidden farmers, at least under traditional conditions, because of the precarious equilibrium of the shifting regime. If their population increases they must, before long, spread out more widely over the countryside in order to bring more land into cultivation; otherwise the deterioration to savannah process which results from too rapid recultivation will set in and their position will become even more untenable. To some extent, such horizontal expansion is, of course, possible for traditional wet-rice agriculturalists as well, and has in fact (though more slowly and hesitantly than is sometimes imagined) occurred. But the pattern of ecological pressures here increasingly encourages the opposite practice: working old plots harder rather than establishing new ones.

The reasons for this introversive tendency follow directly from the listed systemic characteristics. The stability of the rice terrace as an ecosystem makes the tendency possible in the first place. Because even the most intense population pressure does not lead to a breakdown of the system on the physical side (though it may lead to extreme impoverishment on the human side), such pressure can reach a height limited only by the capacity of those who exploit it to subsist on steadily diminishing per capita returns for their labor. Where swidden "overpopulation" results in a deterioration of the habitat, in a wet-rice regime it results in the support of an ever-increasing number of people within an undamaged habitat. Restricted areas of Java today—for example, Adiwerna, an alluvial region in the north-central part of the island—reach extraordinary rural population densities of nearly 2,000 persons per square kilometer without any significant decline in per-hectare rice production. Nor does there seem to be any region on the island in which wet-rice growing was employed effectively in the past but cannot now be so employed due to human overdriving of the landscape. Given maintenance of irrigation facilities, a reasonable level of farming technique, and no autogenous changes in the physical setting, the *sawah* (as the Javanese call the rice terrace) seems virtually indestructible.

Second, the "medium-focused" quality of the regime limits it fairly sharply to those areas in which topography, water resources, and soluble nutrients combine to make the complex ecological integration of sawah farming (whatever that may turn out in detail to be) possible. All agricultural regimes are, of course, limited by the environmental conditions upon which they rely. But wet-rice cultivation, particularly under premodern technological conditions, is perhaps even more limited than most and, within Indonesia, certainly more than swidden, which can be carried out over the greater part of the archipelago, including, as it once was, most of those parts now pre-empted by sawah. Swidden can be pursued on rugged hillsides, in wet lowland forests, and in relatively dry monsoon country where, at least without the assistance of modern methods of water control, conservation, and regulation, sawah cannot. Exact data are difficult to obtain but the great extension of irrigated rice-farming in Indonesia and the rest of Southeast Asia during the last hundred years or so as a result of the application of Western technology ought not to obscure the fact that before the middle of the nineteenth century such farming was restricted to a few, particularly favorable areas. In 1833, when Java was just on the eve of her most diastrous period of social change, the island, which today has about three and a half million hectares of sawah had only slightly more than a third that much.[19]

Yet there is another introversive implication of the technical complexity aspect of traditional wet-rice cultivation. Because productivity is so dependent on the quality of water regulation, labor applied to the improvement of such regulation can often have a greater marginal productivity than that same labor applied to constructing new, but less adequately managed, terraces and new works to support them. Under premodern conditions, gradual perfection of irrigation techniques is perhaps the major way to raise productivity not only per hectare but per man. To develop further water works already in being is often more profitable than to construct new ones as the established technical level; and, in fact, the ingenious traditional water-control systems of Java and Bali can only have been created during a long period of persistent trial-and-error refinement of established systems. Once created, an irrigation system has a momentum of

---

[19] The contemporary figure is from Central Bureau of Statistics of Indonesia 1957:46; the 1833 figure (1,270,000 ha.) from van Klaveren 1955:23.

its own, which continues, and even increases, to the point where the limits of traditional skills and resources are reached. And, as the gap between the first rainfall, stream-bank, or swamp-plot sawah and those limits is usually great, economic progress through step-by-step technological advance within a specifically focused system can be an extended process, as shown in the following description of a Ceylonese system:

> . . . the Kalāwewa canal system—now has a giant tank at its head which leads into a fifty-five mile long watercourse, which in turn feeds into three large tanks which provide water for the ancient capital of Anuradhapura. It all looks like a colossal and highly organized piece of bureaucratic planning, the work of one of Wittfogel's idealised Oriental Despots. But if so, the planning must have been done by a kind of Durkheimian group mind! The original Tissawewa tank at the bottom end of the system was first constructed about 300 B.C. The Kalāwewa tank at the top end of the system was first constructed about 800 years later and elaborations and modifications went on for at least another 600 years (Leach 1959).

However, as mentioned, it is not only with respect to ancillary waterworks that wet-rice agriculture tends toward technical complexity, but on a more microscopic level with respect to the individual terrace itself. In addition to improving the general irrigation system within which a terrace is set, the output of most terraces can be almost indefinitely increased by more careful, fine-comb cultivation techniques; it seems almost always possible somehow to squeeze just a little more out of even a mediocre sawah by working it just a little bit harder. Seeds can be sown in nurseries and then transplanted instead of broadcast; they can even be pregerminated in the house. Yield can be increased by planting shoots in exactly spaced rows, more frequent and complete weeding, periodic draining of the terrace during the growing season for purposes of aeration, more thorough ploughing, raking, and leveling of the muddy soil before planting, placing selected organic debris on the plot, and so on; harvesting techniques can be similarly perfected both to reap the fullest percentage of the yield and leave the greatest amount of the harvested crop on the field to refertilize it, such as the technique of using the razor-like hand blade found over most of inner Indonesia; double cropping and, in some favorable areas, perhaps triple cropping, can be instituted. The capacity of most terraces to respond to loving care is amazing. . . . A whole series of such labor-absorbing improvements in cultivation methods have played a central role in permitting the Javanese rural economy to soak up the bulk of the island's exploding population.

Finally, independently of the advantages of technical perfection, the mere quantity of preparatory (and thus not immediately productive) labor in creating new works and bringing them up to the level of existing ones tends to discourage a rapid expansion of terraced areas in favor of fragmentation and more intensive working of existing ones. In developed systems, this is apparent; a people who have spent 1,400 years in building an irrigation system are not likely to leave it readily for pioneering activities, even if the established system becomes overcrowded. They have too much tied up in it, and at most they will gradually create a few new terraces on the periphery of the already well-irrigated area, where water resources and terrain permit. But this reluctance to initiate new terrace construction because of the heavy "overhead" labor investment is characteristic even of areas where irrigation is still undeveloped, because of the inability or the unwillingness of peasants to divert resources from present production. In contemporary Laos, for example,

> Most villagers are only semi-permanent and forest land is still available. The irrigated rice fields have become fragmented because their yields are more reliable than those of the [swidden]. The creation of new [sawahs] is not easily done, for it involves the extension of irrigation ditches and major investment of labor. This labor must be hired or supplied by the family itself, and implies existing fluid capital or a large extended family containing a number of able-bodied workers. Neither of these situations commonly occurs among Lao peasants, and therefore the progressive division of existing [wet rice] land and cultivation of [swidden] which requires less initial labor (Halpern 1961).

Therefore, the characteristics of swidden and sawah as ecosystems are clear and critical: On the one hand a multicrop, highly diverse regime, a cycling of nutrients between living forms, a closed-cover architecture, and a delicate equilibrium; on the other, on open-field, monocrop, highly specialized regime, a heavy dependency on water-born minerals for nutrition, a reliance on man-made waterworks, and a stable equilibrium. Though these are not the only two traditional agricultural systems in Indonesia, they are by far the most important and have set the framework within which the general agricultural economy of the country has developed. In their contrasting responses to forces making for an increase in population—the dispersive, inelastic quality of the one and the concentrative, inflatable quality of the other—lies much of the explanation for the uneven distribution of population in Indonesia and the ineluctable social and cultural quandaries which followed from it.

BIBLIOGRAPHY

Bates, M.
  1952 *Where Winter Never Comes.* New York: Scribner's.
Beukering, J. A. van.
  1947 *Het Ladangvraagstuck, een Bidrijfs- en Sociall Economische Probleem.* Mededeelingen v.h. Department v. Economische Zaken in Nederlandsch-Indie, No. 9. Batavia.
Central Bureau of Statistics of Indonesia
  1957 *Statistical Pocketbook of Indonesia.* Djakarta: Biro Pusat Statistik.
Clarke, G.
  1954 *Elements of Ecology.* New York: John Wiley.
Collins, W. B.
  1959 *The Perpetual Forest.* Philadelphia, New York: Lippincott.
Conklin, H.
  1954 "An Ethnoecological Approach to Shifting Agriculture." *Transactions of the New York Academy of Sciences,* Series II, 17: 133–42.
  1957 *Hanunóo Agriculture in the Philippines.* Rome: Food and Agricultural Organization of the United Nations.
  1959 "Shifting Cultivation and the Succession to Grassland," in *Proceedings of the 9th Pacific Science Congress (1957),* Vol. 7. Bangkok.
Dobby, E. H. G.
  1954 *Southeast Asia,* Fourth Edition. London: University of London Press.
Freeman, J. D.
  1955 *Iban Agriculture.* London: Her Majesty's Stationery Office (Colonial Research Studies No. 18).
Geddes, W. R.
  1954 *The Land Dayaks of Sarawak.* London: Her Majesty's Stationery Office (Colonial Research Studies No. 14).
Goethals, P. R.
  1961 *Aspects of Local Government in a Sumbawan Village.* Ithaca: Cornell University Press, Modern Indonesia Project Monograph Series.

Gourou, P.
  1953a *L'Asie*. Paris: Hachette.
  1953b *The Tropical World* (trans. E. D. Laborde). New York: Longmans Green.
  1956 "The Quality of Land Use of Tropical Cultivators," in W. L. Thomas (ed.), *Man's Role in Changing the Face of the Earth*. Chicago: University of Chicago Press.
Grist, D. H.
  1959 *Rice*, Third Edition. London: Longmans Green.
Halpern, J. M.
  1961 "The Economies of Lao and Serb Peasants: a Contrast in Cultural Values." *Southwestern Journal of Anthropology*, 17: 165–77.
Hose, C., and W. MacDougal
  1912 *The Pagan Tribes of Borneo*. London: Macmillan.
Kampto Utomo
  1957 *Masjarakat Transmigran Spontan Didaerah W. Sekampung (Lampung)*. Djakarta: P. T. Penerbitan Universitas.
Klaveren, J. van
  1955 *The Dutch Colonial System in Indonesia*. Rotterdam.
Leach, E.
  1954 *Political Systems of Highland Burma*. Cambridge: Harvard University Press.
  1959 "Hydraulic Society in Ceylon." *Past and Present*, 15: 2–25.
Matsuo, T.
  1955 *Rice Culture in Japan*. Tokyo: Yokendo.
Metcalf, J.
  1952 *The Agricultural Economy of Indonesia*. Washington, D.C.: U. S. Department of Agriculture, Monograph 15.
Mochtar, R., et al.
  1956 "The Population of Indonesia." *Ekonomi Dan Keuangan Indonesia* (Economics and Finance in Indonesia), 9: 90–115.
Murphey, R.
  1957 "The Ruin of Ancient Ceylon." *Journal of Asian Studies*, 16: 181–200.
Odum, E. P.
  1959 *Fundamentals of Ecology*, Second Edition. Philadelphia and London: Saunders.
Ormeling, F. J.
  1956 *The Timor Problem*. Groningen, Djakarta, and s'Gravenhage: Wolters and Nijhoff.
Pelzer, K. J.
  1945 *Pioneer Settlement in the Asiatic Tropics*. New York: Institute of Pacific Relations.
Pendleton, R. L.
  1947 *The Formation, Development and Utilization of the Soils of Bangkok Plain*. Bangkok, Natural History Bulletin of the Siam Society, 14.
Richards, P. W.
  1952 *The Tropical Rain Forest*. Cambridge: Cambridge University Press.

Robequain, C.
  1954 *Malaya, Indonesia, Borneo and the Philippines* (trans. E. D. Laborde). New York: Longmans Green.
Spate, O. H. K.
  1945 "The Burmese Village." *The Geographical Review,* 35: 523–43.
Steenis, G. van
  1935 "Maleische Vegetatieschetsen." *Tijdschrift van het Nederlandsch Aardrijkskundig Genootschap,* Series II, 52: 25–67, 171–203, 263–98.
Sumaniwata, S.
  1962 *Sensus Penduduk Republik Indonesia,* 1961 (preliminary report). Djakarta: Central Bureau of Statistics.
Terra, G. J. A.
  1958 "Farm Systems in South-East Asia." *Netherlands Journal of Agricultural Science,* 6: 157–81.
Wittfogel, Karl
  1957 *Oriental Despotism.* New Haven: Yale University Press.

2 AN APPROACH TO THE BIOENERGETICS
OF RURAL WEST BENGAL

Dwain W. Parrack

INTRODUCTION

FOR SEVERAL decades, ecologists have been concerned with the flow of energy through ecosystems, or biotic communities. This is a complex problem and requires, among other things, a knowledge of the number and kinds of organisms in the community, their size, metabolism, reproduction, growth rates, etc. Much of the early work was confined to describing what eats what in food chains or food webs or calculating pyramids of numbers which demonstrated that each succeeding trophic or nutritional level in the community tends to contain fewer individual organisms and less biomass. Such work on food chains and pyramids is useful in that it indicates energy relationships, but it rarely includes quantification of these relationships in much detail. It is rather easy to make diagrams showing that mice eat grass seeds and that owls eat mice. It is something else to determine how much energy is available to a mouse in a gram of seeds and how the mouse uses that energy, or how much energy an owl derives from a mouse and how much it spends in hunting mice.

Aquatic biologists, dealing chiefly with lakes, were able to work out rather well quantified relationships, and some success has been achieved in terrestrial communities. For the most part, however, these terrestrial communities have been simple in having relatively few species of organisms, and the studies usually have not considered large groups of organisms such as insects, or the myriad inhabitants of the soil. And no study has involved

---

This is an original article appearing for the first time in *Environment and Cultural Behavior*.

man as part of a community. "Natural" communities are difficult enough to study, and those communities in which man has a major role are even more so. But since man has become a part of, or interfered with, almost every biotic community on earth, it is becoming increasingly evident that ecologists must consider man in their studies.

The object of this paper is not to present the results of an overall ecological study of West Bengal, for there has been none. Rather, its object is to attempt to gather information from a number of sources and to interpret it in the framework of ecological concepts. It is hoped that in doing so, the paper will point out the need for precise studies. The available data are not always very useful for an ecological approach because they were gathered and published with different aims and views in mind. Where there are no data, and that is rather often, I have either said nothing, or I have made guesses.

It takes little originality to say that the world is burdened with many problems. A large proportion of the human population is underfed and overcrowded. West Bengal is one of those areas which by Western standards is chronically underfed. Occasionally this condition becomes acute and famine results. Of course, famines are nothing new here; they are reported as far back as history of the area goes. Hunter (1868:20–26), for instance, describes a famine which occurred in 1769–70 in the early days of British occupancy and says that about one third of the inhabitants of the province died of starvation, and that this was by no means the first famine in the area. Since Hunter's time there has hardly been a decade which has been free of food shortages of one degree or another, so delicately balanced is the ecology of the area and the interrelationships of the elements of the biotic community.

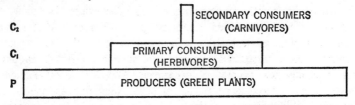

Figure 1   Generalized community structure showing the relationship of numbers of individuals or biomass of the organisms at the different nutritional (trophic) levels

Figure 1 represents the generalized structure of a biotic community. It can apply to aquatic communities as well as to terrestrial ones. The length of the bars represents the relative biomass, or total protoplasm, of each of the three major trophic levels (producers-green plants; consumers-herbivores; and secondary consumers-carnivores). Several organisms such as dogs and foxes are omnivorous and do not actually fit into this classification very neatly. One major component of the community, the decomposers, has been omitted from this figure.

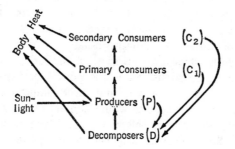

Figure 2   Generalized flow of energy through an ecosystem

Figure 2 represents the flow of energy through the system. Some of the radiant energy entering the system is trapped by green plants and a portion of that energy is passed on to the primary consumers, which in turn pass on a fraction of their energy to the secondary consumers. The energy coming into a trophic level is used in growth, respiration, movement, reproduction, etc. and only a fraction actually enters the next higher level. The dead bodies of all levels are broken down by the decomposers (except those which are eaten by scavengers) and their materials re-enter the system. The metabolism of all levels produces heat, most of which is dissipated into the atmosphere.

THE ECOSYSTEM IN WEST BENGAL

As mentioned earlier, there has been no study of a complete biological community in West Bengal. I have chosen a hypothetical area of one square mile, typical of the land in the vicinity of Singur, as a convenient area for discussion. Singur is a small town about thirty miles northwest of Calcutta proper. It is ten or twelve miles to the west of the Calcutta metropolitan area which follows the Hooghly River. Singur is the major market town for a dozen or so villages and is connected with the Calcutta-Howrah complex by rail and a paved highway. Many shops and a few residences in the town have electricity, but most of the surrounding villages do not. The town is the center of the Singur Health Union, which includes the local villages. A large body of statistical information on the area has been gathered by the All India Institute of Public Health and Hygiene, and this paper draws heavily from it.

The hypothetical sample area has no electricity and is connected to Singur by dirt roads and paths. Automobiles rarely enter the area, except for those of health officials. The area includes several clusters of houses, usually surrounded by trees, agricultural plots which take up most of the land, some bamboo groves, banana plantations, numerous ponds, perhaps an irrigation canal, and a variety of trees and shrubs lining the roads and pathways. An area of this size would contain about 2100 human beings, or almost thirty people per acre. The number of other animals, wild and domestic, will have to be guessed at.

The soil of the area is a rich, clayish alluvium carried down from the Himalayas by the Ganges. As the terrain is flat, there is little erosion, except at the sides of some ponds. Most of the annual rain comes during the monsoon season, which begins about mid-June and tapers out in October. Winters are mild and there is no frost. Summers are hot and temperatures of 100° F or more are common.

1. Radiant Energy

The amount of solar energy striking the sample area is not known, but it must be large. Washington, D.C. under "average cloud conditions" receives from about 1.7 kilowatt-hours per square meter in December to about 5.9 kilowatt-hours per square meter in June (Allee et al. 1949:89). In Bengal the solar input into the biotic community must be considerably higher, since sunlight at that latitude is less filtered than in Washington.

2. Producers, the Green Plants

Only a small fraction of the available radiant energy is converted by plants into tissue or "food energy." The photosynthetic efficiency of the world as a whole (total radiant energy striking the world versus energy converted into plant tissue) is about 0.18 per cent (Spector 1956), but as a general rule for inhabited areas the efficiency of converting the light absorbed by the photosynthetic machinery into food is about 1 to 5 per cent (Odum 1963). Transeau (1926, cited by Allee et al. 1949:506) calculated that an acre of corn converted about 1.6 per cent of the available solar energy into glucose. Golley (1960) worked out the energy relationships in an old-field community in Michigan and found that about 1.1 per cent of the solar energy available during the growing season was converted by the plants into plant material (net production).

The most conspicuous plants in this community are the trees and the crops. Of the trees, a number of species such as coconuts, bananas, mangos, and jackfruits produce fruits that are consumed by man and other animals. After a banana tree has borne fruit, it is chopped into small pieces and used as fodder for the cattle. Bamboos are used in construction and are sometimes sold to builders outside the villages. Dead trees are used as fuel and villagers often cut leaves from living trees for their cattle and goats.

A variety of vegetables are cultivated: potatoes, cabbages, cauliflower, okra, eggplants, tomatoes, and several forms of *dahl* (pulses). The majority of the vegetables seem to be consumed locally, but no figures on this are available.

Jute is the major cash crop of the area and a large amount of the land is given over to its cultivation. In the fall the jute is cut and tied into bundles which are sunk in ponds and ditches until decomposition has loosened the fibers which surround the pithy core of the stem. The fibers are then stripped from the core and sent to the Calcutta area. The cores remain in the community.

The chief cereal is, of course, rice. In Bengal there are two crops: early (*aus*) and late (*aman*). The early crop is the smaller one and is planted in May and harvested in October. The late crop, by far the most important, is planted in June and harvested in December. There are no figures on the rice yield for the Singur area, but my guess, based on reports from farmers, is that in a good year a typical square mile would yield about 360,000 kg. of rice.

The portion of the rice crop which remains in the area for local consumption is likewise not known. For the nation as a whole, about 70 per cent stays in the village which produced it and about 30 per cent is sold in cities and towns. This varies from year to year and from area to area. Sarma (1960:181) reported that an unnamed village near Singur did not grow enough rice to feed its people throughout the year. We can arbitrarily say that our hypothetical area sells 10 per cent of its rice during good years.

The total biomass of the producers has not been determined, so far as I know, for any terrestrial community, but considering the extensiveness of root systems, the number of leaves on an average tree or shrub, and the number of rice or jute plants in a field, the figure for the sample area must be astronomical.

3. *Primary Consumers, the Herbivores*

Insects and other invertebrates will be mentioned only in passing. Their omission is not meant to suggest that they are unimportant. Their numbers and biomass, even in the temperate zone, are enormous. Elton (1960), for example, states that the biomass of wood ants alone is about 400 grams per acre of pine forest, or about 256 kg. per square mile. This figure is included here merely to indicate that whatever the precise biomass of invertebrates in the Singur area, it must be very considerable.

Humans. Although approximately 96 per cent of the humans in the Singur area consider themselves non-vegetarians, we will classify humans as predominantly primary consumers, because almost all of their diet is plant material. Of the average daily caloric intake (2326 cal.) only 130 cal. (about 6 per cent) is of animal origin (Seal et al.). Therefore, of the population of 2100, 94 per cent or 1974 are for our purposes primary consumers.

Most of the following general statements about the people of the Singur area are taken from the report by Seal et al. The inhabitants are of light weight, the average adult man weighing 98.4 lbs. (44.7 kg.) and the average adult woman 86.5 lbs. (39.3 kg.). The report assumes the total value of a balanced diet as 2710 calories per day for adults. In 1957, the average intake was about 2300 calories (about 15 per cent lower), and the intake has probably decreased since then because of poor harvests in 1965 and 1966.

The people are subject to numerous infectious diseases, such as diarrhea, diphtheria, influenza, and dysentery, as well as to parasites such as hookworms and ascaris (Chowdhury and Schiller 1968; Chowdhury, Schad, and Schiller 1968). Still, they are probably healthier than most villagers throughout the nation because of actions of the Central Government and the Government of West Bengal. The drilling of wells has freed many villagers from drinking pond water, and campaigns of immunization, education, and treatment have been in effect for a number of years. Infant mortality dropped from 137 per 1000 live births in 1944 to about 95 per 1000 in 1957. This trend has probably continued since then. The overall death rate was 13.1 per 1000 in 1957, and is probably somewhat lower now. In our hypothetical area about 22 deaths would be expected each year. The crude birth rate in 1944 was about 44 births per 100 population and had changed very little by 1957, when it was about 42 per 1000. With the government's emphasis on family planning during the last several years, this figure has probably decreased also.

Most dwellings are made of mud and have tile or thatched roofs. Due chiefly to the reduced death rate, the number of individuals per household rose from 4 in 1944 to 6 in 1957, and by 1957, two thirds of the households had less than thirty-six square feet of floor space per person.

Although most drinking water now comes from drilled wells, the ponds continue to be important in the daily lives of the villagers, most of whom use them for bathing and for washing clothing and dishes. The ponds are stocked with fish and thereby supply a vital source of protein to the people. The precise role of the ponds in the ecosystem cannot be considered in this paper because of the lack of data.

The construction of latrines is encouraged by health officials, but, in the hypothetical sample area, the number of latrines is small. Almost all defecation takes place in bamboo groves, in banana plantations, or at the edge of fields.

Farming is the most common occupation of the area and accounts for 24 per cent of adult males (adults being anyone over fifteen years old), although 29 per cent of adult males are assigned to an undefined category: "at home." About 19 per cent are in school. The remaining 28 per cent earn their living as teachers, physicians, shopkeepers, laborers, and artisans. Some people, especially clerks and accountants, find employment in Calcutta and commute daily by train from Singur. There is a tendency for some villages to specialize in certain occupations. One village may produce pottery, another may specialize in fishing or in dairy farming. It appears that few farm owners work their fields themselves. Instead they rent the land to sharecroppers or hired laborers, thus creating another niche.

The large number of non-adults complicates any attempt to estimate the human biomass in our square mile. Since the average adult weight is 92 lbs. and most of the population is young, it seems safe to guess that the overall average is about 50 lbs. (23 kg.). The human biomass, then, is around 105,000 lbs. (47,730 kg.).

Cattle. To some people the terms "India" and "sacred cow" are almost synonymous. Most westernized Indians and foreigners feel that India has far too many cattle and that the veneration of cattle is a prime example of man's ability to maintain religious beliefs which are detrimental to man's well-being. Radhakamal Mukerjee (1938:142–43), for instance, states that "veneration for the cow has had a positive effect in protecting the cattle, and large numbers of useless animals are now being maintained even in crowded areas of the [Gangetic] plain, leading to chronic shortage of fodder and deterioration of breed." Writers such as Mukerjee favor control of the numbers of the animals. At the opposite end of the spectrum are some traditional Hindus who advocate a nationwide ban on cow slaughter. The average farmer falls somewhere between these two extremes, his attitude changing with his economic condition. In periods of famine he will, as a last resort, slaughter and eat his own cattle. At other times, he will not, although he may still sell a cow or ox knowing that it may be slaughtered.

Harris (1966) has presented a forceful argument that the Western idea mentioned above is basically false and that India's cattle serve a vital role in the ecology of the country. His thesis is that "insufficient attention has been paid to such positive-functioned features of the Hindu cattle complex as traction power and milk, dung, beef and hide production in relationship to the costs of ecologically viable alternatives" (Harris 1966:59). In my opinion, this quite reasonable interpretation, if followed up by actual studies in the villages, can lead to policies with beneficial results.

The cattle of India can be divided into three functional categories: working cattle, which includes those which pull the plows and carts, produce milk, etc.; breeding cattle, which includes some of the workers (the offspring being sold to farmers who need workers); and useless cattle, which is almost restricted to those kept in special facilities for aged cattle.

The general physical condition of animals in all three categories is wretched. They are underfed, poor breeders, and poor producers of milk. The number of working cattle is far greater than the other two categories combined, and I would guess that the number of cattle in the facilities for aged animals is very small in proportion to the total population. It seems likely that some observers have mistakenly regarded as "useless" some cattle still being used for breeding.

For our purpose we can look on the farmer and his ox in terms of energy. Energy is expended by the man (E_1) and by the animal (E_2) in the production of rice which contains energy (E_3) in the grain and the straw.

$$E_1 + E_2 \rightarrow E_3$$

The man and the ox work together as a unit, the man unable to plow the fields and do the other tasks of cultivation by himself, since the expenditure of energy would be more than the yield. Most of the rice seeds are consumed by the man; the ox gets little or none. The straw, which is inedible as far as man is concerned, goes to the ox.

$$\overleftarrow{E_1} + E_2 \overleftrightarrow{} E_3$$

The amount of food given to the ox is not enough to make the animal fat, but it is enough to keep it going.

The role of the cattle does not end there. Unlike tractors, cattle produce valuable excrement. The dung is used as fuel for cooking the rice and as fertilizer for growing more rice. And when the ox or cow dies, its skin is often made into leather.

Although cows do not usually serve as draft animals, they do occasionally produce calves, some of which become draft animals.

Female calves are often allowed to starve (Mukerjee 1958), while the males are castrated to become field workers. The cow also produces a little milk. The average yield for the Singur area is apparently about 30 kg. per year, the average for Madhya Pradesh, since farmers say that they get about one liter per day during periods of lactation. Compared to the Western average of 2280 kg. per year (Harris 1966), these yields are poor, but they are not likely to improve until the supply of fodder is increased.

Mention was made earlier of the use of dung as fuel and fertilizer.[1] Although estimates vary, it seems that about 40 per cent of the dung is used as fuel, 40 per cent for field manure, and 20 per cent remains along roadsides (Spate 1954; cited in Harris 1966). The annual amount used as fuel in India is estimated to be equivalent to 35,000,000 to 131,000,000 tons of coal. Even if the lower figure is accepted, this is somewhat over one half of the total coal production of the nation in 1963 (Ministry 1964). The dung used as fuel is also estimated to be equivalent to at least 68,000,000 tons of wood. The loss of fuel dung would pose a serious threat to the nation's forests.

It seems to me that any significant reduction in the number of cattle will have to follow, rather than precede, improvement in: the cost and availability of cooking fuels, artificial fertilizers, and tractors; the size of agricultural plots; the patterns of land ownership; and the density of the human population of the country.

Rodents. Less conspicuous than either the humans or cattle as primary consumers are the rodents. In our area there are four main species of rats: the house rat (*Rattus rattus*), the greater bandicoot (*Bandicota indica*), the lesser bandicoot (*Bandicota bengalensis*), and, less common, the Indian gerbil (*Tatera indica*). Neither species of bandicoots is often found in houses in this area, but most buildings are infested with house rats. Both species of the bandicoots live in and around fields and the gerbil is usually found in bushy areas.

In homes and buildings the house mouse (*Mus musculus*) is

---

[1] Macfadyen (1964) estimated that cattle, presumedly in Europe, utilized about 33 per cent of their energy intake in respiration, 4 per cent in producing protoplasm, and that 63 per cent was excreted. No comparable figures for Indian cattle are available.

common, and outside, especially in grassy areas, two other species of the same genus occur in considerable numbers. The palm squirrel (*Funambulus*) is fairly common.

No one knows how many rats there are in India, or any other country, although several estimates have been made for the nation. The widespread idea that there is one rat per person is an old wives' tale. Davis (1949) did a painstaking estimate of the rat population of New York City and concluded that there was about one rat for thirty-six humans. The number of rats in our area in India is probably considerably higher, but how much higher is not known.

Everyone agrees that rodents consume a great deal of grain. Majumder and Parpia (1966) estimate that 50 per cent of India's cereals is lost to birds, insects, or rodents. Patnaik (in press) has reviewed the estimates of foodgrain loss due to rats and mice in India. The estimates of loss vary from 2.4 million to 26 million tons per year. Daily consumption has been reported to be 20, 25, 30, and 60 grams per day per rat (Patnaik, in press). It is not clear whether these figures include hoarding as well as actual consumption. The lesser bandicoot is a great hoarder and under certain conditions a single animal consumes and hoards over 100 grams a day.

Miscellaneous herbivores. Our community contains a few buffaloes, kept only for their milk production. A few people in the Singur area raise pigs, but the number is so small that for our purpose these animals can be ignored. Chickens are outnumbered by ducks, but no one in the area raises large numbers of either. Goats are rather common, something on the order of one goat per human family. They feed on grass, shrubs, and rubbish, but there is no evidence of their seriously harming the habitat as they have done in Rajastan and the Middle East.

Many buildings have one or more mush shrews (*Suncus murinus*), sometimes mistaken for rats. Although these animals are assigned to the order Insectivoria, their diet is not limited to insects or even to animal material. They eat all sorts of table scraps when in houses, but are basically carnivorous when they live elsewhere.

There are a few colonies of the giant fruit bat (*Pteropus giganteus*) in the Singur area, but none of these colonies is large. Great numbers of grain- or fruit-eating birds occur in the area, such as sparrows, parakeets, and koels.

Monkeys are very rare. An occasional family of langurs may pass through the area, but these animals are not ecologically significant. The rhesus monkey, once common, has been entirely trapped out for export.

Even though the discussion has been largely limited to the vertebrates, the snails of the area should be mentioned. In the rice fields and ponds there are several species, including a giant species that occurs in large numbers and undoubtedly consumes much vegetation.

4. *Secondary Consumers, the Carnivores*

Humans. As mentioned earlier, humans in the Singur area are not particularly carnivorous. It is interesting to note, however, that the amount of animal protein in the diet is not always related to income (Seal et al.:207). The economic level classified as "upper middle" (the highest of five classes) consumed less animal protein than even the "very poor" (the lowest class). Some low-caste or casteless people, not restricted by the dietary regulations of the upper castes, occasionally eat snails, clams, rats, and fruit bats. The Shantals, a tribal group, a few of whom live near Singur, are hunters as well as farmers and have such dietary freedom that it is easier to list the foods which are forbidden to them rather than those which are permitted. According to Bodding (1940:477–82), they refuse to eat monkeys, horses, hyenas, vultures, kites, parakeets, and adult crows. All other vertebrate animals, including shrews, rodents, pythons, and cattle, are acceptable. Although these people are near the bottom of the social ladder, they are in some ways more fortunate than their superiors with regard to diet. The protein of non-tribal people comes chiefly from goat meat and fish and occasionally from eggs and chickens.

Other carnivores. Some families keep dogs, but the food given to them is mostly vegetable. Stray dogs are common and, along with jackals, will be discussed with the scavengers. A few foxes (*Vulpes bengalensis*) occur in the area. Cats are less common as pets than are dogs. Some are feral and are said to interbreed with the jungle cat (*Felis chaus*) which lives in little patches of woods. Among the civets, the toddy cat (*Paradoxurus herma-phroditus*) and the small Indian civet (*Viverricula indica*) are found in our square mile. The civets are carnivores but, like foxes, will also eat fruit. The small Indian mongoose (*Herpestes auropunctatus*) and the so-called common mongoose (*Herpestes edwardsi*) are seen from time to time. Several forms of insectivorous bats and one carnivorous species are also to be found here, as are numerous insectivorous birds. Owls and other hunting birds are also present.

The area is rich in reptiles. All buildings have several resident lizards (*"tick-ticks"*) which cling to the walls and ceilings and eat insects. Less commonly seen are the iguanids and monitors of the fields. Of the poisonous snakes, kraits and Russell's vipers are the most common. Cobras are said to be in the area. Much more common than the venomous forms, of course, are the harmless snakes of which the rat snake (*Zamenis sp.*) is the most conspicuous because of its large size.

Frogs and toads occur in large numbers and undoubtedly consume tons of insects during the rainy season.

Although there are no detailed studies of the food consumption of the carnivores of the Singur area, it seems probable that rodents constitute a major part of the diet of the non-insectivorous species.

Scavengers. The carcass of a dead animal very quickly draws the attention of vultures, kites, crows, and dogs, which reduce it to bones in a short while. Jackals apparently get what little is left, but not much is known of the habits of these nocturnal animals.

5. *The Decomposers*

Very little is known of the organisms which decompose the dead tissue and excrement of the other trophic levels in our community. For the sake of convenience, dung beetles and other coprophagous organisms will be included here with the bacteria and fungi.

According to Macfadyen (1963:39), the respiration of the decomposers of three forests in Holland and Denmark accounted for about half of the total respiration of the communities. This does not mean, however, that the biomass of the decomposers is half the total biomass of the community, for the decomposers are small organisms and have a higher metabolic rate per unit weight than do larger organisms.

BIOMASSES

An attempt has been made to estimate the biomass of the vertebrates of the herbivorous and carnivorous sections of our hypothetical community. This has been done by multiplying the estimated numbers of individuals of each species by their approximate weights. The resulting figures are largely guesswork and are probably much too low. I hope, however, that the ratio between the two biomasses is fairly accurate. By my estimate, the biomass of the primary consumers (C_1) is no less than 166,000 kg. per square mile and that of the secondary consumers (C_2) is at least 3,700 kg. per square mile, the biomass of the carnivores being about 2 per cent of that of the herbivores (Table 1

Table 1. A comparison of the biomass of carnivores (C_2) and herbivores (C_1) in three localities (kg. wet wt. per mile^2).

	BENGAL	ARIZONA (Leopold 1933)	MICHIGAN (Golley 1960)
C_1 Carnivore	3,700	80	21
C_2 Herbivore	166,000	5,000	360
$C_1/C_2 \times 100$	2%	1–2%	6%

and Fig. 3). Comparative figures from other communities are hard to find. Leopold (1933, cited by Clarke 1954:472) lists the estimated numbers of vertebrates inhabiting one square mile of the Santa Rita Range Reserve in Arizona. By guessing at the weight of these animals, I calculate the biomass of the herbivores to be about 5000 kg. and that of the carnivores to be about 80 kg. and the mass of the carnivores to be between 1 and 2 per cent of that of the herbivores (Table 1). Applying even more guesswork to the data of Golley (1960) on field mice (the herbivores) and least weasels (*Mustela frenata*) (the carnivores) in an old-field community in Michigan, I calculate the herbivore and carnivore masses to be about 21 and 360 kg. per square mile respectively, with the carnivores' mass being about 6 per cent of that of the herbivores. These three figures agree rather well, but the striking similarity between the Bengal and Arizona figures may not be very meaningful, since the climates of the two areas are so dissimilar. All three figures accord reasonably well with the general idea that about 10 per cent or less of the energy (not necessarily biomass) at one level is used by the next level for the production of protoplasm and for general metabolic activity.

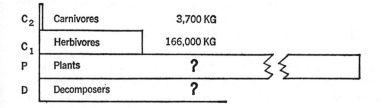

Figure 3 Estimated biomass of the trophic levels in an ecosystem of one square mile in West Bengal

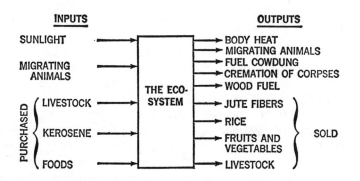

Figure 4 Diagrammatic representation of the ecosystem in rural West Bengal

The inputs and outputs of the ecosystem are represented graphically in Fig. 4. The essential input is, of course, sunlight, and this has remained relatively constant over a long period of time. The coming and going of migrating animals such as birds bring about seasonal gains and losses in the total biomass and energy of the system. The other inputs are man-made, and are subject to historical variation. For instance, it has long been the practice of farmers to purchase cattle from outside the sample area when the breeding of their own worker cattle do not meet their demands. The purchase of kerosene, on the other hand, is relatively new, and the purchase of artificial fertilizer is newer still and is of great importance to the biotic community. There are no figures available on the amount of fertilizer brought into the Singur area, but the amount is probably still very low, even though the use of fertilizers has become increasingly popular during the last several years.

Until the input of fertilizers is greatly increased, the total output of the system will remain greater than the input. However, the removal of agricultural products from the area is not a total loss, for these products are exchanged for money, some of which is used to bring in energy in the form of fertilizers, cattle, and foods. Even so, the net result appears to be a loss to the biotic community, with the reserves of the soil being used faster than they are being replenished. However, the rate at which the ecosystem is running down is not known. It would be interesting to compare the situation in Bengal with that of Iowa or of the Nile delta where annual floods bring in an influx of organic and inorganic materials.

From man's standpoint, the ecosystem in Bengal is not stable. This is indicated by the periodic occurrence of acute food shortages. The chief weakness of the system is that the demands of the herbivores upon the producers is so great that there is little surplus left for the lean years when the monsoon is poor.

The ratio of demand and supply can be altered in several ways. The most obvious is to reduce the number of herbivores (humans, cattle, insects, rodents). And it is a certainty that this will be done, either by nature or by man. Hopefully, if man does the reducing, he will be more selective than nature will be. A second approach is to increase the usable portion of the producer level. Both approaches are being employed. Family planning is being encouraged, but there is at the same time a rising survival rate. New methods of farming are increasing the production of food. An immense effort to bring the producers and the herbivores into a better balance is being made by man, but it remains to be seen whether man or nature will finally accomplish it.

BIBLIOGRAPHY

Allee, W. C., A. E. Emerson, O. Park, T. Park, and K. P. Schmidt
  1949 *Principle of Animal Ecology.* Philadelphia: Saunders.
Bodding, P. O.
  1940 "Studies in Santal Medicine and Connected Folklore, Part III, How Santals Live." *Memoirs of the Royal Asiatic Society of Bengal* 10: 427–502.
Chowdhury, A. B., and E. L. Schiller
  1968 "A Survey of Parasite Infection in a Rural Community Near Calcutta." *American Journal of Epidemiology,* 87: 299–312.
Chowdhury, A. B., G. A. Schad, and E. L. Schiller
  1968 "The Prevalence of Intestinal Helminths in Religious Groups of a Rural Community near Calcutta." *American Journal of Epidemiology* 87: 313–17.
Clarke, George L.
  1954 *Elements of Ecology.* New York: John Wiley.
Davis, D. E.
  1949 "The Rat Population of New York." *American Journal of Hygiene* 52: 147–52.
Davis, D. E., and F. B. Golley
  1963 *Principles in Mammalogy.* London: Reinhold.
Elton, C.
  1960 *The Ecology of Animals* (First publication, 1933). New York: Methuen.
Golley, F. B.
  1960 "Energy Dynamics of a Food Chain of an Old-field Community." *Ecological Monograph,* 30: 187–206.
Harris, M.
  1966 "The Cultural Ecology of India's Sacred Cattle." *Current Anthropology,* 7: 50–59.
Hunter, W. W.
  1868 *The Annals of Rural Bengal.* Calcutta: Indian Studies Past and Present.
Leopold, Aldo
  1954 See Clarke, George L.

Macfadyen, A.
1963 "The Contribution of the Microfauna to the total Soil Metabolism," in J. Doeksen and J. van Der Drift (eds.), *Soil Organisms.* Amsterdam: North-Holland Pub. Co.
1964 "Energy Flow in Ecosystems and Its Exploitation by Grazing," in D. J. Crisp (ed.), *Grazing in Terrestrial and Marine Environments.* Great Britain: Adlard and Son.

Majumder, S. K., and H. A. B. Parpia
1966 "Possible Losses of Foodgrains In India." *Vijnan Karmee* 18: 2–7.

Ministry of Information and Broadcasting
1964 *India, 1964.* Delhi: Publishing Division, Government of India.

Mukerjee, Radhakamal
1938 *The Regional Balance of Man: An Ecological Theory of Population.* Madras: University of Madras.

Mukerjee, Ramkrishna
1958 "Six Villages of Bengal." *Journal of Asiatic Society* (*Science*) 24: 1–220.

Odum, E. P.
1963 *Ecology.* New York: Holt, Rinehart & Winston.

Patnaik, K. C.
In Press "The Role of Rodents in Problems of Food and Health in India." *Proceedings of the Indian Rodent Symposium.*

Sarma, Jyotirmoyee
1960 "A Village In West Bengal," in M. N. Srinavas (ed.), *India's Villages.* Bombay: Asia Publishing House.

Seal, S. C., K. C. Patnaik, P. C. Sen, L. M. Bhattachaji, et al.
No Date *Report of the Resurvey of Singur Health Unit Area: 1957–58.* Calcutta: All India Institute of Hygiene and Public Health.

Spate, O. H.
1954 *India and Pakistan: A General and Regional Geography.* London: Methuen.

Spector, W. S.
1956 *Handbook of Biological Data.* Philadelphia: Saunders.

Transeau, E. N.
1926 "The Accumulation of Energy by Plants." *Ohio Journal of Science* 26: 1–10.

3 !KUNG BUSHMAN SUBSISTENCE: AN INPUT-OUTPUT ANALYSIS[1]

Richard B. Lee

I. INTRODUCTION

THIS PAPER EXAMINES the ecological basis of a hunting and gathering economy through an input-output analysis of work and consumption. The first goal of this exercise is to outline the subsistence strategy that enables the !Kung Bushmen, with only the simplest of technologies, to live well in the harsh environment of the Kalahari Desert. The second goal is to show that the Bushmen exhibit an elementary form of economic life. And the third goal is to trace, from a primate baseline, the origin and evolution of human energy relations.

The methodology I have used is adapted from the transactional models of input-output economics (Leontief 1966) and ecological energetics (Gates 1962; Kleiber 1961). At the outset an essential

Reprinted by permission of the author and publisher from *Ecological Essays: Proceedings of the Conference on Cultural Ecology, National Museum of Canada, 1966*, David Damas, ed., National Museum of Canada Bulletin No. 230, Ottawa: National Museum of Canada, in press. The author has made minor revisions in the paper for publication in the present volume.

[1] The Bushman field research (August 1963 to January 1965) was generously supported by a U. S. National Science Foundation grant entitled "Studies in the Evolution of Human Behavior." To Irven DeVore, the principal investigator for this project, I owe special thanks for his unfailing support and good advice. Earlier versions of this paper were presented at the Conference on Cultural Ecology, Ottawa, August 1966, and at the University Seminar on Ecological Systems and Cultural Evolution, Columbia University, January 1967. For constructive criticism I owe a debt of gratitude to: Sally Bates, Mario Bick, David Damas, Henry Harpending, Marvin Harris, June Helm, Nancy Howell Lee, G. P. Murdock, Robert Murphy, Robert Netting, Roy Rappaport, R. H. S. Smithers, Louise Sweet, A. P. Vayda, and E. Z. Vogt.

distinction should be made between these two approaches. Ecologists take as their unit of study a species which has energy relations with other species within an ecosystem. A population is maintained by the energy absorbed in the course of food-getting activities of its members. The focus here is on *interspecific* trophic exchanges (Rappaport 1967:18–19). Economists, by contrast, focus on the exchange relations within a single species. A productive unit, such as an industry in the American economic system, is maintained by the inputs from other productive units, and in turn allocates its outputs to other like units or to the "final demand" sector of the economy (Leontief 1966:14–20). Viewed ecologically, these transactions can be considered as a highly evolved form of *intraspecific* exchange.

At first glance, the connection between, for example, the relations between predator and prey in an African savannah and the relations between industrial units in the American economy seems too remote to be worth considering. Yet this connection becomes meaningful when viewed in evolutionary terms. First of all, a human population, like all animal populations, has to expend energy in work in order to incorporate energy through consumption. In this respect energetics would apply equally well to the study of man as to the study of other animals.

However, in one important respect, human energy relations are unique among the higher animals. Whereas each adult non-human vertebrate organism is a self-sufficient subsistence unit, a large percentage of a man's energy expenditure goes to feeding others, and a large percentage of an individual's consumption is of food produced by others. Thus for humans, the minimal self-sufficient subsistence unit includes at least a social group, such as a family or "band," and at most includes economies involving hundreds of millions of persons. This central fact of cooperative consumption has been termed "division of labor" and "economic interdependence," and the study of the transactions and allocations so generated forms the foundation of economic science. In man alone, these intraspecific exchanges have become extraordinarily pervasive and complex, so much so, in fact, that we take them for granted! Yet it is precisely in this form of trophic exchange that animal adaptation and human adaptation first part company. And it is here that the study of energetics and economics converge.

In evolutionary terms the origin of what we call an economic system is a relatively recent phenomenon. It appears in the Pleistocene, probably less than two million years ago, when early man began to pool resources and thereby break down individual animal self-sufficiency. Women are usually thought to be the original "scarce good," or medium of exchange (White 1949:316; Lévi-Strauss 1949:35–86). It is more likely, however, that food was the original medium of exchange and that such exchanges are the foundation of social life.

Many economic transformations have occurred since the basic form of human exchange originated in the Pleistocene. Plant and animal domestication, the development of the market and money, and the harnessing of fossil and nuclear fuels have all contributed to making human energy exchange relations more complex.[2] The evolution of economic organization has reached the point at which an individual's productive activity is usually at the *n*th removed from the ultimate source of the food he consumes. He sells his labor (input) to the market and receives his consumption (output) in the form of cash, or some other convertible standard of value (Bohannan and Dalton 1962:9).

However, economies have evolved at different rates in various parts of the world. In some contemporary societies a much more elementary form of economic life can still be observed. I use elementary in the sense of an economy which exhibits the basic human pattern of exchange, without further elaboration.

In input-output terms, an economy exhibits an elementary form when the relation between the production and consumption of food is immediate in space and time. Such an economy would have the following properties: minimal surplus accumulation; minimal production of capital goods; an absence of agriculture and domestic animals; continuous food-getting activities by all able-bodied persons throughout the year; and self-sufficiency in foodstuffs and generalized reciprocity within local groups.

Although no contemporary society exhibits all these properties, the !Kung Bushmen of the Dobe area of Botswana are a close approximation. The !Kung have a simple, small-scale, self-contained economy of a type that may have been characteristic of

---

[2] The implications of these developments have been documented by Marx (1867), Childe (1951), Polanyi (1944, 1957), and White (1949, 1959).

early man. Extreme isolation and a marginal environment have
been responsible for the persistence of this form to the present.
The Dobe area is surrounded by waterless desert, and the Bushman
population within it is largely self-sufficient in terms of subsistence.
The economy lacks trading posts, trade in foodstuffs, wage labor,
cash, conversions, and markets—the features which are commonly
taken to indicate economic interdependence (Bohannan and Dalton 1962:1–26). Because the !Kung are hunters and gatherers,
without agriculture and domestic animals (except for the dog),
and because they do not amass a surplus of foodstuffs, the relation
between local food production and consumption is an immediate
one. A diagnostic feature of their subsistence economy is: *food is
almost always consumed within the boundaries of the local group
and within forty-eight hours of its collection.* This immediacy of
consumption makes the !Kung Bushman an apt case for input-output analysis, since the level of work effort in a given period is a direct reflection of the food requirements of the local group. Such
an analysis would be more difficult in a complex economic situation in which the work effort during a given period is dictated
by the need for surplus accumulation for ceremonial purposes
(Wolf 1966:7), for the conversion of subsistence goods into
prestige (DuBois 1936), or for delayed consumption at a later
period (Richards 1939:35–37).

Sections II through VI of this paper present the descriptive
material on Bushman ethnography, demography, and subsistence
strategies. These serve as a necessary introduction to the input-
out analysis itself, presented in Sections VII and VIII. A con-
cluding section (IX) returns to the problem of defining the properties of an elementary form of economy, and attempts to place
the discussion in a comparative and evolutionary perspective.

II. ETHNOGRAPHIC BACKGROUND

The Dobe area lies in the northwestern corner of the Republic
of Botswana and in adjacent areas of Southwest Africa. During
my field work (1963–65), some 336 !Kung Bushmen were resident in the area, along with 340 Bantu pastoralists, mainly of
the Herero and Tswana tribes.

!Kung Bushmen are known to have lived in the Dobe area

for at least 100 years. Late Stone Age materials of Wilton Horizon are found at several localities, indicating that some hunting peoples have lived there for many hundreds of years (Malan 1950). There is no evidence that the present-day !Kung are recent refugees from other areas (Lee 1965:38–68). The introduction of metal tools and weapons can be provisionally dated to the period 1880–90 when iron replaced bone as the primary material for arrowheads and spears.

The first European known to have penetrated the area was Hendrick van Zyl in 1879 (Silberbauer 1965:115). The Tswana cattle herders appeared soon after, and from the 1890s onwards the area was used as a regular summer grazing ground by these pastoralists. The first year-round settlements by non-Bushmen were not established until 1925 when two Herero families set up a cattle post at !angwa. Effective administrative presence is even more recent, dating from 1948, the year in which a resident Tswana Headman was appointed by the Paramount Chief of the Batswana Tribal Administration. Apart from brief annual patrols by the British Colonial government starting in 1934, almost nothing was known of the Dobe area until the 1950s.

In 1952, for example, Sillery wrote:

> Not far from the border of South West Africa, near latitude 20° south, is a group of caves which occur in the limestone there. These caves have been visited by few white people. The journey involves a long and arduous trek across sandy country through which no road passes and a competent guide is essential. . . . The country in the vicinity of these caves is probably the least known in the whole Protectorate and Bushmen and wild animals have it to themselves (1952:198).

The Marshall family of Cambridge, Massachusetts, were the first "Europeans" to spend more than a few weeks in this area. Their expeditions (1951–59) focussed on the adjacent Nyae Nyae !Kung in Southwest Africa and their reports form the most complete and detailed record for any Bushman group (Lorna Marshall 1957, 1959, 1960, 1961, 1962; John Marshall 1956; Thomas 1959).

In 1960, the South African government initiated a scheme to

settle the !Kung Bushmen of the Nyae Nyae area. By 1964 over 700 Bushmen had moved into the government station at Tsumkwe S. W. A. and were being instructed in agricultural and stock-raising techniques. As a result of political pressures, the South Africans have not permitted the !Kung Bushmen of the formerly British Bechuanaland Protectorate to participate in this settlement scheme.

The situation in the mid-1960s finds the !Kung on the Botswana side of the border primarily dependent on hunting and gathering for their subsistence. The Bushmen have now obtained some blankets, clothing, and cooking utensils from their Bantu neighbors. There is an inexhaustible supply of metal for arrowheads which are hammered out from scraps of fencing wire from the cattle enclosures built by the Botswana Veterinary Department. However, the !Kung still lack firearms, livestock, and agriculture. About 7 per cent of the Bushwomen have married Bantu; and 20 per cent of the young men are working for Bantu as cattle herders. Serious disputes, usually involving Bush-Bantu labor relations, are adjudicated by the Tswana Headman. Capital offenders are sent to Maun, the tribal capital, for trial. European presence amounts to a brief patrol once every six to eight weeks. The important point is that the Bushmen continue to hunt and gather because there is no viable alternative available to them.

III. POPULATION DYNAMICS

In a census made in November 1964, the resident !Kung population stood at 336. Of the 336 residents, 248 were organized into fourteen independent camps, ranging in size from nine to twenty-nine members (see Table I). The size of each camp is a statistical abstraction because individuals and families were constantly shifting from camp to camp. Subsistence at the camps was based on hunting and gathering. The remaining eighty-eight residents were associated with Herero and Tswana cattle posts (Table IIa). These people did some work for the Bantu and ate some of their foods, including milk, cheese, and meat. Because part of their diet came from external sources, these Bantu-associated Bushmen groups are not included in the input-output analysis. In addition to the residents, fifty-five !Kung alternated

Table I Dobe area census by living units: resident camps

No. place and name	Males			Females			Total			% Effect.
	Y*	A	O	Y	A	O	T	Effect.**	Dep	
1. Dobe—n≠eisi	0	4	1	1	4	1	11	8	3	72.7
2. Dobe—≠oma//gwe	5	7	2	6	5	1	26	12	14	46.2
3. !angwa—bo	1	6	0	3	5	1	16	11	5	68.8
4. Bate—!xoma	3	7	0	3	5	1	19	12	7	63.2
5. Bate—Liceku	1	5	0	1	4	0	11	9	2	81.8
6. !ubi—Kamburu	3	5	0	1	10	0	19	15	4	79.0
7. !gose—/ise	1	7	0	5	7	2	22	14	8	63.6
8. !gose—/ilay	0	6	0	1	4	0	11	10	1	90.9
9. !gose—Konguroba	3	4	0	5	7	0	19	11	8	57.9
10. /ai/ai—//aunla	1	2	1	3	4	1	12	6	6	50.0
11. /ai/ai—/aiha	1	1	1	3	2	1	9	3	6	33.3
12. /ai/ai—≠oma!xwa	4	9	1	3	10	2	29	19	10	65.5
13. /ai/ai—x!am	2	3	1	5	5	1	17	8	9	47.1
14. /ai/ai—≠omazho	4	6	2	6	8	1	27	14	13	51.9
Total in Resident Camps	29	72	9	46	80	12	248	152	96	61.3%

* Age Divisions: Y=Young, 0–15 years
  A=Adult, 16–59 years
  O=Old, 60+ years

** Effectives=Adults
   Dependents=Young and Old

in and out of the Dobe area (Table IIb) and thirty-four others
emigrated permanently from the area (Table IIc). Thus the
grand total of Bushmen enumerated in 1964 was 425.

Table II   Dobe area census by living units: other groups

IIa	*Residents living with Bantu*	Males			Females			Totals
		Y	A	O	Y	A	O	T
	21 living groups	11	27	2	9	38	1	88
IIb	*Alternators*							
	6 living groups	13	14	0	12	15	1	55
IIc	*Emigrants*							
	3 living groups	10	7	0	6	11	0	34
	Total IIa, IIb, IIc	34	48	2	27	64	2	177
Grand Total of Population		63	120	11	73	144	14	425

In the census, the population is divided by sex, and by age into
three divisions: young, 0–15 years; adult, 16–59 years; and old,
60+ years. Several important demographic features should be
noted. Eight per cent of the population in camps (21 of 248)
was determined to be over sixty years of age.[8] These data con-
tradict the view that Bushman life expectancy is short. Silberbauer, for example, says of the G/wi of the Central Kalahari
that "life expectancy among Reserve Bushmen is difficult to
calculate, but I do not believe that many live beyond 45"
(1965:17). Among the Dobe area !Kung, every camp had at least
several members over forty-five years of age, and ten of the fourteen camps had members over sixty years old; the oldest person
was estimated to be 82±3 years. These old people, although non-
productive in terms of food, played an important role in the
social and ritual activities of the camps.

Since persons under fifteen and over sixty years of age do not
contribute significantly to the food supplies of the camps, it is
possible to use the census data to calculate the percentage of

---

[8] The age estimates are based on a relative age ranking of the population
from youngest to oldest; an event calendar was used to establish birth
dates. The accuracy of estimation is ± 3 years.

effective food producers and the percentage of dependents. The effectives comprised 61.3 per cent (152 of 248) of the total population in camps, in other words, every three effectives supported themselves and two dependents in subsistence. What is surprising is the wide variation in the percentage of effectives from camp to camp. In camp No. 11 (Table I), for example, three effectives supported themselves and six dependents (33.3 per cent effective), whereas in camp No. 8, ten of the eleven members (90.9 per cent) were effective. These variations were more apparent than real, however, since groups were constantly shifting in composition and the net effect was to produce work groups in which the ratio of effectives to dependents approached the mean.

In addition, these data show an unusual sex ratio favoring females. In the total population, the sex ratio is eighty-four males per hundred females. The ratio for each age group is:

> Young 86 males/100 females
> Adult 83 males/100 females
> Old 80 males/100 females

These data indicate a higher mortality rate for males in all age groups; although it is possible that the sex ratio at birth is anomalous, producing an initial excess of female over male live births. Another possible explanation is the practice of male infanticide. However, the overall incidence of infanticide (as well as invalidicide and senilicide) is so low that it is unlikely that this practice alone would account for the skewed sex ratio in the immature age group.

IV. SEASONAL SUBSISTENCE PATTERNS

The northern Kalahari Desert is characterized by a hot summer with a five-month rainy season from November to March, a cool dry winter from April to August, and a hot dry spring in September and October. During the spring and summer the diurnal temperature range is from a low of 60° F to a high of 100° F, with shade temperatures of as high as 108° F recorded. In the

winter the diurnal range is from a low of 30° F to a high of 78° F.
The annual rainfall varies from six to ten inches. The loose
sandy soils support a surprising abundance of vegetation, in
spite of the fact that the porosity of the sand is such that rainfall
is rapidly absorbed and surface runoff is minimal. Permanent
waterholes exist only where the underlying limestone strata have
been exposed.

Because of these soil factors, the distribution of water sources
is by far the most important ecological determinant of Bushman
subsistence. The availability of plant foods is of secondary importance and the numbers and distributions of game animals
are only of minor importance. Since the Bushman camps, of
necessity, are anchored to water sources they can exploit only
those vegetable foods that lie within a reasonable walking distance of water. Food sources that lie beyond a reasonable walking distance are rarely exploited.

The life of the camps surrounding the eight permanent waterholes are shown as solid dots on Figure 1. During the seven dry

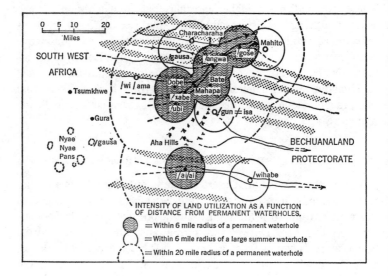

Figure 1 Intensity of land utilization as a function of distance from permanent waterholes

months of the year, April through October, these wells were the only sources of standing water and all the Bushmen camps were located within a mile of a well. During the summer rains (November–March) seasonal pools of water developed elsewhere, and virtually all the Bushmen went out to live at them.

The necessity for drinking water strictly defined the areas that people could exploit for food. On Figure 1 three divisions are plotted: (1) The shaded circles cover all the areas that lie within a day's walk, i.e., a six-mile radius of a permanent waterhole. This area of about 600 square miles supports all of the 248 Bushmen in camps for half the year. Thus the effective population density for the dry season is 42/100 square miles. (2) The unshaded circles enclose an additional 400 square miles that lie within a six-mile radius of a large, seasonal summer waterhole. These areas support most of the resident population for the other half of the year. (3) Finally, the dotted line encloses all the areas that lie within a twenty-mile radius of permanent water. None of the Bushmen were observed to camp or forage *outside* of this dotted line, and in fact the additional areas, so defined, were rarely utilized by the Bushmen. Therefore about 1000 square miles was sufficient to support the entire population, plus visitors, at an effective density of 25 per 100 square miles, or four square miles per person.

Table III shows the actual numbers resident at each waterhole during the dry season of 1964. Two of the waterholes, !xabe and Mahopa, did not have an independent camp resident. The other six waterholes supported all of the 248 Bushmen in camps. The mean standing population per waterhole was forty-one and the range was from a low of sixteen at !angwa to a high of ninety-four at /ai/ai. These differences in standing population may reflect differences in the density of foodstuffs. It is probable that /ai/ai with ninety-four residents had more food closer to home than did !angwa, with only sixteen residents. Dobe with a standing population of thirty-seven was closest to the mean and was the subject of an intensive investigation of the relation of subsistence effort to food consumption.[4]

---

[4] The ecological and demographic determinants of group structure will be discussed in another paper.

V. PATTERNS OF CONSUMPTION

The camp serves as a home base for its members. Each morning some people move out to collect plant food and/or hunt game, and each evening the workers return to the camp and pool the collected resources with each other and with the members who stayed behind. Food getting is not a cooperative activity. Collectors go out in twos and threes and each woman gathers plant foods on her own. Hunters usually work individually or in pairs and the success of the hunt is dependent largely on an individual's tracking ability and on the enthusiasm of his hunting dogs; there is no evidence of coordinated effort producing more meat than individual effort.

Cooperation is clearly in evidence, however, in the consumption of food. Not only do families pool the day's production,

Table III The numbers and distribution of the resident Bushmen and Bantu by waterhole

Name of Waterhole*	No. of Camps	Population of camps	Other Bushmen	Total Bushmen	Bantu
Dobe	2	37	—	37	—
!angwa	1	16	23	39	84
Bate	2	30	12	42	21
!ubi	1	19	—	19	65
!gose	3	52	9	61	18
/ai/ai	5	94	13	107	67
!xabe	—	—	8	8	12
Mahopa	—	—	23	23	73
Totals	14	248	88	336	340

* For locations refer to Figure 1.

but the entire camp—residents and visitors alike—shares equally in the total quantity of food available. The evening meal of any one family is made up of portions of food from the supplies of each of the other families resident. Foodstuffs are distributed raw or are prepared by the collector and then distributed. There is a constant flow of nuts, berries, roots, and melons from one family fireplace to another until each person resident has received an equitable portion (cf. Marshall 1961). The following morning a different combination of foragers moves out of camp and, when they return late in the day, the distribution of foodstuffs is repeated. Except in the case of windfalls, such as the killing of a large ungulate, food rarely moves beyond the boundaries of a camp. People, however, move frequently from one camp to another. The boundary of the camp, therefore, can be considered to define the boundary of the co-consuming group; and the size of the consumption unit will depend on the number of personnel on hand in a given day.

The food resources of the Dobe area were both varied and abundant. I tabulated over 200 plant and 220 animal species known and named by the Bushmen (Lee 1965:98–121). Of these, eighty-five plant species and fifty-four animal species were classified by the Bushmen as edible. The basic food staple is the mongongo (mangetti) nut, *Ricinodendron rautanenii Schinz;* alone it accounted for one-half to two-thirds of the total vegetable diet by weight. This species was so abundant that millions of the nuts rotted on the ground each year for want of picking. The energy yield of the nut meat is remarkably high: 600 cals./ 100 gms. (see Section VIII below).

Of the fifty-four animals classified as edible, only ten species of mammals were regularly hunted for food. The ten species, listed in order of their importance in the diet, are: wart hog, kudu, diuker, steenbok, gemsbok, wildebeeste, spring hare, porcupine, ant bear, and common hare.

VI. FORAGING STRATEGY

The Bushmen were observed to be highly selective in their food habits. They stated strong likes and dislikes in foods and all of the eighty-five edible species of vegetable food were clearly ranked by the Bushmen on criteria of desirability: tastiness, nutritional value, abundance, and ease of collecting. As a rule people tended to eat only the most palatable and abundant foods available and to bypass the less desirable foods. Since the other major factor in subsistence was the distance between food and water, it is possible to summarize the basic principle of Bushman foraging strategy in a single statement: *At a given moment, the*

members of a camp prefer to collect and eat the desirable foods
that are at the least distance from standing water.

Given this principle, the optimum situation occurs when standing water and mongongo nuts are close together, and the worst
situation occurs when water and nuts are far apart. The dynamics
of the subsistence situation are made clear when we realize that
the food that can be eaten in one week is a function of the food
that has already been eaten in previous weeks.

The Bushmen typically occupy a camp for a period of weeks
or months and eat their way out of it. For instance, at a camp in
the nut forests (which form narrow belts along the crests of fixed
dunes, see Figure 1), the members will exhaust the nuts within
a one-mile radius during the first week of occupation, within
a two-mile radius the second week, and within a three-mile radius
the third week. As time goes on, the members of the group must
travel farther and farther to reach the nuts, and the round-trip
distance in miles is a measurement of the "cost" of obtaining
this desirable food.

In Figure 2, the cost of obtaining mongongo nuts is plotted

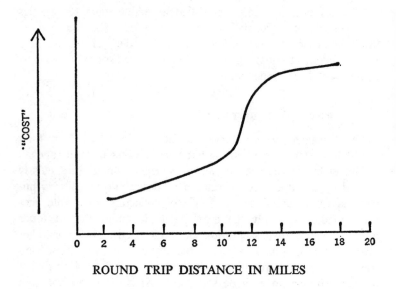

Figure 2   The cost curve for obtaining mongongo nuts

against distance. The cost curve for nuts rises slowly as the round-trip distance increases from two to twelve miles, climbs sharply from twelve to sixteen miles, then levels off for longer distances. The reason for the inflection in the cost curve is the difference between one-day trips and overnight trips. A round trip of up to twelve miles can be accomplished in a single day, but for trips to more distant points an overnight hike must be organized, involving the packing of drinking water and the carrying of heavy loads over long distances.

The alternative tactic to the longer trips is to stay at the home base, and to exploit foods of lesser desirability in terms of taste, ease of collecting, and abundance. At a given dry season camp one sees both alternative tactics in evidence. The older, less mobile members of the camp stay close to home and collect the less desirable foods, while the younger, more active members make the longer trips to the nut forests. As the water—nut distance increases, more and more attention is given to the lesser foods.

During the rainy season, a different and less costly strategy is employed. Since temporary pools of water form at a number of localities, when nuts are exhausted within a few miles of one pool the entire group moves camp to another where water and nuts are still abundant. Thus the "cost" of obtaining nuts during the rainy season never exceeds the level of a six-mile round trip. Towards the end of the rainy season, a temporary pool may dry up before the nuts in its immediate vicinity become exhausted. In this case the residents move camp to one of the large summer waterholes which usually persist until early autumn (April or May). When these latter pools dry up, then the entire population moves back to the areas around the eight permanent waterholes to spend the winter and spring dry season.

It is evident that the crucial factor in the annual subsistence cycle is the distance between food and water. Basically, the Dobe area !Kung face three different sets of conditions through the year.

(1) Food Abundant and Many Water Points

During the rainy season (November–April) all the people live at the temporary pools in the midst of the nut forests. The water–food distance is short and the subsistence effort is minimal. This is also the season of plant growth when seasonal foods such as berries and leafy greens are available.

(II) Food Abundant but Only Eight Water Points

In the early half of the dry season (May–July), all the groups are based at the permanent waterholes. They eat out an increasing radius of desirable foods. As the water–food distance increases, the subsistence effort increases.

(III) Food Scarce and Only Eight Water Points

By the end of the dry season (August–October) the water–food distance approaches an annual maximum. People must either walk long distances to reach the nuts, or be content to eat the less and less desirable foods, such as bitter melons, roots, Acacia gum, and the heart of the vegetable ivory palm. The diet is most eclectic at this time of year.

With the onset of the first rains in late October or November, a new cycle of plant growth is initiated and seasonal pools again form in the hinterland. The subsistence effort decreases to the level of condition I.

VII. INPUT-OUTPUT: THE SUBSISTENCE EFFORT

As stated earlier, the purpose of Bushman work is to get food, and the amount of work expended is therefore a measure of the effort required to feed the group. In addition, the food gathered is equitably distributed among all members of the camp and rarely moves beyond camp boundaries. With these points in mind, we can apply the framework of input-output analysis to the Bushman data. The work input, or subsistence effort, is a compilation of all the days of work carried out by members of a group within a specified period of time. The subsistence effort could be stated in terms of the number of work days per week per hunter or gatherer. This, however, is a crude measure, since it does not define the size of the consumption unit. In addition one should know the number of dependents who are being supported by the work. The consumption unit, therefore, is defined by adding together the total number of effectives and the total number of dependents resident at a camp during a specified period.

I have found useful the following formula for measuring "S," the index of subsistence effort:

$$S = \frac{W}{C}$$

where W=the number of man-days of work and
where C=the number of man-days of consumption.

Example 1 Consider a hypothetical population of ten people subsisting for a thirty-day period. Since everyone eats every day, the value of "C" (man-days of consumption) is:

$$C = 10 \times 30$$
$$= 300$$

How many man-days of work will be necessary to provide 300 man-days of consumption? If every person worked every day of the thirty-day period, then:

$$W = 10 \times 30 \qquad \text{and} \qquad S = \frac{W}{C}$$
$$= 300 \qquad\qquad\qquad = \frac{300}{300}$$
$$= 1.00$$

Since every person works every day in order to eat every day, the value of "S" is unity.

Example 2 If everyone worked on alternate days, then:

$$S = \frac{10 \times 15}{300}$$
$$= .5$$

Example 3 If half the people worked every day and half the people were dependents, then:

$$S = \frac{5 \times 30}{300}$$
$$= .5$$

Example 1, in which everyone works every day, is not merely a hypothetical case. In fact, "S=1.00" approximates the situation among the non-human primates (and most other vertebrates) in which every animal (save nursing infants) forages for its own food on every day of the year. For monkeys and apes (DeVore 1965) the value of "S" approaches unity and the actual value of "S" is simply a function of the percentage of nursing infants in the population.

A baboon troop, for example, leaves the sleeping area each morning and spends the day moving as a group through its range (Hall and DeVore 1965:70). Although the spatial cohesion of the group is maintained, each troop member acts as a self-sufficient subsistence unit, collecting and eating its own foods as it moves. There is no *exchange* of food between individuals, and this is truly a "hand-to-mouth" existence. The foregoing is not meant to imply that subsistence is precarious for baboons and other primates. On the contrary, the individual animal may spend only a few hours a day picking food, and this activity is interspersed with periods of social grooming, sexual and dominance behaviors, and sleeping. The point is that the work rhythm is such that every individual must do some subsistence work on *every single day of his adult life.*

The work rhythm of human groups is radically different. All human societies allocate some days to work and others to leisure, and in all human societies some people work harder than others. However, the condition "S=1.00" can be regarded as the baseline from which man evolved. The sharing of food is part of a cluster of basic human institutions which also include the division of subsistence labor, the home base, the primary carrying device (for transporting foods to the home base for distribution), and the prolonged support of non-productive young and old people. These developments represent a quantum step in human affairs, for their presence means that not *all* of the people have to work *all* of the time.

The immediate implication of division of labor was that the value of "S," the index of subsistence effort, must have dropped radically during the early phases of hominid evolution. It is at this point that human economics parts company with animal energetics. The long-term implications of division of labor are manifold. Exchange opens up the possibility of more and more complex forms of surplus accumulation, either for the purpose of distribution to a wider social group or for the purpose of consumption by the producers themselves at a later date. Therefore one of the important dimensions along which economic evolution can be traced is the increasing separation between the production of food and its allocation to consumers.

Formally, the !Kung Bushmen economy corresponds to an early stage in this trend since the relation between production and consumption of food is immediate in space and time. Food produced by the local group is consumed within its boundaries, usually within forty-eight hours of production. The major concern, therefore, is to use the formula $S = \dfrac{W}{C}$ for the analysis of !Kung subsistence.

In any self-sufficient human group the magnitude of "S," the subsistence effort, is a function of the ease or difficulty of feeding the group. One would assume that hunter-gatherers such as the !Kung Bushmen, with a simple technology, living in a marginal desert environment, would have a difficult time getting food; therefore the index of subsistence effort should be relatively high.

For instance, in a group of ten people, if the six adults had to work 5½ days per week to support themselves and four dependents, then the value of "S" would be ca. .5. A 5½ day work week is not excessive by Western industrial standards. On the other hand, if the work week were only three days long, then the value of "S" would fall to .26.

The calculation of the actual level of subsistence effort is, of course, an empirical question. Table IV tabulates the four-week work diary for the Dobe camp during the period July 6 to August 2, 1964. This period was chosen because it was neither the easiest nor the most difficult time of the year for subsistence, and it covered the period of transition from better to worse conditions.

Column (1) shows the number of adults at the camp on each day and column (2) the number of children. Column (3) tabulates the number of man-days of consumption (and incidentally documents the daily variations in group size). Column (4) counts the number of people who went out for food each day. Column (5) lists the meat output, in pounds of edible raw portion, for each day.

Table IV   Dobe work diary: a record of the activities at the Dobe camp for the 28-day period 6 July–2 August, 1964

Week	Date		(1) Adults	(2) Children	(3) Man-days of consumption*	(4) Man-days of work	(5) Meat output pounds
I	July	6	18	9	27	9	—
		7	14	9	23	6	92
		8	15	9	24	2	—
		9	15	9	24	3	12
		10	16	9	25	7	—
		11	18	11	29	3	—
		12	18	9	27	7	—
II**		13	20	11	31	5	—
		14	16	9	25	0	—
		15	16	9	25	1	—
		16	14	9	23	0	—
		17	19	12	31	11	80
		18	17	9	26	3	—
		19	23	14	37	2	—
III		20	26	14	40	9	110
		21	24	11	35	3	24
		22	19	13	32	3	—
		23	18	11	29	4	27
		24	23	13	36	10	16
		25	22	10	32	6	—
		26	24	12	36	7	—
IV		27	22	13	35	12	7
		28	27	13	40	12	80
		29	26	13	39	9	10
		30	24	11	35	16	12
		31	22	10	32	4	20
	Aug.	1	24	11	35	8	—
		2	22	11	33	16	—

* Each entry in column 3 equals the sum of the entries in columns 1 and 2 for the given date.

**Week II (July 13–19) shows an unusually *low* work output. The investigator contributed food on July 12 and 17, resulting in a decreased subsistence effort for the seven-day period. Week II therefore has not been included in final calculation of the S ratio (see Table V).

Table V is a summary, by week, of the work diary. Mean group size (column 1) varies from 25.6 to 35.6; the actual count of personnel on hand was rarely the same two days running. The work week (column 7) varies from 1.2 to 3.2 work days per adult. In other words, each productive individual supports herself or himself and dependents and still has 3½ to 5½ days available for other activities. The Index of Subsistence Effort (column 8) varies from .11 to .31. For instance, during Week I (July 6–12), thirty-seven man-days of work were expended to provide 179 man-days of consumption. The value S=.21 indicates twenty-one days of work per hundred man-days of consumption; or each day's work provided food for the worker and four other people. During Week IV (July 27–August 2), seventy-seven man-days of work provided 249 man-days of consumption for an "S" value of .31 (31 work days per 100 consumption days). The work input during Week IV is 50 per cent higher than in Week I. This rise reflects an increased difficulty in reaching food, although, in terms of actual time devoted to the food quest, the average rises from two days per week to three per week per individual producer.

In calculating the overall average value of "S" for this period, I have omitted Week II for the reason noted (Table IV, note 2); therefore the Index of Subsistence Effort for this camp of !Kung Bushmen is .23. Since the non-productive members comprised 35 per cent of the population, another way of expressing the Index is to say that 65 per cent of the people worked 36 per cent of the time, and 35 per cent of the people did no work at all.[5]

Two of the ecological conditions noted above are represented in the work diary. The first week is condition II, in which food is abundant but only eight water points are available. People are making the daily round trips to the nut forests, giving an "S" value of .21. By the fourth week condition III has appeared; it is no longer possible to reach the nuts in one day, since a radius of over seven miles has been eaten out. The round-trip distance

---

[5]In calculating the Index, I have taken into account only the work actually devoted to getting food. The time spent on manufacturing the tool kit has not been included, nor has the time spent on processing food. However, in calculating the caloric requirements (Section VIII), I have included a value for the energy expended in such activities.

Table V Summary of Dobe work diary

Week	(1) mean group size	(2) adult-days	(3) child-days	(4) total man-days of consumption	(5) man-days of work	(6) meat lbs.	(7) work week	(8) Index of Subsistence Effort
I (July 6–12)	25.6 (23–29)	114	65	179	37	104	2.3	.21
II (July 13–19)	28.3 (23–37)	125	73	198	22	80	1.2	.11
III (July 20–26)	34.3 (29–40)	156	84	240	42	177	1.9	.18
IV (July 27–Aug. 2)	35.6 (32–40)	167	82	249	77	129	3.2	.31
4-wk. Totals	30.9	562	304	866	178	490	2.2	.21
Adjusted* Totals	31.8	437	231	668	156	410	2.5	.23

* See note** in Table IV

KEY: Column 1: mean group size = total man-days of consumption
$$\frac{\text{total man-days of consumption}}{7}$$

Column 7: work week = the number of work days per adult per week

Column 8: Index of Subsistence Effort = $\dfrac{\text{man-days of work}}{\text{man-days of consumption}}$

(e.g., in Week I, the value of "S" = .21, i.e., 21 days of work per 100 days of consumption or 1 work day produces food for 5 consumption days) to the nearest nuts is over fourteen miles and the "cost" curve of nuts has turned sharply upwards (see Figure 2). The higher value of "S" (.31) reflects the marked increase in overnight trips to reach the nut forests.

VIII. INPUT-OUTPUT: CALORIC LEVELS

Having considered the level of work effort required to feed the group, it is necessary to determine the quantity of energy yielded by this work effort. Since the actual time devoted to subsistence is modest, the question arises whether this low work effort produces a substandard diet.

The major constituents of the diet by weight during this period were:

1.	mongongo nuts	33%
2.	meat	37%
3.	other vegetable foods	30%
		100%

During field work no direct caloric observations were made. It was difficult to measure a single individual's daily food intake, since this was eaten over a period of several hours in the late afternoon and evening and was made up of small portions from the supplies of different families. However, since foodstuffs are shared equitably throughout the camp, it was possible to measure gross per capita intake by estimating the total weight of food brought in and dividing it by the number of people on hand. A net per capita intake figure was calculated by deducting values for waste (inedible portions, bones, nutshells, etc.) and allowing for loss through cooking. An account follows of the methods and results.

1. The staple mongongo nut is particularly suitable for this kind of analysis; it is easy to count and weigh, and the percentage of edible constituents is precisely known. The nut consists of a hard outer shell and a soft inner shell (both inedible) and a core of edible nut meat. The whole nut weighs 5.0 gm. and the nut meat comprises 14 per cent of the total weight, or 0.7 gm. (Anon. 1917; author's field observations).

There are approximately 200 whole nuts per kilogram (91

nuts per lb.). Each kilogram of whole nuts yields 140 gm. of nut
meats (64 gm. per lb.). I weighed the total back load of nuts
brought in by a sample of women each day. A woman's daily
collection of whole nuts weighed between 10 kg. (22 lbs.) and
15 kg. (33 lbs.), although back loads of as much as 20 kg.
(44 lbs.) of whole nuts were recorded. Each back load contained
on the average 2500 whole nuts, as well as smaller quantities of
other foodstuffs. Since the edible portion of whole nuts is 14 per
cent, each 12.5 kg. back load of nuts contained 1750 gm. of edible
nut meats.

Records were also maintained for the number of nuts cracked
and eaten by individuals and families on a single day. Women
roast a quantity of nuts in the coals of the fire for a few minutes before cracking. The nuts are equally palatable when raw,
but the brief roasting serves to drive off some of the moisture
and makes the hard outer shell easier to crack. The nut is then
cracked open, using a fist-sized limestone cobble as a hammer-
stone and a larger flat limestone block as an anvil. The shell is
extremely hard, which accounts for the remarkable storage properties of the mongongo. Nuts are still perfectly edible after having lain on the ground for a year.

The cracking and shelling rate averages five or six nuts per
minute and varies little from one woman to another. In one hour
a woman cracks and shells 300–360 nuts, or one-eighth of a back
load, and an hour's cracking yields 210–252 gm. of edible nut
meats. On the basis of observations of cracking rates and time
devoted to cracking, and on the basis of total weights of whole
nuts brought into the camp, Bushmen were observed to eat about
300 nuts per person per day, yielding 210 gm. of nut meats. Thus
one back load of whole nuts would feed a family of four for two
days, with a little left over for the third day.

The constituents of the nut meat have been determined
(Wehmer 1931, vol. 2:678)[6] and the nutritional yield can be
calculated (Oser 1965:1336).[7] The yield is 600 (±1 per cent)
cal. per 100 gm. of edible portion and the protein yield 27 gm. per
100 gm. The caloric value of mongongo compares favorably with

---

[6] Fats 59.4%, Protein 27.0%, Crude Fiber 5.9%, Water 4.7%, Ash 3.02%.
[7] Modified Atwater formulas used by the F.A.O. were employed, based on
the following values: 8.37 cal./gm. of fat, 3.4 cal./gm. of protein.

that of domesticated species of nuts such as almonds (600 cal. per 100 gm.), brazil nuts (653), cashews (563), and peanuts (583). In proteins, however, it exceeds the levels for these other nuts (27 per cent for mongongo vs. an average of 19 per cent for other species).

2. Complete records were kept for kills of game animals, and for the quantities of meat brought into the Dobe camp during the twenty-eight-day period of the work diary. Eighteen animals, totalling 206 kg. (454 lbs.) of edible meat, were killed and consumed by members of the camp.[8] In addition, 16 kg. (36 lbs.) of meat were brought into Dobe by visitors from other camps, for a total of 222 kg. (490 lbs.) of meat. Dividing this figure by the 866 man-days of consumption (see above) gives a daily allotment of 256 gm. (9.1 oz.) of uncooked meat per person. Even allowing for a 10 per cent shrinkage in cooking, the caloric yield of this allotment is estimated at 690 calories (based on a rate of 300 cal. per 100 gms., cooked). The protein content is estimated to be 15 per cent by weight, or 34.5 gms. per cooked portion.

3. The remaining vegetable portion of the diet consisted of small quantities of twenty species of roots, melons, gums, bulbs, and dried fruits. No caloric observations were made for these foods and their total caloric yield is estimated at 100 cal. per 100 gm. Protein yield is negligible, and is estimated at 1 per cent.

In Table VI the three main food sources (meat, mongongo nuts, other vegetable foods) are brought together in order to show the contribution each makes to the Bushman diet and to derive an estimate of daily per capita intake of calories and proteins. The results show a daily allotment of 2140 calories and 93.1 grams of proteins per person. Because of the high protein values for mongongo, the protein intake is unusually high even by American standards. It is also unexpected that a hunting people should get such a high proportion of their proteins from vegetable rather than from meat sources.

Does a per capita intake of 2140 calories meet the energy requirements of the group? The Bushmen are small in stature and

---

[8] Edible/waste ratios for various mammals were calculated by R. H. S. Smithers.

weight. The average height and weight for adult males are 157 centimeters (5ft. 2 in.) and 46 kilograms (101 lbs.) and for adult females 147 centimeters (4ft. 10 in.) and 41 kilograms (91 lbs.) (Bronte-Stewart et al. 1960). Basal metabolic requirement for individuals of such heights and weights are calculated

Table VI Caloric and protein levels in the !Kung Bushman dietary, July–August, 1964

Class of food	Percentage Contribution to Diet	Per Capita Consumption		Calories per person per day
		Weight in grams	Protein in grams	
meat	37%	230	34.5	690
mongongo nuts	33%	210	56.7	1260
other vegetable foods	30%	190	1.9	190
Total, all sources	100%	630	93.1	2140

at 1400 cal. per day for males and 1100 cal. per day for females (Taylor and Pye 1966:45–48). Given an activity regime that varies from light–moderate to severe exercise (including an hour of nut-cracking per day and two ten-mile hikes per week), the caloric requirements can be estimated at 2250 calories for males and 1750 calories for females, per day of an average work week. These figures apply to adults thirty years of age and would necessarily be less for middle-aged and elderly persons. For children I have taken a median age of eight years for all individuals under age fifteen and estimate the daily requirements at 2000 calories (Taylor and Pye 1966:463).

To calculate the daily caloric requirement for the study group as a whole, it is necessary to take an average weight according to the percentage of each age-sex class in the population. Since the population consists of 30 per cent adult males, 35 per cent adult females, and 35 per cent children under fifteen years (see Tables I and II), the mean daily energy requirement for a group of thirty-one persons is 61,300 calories, and for each group member, about 1975 calories.

The per capita yield of foodstuffs during the study period

was estimated to be 2140 calories (Table VI) and therefore it is clear that food output exceeds energy requirements by about 165 calories per person per day. The conclusion can be drawn that the Bushmen do not lead a substandard existence on the edge of starvation as has been commonly supposed.[9]

A portion of these extra calories is absorbed by the food allocated to the maintenance of hunting dogs. The dog population of Dobe varied from five to eight animals. The dogs eat what is left over when people have eaten their fill, and it is worth noting that the physical condition of the animals seemed to show more seasonal variation than the conditions of the humans. It may be possible that, in input-output terms, Bushman dogs absorb most of the marginal variation in abundance of foodstuffs brought into the camp.[10]

The remainder of the extra calories may go into physiological accumulation of fat by the Bushmen during the good season, an accumulation which is then metabolized during the worst season of the year (September–October). Future research should include the weights and skin-fold measurements of individuals taken each month through the annual cycle. During the lean season of the year, the availability of the staple mongongo nut reaches an annual low, and the people have to walk farther and work harder in order to maintain an adequate diet. In other words, a higher energy input yields a relatively lower caloric output.

The significance of the differential activities of young and old people can now be appreciated. The more able, more mobile members of the group have higher energy requirements and they have the means to meet these by making the long hikes to the mongongo nut forests. The old people, with more modest energy requirements, remain close to home and gather a more eclectic diet

---

[9] The possibility that the Bushmen were enjoying an exceptionally good year can be discounted. The observations were made during the second year of a severe drought, which seriously dislocated the pastoral and farming economics of the Bantu, but apparently did not seriously affect the foraging economy of the Bushmen. If drought conditions demanded a three-day work week from the Bushmen, then one would have to postulate an even lower work input during years of average or higher rainfall.

[10] Pigs may play a similar role in the subsistence economy of Melanesians (Vayda et al. 1961; Rappaport 1967). Unlike the Melanesians, who eat their pigs, the Bushmen have never been known to eat their dogs.

of low-yield roots, bulbs, and edible gums. The group as a whole distributes the collective resources in such a way that the caloric needs of each age-sex class are met. In input-output terms this is a way of restating the classic dictum: *from each according to his means and to each according to his needs.* In principle the Bushman camp is a communistic society. In practice, sharing is never complete, but conflicting parties have the option of rearranging themselves spatially so that, when sharing breaks down, new groups can be constituted to ensure parity of production and consumption.

The input-output approach to subsistence has shown that !Kung Bushmen in the Dobe area can derive an adequate living from only a modest expenditure of their time and effort. The analysis may help to correct the impression that their life is a constant struggle, maintained in the face of adversity, and ending in early death. As Sahlins (1968:85–89) has pointed out in a recent discussion, our view of the hunter has been conditioned by the traditional wisdom of the economics of scarcity. We have tended to equate poverty with the absence of material wealth. Sahlins suggests the alternative interpretation that hunters may be simply in business for their health, and that this modest end can be achieved even with the rudimentary technical means at their disposal. The result is that hunters may actually enjoy more leisure time per capita than do peoples engaged in other subsistence activities (see also Service 1966:13). In the Bushman case, food-getting is the primary productive activity, but the majority of the people's time (four to five days per week) is spent in other pursuits, such as resting in camp or visiting other camps.

Since the northern Kalahari Desert is by any account a marginal habitat for human occupation, it is likely that hunters in the past would have had an even more substantial subsistence base. Today the remaining hunters are confined to the least attractive environments of the world, but in Pleistocene times they would have had their pick of the richest areas, in terms of game, plant foods, and water supply.[11]

---

[11] The reconstruction of the prehistoric habitats of hunter-gatherers has been discussed in detail elsewhere (Lee 1963 and 1968).

IX. ELEMENTARY FORMS AND THE LOGIC OF GENERALIZED RECIPROCITY

One of the most striking cross-cultural regularities yet discovered is the almost universal practice of voluntary food sharing among small-scale hunter-gatherers.[12] Sahlins has labelled this practice generalized reciprocity, and defines it as the giving of food, or other goods, without a definite expectation of return (1965:147). It is the kind of transaction that obtains in our own society between members of the nuclear family, and it falls at the solidary (sociable) extreme of Sahlins' continuum of reciprocities, ranging from generalized, through balanced, to negative reciprocity, the latter being the unsociable extreme (1965:147–49).

Viewed as a system of allocations, generalized reciprocity may be a necessary sociological outcome of the elementary form of economic life defined in Section I of this paper. The clue lies in the implications of this practice for the organization of subsistence. The obverse of sharing is, of course, hoarding, or withholding. The latter is reported to be a cardinal sin among hunter-gatherers (Service 1966:18; Sahlins 1965:200–1, 215–18). Yet hoarding is but a morally negative paraphrase of the respectable economic term "surplus accumulation." The act of setting aside a portion of one's production for consumption or distribution at a future date is the essence of bourgeois economics ("savings"), but it is regarded as stinginess or hard-heartedness among the hunters. Since everyone in a hunter camp must be fed from the food supply on hand and since no one can be refused, the constancy of demand tends to keep food inventories at a minimum. It also tends to maintain "wealth" differences between people at an exceedingly low level. Constant turnover and low inventories are simply different facets of the earlier definition of an elementary form as an economy in which food production and consumption are immediate. In such an economy, the withholding of

---

[12] Some of the evidence has been brought together by Sahlins in his excellent review on reciprocity (1965:186–91, 200–1, 215–18). The practice of generalized reciprocity within local groups is found among: Mbuti Pygmies, Andaman Islanders, Australian Aborigines, Eskimos, Semang, and Great Basin Shoshone. For references consult Sahlins (*op cit.*).

food by even one party would be incompatible with the model of generalized reciprocity. Only if all parties are equally wealthy—or, to be more accurate—equally poor, can the economic equilibrium be maintained.

What would happen if one individual in such an economy, against the expectations of his fellows, were to husband his resources and allocate his production to savings rather than to sharing? The short-term result of such a move would probably be ostracism for the individual; but if enough of his fellows were able to follow his example and did so, then the social fabric would be preserved and a new economic equilibrium would be established at a higher level of surplus accumulation. Wealth disparities would now become possible, and an avenue for the conversion of subsistence goods into prestige would open up. Such a society would have embarked on the road to "economic development."

In human energy relations, no individual is self-sufficient. Human existence is made possible by the work effort of individuals, but social life is founded upon the principle of cooperative consumption of resources. It is fortunate for anthropologists that in some contemporary societies, the rudimentary forms of exchange may still be observed. In other societies higher orders of complexity can also be observed, enabling the analyst to trace the evolution of economic systems.

Starting from the primate baseline of a "hand-to-mouth" existence, one can discern several secular trends in human social evolution. One such trend leads to an increasing separation between the production of food and its final allocation in consumption. Another is in the direction of conversion of an increasing proportion of subsistence output into the production of durable goods. And a third trend is towards a greater and greater disparity in the distribution of wealth among individuals.

On all of these dimensions, the !Kung Bushmen exhibit an elementary form. Although the ideology of exchange is complex, the formal aspects of exchange are simple. Using input-output analysis may contribute, on a quantitative level, to our understanding of the origins and evolution of economics.

BIBLIOGRAPHY

Anonymous
  1917 "Manketti Nuts from South-West Africa." *Bulletin of the Imperial Institute,* 15: 35–38.
Bohannan, Paul, and George Dalton (eds.)
  1962 *Markets in Africa.* Evanston: Northwestern University Press.
Bronte-Stewart, B., O. E. Budtz-Olsen, J. M. Hickley, and J. F. Brock
  1960 "The Health and Nutritional Status of the !Kung Bushmen of South West Africa." *South African Journal of Laboratory and Clinical Medicine,* 6: 187–216.
Childe, V. Gordon
  1951 *Social Evolution.* New York: Schuman.
DeVore, Irven (ed.)
  1965 *Primate Behavior: Field Studies of Monkeys and Apes.* New York: Holt, Rinehart & Winston.
DuBois, Cora
  1936 "The Wealth Concept as an Integrative Factor in Tolowa-Tututni Culture," in R. H. Lowie (ed.), *Essays in Anthropology Presented to A. L. Kroeber.* Berkeley: University of California Press.
Gates, David Murray
  1962 *Energy Exchange in the Biosphere.* New York: Harper & Row.
Hall, K. R. L., and Irven DeVore
  1965 "Baboon Social Behavior," in I. DeVore (ed.), *Primate Behavior.* New York: Holt, Rinehart & Winston.
Kleiber, Max
  1961 *The Fire of Life: an Introduction to Animal Energetics.* New York: John Wiley.
Lee, Richard B.
  1963 "Population Ecology of Man in the Early Upper Pleistocene of Southern Africa." *Proceedings of the Prehistoric Society,* 29: 235–57.
  1965 *Subsistence Ecology of !Kung Bushmen.* Unpublished Ph.D. Dissertation, University of California, Berkeley.
  1968 "What Hunters Do for a Living, or, How to Make Out on Scarce Resources." in R. B. Lee and I. DeVore (eds.), *Man the Hunter.* Chicago: Aldine.

Leontief, Wassily
1966 *Input-Output Economics.* New York: Oxford University Press.
Lévi-Strauss, Claude
1949 *Les Structures élémentaires de la parenté.* Paris: Presses Universitaires de France.
Malan, F.
1950 "A Wilton Site at Kaikai, Bechuanaland Protectorate." *South African Archaeological Bulletin,* 5: 140–42.
Marshall, John
1956 *The Hunters* (film). Film Study Center, Peabody Museum, Cambridge, Mass.
Marshall, Lorna
1957 "The Kin Terminology System of the !Kung Bushmen." *Africa,* 27: 1–25.
1959 "Marriage Among !Kung Bushmen." *Africa,* 29: 335–65.
1960 "!Kung Bushman Bands." *Africa,* 30: 325–55.
1961 "Sharing, Talking, and Giving: Relief of Social Tensions among !Kung Bushmen." *Africa,* 31: 231:49.
1962 "!Kung Bushman Religious Beliefs." *Africa,* 32: 221–52.
Marx, Karl
1867 *Das Kapital.* New York: Random House (Modern Library Edition).
Oser, Bernard L. (ed.)
1965 *Hawk's Physiological Chemistry,* Fourteenth Edition. New York: McGraw-Hill.
Polanyi, Karl
1944 *The Great Transformation.* New York: Rinehart.
1957 "The Economy as an Instituted Process," in K. Polanyi, C. W. Arensberg, and H. W. Pearson (eds.), *Trade and Market in the Early Empires.* Glencoe, Ill.: The Free Press.
Rappaport, Roy A.
1967 "Ritual Regulation of Environmental Relations Among a New Guinea People." *Ethnology,* 6: 17–30.
Richards, Audrey I.
1939 *Land, Labour and Diet in Northern Rhodesia.* London: Oxford University Press.
Sahlins, Marshall D.
1965 "On the Sociology of Primitive Exchange," in *The Relevance of Models for Social Anthropology.* A. S. A. Monographs 1. London: Tavistock; New York: Praeger.
1968 "Notes on the Original Affluent Society," comment in R. B. Lee and I. DeVore (eds.), *Man the Hunter.* Chicago: Aldine.
Service, Elman R.
1966 *The Hunters.* Englewood Cliffs, N.J.: Prentice-Hall.
Silberbauer, George B.
1965 *Report to the Government of Bechuanaland on the Bushman Survey.* Gabarones: Bechuanaland Government.

Sillery, Anthony
1952 *The Bechuanaland Protectorate.* London: Oxford University Press.
Taylor, Clara M., and Orrea F. Pye
1966 *Foundations of Nutrition,* Sixth Edition. New York: Macmillan.
Thomas, Elizabeth Marshall
1959 *The Harmless People.* New York: Knopf.
Vayda, Andrew P., Anthony Leeds, and David P. Smith
1961 "The Place of Pigs in Melanesian Subsistence," in V. E. Garfield
(ed.), *Proceedings of the 1961 Annual Spring Meeting of the American Ethnological Society.* Seattle: University of Washington Press.
Wehmer, Carl
1931 *Die Pflanzenstoffe,* 2 vols. Second Edition. Jena: Fischer.
White, Leslie A.
1949 *The Science of Culture.* New York: Farrar, Straus.
1959 *The Evolution of Culture.* New York: McGraw-Hill.
Wolf, Eric
1966 *Peasants.* Englewood Cliffs, N.J.: Prentice-Hall.

4 ECOLOGY AND ADAPTATION
TO PARASITIC DISEASES[1]

Alexander Alland, Jr.

THE STUDY OF disease and disease-related behavior in preliterate societies has two important values: (1) it serves as
an aid in the analysis of demographic factors which often lie at
the base of more complicated ethnological problems; (2) it allows
the investigator to test hypotheses related to the survival value of
cultural practices associated with disease.

An objective study of disease-related behavior must go beyond
"ethnoscience" (in which only native medicine is considered) to
a full analysis of encounters in the real world between man
and his parasites. The morbidity profile of any population is
dependent upon such encounters, the complexity of which, more
often than not, will go beyond any existing native medical
theory. What I am suggesting is that even in such cases where
relationships between certain cultural practices and disease are not
understood by a population, such practices will have an objective
effect on morbidity rates.

In this paper I shall outline a series of biological factors which
intersect with cultural practices to produce particular disease patterns. I shall also offer a brief illustration, drawn from my own

This is an original article appearing for the first time in *Environment and
Cultural Behavior.*

[1] The research on which this paper is based was supported by grants
from the Yale University Department of African Studies and the Yale
University Department of Anthropology in the summer of 1960 and by
the United States Public Health Service—National Institute of Mental
Health (Grant Number M-5512) in the fall, winter, and spring of
1961–62.

field work in West Africa, of these factors as they affect a specific population.

For purposes of analysis, pathologies may be divided into three broad categories: (1) functional diseases, including genetic disorders; (2) nutritional diseases; (3) parasitic diseases. Each category presents its own problems for study, and each has some effect on the others, but in this paper I shall deal only with parasitic diseases. These are pathologies caused by the invasion of a host by foreign organisms which interfere with the normal functioning of the host. These organisms include viruses, bacteria, fungi, protozoa, helminths, and arthropods.

Among the biological characteristics to be outlined below, some are concerned with properties of the host, others with properties of the parasites themselves. While these characteristics are discussed separately, it must be understood that the specific disease pattern which occurs in a population depends upon the combined effect of these characteristics and the cultural practices which may be related to them.

SIZE, DENSITY, AND MOVEMENT OF POPULATIONS

Epidemics like people. That is, there are certain optimal numbers which make a population more susceptible to the rapid spread of epidemic disease. The higher the population density, the greater the chance that microorganisms will make a successful transfer from host to host.

Beyond the factor of size, the arrangement of living space has a great deal to do with the spread or containment of disease. Thus the type and arrangement of houses, the number of rooms per dwelling, and the number of occupants per room are all important factors in disease ecology.

Social isolation of various sub-groups may also play a role in the epidemiological pattern displayed by disease. A rigid caste system with minimal social and physical contact between groups may affect epidemic routes in a community for at least some diseases.

Population movement is another important variable. Nomads tend to leave their waste products behind them. Sedentary peoples live in more or less constant contact with their own refuse. Where and how they dispose of this refuse is itself a factor in disease ecology.

Nomadic populations may also carry certain diseases over long distances. Visiting patterns within and between villages are important. Area-wide attendance at funerals and the length of such ceremonies may affect the level and distribution of infection during epidemics. Markets are a good place for the exchange and redistribution of disease organisms as well as goods and services. Contact between different cultural groups may bring about cross-infection.

THE ORGANISMS' ENVIRONMENT OUTSIDE OF THE HUMAN HOST

Most organisms associated with infectious disease spend a part of their life cycle outside their human hosts. Those carried by vectors (organisms carrying parasites to the host) may reproduce and pass through morphological stages in an animal or insect carrier. Others inhabit water, still others soil, and some are found only in human and/or animal excrement. Cultural practices which effectively separate man from the organisms' extra-human environment act to control the incidence of disease in human populations. If human and animal carriers are denied access to such environments, the disease cycle may be broken. Deep latrines offer protection against many intestinal infections which are spread through contact with waste products. Care of the water supply or its location away from domestic animals and human habitation protect against the contamination of water. The penning of domestic animals so that their feces will not spread throughout the village, or the removal of such fecal material, will substantially reduce the chance of transference of enzootic and epizootic diseases to man.

VIABILITY OF THE ORGANISM

The viability of microorganisms depends upon geographical factors and certain features of the host population which are themselves variable, but within any one environment and time period these may be quite stable. Organisms may be rated from highly viable (many viruses) to least viable (organisms of venereal disease). Organisms which spread in the air and which are resistant to long desiccation are particularly difficult to eliminate from a population. Organisms which survive only in a liquid or semi-liquid environment (food, water, feces, and other waste) may be eliminated by boiling or cooking in the case of food and water, or burying in the case of offensive matter. Personal and village hygiene levels are both directly related to the spread or containment of specific diseases, and organisms of low and moderate viability are most susceptible to general hygienic measures.

MODE OF INFECTION

Organisms may gain entry into the host through the unbroken skin (such helminths or worm infections as schistosomiasis and ancylostomiasis), the mouth (most intestinal parasites, guinea worm, the dysenteries), the nose (viruses carried in the air, such as influenza; bacteria causing pneumonia and bronchitis), injection from carriers (encephalitis, malaria, yellow fever, plague, leishmaniasis, dengue, relapsing fever, filariasis), wounds (yaws, gangrene, tropical ulcer, tetanus), or contact with the mucous membrane (venereal diseases). They may also affect the surface of the body (fungus and arthropod infections).

The avoidance of infected streams is the only protection against schistosoma (bilharzia). Aerosol infections may be prevented by isolating the sick. Promiscuous spitting increases the probable spread of viruses and mycobacterium tuberculosis. Protection against injection depends upon an understanding of the host-vector relationship and/or practices which tend to discourage the insect population. Wounds must be covered and contact between infected and normal individuals avoided. Venereal patients must be isolated or refrain from sexual intercourse. Polygyny in combination with adultery and other forms of promiscuity may increase the frequency of contact between infected and normal individuals. Fungus infections may be discouraged by avoiding contact with sick individuals, by boiling contaminated water, through frequent washing (except where the fungus is waterborne), and in certain conditions by shaving body hair.

Certain organisms (anaerobic bacteria such as Clostridium tetani, the organism of tetanus) cause infection only if they gain entry to the host through deep puncture wounds. The type of tools used and kind of work done by members of a society may influence the frequency of this type of injury.

VIABILITY AND TYPE OF VECTOR

Vectors may be divided into two types: mechanical, when the disease organism is merely transported by the vector; or breeding, when the organism depends on the vector for part of its life cycle. The range and habitat of vectors vary considerably. Fleas and lice live on the body of the host, but fleas jump readily from one host to another while lice spread primarily via shared clothing or bedding. Tailored clothing presents a better environment for lice than loose togas. Tapa cloth which must be replaced frequently is the least favorable environment for these vectors. Flies and mosquitoes are highly mobile, but mosquitoes prefer to fly at night, flies in the daytime. One rarely needs protection against mosquitoes in the heat of day, and eating at night or early in the morning may protect food from fly-borne contamination. Some ticks live in the underbrush generally away from human habitation; others are domestic, preferring the cracks in mud walls and house roofing to the bush. The clearing of paths around villages is good protection against ticks of the first type.

Some rodents are also domestic, living in intimate contact with man; others normally live away from human habitation but act as disease reservoirs, sometimes passing infections to the domestic rodent population.

Even mosquitoes may be classified as wild or domestic, in that some breed best in and around villages in trash heaps (Aedes is a good example), while others require natural habitats (most anophelenes). The flight patterns of biting insects is important. Some have very limited flight ranges (sand flies, certain varieties of Glosina, tsetse flies, and Aedes mosquitoes); others cover a wide area (Culex mosquitoes). Certain insects prefer human victims; others bite a range of domestic and wild animals. When the latter is the case, it is possible that much infection is diverted to domestic animals living with man, but such animals also constitute a reservoir of infection. This is true, for example, of yellow fever, which infects monkeys as well as human beings.

Snails, the carriers of schistosomiasis (bilharzia), and cyclops, a microscopic crustacean, the carrier of dracunculosis (guinea worm), are limited to a particular sort of watery environment. Irrigation increases the spread of schistosoma-carrying snails, while the technique of wet rice cultivation leads to frequent contact between human hosts and the parasite environment. Wells, if they are covered, discourage guinea worm, unless infected individuals bathe their sores at well side. Deep latrines or the burial of fecal material keep flies from spreading a wide range of intestinal parasites. Domestic animal populations within the village increase the possibility of parasitic contamination. Dogs, for example, carry the organism of creeping eruption in man.

INCUBATION PERIOD

The incubation period between time of contact and the development of symptoms varies to an extraordinary degree. Where incubation periods are short and the disease severe, nomadic populations or traveling merchants are less likely to spread a disease than when incubation periods are long and the host has time to cover considerable distances before coming down with the disease.

SYMPTOMS AND PRODROMAL SYMPTOMS

The recognition of symptoms is both a biological and cultural problem. A people's classificatory concepts may affect their ability to recognize disease and to isolate individuals before contagion becomes a problem. Where prodromal symptoms are recognized as a preview of incipient disease, isolation may be particularly effective when practiced.

Certain diseases have more discrete symptomologies than others. Measles, chicken pox, and smallpox may be confused in some cultures and distinguished in others. The various forms of leprosy, yaws, and syphilis may be recognized as manifestations of these same three diseases, or each symptom category may be used to tag a separate, ethnically defined illness. Symptoms may be seen as discrete units (headache unrelated to fever, unrelated to rash), or they may be combined to describe a specific condition. The ability to recognize symptoms is important in the effective treatment of disease and effective treatment in turn influences not only the rates of a particular treated condition, but over-all health within any given population. Treatment of one condition may act as an effective barrier against one or more other conditions.

NON-GENETIC FACTORS IN RESISTANCE

Even when the viability of the organism is constant, the receptivity of the host may vary. Diet, work loads, sleep, and exposure are all factors which affect resistance.

IMMUNITY

The incidence and severity of disease may also depend upon the availability of non-immunes within a population. Epidemics of such diseases as measles cycle predictably through time, striking only when a new generation of non-immunes takes its place in the community. A correlation between the ceremonial calendar and this type of cycling may spread disease among a gathering of celebrants. The incidence of epidemics in societies which practice age-grade initiations might well be worth looking at.

THE EXISTENCE OF HUMAN CARRIERS

The occupational role of human carriers in disease is well known in our society from such famous cases as Typhoid Mary. Other diseases such as amoebic dysentery and hepatitis are spread by carriers. Little is known about the role of carriers in other societies. Are they recognized? Do certain occupations make individuals prone to both disease and the possibility of becoming carriers? What is the strategic position of carriers in various societies?

An investigation of the role of carriers in societies stratified according to castes, professions, or social classes might provide interesting data for the field of epidemiology.

COMBINATION OF THESE FACTORS

An epidemiological study must take account of the permutations and combinations resulting from these various biological and cultural factors acting together. To take one example: plague is caused by the bacterium Pasteurella pestis. The organism has low resistance outside of the host. It is carried by rat fleas and does not usually affect a human population until the fleas have no more rats to feed upon. The disease has a short incubation period, a high mortality rate, rather obvious symptoms, and, in its bubonic form, is not transmitted from man to man directly. The rat population varies according to the type and duration of human occupation. This applies not only to the size of the rat population, but to the rat species which is most frequent. Rattus rattus, the principal carrier of the plague vector, may be replaced by other breeds of rat which are less commonly associated with the disease. The short incubation period and high mortality rates of the disease mean that infected populations are not likely to spread the plague directly through population movement, although rat migrations do affect its motility. Isolation of the sick has little effect on the incidence of plague and most hygienic measures offer little protection against epidemics once they have begun. Hygiene practices must be directed specifically to the elimination of rats and fleas. The same disease in its pneumonic form presents an entirely different epidemiological picture, since the rat-flea vectors are eliminated from the disease cycle. Pneumonic plague may develop from the bubonic form and pass rapidly from host to host through direct contact. Total isolation of infected persons then becomes necessary.

A list of the behavioral factors which influence disease patterns may be expanded almost infinitely. My purpose here has been merely to illustrate the kinds of relationships which exist between behavior and certain characteristics of parasites and their hosts. I shall now present a brief outline of key items of behavior which affect health levels and disease patterns of a particular people among whom I have done field work: the Abron of the Ivory Coast. These behaviors represent concrete examples of the interaction between biological and cultural factors discussed in the first part of this paper.

The Abron live in the transitional zone between tropical forest and savannah about 250 miles north of the Atlantic Ocean. Their territory, which encompasses about 3000 square miles, extends westward thirty miles from the Ghana border. Living north of the rain forest, they are less subject to yaws and some fungus infections than forest dwellers, although these conditions do occur. On the other hand, Abron territory lies south of the true savannah where trachoma and meningitis are so common. Climatic and physiographic conditions in Abron country are ideal for the normal run of tropical diseases, excluding only those which are generally associated with long dry periods.

Health levels within the population were found to be affected by a number of cultural practices, many of which were not recognized by the people themselves to have medical significance. Among the Abron positive protection is afforded by the use of deep latrines located well outside the village, reasonable work loads for most adults, the lack of milk cattle in an area where undulant fever and bovine TB would normally be a problem, ample living space (one room per adult male; one room per adult female with her young children), relative social isolation for men, adequate clothing and shelter for most adults, a relatively well-balanced diet for most adults, a high level of personal and village hygiene, frequent and thorough bathing, frequent washing of dress clothing, isolation of the sick in the case of smallpox only, adequate cooking, a taboo on carrion as food, and the wearing of untailored clothing which affords a less favorable living space for the body louse than tailored clothing.

Features of Abron culture which operate negatively in terms of health are: non-isolation of sick animals, where epizootics might turn into epidemics; poor diets for children; lack of insect control outside of the village; use of polluted water; the custom of visiting sick relatives; the wearing of tailored, often dirty work clothes; visits to funerals in other villages during epidemics; agricultural techniques which allow mosquito breeding in cleared areas, thus increasing the population of the vector for falciparum malaria; the chewing of kola with its attendant spitting (although this might reduce hookworm infection by expelling parasites); a predominantly starch diet highly spiced with cayenne pepper which may have some effect on the frequency of amoebic lesions.

Behavioral patterns in Abron society offer varying degrees of protection against parasitic diseases. The types of disease which occur in the population may be ordered in a rough scale arranged in descending order according to the efficacy of existing preventive medical behaviors. The Abron are *best* protected against parasitic diseases spread either by ingestion of undercooked food or through careless disposal of human feces. The one exception to this is the high level of ascaris infection, which is probably spread by infants and young children before toilet training, a practice which comes rather late in the life of the child. The Abron are *well* protected against diseases which are mildly contagious and which require prolonged contact for transmission. They are *fairly well* protected against infectious diseases spread by contaminated water supplies, except in the case of guinea worm. The protection of adults against infectious parastic disease is superior to that of children, and the protection of men superior to that of women. Cultural practices of the Abron provide *little* protection against highly contagious diseases, diseases of children, diseases spread by insect vectors—especially breeding vectors—and venereal diseases.

Those items of behavior and their relationship to epidemiological patterns in Abron society suggest several problems for future research, among which are the following: (1) Is there some underlying regularity which can be used to explain why some behaviors are medically adaptive and others are medically maladaptive? (2) How does the relatively poor protection for children and women affect the genetic structure of the adult population in relation to disease and resistance and the sex ratio? (3) Has the behavioral-epidemiological situation in this society led to some sort of population balance and accommodation to the environmental setting?

Questions of this sort can be investigated in individual societies but the development of valid generalizations concerning disease and human ecology will require cross-societal comparisons of different behavioral systems in similar and disparate environmental settings. The biological and cultural factors presented in this paper have been offered as a guide for such research. While they are not exhaustive, it is hoped that they will act as a stimulus for further study.

5 CULTURAL AND NATURAL CHECKS
ON POPULATION GROWTH

D. H. Stott

THE STUDY OF the ways in which animal populations limit themselves to their means of subsistence has yielded many surprises, and explained many hitherto anomalous features of physical growth and behavior. The theme of the present contribution is to examine some of this work, and to ask whether certain unexplained, or poorly explained, features of human development and behavior may be similarly understood. The writer has in mind in particular the regular appearance of reproductive casualties—infertility, stillbirth, infant death, malformation, mental deficiency, constitutional ill-health—which are commonly regarded as biological accidents or genetical vestiges of no value to the species. To these must be added the behavioural maladjustments which, as the term implies, are viewed as failures to adapt to not very uncommon situations. Behavioural breakdown would have been many times more disastrous under primitive conditions; the capacity for maladjustment cannot thus be regarded even as a genetic survival. We must ask why, with the minutely fine instinctual equipment which regulates animal behavior, human beings never evolved breakdown-immune patterns of conduct. The application of the criterion of survival-value to these human phenomena consequently leaves many facts unexplained.

For the individual, perinatal death, infertility, malformation, behaviour-disturbance, could obviously have no survival-value. But, as Simpson (1958) points out, "selection favors successful reproduction of the population and not necessarily of any or of

Reprinted by permission of the author and publisher from *Culture and the Evolution of Man*, M. F. Ashley-Montagu, ed., pp. 355–76, New York: Oxford University Press (Galaxy Book), 1962.

all particular individuals within it." It may seem implausible to suggest that the appearance of lethal disabilities could have survival-value even for the population as a whole, but if the limitation of fertility can be of advantage this might be the case. Similarly an increase in efficiency by natural selection may endanger the whole population if it reaches the point where the source of food is wiped out. A curb upon the presumed evolutionary trend towards greater hunting skill would therefore be of advantage. For human beings we thus reach the paradoxical conclusion that in times of the pressure of population on food resources any process which tended to *lower* the mental capacity, physical dexterity or perceptual acuity of a certain number of individuals might mean the saving of the race.

That the amount of food available sets the ultimate limit to the growth of all animal and human populations cannot be disputed. But this apparently self-evident proposition only holds good in a very rough way over a long period. The popular Malthusian notion that the number surviving from year to year is determined by the current supply of food, with the excess dying from starvation, is no longer supported by any student of natural populations. Even David Lack (1955), who among the authorities in this field lays the greatest emphasis upon food supply as the limiting factor, recognizes that the relationship is a complicated one. Food shortage severe enough to impair functional efficiency is critical, not because more members of the species may die than need do in order to restore the ecological balance—a state of affairs that can and often is quickly made good by the excess reproductive capacity possessed by all species—but because a general weakening threatens total annihilation from predators. Thus Chitty (1952b), one of the best known students of animal populations, argued that "a species which frequently exhausted its food supply might be supplanted by one whose population densities were controlled at a safer level." This caused him to look for the alternatives to starvation as the regulating factors.

All the animal populations which have been the subject of observation have been found to suffer periodic declines in numbers which are not generally the result of starvation. These declines often continue in successive generations under conditions in which there could be no question of a shortage of food, and yet may result in the near-annihilation of a local population.

The possibility that they may be due to epidemic diseases has been closely examined, but no greater incidence of such has been found in "dying" populations; and the pattern of the decline and recovery does not correspond to the progress and recession of an epidemic.

Lack (1954) suggests that the fluctuations may reflect predator-prey cycles: overpopulation of the "consumers" reduces their food supply, whether it be animal or vegetable, to the point where recovery is slow. Consequently there is widespread starvation among them, until their numbers are so small that their source of food can recover. As will be noted in the discussion of the field-studies, this explanation does not fit the facts, since the "crashes" often occur when food is abundant, and the mass emigrations which sometimes mark their beginning almost invariably take place in the late summer and autumn, when food is plentiful, rather than in winter. There is in addition a theoretical reason why predator-prey cycles could not be the rule. Any major advantage gained by the "consumer" species over its prey implies that it has been able to make significant inroads into the numbers of healthy adults. If though only a more efficient minority of the predator-species are able to do this, their increased hunting capacity would spread by natural selection, and still further inroads, without limit, would be made into the numbers of the prey, until they, and the predators themselves, were exterminated. It seems that predators only take a marginal toll in the form of the weakly and young animals (and the latter are naturally only at risk for a critical few weeks of their life). In his comprehensive collation of the evidence on predation Errington (1946) quotes authorities on many wild animals to the effect that, on the whole, healthy adult populations suffer little from predators. In their home ranges at normal densities he observed that adult muskrats lived in noticeable security. The larger ungulates "suffer from sub-human predation chiefly when immature, aged, crippled, starved, sick, or isolated from their fellows." He advanced the theory of the *intercompensation* of factors limiting population: if predators and disease took little toll, self-limiting mechanisms came into operation to check the growth of numbers; if losses were great from external causes these mechanisms did not come into play. He concluded that "regardless of the countless individuals or the large percentages of populations who may annually be killed by predators, predation looks ineffective as a limiting factor to the extent that intraspecific self-limiting mechanisms basically determine the population-levels maintained by the prey." One might add that if predators only succeed in catching the vulnerable minority the balance would be smoothly maintained rather than cyclic, for a fairly constant proportion of the prey, other things being equal, would be eaten each year. (This argument does not hold in the case of a newly introduced predator, since time would be needed for a balance to occur by natural selection. There is also some anecdotal evidence that some ungulates, who rely for protection upon herding and flight, have at times been known in the absence of predators to eat up herbage to the point of starvation. In their case predators may be able to catch healthy adults, but since only one in a herd can be taken at a time, and the predators would be thinly spaced by territory, the toll might never exceed the replacement rate under normal conditions of abundance, and yet suffice to render other means of limiting numbers unnecessary.)

A record of typical population-cycle, that of the snowshoe hare, made by Green and Evans (1940), is given in Table 1. It is seen

Table 1

	Early spring population	Young born during summer	Per cent of yearlings surviving
1932		600	
1933	478 (peak)	1049	23
1934	374	818	29
1935	356	779	18
1936	246	541	12
1937	151	330	8
1938	32	66	91
1939	73	158	

that the decline extended over five years, and then in 1938, when extinction seemed near, the trend was reversed. In their review of possible causes the authors of this, as of similar studies, discount the likelihood of an epidemic because the mortality did not abate after a first rapid spread. Nor could the losses have been due to emigration or an encroachment into adjoining regions: the snowshoe hares were seldom found more than one-eighth of a mile from the point where they were first trapped, even after a year or more.

The decline was chiefly a matter of the poor survival of the immature hares, as shown strikingly in the last column of the table.

It is indeed remarkable that the mortality among the yearlings should be so catastrophic in 1937, four years after the presumed overpopulation, and that this should occur during the summer months, whereas the greatest mortality of adult hares was, as would be expected, during the winter. Food shortage would thus seem to be ruled out as the immediate cause of this youthful mortality. That the young born during the summer of 1937 were still severely affected despite the fact that the parental population was little over half the peak density suggests that the noxious factors persisted through four generations.

During the peak, before the decline became general, occasional hares were found dead in the traps, the cause of which Green and Larson (1938) diagnosed as "shock disease." As the decline became widespread during 1935 and 1936 this condition was observed over the entire area. The wider significance of this finding will be discussed later, but it may be noted at this stage that the parent-hares were found to be in a poor condition during the breeding season in which the generation of poor viability were produced.

In his study of a population cycle of ruffed grouse in Ontario, Clarke (1936) was similarly struck by the poor viability of the young, and by the fact that "even though the first year of dying off in an area has reduced numbers to a point where the birds may be regarded as scarce, the succeeding year may show a similar reduction of summer flocks."

From the study of a number of widely dissimilar species of animal one conclusion emerges with tolerable certainty: when population density reaches a certain point, even without actual shortage of food, changes take place which have the effect of reducing the population. These changes may even be in bodily form. Wilson (1938) observed that when aphides become crowded on a plant the next generation grow wings to allow emigration. Uvarov (1928) reported analogous physical changes in the locust. Preparatory to swarming and emigration locusts "moult" and change their exteriors from predominantly green to a brownish colour, the two forms being originally thought to be different species. When studied in the laboratory this change was found to depend only on the density of population in a cage, and was notably independent of temperature, light or other obvious factors. The swarming is in no sense a migration, since it occurs irregularly in cycles of years. Nor, Uvarov points out, can they be driven by hunger, since they leave rich vegetation to enter the desert.

Among mammals the well known "suicidal" mass wanderings of the lemming offer a close parallel. Once again, as Elton (1942) and others have shown, they occur in three to four year cycles, in periods of apparent high population in the home locality. Their emigration might be described as a behavioural aberration taking the form of always wandering downhill, which brings them to the sea, into which they then plunge, so that they are mostly drowned. The result is a periodic drastic thinning of the resident population, since none of the emigrants find their way back.

Lack draws attention to the genetic problem which these "suicidal" emigrations raise: if those who respond to this urge are eliminated while those in whom it is absent survive, why is it not rapidly eliminated by natural selection? If, however, the sacrificed individuals are the yearlings, their parents, who would as a whole be of the same genetic constitution, would have a certain advantage over other parent animals whose young caused dangerous overcrowding. In this way an inherited tendency to self-elimination, confined to the young, would be perpetuated by natural selection.

The reproductive behaviour of several species of birds shows puzzling features which can only be convincingly explained as population regulatory mechanisms. Lack draws attention to the fact that among many species of birds—the hawks, owls, storks, crows, etc.—incubating starts as soon as the first egg is laid. Consequently the earlier hatched nestling will always be stronger than the later hatched, with the result that each younger one can only get fed when its elder sibling has had so much that it is replete and inactive. The whole brood survive only when food is very abundant. Lack (1954) argues that "if all the chicks had hatched on the same day and been of the same size, the food might have been divided equally between them, and all might have died." Since the passerine birds do in fact defer incubation until the clutch is complete and so produce a brood who share the available food more or less equally, this reason for a different child-rearing practice among the larger predators seems unconvincing. It would surely have been more economical for them to have evolved a slower growth rate and smaller daily food intake so that the whole brood could survive. This indeed happens among those passerines who nest in holes or roofed nests, where the young are safe from predators and there is no need for the nestling stage to be got through as quickly as possible. The ultimate value of the successive hatching would thus seem to ensure not that such of the particular brood survive as their immediate food-supply permits, but that the number of young raised should not produce a general overpopulation in the region.

Brown's study (1955) of various species of eagles within a district in Kenya has brought to light yet another regulatory mechanism (that of successive hatching not being applicable because the species in question only incubate one egg). He found that in some years certain pairs failed to breed, although they were in secure possession of territories in which they had bred in previous years. This could not be related to variations in the weather, changes of mate, exigencies of nest-building or to shortage of food; but the off-years tended to follow one or two productive years. Thus the periodic infertility can best be explained, not as an adaption to contemporary food-supply, but as a means of checking population numbers before the danger-point is reached.

Errington's study (1954) of cyclic fluctuations in muskrat populations enables us to see, for this mammal at least, something of the detail of the interaction between crowding and the regulatory mechanisms. It would appear that at a certain degree of density the muskrats become intolerant of each other, as shown in greater dispersal, savage fighting among adults and attacks upon helpless young. It was significant that the friction was not a simple reaction to a threshold density-level, but seemed rather to be a "state of nerves" persisting during the phase of population decline. During the cyclic upgrade, the muskrat population congregated within the choicer feeding grounds, at a density of about ten breeding pairs per acre, while leaving the unattractive areas uninhabited. But during the peak and decline the strife was so great that they distributed themselves at densities of about one pair per acre through good and bad habitat alike.

The last of the field-studies to be considered, that of Chitty (1952a) in respect of voles upon a plantation in Montgomeryshire, contains an important suggestion as to the nature of the regulatory mechanism involved. He found that the offspring of the peak-generation either died prematurely or were infertile, as also was the case during the cyclic decline of the snowshoe hare. He concluded that, "in order to account for this decrease in viability and reproductive performance it is necessary to postulate a delayed effect of some previous condition . . . We cannot at present be more precise about this supposed condition than to imagine some disturbance of the hormonal balance of the mother which in some way affected the foetus." He drew attention to the strife among the adults during the early part of the season in which the affected generation were born. That this caused congenital damage may be considered a bold hypothesis, but evidence is quoted below that the harassment and strife attendant upon overcrowding may produce psychosomatic illness in animals. Chitty arrived at his theory of prenatal damage only after reviewing and dismissing all other feasible causes, such as disease, food shortage, predation and migration.

In an experiment with wild rats Calhoun (1952) showed that the regulatory mechanism consisted mainly of changes in social behaviour. He bred a colony from a few individuals in a pen of 10,000 square feet, allowing them an abundance of food at all times. If over the 28 months of the experiment they had realized their breeding potential they would have numbered 50,000. If they had been content with the two square feet per rat allowed for caged rats in laboratories there could have been 5,000. In fact the population stabilized itself at less than 200. The social behaviour of the colony limited population growth in three ways. First, the rats split themselves up into local sub-colonies, between which were maintained buffer zones without burrows. Second, with crowding the normal dominance hierarchy broke down, leading to unstable groups. The effect of this was reduced frequency of conception and poor viability of the suckling young. Of the few which survived beyond weaning very few in turn had progeny of their own. Third, crowding caused increased attack upon the young, and those who received severe punishment were likely to succumb.

The behavioural breakdown of the rats living under conditions of social stress seems to have been manysided. Those which had suffered excessive punishment no longer made favourable use of their environment, that is, became "maladjusted," notably by losing their food-storage habits. The collapse of the social pattern also had a detrimental effect on fertility. Under conditions of crowding the dominant rats could no longer guard their own females from intruding males, for the latter pursued them and copulated frequently. Why the outcome was infertility may be gathered from the analogy of Bruce's (1960a, 1960b) experiments with mice. From a chance observation that pregnancy sometimes unaccountably failed in the laboratory she was able to establish the cause as contact with a strange male. After mating with their familiar sire the females suffered a "blocking" of the pregnancy even if they only detected the odour of the intruder on nesting material. After some five days they came on heat again and could conceive, but a breakdown of social dominance and exposure to a succession of strange males would presumably inhibit pregnancy indefinitely.

A further effect of crowding in Calhoun's experimental colony was that "more and more individuals were stunted despite having plenty of food available. Such stunted rats seemed healthy . . . they simply failed to grow very large and attained their mature weight very slowly." These stunted rats were also characterised by behaviour-disturbances. Again one might infer prenatal damage, with a hint of the pregnancy/multiple-impairment syndrome hypothesized by the present writer in respect of human beings (Stott 1957).

The regulatory mechanisms which Calhoun observed in rats, and Bruce's "pregnancy-block" in mice, originated in the animals' becoming aware that something was "wrong" in their environment. No doubt to avoid the controversial term "psychological," Bruce described this type of influence as exteroceptive. Leaving terms aside, it can be said that a situation of a certain type, namely a relationship with other animals of their own species, was appraised as unfavourable, and that this act of appraisal initiated physiological processes which culminated in infertility. Barnett has carried out experiments which showed that the male rats in the unfavourable situation of being bullied become subject to adrenal cortical depletion, which may be followed by death, even though they suffer no actual wounding (Barnett 1958; Barnett et al. 1960). It would appear that he induced in these bullied rats the condition of "shock-disease" which Green and Evans described in the snowshoe hare during the phase of population decline. With Larson, Green made a physiological study of a number of afflicted animals, and Christian (1950) recognized their description of the disease as similar to Selye's stress adaptation syndrome: the animals had died of adreno-pituitary exhaustion.

Such a psychosomatic reaction to a situation appraised as unfavourable or disastrous does not, in itself, account for the continuance of the shock-state in subsequent generations, which did not experience the overcrowding. This could, however, result if the state of shock interferes with the reproductive processes, causing the next generation to suffer damage at the foetal stage. Two critical experiments demonstrate that the offspring can suffer prenatal damage as a result of the mother-animals' being subjected to exteroceptive or "psychological" shock. Thompson and Sontag (1956) subjected pregnant rats to the constant ringing of an electric bell, to the extent that they broke down in convulsions. To eliminate the possibility that the after-effects upon the mothers retarded their young postnatally, the latter were changed around with the young of a control-group of unshocked rats. The offspring of the rats shocked in pregnancy were found to be significantly slower at maze-learning. Thompson (1957) carried out a further experiment to test the effects of anxiety pure and simple during pregnancy upon the offspring. Female rats were trained to expect an electric shock on hearing the sound of a buzzer, and to escape by opening a door. After being mated they were placed each day in the same compartment, without the electric shock being applied. But the escape-door was locked, so that they were reduced to a state of fear. Once again their offspring were randomly switched with those of control-rats. The young born to the rats which had been subjected to anxiety were much more sluggish, took twice as long to reach food when hungry, and nearly three times as long before they would venture forth from an open cage. In human terms we would say that they were suffering from a congenital impairment of motivation. Their timidity and "unforthcomingness" resembled a type of personality-defect which the present writer found to be associated with pregnancy-stress in the human mother. It is reasonable to suppose that such "substandard," unassertive young would be the bullied animals, which would succumb to attacks during the strife generated in phases of overcrowding. If so, the congenital damage they suffered might rank as a mechanism for the limiting of population.

The defence of territory is found in some form among almost all animals, and must therefore have been a powerful factor in survival. Howard (1920) put forward the most apparent reason why this should be so, that by defending a territory a nesting pair guarantees its family larder. Lack (1953) disputes this view, pointing out that the "territories" of some of the gregarious birds, such as the guillemot and heron, consist of a few feet or yards around their nests, which could not possibly serve as a source of food. He also draws attention to many anomalies: encroachment for feeding takes place regularly; during hard weather territoriality is suspended and birds congregate around any provision of food; and finally territories vary greatly in size for the same species (the largest held by the robins he studied being five times greater than the smallest). These anomalies can better be explained if territorialism is seen as primarily a mechanism for the regulation of population-numbers. Just as it was previously suggested that successive hatching in the larger predators serves to limit the population in general to the resources of the region rather than adjust the number of mouths in a particular brood to the resources of the moment, so the defending of territory may limit the population-density over the region as a whole from generation to generation. This is effected by preventing more than a certain number of birds from breeding. That some fail to do so is shown by the rapidity with which a new mate is forthcoming when the former one dies. Lack has himself shown that in a covered aviary, where there was insufficient space for two territories, the non-dominant pair of robins failed to breed. The territories in miniature maintained by sociably breeding birds around their nests, and the destruction by rooks of "unpermitted" additions to their rookery, would have the analogous effect of limiting the number of birds who could forage over a day's flight or over the available fishing ground. The balance of evidence thus seems to favour the view of Huxley (1933) that territorialism is "one of the more important of the factors determining the population of breeding pairs in a given area"; and of Carpenter (1958) that it is "an important condition for optimal population density."

It has been seen that the postulated mechanisms for the limitation of population tend to centre around reproduction and the viability of the young, these being the stages at which they could operate most economically. This consideration brings us to another sphere of biology which is fraught with unsolved problems: the study and experimental production of congenital malformations. Traditionally these have been regarded as genetic in origin, but the most persistent attempts to fit their appearance into any of the known Mendelian patterns of inheritance have met with little success. Examples of standard types of malformation crop up in a strain of animal or human being without antecedents, and even where a certain familial tendency is observed the malformation, with a few exceptions, does not occur with the regularity that would be expected if it were entirely genetically-determined. The labelling of the isolated malformation as a "phenocopy" of the true genetic prototype, or the explanation of the sporadicity in terms of the varying "penetrance" of a gene, has brought little additional understanding of the causes of malformation. In the early years of the present century Stockard (1910) observed that malformations could be produced in fishes by treating their eggs with a weak solution of alcohol and other noxious substances. It was not until 1935 that an analogous discovery was made in a mammal: Hale (1935) demonstrated that pregnant sows deprived of vitamin A produced piglets with a tendency to severe malformation of or total lack of eyes, together with other malformations. These findings have been abundantly confirmed in respect of a number of species of animals. The degree of deprivation proved important. Summarizing his extensive work in this field Warkany (1947) reported that, "a borderline deficiency is required to induce malformations; a slight improvement of the dietary situation may result in normal offspring, while a further deterioration may lead to embryonic death." Similarly Sobin (1954) found that congenital heart disease could be induced in the offspring by revolving the pregnant rat 200 times in a drum; but if it was subjected to 800 revolutions no live offspring at all were produced. The effect of these phenomena under natural conditions would be to limit population-growth in times of short-age, and the greater the shortage the more severe would be the block to fertility. It is also significant that besides vitamin depriva-tion the administration of hormones such as cortisone and thyroxine tends to produce malformation. With the known effects of rage and fear on the endocrine system, strife and harassment resulting from shortage and overcrowding might thus be expected to reduce fertility.

A big advance in the study of malformation was made when it was realized that they were the result, not of either genetic or environmental influences as the case may be, but of an interaction of both. This was first hinted at by Malpas in 1937: "The role of an unfavourable maternal environment is to facilitate the emergence of certain lethal genetic factors" (Malpas 1937). Since then this concept of the *facilitation* of a genetic propensity to malformation has been experimentally confirmed by Landauer and by Clarke Fraser and his co-workers: the appearance of mal-formation under conditions of stress was found to depend on the genetic constitution of both mother and foetus (Landauer and Bliss 1946; Fraser et al. 1954). It would thus appear that there is *regular genetic provision* for the production of mal-formation, or poor viability, in the offspring in times of stress. This is consistent with the view that malformation must be ac-counted one of the mechanisms for adapting population-numbers to the resources of the environment, and as such to have survival value.

The existence of mechanisms for limiting population in man cannot be assumed because they are found in animals. On the other hand the fact that changes in viability and in fertility as well as aberrations of behaviour leading to reduction in numbers are widespread among animals indicates a strong probability that such will be found among the human species. Moreover these mechanisms were found in their most intricate level of develop-ment—in variations of instinctive behaviour—among the large predator birds; and primitive man was the super-predator, who must have been reasonably safe against other predators in many regions of the earth.

The most evident devices for limiting human population are cultural in character. In the case of infanticide it is a self-con-scious one. Among the Polynesians for example not only was any weakly or malformed child disposed of as a matter of course, but it was by no means taken for granted that even a healthy child would be allowed to live; it was left for the father to decide as a matter of policy (Danielsson 1956). In many cultures the taboo upon sexual intercourse during lactation, and the long nursing period, would have the effect of spacing out births. The institution of marriage, and the customs and sexual morality that go with it, must have the effect of limiting the number of children. If a bride has to be bought, or only a suitor of substantial means is acceptable, young wives would tend to get paired with old men. In peasant communities marriage had to be postponed until the suitor got possession of a holding, and by the custom of gavelkind (gable-child) the youngest son was expected to remain unmarried to work his parents' holding until eventually, at a mature age, he inherited it himself (Rees 1950). In former times in England marriage was not socially sanctioned until the couple were able to get their own cottage, which usually meant waiting many years. Just what social institutions in each civilization have militated against population-increase would be a fruitful subject of study. Under the feudal system there was a residue of landless and homeless serfs or semi-slaves, innferior in status to the peasant, who slept around the log fire of the manorial hall, and who thus had no family life. In the ancient world the institution of slavery would similarly have made marriage and reproduction out of the question for a large section of the population, not to mention the effects of physical hardship and ill-treatment. In his historical novel, *Salammbô,* Gustav Flaubert (1874) makes Hamilcar, prince of Carthage, express surprise at the small number of children among his slaves. He commanded that their quarters should be left open at night so that the sexes might mix freely. Since Flaubert was noted for the thoroughness and accuracy of his historical research, it is unlikely that he invented this episode.

The aborigines of Australia are of unique scientific interest from the point of view of the limitation of numbers, since they were at the time of their discovery by Europeans the only extant example of a human population at the food-gathering stage covering a complete land mass, without anywhere to emigrate. Being subject to no predatory wild animals, they presented the exact human counterpart of the large birds of prey. If, therefore,

mechanisms for the limitation of human populations exist they
should be found among them. That the density of the aboriginal
population was closely related to the available food was cleverly
demonstrated by Birdsell (1953). He found that the lower the
rainfall, and hence the poorer the vegetation and the fewer the
animals able to live on it, the larger was the area occupied by
each tribe. This was all the more striking among tribes without
any water or shore from which to get food.

Birdsell found a remarkable correspondence between rainfall
and the practices of circumcision and subincision. These were the
rule in the driest central areas. The eastern boundary of the
region throughout which subincision was practised followed the
eastern 8- and 10-inch rainfall line with a closeness which made
a chance relationship out of the question. That for the practice
of both circumcision and subincision ran further west, along the
5-inch rainfall line. Since these rites do not impair the fertility of
the affected males, it must be asked what connection they can
have with austere living conditions. The explanation which will
be proffered involves reference to findings which will be described
more fully below. These are that the commonest form of impairment of a disturbed pregnancy is to render the infant
weakly and more liable to common infections. Under unhygienic
conditions the chances of survival of such weakly children would
be poor. Even in 20th century Britain, the writer observed that
among mentally sub-normal children—who are very liable to infection in infancy—those coming from the lowest-standard of
home had the best health-records, for the reason that the poorly
children in such homes would have died in infancy. Similarly it
is reasonable to suppose that under primitive conditions the in-
fliction of wounding by the above rites, and similar operations
upon the girls, would eliminate those of delicate health. In times
of food shortage, with the consequent harassment, fatigue and
anxiety, many more delicate children would be born, so that the
numbers of the rising generation would be significantly reduced.
Birdsell in fact found that along the boundary marking the edge
of the diffusion of these rites the tribes practising them were less
numerous than those not doing so. Yet paradoxically the area
in which the rites were practised had become progressively extended, which suggests that the numerically smaller tribes had
gained an advantage in times of scarcity by avoiding starvation.

Circumcision, subincision, and indeed the widely prevalent superficial mutilation inflicted during initiation ceremonies, may therefore be culturally effective means of adapting the size of primitive human populations to their food resources.

In the light of the work on animal populations, it would be surprising if there were no regulatory mechanisms in human beings operating at the physiological level. An observation by Smith (1925) on the Ao Naga tribe of Assam may have wide implications: "The number of childless marriages is usually large, and very few women have large families. The Nagas take a pride in the strength and endurance of their women, saying they are inferior to the men by a narrow margin only. These qualities have no doubt been developed by the life of toil to which they have been accustomed from their earliest youth, but they have paid the price in a weakening of the reproductive power." Of all the hill tribes he writes, "The young women are generally stocky and plump; but this does not last long, because the hard life of carrying wood from the jungle, doing cultivation work, raising children and performing other hard tasks soon make old hags of them." Such a picture, with the women doing the hard work and the carrying, while the menfolk sit around and talk except for seasonable bursts of activity, is typical of primitive and many peasant agricultural communities. It may be that this unequal division of labour to the disadvantage of women is a cultural provision which has had survival-value by the limitation of fertility. In a study of pregnancy-factors among over 3000 women at the Watford Maternity Hospital near London, McDonald (1958) found that "a statistically significant excess of mothers of children with major defects had been engaged in work they described as heavy—particularly laundry work"; work involving heavy pulling or lifting was reported in 20 per cent of the cases where the children were malformed, but in only 8 per cent where the children were normal.

If physiological mechanisms for limiting numbers in man exist, one would expect the reproductive rate to be sensitive to the quality of nutrition during pregnancy. Even in a middle-class population in Boston, women who had poor feeding habits during pregnancy were found much more likely to give birth to stillborn, malformed or otherwise defective children compared with mothers whose diet was good (Burke et al. 1943). In Aberdeen, women belonging to the poorer sections of the community had twice as many premature babies, three times as many stillbirths and lost their infants in the first month four times as frequently, when compared with well-to-do women in a nursing home (Baird 1945). In Toronto it was found by a carefully controlled experiment that miscarriage, prematurity and stillbirth among ill-nourished women could be reduced to a small fraction of what it would otherwise have been by giving them a supplementary diet during pregnancy (Ebbs and Moyle 1942; Ebbs et al. 1942).

As early as 1812 a doctor, Jacob Clesius, remarked that malformations were more frequent in times of war. Of the Thirty Years' War in Germany, Gustav Freytag wrote: "The effects which such a life, full of uncertainty and terror, exercised upon the minds of country people were very dire . . . one observed the signs of terrible misery in numerous malformations." After the siege of Paris in 1870–71 the French doctor de Saulle reported a crop of malformations (Gesenius 1951). Systematic evidence of this phenomenon comes from studies in several centres in Germany of the incidence of malformation during the war and in particular during the post-war phase of acute hardship, housing shortage and despondency. The malformation rate in 55 German hospitals (Eichmann and Gesenius 1952) showed a startling rise after the war—the average for 1946–50 being 6.5 per cent, but there was a smaller rise for the war years themselves (2.58 per cent compared with 1.43 per cent during the pre-war and pre-Hitler Weimar period). This began from the start of the war, when there was no question of food shortage. There would however have been many reasons for anxiety and fear among the civilian population; besides the bombing, husbands and sons would have been called up, reported killed, wounded or missing and so on. From the point of view of the role of anxiety in inducing malformations, it is also noteworthy that the rate reached a minor peak during 1933, in the January of which year Hitler seized power and loosed his Storm Troopers upon the Jews and the politically opposed sections of the population; during the whole period of the Hitler terror up to the outbreak of the war (1933–39) the average rate was nearly double that obtaining during the last seven years of the democratic Weimar period. For Britain no general figures of incidence of malformation are published, but an indirect indication of the trend can be had from the death rate from malformation in the first month of life (Registrar-General of England and Wales 1932–57). For both male and female infants it was fairly stable for the years 1932–39, but moved to a peak-level during 1940–43, the years of the heavy bombing and severest fighting, with the resulting news of casualties. Owing to full employment and the equalising effect of an efficient rationing system, the general standard of nutrition, especially of pregnant and nursing mothers, was above the level of the pre-war years (Garry and Wood 1946). One can only conclude that the increase in malformations was due to the prevalence of fear and anxiety. A study by MacMahon, Record and McKeown (1951) in Birmingham confirmed the existence of a distinct peak during the years 1940–43 for anencephaly and spina bifida, the malformations which seem to act as barometers of social stress. In Scotland, where there was very little bombing, there was no significant wartime peak but only the post-war downward trend presumably reflecting the general improvement in the standard of livng and social security throughout Britain as a whole.

A remarkable inverse correlation has in fact been found between social amenities and the incidence of anencephaly (Anderson, Baird, and Thompson 1958). It is highest in Glasgow (3.1 per 1000) where overcrowding is worst, and lower in regular succession in the other three chief cities of Scotland placed in order of amenities. In the widely spaced communities of the Highlands the rate was found to be only 1.29 per 1000. Edwards (1958), also in Scotland, showed that the anencephaly rate was about four times as high among unskilled town labourers as in the highest social class. Both in the United States (Pasamanick and Knobloch 1957) and in Britain (Drillien and Richmond 1956) prematurity is significantly more frequent in the lower social classes, and Stewart has shown that the same also applies to death of the infant in the first month.

There are, some telltale findings concerning the greater risks attached to extramarital conception (illegitimacy and premarital conception). Stewart found prematurity to be over twice and death of the infant in the first month nearly three times as frequent among such children compared with those conceived after marriage. These findings may link up with some suggestive and unexplained features of the anencephaly studies referred to above. McKeown and Record (1951) report a consistently greater risk of this malformation in *first-born* children conceived during the summer months. This could not have been due to a greater physiological risk in first-born, otherwise the tendency would have been equally apparent in winter-conceived first-borns; nor could it have been due to seasonal infections, for second-born children conceived in the summer were not affected. But extramarital conception, owing to the greater opportunities for outdoor lovemaking, is probably more frequent during the summer months, and the resulting children would mostly be first-borns. It might be that the mental stress consequent upon becoming pregnant in the unmarried state can be one of the causes of this malformation.

This suggestion received confirmation in the above-mentioned study of anencephaly in Scotland by Edwards. Despite the general improvement in social conditions there was virtually no change in the rate between 1939 and 1956. But this global incidence disguised two opposing trends which cancelled each other out. During the peak period of the war, 1939–43, the figure for later births was consistently high, and indeed higher than for first-births. This would reflect wartime stresses. But that for first-births became markedly greater in 1944 and 1945, and except for two years when the rates were about equal, remained greater thereafter. This may well be the result of an increase in extramarital conception due to a measure of breakdown in traditional sexual morality. It is perhaps relevant that the Chief Medical Officer for England and Wales, in his Report for 1959, infers an increased tendency to sexual promiscuity, especially among young people, from the steady rise in the number of new cases of gonorrhea in recent years.

It is, in short, apparent that sections of a population subjected to adverse social conditions tend to suffer more reproductive casualty. And there seems some evidence that, as in the case of some animal populations, the physiological process responsible is triggered off by exteroceptive stimuli which arouse anxiety or other emotion calculated to lead to adreno-pituitary exhaustion. That absolute infertility can be brought about by severe emotional stress was conclusively demonstrated by the well-known German anatomist, Stieve (1942, 1943). In the bodies of women who had been imprisoned during the Nazi terror and subsequently executed he found unmistakeable signs of degeneration in their reproductive organs which, he pointed out, must have been due exclusively to nervous shock, as they were in a well-nourished condition at the time of their death.

In his pioneer work on the effects upon the foetus of emotional disturbance in the mother Sontag (1941, 1944) observed that the children tended to suffer from gastro-intestinal illnesses. He suggested that these were in many instances of autonomic origin. In other words, the children may have already been born in the state of shock-disease found by Green and Larson in snowshoe hares during the phase of population decline. Striking also is the parallelism with Chitty's conclusion, that the poor viability in young voles during the population decline could best be accounted for by foetal damage.

The present writer made a study of 102 mentally subnormal children by case-study methods in order to make comprehensive soundings of causative factors (1957). The pregnancy was disturbed by either illness or emotional upsets in 66 per cent of the cases, compared with only 30 per cent among the mentally normal controls. Where there had been pregnancy-stress 76 per cent of the mentally retarded children were weakly and ailing or had serious illnesses other than epidemics during their first three years, as against only 29 per cent of those retarded children of whom no pregnancy-stress was reported. Among the 450 controls of normal mental ability a similarly close relationship between disturbed pregnancy and early illness was observed. Malformations in both groups followed the same pattern.

Of the pregnancy-stresses emotional upsets were more than twice as frequent as illnesses, and these showed a curious parallelism with the conditions attendant upon overcrowding in animal communities, namely strife, harassment and personal difficulties over having to share housing accommodations, shocks and anxiety-states. It is also significant that of the 24 maternal illnesses in pregnancy, 20 of which resulted in unhealthy children, all but three were stress-diseases, notably gastric ulcer, chronic heart disease, severe sickness and vomiting, and toxaemia.

It has been commonly observed that mentally retarded children tend to suffer from a multiplicity of handicaps; this was not only confirmed in the above study, but each handicap was related so closely to pregnancy-stress that the latter could be reckoned to be the common causative factor. This syndrome of pregnancy/ multiple impairment, thus named, included impairment of temperament. Of this the most prevalent type was "unforthcomingness," seen in extreme unassertiveness, timidity and general lack of motivation (Stott 1959). It resembled the behaviour of the offspring of the rats which Thompson subjected to anxiety during pregnancy. There can be little doubt, also, that the other main type of impairment of temperament found in backward children, which one might term disorganized motivation (abnormal restlessness and inability to concentrate, and excitability), can also be congenital. In the important series of Baltimore studies conducted by Pasamanick, Lillienfeld and their co-workers behaviour-disturbance in the children, especially of the hyperactive, disorganized type, was found to be significantly related to certain stress-conditions of pregnancy (toxaemia and bleeding) (Pasamanick, Rogers, and Lillienfeld 1956). It goes without saying that these unforthcoming or disorganized children would have a very poor chance of survival under primitive conditions, and would be bullied and rejected in times of stress.

Even closer parallels can be seen between the behaviour-deterioration of animals during population-declines and that of human beings under stress. Before he was interested in the mechanics of the former, the writer, in his studies of the types of family-situation leading to maladjustment and delinquency, described the "irritable-depressive non-tolerance . . . in a severely overburdened or nervously exhausted mother (which) can assume the form temporarily of a heartless rejection of her child." During the phases of irritable-depressive character-change "the mother may express the greatest dislike of the child, or even commit some hostile act against it which earns her a prison sentence" (Stott 1956). Such a reaction may be cognate with the attacks of the adult muskrats upon the young during the strife-phase of the population-cycle observed by Errington.

In the child who is the victim of parental rejection can be observed a typical and apparently instinctive behavioural-change, described as "an attitude of active hostility (which) it is hard to explain otherwise than as calculated to make its position in the family impossible." This was designated "a self-banishing reaction." Considering that at the food-gathering stage each family would need many square miles of territory per head, and that shortage and overpopulation would be likely to be general in a whole region, the chances of a rejected child being able to reattach itself to another family would be small indeed. The break-away from its own group would therefore be virtually suicidal in the same way as is that of the lemming. It is noteworthy that along with or alternative to this hostility-reaction the writer observed a "removal impulse," which had surprisingly recurrent features: a dislike of the home-locality, wanting to go to sea, join the army, or to get work on a farm or with a travelling fair, besides actually running away from home or committing such flagrant offences as will secure removal from home. In a study of approved-school boys the writer found that this unconscious urge for removal was the commonest motive underlying their delinquency (Stott 1950).

The most drastic way in which the reproductive capacity of a population can be reduced, short of sterility, is to limit the number of females born. In fact the incidence of anencephaly, which is a lethal malformation and the commonest of those which are sensitive to social environment, is three times as high among females. The slight preponderance of males born probably reflects the tendency for female embryos to be more subject to lethal anomalies; hence no doubt also the slight rise in the male-female sex-ratio during the war years, which has been explained by the myth that Providence supplies more males to replace those killed. The wartime rise in deaths of infants of under four weeks from malformation was more marked for female infants: the increase in the rate during the stress-years of 1940–42 compared with the eight pre-war years was 7.5 per cent for boys and 14.3 per cent for girls.

On the other hand, non-lethal malformations and liability to disease in childhood are more common among boys. Among the 450 normal children studied by the writer, infantile ill-health was over twice as common among the boys, and it appeared that a greater degree of pregnancy-stress is needed to produce an unhealthy girl than an unhealthy boy. Boys are also more frequently mentally subnormal, and if their ten times greater proneness to delinquency is taken as an index thereof, they are much more liable to behaviour-disturbance. (Contrary to popular impression and certain sociological theories, the great majority of delinquents are emotionally disturbed [Stott 1960a].)

In seeking an explanation of why males thus seem constitutionally to be the more vulnerable sex, it must be borne in mind that under primitive conditions the male was the chief predator. If a predatory species becomes too efficient it eats up its food resources and so exterminates itself. Consequently it would be of advantage to the species in times of too great numbers, when the prey would be over-hunted, for the predators to become less competent. The effects of pregnancy-stress on the male offspring is to make him more stupid, physically less robust, temperamentally less aggressive, and possibly more myopic and more gawky. There is indeed some evidence that deficiencies of diet in a poor community depress the level of intelligence. Harrell and Woodyard supplemented the diet of a group of pregnant and lactating women in Virginia (predominantly Negro); at the ages of 3 and 4 years their children had an average I.Q. five points higher than those whose mothers had only received dummy diet supplements (Harrell, Woodyard, and Gates 1955). Among a similar group of White women in Kentucky, the average I.Q. of whose children was 107.6, the vitamin supplement made no significant difference, presumably because the untreated diet was above the level which under primitive conditions would have indicated food-shortage. Evidence that eclampsia and pre-eclampsia, which are stress-conditions of pregnancy, may result in a certain impairment of intelligence in the children has been provided by Margaret Battle (1949) in her study of school children in Rocky Mountain City. It may seem paradoxical that a lowering of intelligence in the next generation should be the biological response to stress, but this is consistent with the need to maintain ecological balance.

In yet another respect the handicaps following stress during pregnancy suggest a regulatory mechanism. Those children who suffer from early chronic ailments seem to grow out of them— hence no doubt the folklore that a child's health will change for the better at 7 or 14 years. The writer has also observed that pathological unforthcomingness is often replaced at puberty in boys by normal assertiveness and confidence. Of these children who have overcome their initial handicaps one might say that under natural conditions their poor viability would have been only a provisional "death sentence": if the hardships which caused the impairment were replaced by communal well-being, so that a larger population could be tolerated, these children would be re-prieved. The writer also found evidence that boys were more likely than girls to outgrow handicaps of intelligence (Stott 1960b).

The tendency, to which Tanner (1955) has drawn attention, for puberty to begin progressively earlier in recent generations would also seem to reflect a mechanism for the adaptation of numbers to food resources. Hammond (1955), the leading British authority on farm animals, points out that high-plane nutrition brings earlier sexual maturity in poultry and cattle: "With seasonal breeding species like sheep, lambs reared on low-plane nutrition may completely miss the first breeding season and not come on heat for the first time until a year later."

Once one gets the bit of a theory between the teeth there is no limit to the intriguing speculation in which one may indulge. The test is whether, having caused new questions to be asked, the theory can predict the answers to them better than other theories, and whether it can link into a meaningful whole what was previously thought of as separate, accounted for in a number of different ways, or just taken for granted. The case for the theory can be briefly summed up. Animal-populations would seem to be adapted to their food resources by a variety of built-in physiological and instinctive mechanisms rather than by starvation, and these come into play in response to signals of incipient over-crowding in advance of serious shortage of food. Among these signals are certain exteroceptive or "psychological" stimuli; that is to say, the perception by the animal of some factor in its en-vironment—presumably unfavourable in the biological sense—triggers off a physiological or instinctive mechanism which has the effect of reducing fertility or the survival-rate of the young.

There was also some evidence that the same sorts of population-limiting mechanisms are found in animals and in man. In both, the severity of reproductive casualty is geared to the degree of stress upon the mother during and possibly prior to pregnancy. The most unfavourable conditions induce sterility or stillbirth; the somewhat less harsh result in a multiplicity of impairment in the young which reduces the chances of survival; more moderate hard-ships—sub-optimal diets, insufficient living space, strife and har-assment—bring a reduction in competence, vigour or strength of motivation in the young. Perhaps the most striking and unexpected parallel is in the appearance of behavioural aberration, or perhaps more accurately, the substitution of the normal behaviour-pattern by a special pattern of stress-behaviour. In the adult this takes the form of increased irritability and intolerance of congeners, in particular of the young, who may—whether animal or human—be viciously attacked. In the young themselves the behavioural aberration is seen on the one hand in "unforthcoming-ness" and on the other in disorganized hyperactivity and an emigratory or "removal" urge.

The chief implication of the theory is that the predicted catastrophe of a world population increasing by geometrical progression to the point of starvation is unlikely to occur. It will be forestalled, if not by conscious human design, by the physiological mechanisms which have been evolved to obviate just such a calamity. Indeed we see that these mechanisms are already insidiously at work, and as in one region or another overpopulation and crowding cause increased hardship, so we may expect to find them more in evidence. Even among sections of the White populations of Britain and America reproductive efficiency is significantly reduced by sub-optimal living conditions.

This is not to minimize the fact that these mechanisms are themselves highly unpleasant. Nature prescribes happiness only when it has survival-value. If the survival of our species demands a certain amount of sterility, deaths of babies, unhealthy children, malformed and mentally deficient people, criminals and perverts, our feelings about these drastic measures are irrelevant. To man nevertheless is given an answer. We need not wait for the physiological killers and maimers to come upon us. Primitive man was able to evolve cultural means, even though harsh, for limiting populations. Apart from dropping the more barbarous, little real advance has been made on them by modern Western civilization. During the 18th and early 19th centuries in Britain the execution of child-delinquents, their transportation, or their being sent to sea with the poor viability which that entailed, must have been nearly as effective a means of elimination as the emigration of yearling animals. It should not, however, be beyond the capacity of man to develop cultural methods of regulating population-numbers which do not involve distress and unhappiness. The consideration of such is beyond the scope of this essay. All that can be said is that man has the choice of consciously maintaining population at a level, for each stage of economic development, at which welfare, health and ability will be at a maximum, or of allowing Nature to make the adjustment by genetic provisions which have been valuable in man's evolution but which are insensitive and amoral.

BIBLIOGRAPHY

Anderson, W. J. R., D. Baird, and A. M. Thompson
  1958 "Epidemiology of Stillbirths and Infant Deaths Due to Congenital Malformation." *Lancet,* 274 (Vol. 1 of 1958): 304–6.
Baird, D.
  1945 "The Influence of Social and Economic Factors on Stillbirths and Neonatal Deaths." *The Journal of Obstetrics and Gynaecology of the British Empire,* 52: 217–34, 339–66.
Barnett, S. A.
  1958 "Physiological Effects of 'Social Stress' in Wild Rats. The Adrenal Cortex." *Journal of Psychosomatic Research* 3: 1–11.
Barnett, S. A., J. C. Eaton, and H. M. McCallum
  1960 "Physiological Effects of 'Social Stress' in Wild Rats, 2: Liver Glycogen and Blood Glucose." *Journal of Psychosomatic Research,* 4: 251–60.
Battle, M.
  1949 "Effect of Birth on Mentality." *American Journal of Obstetrics and Gynaecology,* 58: 110–16.
Birdsell, J. B.
  1953 "Some Environmental and Cultural Factors Influencing the Structuring of Australian Aboriginal Populations." *American Naturalist,* 87: 169–207.
Brown, L. H.
  1955 "Supplementary Notes on the Biology of the Large Birds of Prey of Embu District, Kenya Colony." *Ibis,* 97: 183–221.
Bruce, H. M.
  1960a "A Block to Pregnancy in the Mouse Caused by Proximity to Strange Males." *Journal of Reproduction and Fertility,* 1: 96–103.
  1960b "Further Observations on Pregnancy Block in Mice Caused by the Proximity of Strange Males." *Journal of Reproduction and Fertility,* 1: 310–11.
Burke, B. S., V. A. Beal, S. B. Kirkwood, and H. C. Stuart
  1943 "Nutrition Studies During Pregnancy." *American Journal of Obstetrics and Gynecology,* 46: 38–52.

Calhoun, J. B.
1952 "The Social Aspects of Population Dynamics." *Journal of Mammalogy*, 33: 139–159.

Carpenter, C. R.
1958 "Territoriality: A Review of Concepts and Problems," in G. G. Simpson and A. Roe (eds.), *Behavior and Evolution*. New Haven: Yale University Press.

Chief Medical Officer for England and Wales
1959 *Report*. London: Her Majesty's Stationery Office.

Chitty, D. H.
1952a "Mortality Among Voles (*microtus agrestis*) at Lake Vyrwy, Montgomeryshire, in 1936–39." *Philosophical Transactions of the Royal Society of London*, B.236: 505–52.
1952b "Population Dynamics in Animals." *The Journal of Animal Ecology*, 21: 340–41.

Christian, J. J.
1950 "The Adreno-pituitary System and Population Cycles in Mammals." *Journal of Mammalogy*, 31: 247–59.

Clarke, C. H. D.
1936 *Fluctuations in Numbers of Ruffed Grouse*. University of Toronto Studies: Biological Series No. 41.

Danielsson, B.
1956 *Love in the South Seas*. London: Allen & Unwin.

Drillien, C. M., and F. Richmond
1956 "Prematurity in Edinburgh." *Archives of Disease in Childhood*, 31: 390.

Ebbs, J. H., and W. J. Moyle
1942 "The Importance of Nutrition in the Prenatal Clinic." *Journal of American Dietetic Association*, 18: 12–15.

Ebbs, J. H., W. A. Scott, F. F. Tisdall, W. J. Moyle, and M. Bell
1942 "Nutrition in Pregnancy." *Canadian Medical Association Journal*, 46: 1–6.

Edwards, J. H.
1958 "Congenital Malformations of the Central Nervous System in Scotland." *British Journal of Preventive and Social Medicine*, 12: 115–30.

Eichmann, E., and H. Gesenius
1952 "Die Missgeburtenzunahme in Berlin und Umgebung in den Nachkriegsjahren." *Archiv für GynäKologie*, 181: 168–84.

Elton, C.
1942 *Voles, Mice and Lemmings: Problems in Population Dynamics*. Oxford: Clarendon Press.

Errington, P. L.
1946 "Predation and Vertebrate Populations." *The Quarterly Review of Biology*, 21: 144–77, 221–45.
1954 "On the Hazards of Over-emphasizing Numerical Fluctuations in Studies of 'Cyclic' Phenomena in Muskrat Populations." *Journal of Wildlife Management*, 18: 66–90.

Flaubert, G.
   1874 *Salammbô*. Paris: Charpentier.
Fraser, F. C., H. Kalter, B. E. Walker, and T. D. Fainstat
   1954 "Experimental Production of Cleft Palate With Cortisone, and Other Hormones." *Journal of Cellular and Comparative Physiology,* 43 (suppl.): 237–59.
Garry, R. C., and H. O. Wood
   1946 "Dietary Requirements in Human Pregnancy and Lactation. A Review of Recent Work." *Nutrition Abstracts and Reviews,* 15: 591–621.
Gesenius, H.
   1951 "Missgeburten im Wechsel der Jahrhunderte." *Berliner Medizinische Zeitschrift,* 2: 359–62.
Green, R. G., and C. A. Evans
   1940 "Studies on a Population Cycle of Snowshoe Hares on Lake Alexander Area." *Journal of Wildlife Management,* 4: 220–38, 267–78, 347–58.
Green, R. G., and C. L. Larson
   1938 "A Description of Shock Disease in the Snowshoe Hare." *American Journal of Hygiene,* 28: 190–212.
Hale, F.
   1935 "Relation of Vitamin A to Anophthalmos in Pigs." *American Journal of Ophthalmology,* 18: 1087–93.
Hammond, J.
   1955 "The Effects of Nutrition on Fertility in Animal and Human Populations," in J. B. Cragg and N. W. Pirie (eds.), *The Numbers of Man and Animals.* Edinburgh: Oliver and Boyd.
Harrell, R. F., E. Woodyard, and A. J. Gates
   1955 *The Effect of Mothers' Diets on the Intelligence of Offspring.* New York: Bureau of Publications, Teachers College, Columbia University.
Howard, H. E.
   1920 *Territory in Bird Life.* London: John Murray.
Huxley, J. S.
   1933 "A Natural Experiment on the Territorial Instinct." *British Birds,* 27: 270–77.
Lack, D.
   1953 *The Life of the Robin.* Harmondsworth, Middlesex: Penguin.
   1954 *The Natural Regulation of Animal Numbers.* Oxford: Clarendon Press.
   1955 "The Mortality Factors Affecting Adult Members," in J. B. Craig and N. W. Pirie (eds.), *The Numbers of Man and Animals.* Edinburgh: Oliver and Boyd.
Landauer, W., and C. I. Bliss
   1946 "Insulin-induced Rumplessness of Chickens." *The Journal of Experimental Zoology,* 102: 1–22.

McDonald, A. D.
1958 "Maternal Health and Congenital Defect." *New England Journal of Medicine*, 258: 767–73.

McKeown, T. and R. G. Record
1951 "Seasonal Incidence of Congenital Malformation of the Central Nervous System." *Lancet*, 260 (Vol. 1 of 1951): 192–96.

MacMahon, B., R. G. Record, and T. McKeown
1951 "Secular Changes in the Incidence of Malformations of the Central Nervous System." *British Journal of Social Medicine*, 5: 254.

Malpas, P.
1937 "The Incidence of Human Malformations and the Significance of Changes in the Maternal Environment in Their Causation." *Journal of Obstetrics and Gynaecology of the British Empire*, 44: 434–54.

Pasamanick, B., and H. Knobloch
1957 "Some Early Precursors of Racial Behavioural Differences." *National Medical Association Journal*, 49: 372.

Pasamanick, B., M. E. Rogers, and A. M. Lillienfeld
1956 "Pregnancy Experience and the Development of Behavior Disorder in Children." *The American Journal of Psychiatry*, 112: 613.

Rees, A. D.
1950 *Life in a Welsh Countryside*. Cardiff: University of Wales Press.

Registrar-General of England and Wales (1932–57).
1932–57 *Reports for England and Wales*.

Simpson, G. G.
1958 "The Study of Evolution: Methods and Present Status of the Theory," in G. G. Simpson and A. Roe (eds.), *Behavior and Evolution*. New Haven: Yale University Press.

Smith, W. C.
1925 *The Ao Naga Tribe of Assam*. London: Macmillan.

Sobin, S.
1954 "Experimental Creation of Cardiac Defects. Congenital Heart Disease." Fourteenth Medical and Research Report of the Pediatric Research Conference, Ohio.

Sontag, L. W.
1941 "Significance of Fetal Environmental Differences." *The American Journal of Obstetrics and Gynecology*, 42: 996–1003.
1944 "Differences in Modifiability of Fetal Behavior and Physiology." *Psychosomatic Medicine*, 6: 151–54.

Stewart, A. M.
1955 "A Note on the Obstetric Effects of Work During Pregnancy." *British Journal of Preventive and Social Medicine*, 9: 159–61.

Stieve, H.
1942 "Der Einfluss von Angst and psychischer Erregung auf Bau und Funktion der weiblichen Geschlechtsorgane." *Zentralblatt für Gynäkologie*, 66: 1698–1708.
1943 "Schreckblutungen aus der Gebärmutterschleimhaut." *Zentralblatt für Gynäkologie*, 67: 866–877.

Stockard, C. R.

    1910 "The Influence of Alcohol and Other Anaesthetics on Embryonic Development." *The American Journal of Anatomy*, 10: 369–92.

Stott, D. H.

    1950 *Delinquency and Human Nature*. Dunfermline, Fife: Carnegie United Kingdom Trust.

    1956 *Unsettled Children and Their Families*. London: University of London Press; New York: Philosophical Library.

    1957 "Physical and Mental Handicaps Following a Disturbed Pregnancy." *Lancet*, 272 (Vol. 1 of 1957): 106–12.

    1959 "Evidence of Pre-natal Impairment of Temperament in Mentally Retarded Children." *Vita Humana*, 2: 125–48.

    1960a "Delinquency, Maladjustment, and Unfavourable Ecology." *British Journal of Psychology*, 51: 157–70.

    1960b "Observations on Retest Discrepancy in Mentally Subnormal Children." *British Journal of Education Psychology*, 30: 211–19.

Tanner, J. F.

    1955 *Growth at Adolescence*: Oxford, Blackwell.

Thompson, W. R., Jr.

    1957 "Influence of Prenatal Maternal Anxiety on Emotionality in Young Rats." *Science*, 125: 698–99.

Thompson, W. R., Jr., and   L. W. Sontag

    1956 "Behavioral Effects in the Offspring of Rats Subjected to Audiogenic Seizure During the Gestational Period." *Journal of Comparative and Physiological Psychology*, 49: 454–56.

Uvarov, B. P.

    1928 *Locusts and Grasshoppers*. London: Imperial Bureau of Entomology.

Warkany, J.

    1947 "Etiology of Congential Malformations." *Advances in Pediatrics*, 2: 1–63.

Wilson, F.

    1938 "Some Experiments on the Influence of Environment upon the Forms of *Aphis chloris* Koch." *Transactions of the Royal Entomological Society of London*, 87: 165–80.

6 DIVINATION—A NEW PERSPECTIVE[1]

Omar Khayyam Moore

THE PURPOSE OF this paper is to suggest a new interpretation of certain kinds of magical practices, especially divination. First, however, I should perhaps explain briefly the motivation for undertaking this analysis. The initial impetus came from experimental investigations of the problem-solving activities of groups.[2] These experiments quite naturally involved the study and classification of ineffective problem-solving techniques, and it appeared that fresh insight into this whole matter might be gained through examining some "classic" cases of ineffective solutions to problems. Magic is, by definition and reputation, a notoriously ineffective method for attaining the specific ends its practitioners hope to achieve through its use. On the surface, at least, it would seem then that magical rituals are classic cases of poor solutions to problems, and for this reason should be of theoretical interest from the standpoint of research on human problem solving.

Reprinted from *American Anthropologist*, Vol. 59 (1965), pp. 69–74, by permission of the author and publisher.

[1] This paper is an indirect outcome of a program of laboratory research on problem solving and social interaction, sponsored by the Office of Naval Research, Group Psychology Branch.

Thanks are due to Alan R. Anderson, Maurice R. Davie, and George P. Murdock, who read preliminary drafts of this paper and made helpful suggestions which were incorporated into the final manuscript.

[2] Under laboratory conditions groups can be observed working out adequate solutions to problems and also becoming enmeshed in futile procedure. I wondered whether magical rites might not possess some of the same self-defeating patterns so often exhibited under experimental conditions, e.g., "cycling," introduction of extraneous material, etc. (See Moore and Anderson 1954a:151–60; 1954b:702–14.)

Most, if not all, scientific analyses of magic presuppose that these rituals as a matter of fact do not lead to the desired results. If the carrying out of a magical rite is followed by the hoped for state of affairs, then this is to be explained on other grounds. Scientific observers, of course, employ the criteria furnished by modern science to judge the probable efficacy of magical activities as methods for producing the ends-in-view of magicians. One of the puzzles most theories of magic seek to resolve is why human beings cling so tenaciously to magic if it does not work. Many contemporary explanations of this puzzle make use of the concept "positive latent function," that is, that even though magic fails to achieve its "manifest" ends, except by accident or coincidence, it serves its practitioners and/or their society in other critically important ways. The position developed here is compatible with the viewpoint that magical rituals may be sustained by numerous latent functions. However, it conceivably could serve as a prophylaxis against the overelaboration of these functions; in any case, it could serve as a supplementary explanation of the phenomena.

Put baldly, the thesis to be advanced here is that some practices which have been classified as magic may well be directly efficacious as techniques for attaining the ends envisaged by their practitioners. Perhaps the best way to render plausible this somewhat counter-intuitive proposition is to consider in some detail an actual magical rite as it has been described by a highly competent anthropologist.[3]

The Montagnais-Naskapi, most northerly of eastern Indian tribes, live in the forests and barren ground of the interior plateau of the Labradorian Peninsula. Speck (1935) has conducted field studies of the Naskapi and in the account that follows, primary reliance is placed upon his reports. According to Speck, "The practices of divination embody the very innermost spirit of the religion of the Labrador bands. Theirs is almost wholly a religion of divination" (1935:127). It is of interest to learn exactly how divination is carried out and what ends the Naskapi expect to achieve through it.

Animal bones and various other objects are used in divination.

---

[3] The Human Relations Area Files proved to be a great help in facilitating my investigation into magical practices.

The shoulder blade of the caribou is held by them to be especially "truthful." When it is to be employed for this purpose the meat is pared away, and the bone is boiled and wiped clean; it is hung up to dry, and finally a small piece of wood is split and attached to the bone to form a handle. In the divinatory ritual the shoulder blade, thus prepared, is held over hot coals for a short time. The heat causes cracks and burnt spots to form, and these are then "read." The Naskapi have a system for interpreting the cracks and spots, and in this way they find answers to important questions.[4] One class of questions for which shoulder-blade augury provides answers is: What direction should hunters take in locating game? This is a critical matter, for the failure of a hunt may bring privation or even death.

When a shoulder blade is used to locate game, it is held in a predetermined position with reference to the local topography, i.e., it is directionally oriented. It may be regarded as "a blank chart of the hunting territory . . ." (Speck 1935:151). Speck states (1935:151) ". . . as the burnt spots and cracks appear these indicate the directions to be followed and sought." If there is a shortage of food, the shoulder-blade oracle may be consulted as often as every three or four days and, of course, the directions that the hunts take are determined thereby.

There are certain other relevant aspects of divination that must be mentioned before turning to an analysis of the ritual. Speck explains (1935:150):

> In divining with the burnt shoulder blade the procedure is first to dream. This, as we shall see, is induced by a sweat bath and by drumming or shaking a rattle. Then, when a dream of seeing or securing game comes to the hunter, the next thing to do is to find where to go and what circumstances will be encountered. And since the dream is vague, and especially since it is not localized, the hunter-dreamer cannot tell where his route is to lie or what landmarks he will find. So he employs the shoulder blade. As one informant put it, the divination rite cleared up the dream. "We generally use the caribou shoulder blade for caribou hunting divi-

---

[4] There are differences among the various bands of the Naskapi (and among persons within bands) with respect to the system used for interpreting the pattern of cracks. The important point is that every interpreter has a system which is independent of any particular occasion of divination.

nation, the shoulder blade or hip bone of beaver for beaver divination, fish-jaw augury for fishing, and so on." Drumming, singing, and dreaming, next divination by scapula, then, combine as the modus operandi of the life-supporting hunt.

It is well to pause at this point to take note of certain features of these rites.

The Naskapi do not control the exact pattering of cracks and spots in the shoulder blade and, furthermore, it would not be in accord with their beliefs about divination to attempt such control; rather, they are interested in observing whatever cracks and spots appear. This means that the final decision about where to hunt, for instance, does not represent a purely personal choice. Decisions are based on the outcome of a process extrinsic to their volition—and this outcome is dependent upon the interaction of a number of relatively uncontrolled variables such as bone structure, temperature of fire, length of time bone is exposed to heat, etc.

It may be clarifying to perform a "mental experiment" in order to analyze some of the possible consequences of basing a decision on the outcome of an impersonal and relatively uncontrolled process. Imagine that the Naskapi carried out their divinatory rites as described with this exception; they did not base their decisions on the occurrence of cracks and spots in the burnt blade. They dreamed, sang, drummed, burned a shoulder blade, but ignored the cracks and spots. Under these hypothetical circumstances, decisions still would have to be made about where to hunt for game.

One question which this "mental experiment" raises is: Would the Naskapi be likely to enjoy more success in hunting if they did not permit decisions to rest upon the occurrence of cracks and spots? Would it not be sounder practice for them simply to decide where, in their best judgment, game may be found and hunt there? Of course, when the Naskapi do have information about the location of game, they tend to act upon it. Ordinarily, it is when they are uncertain and food supplies get low that they turn to their oracle for guidance.

It can be seen that divination based on the reading of cracks and spots, serves to break (or weaken) the casual nexus between final decisions about where to hunt and individual and group preferences in this matter.[5] Without the intervention of this impersonal mechanism it seems reasonable to suppose that the outcome of past hunts would play a more important role in determining present strategy; it seems likely their selections of hunting routes would be patterned in a way related to recent successes and failures. If it may be assumed that there is some interplay between the animals they seek and the hunts they undertake, such that the hunted and the hunters act and react to the other's actions and potential actions, then there may be a marked advantage in avoiding a fixed pattern in hunting. Unwitting regularities in behavior provide a basis for anticipatory responses. For instance, animals that are "overhunted" are likely to become sensitized to human beings and hence quick to take evasive action. Because the occurrence of cracks and spots in the shoulder blade and the distribution of game are in all likelihood independent events, i.e., the former is unrelated to the outcome of past hunts, it would seem that a certain amount of irregularity would be introduced into the Naskapi hunting pattern by this mechanism.[6]

We can indicate the point of the foregoing discussion in the following way. In the first place, the Naskapi live a precarious life; their continued existence depends on the success of their day-to-day hunting. And it is prima facie unlikely that grossly defective approaches to hunting would have survival value. Like all people, they can be victimized by their own habits; in particular, habitual success in hunting certain areas may lead to depletion of the game supply—it may lead, that is, to a success-induced failure. Under these circumstances, a device which would

---

[5] The act of interpreting cracks and spots provides an opening through which personal preferences may enter, especially if the "signs" are of a mixed character. However, according to Speck, they do not "cheat" in reading the cracks and spots any more than we would in reading a table of random numbers. The sacred character of the ritual and the fact that there are conventional agreements about the meanings of cracks and spots serve as some guarantee against purely personal interpretations. In any case, preferences have less opportunity to influence decisions than they would if the Naskapi did not make use of bones in this way.

[6] The interplay between the actions of hunters and the game they hunt is no doubt much more "sluggish" than the interactional relations between men in conflict. When men are in conflict the relative advantage to be gained by avoiding fixed patterns of behavior is potentially much greater than in the conflict between men and animals.

break up habit patterns in a more or less random fashion might be of value. The question is: To what degree, if any, does shoulder-blade augury do this?

It should be remembered that it is difficult for human beings to avoid patterning their behavior in a regular way. Without the aid of a table of random numbers or some other randomizing instrument, it is very unlikely that a human being or group would be able to make random choices even if an attempt were made to do so. The essential soundness of the last statement is recognized in scientific practice. Whenever, in the course of a scientific investigation, it is essential to avoid bias in making selections, every effort is made to eliminate the factor of personal choice. As Yule and Kendall (1948:337) have succinctly stated, "Experience has, in fact, shown that the human being is an extremely poor instrument for the conduct of a random selection."

Of course, it is not maintained here that the burnt shoulder blade is an unbiased randomizing device. It is likely that the bones would crack and form spots in certain ways more often than others. Regularity stemming from this source may to some degree be lessened because the Naskapi change campsites, yet in the rituals they maintain the same spatial orientation of the bones (for, as previously mentioned, the bones are oriented map-like with reference to the topography). Hence, a crack or spot appearing in the same place in the bone on a new occasion of divination at another campsite, would send them on a different route. An impersonal device of the kind used by the Naskapi might be characterized as a crude "chance-like" instrument. It seems that the use of such a device would make it more difficult to anticipate their behavior than would otherwise be the case.

It is not possible on the basis of the available evidence to determine even approximately whether shoulder-blade divination as practiced by the Naskapi actually serves to increase their hunting success, although a plausible argument has been advanced indicating that this might be the case.

If the Naskapi were the only people who engaged in scapulimancy, the question of its efficacy would perhaps not be of general theoretical interest. However, scapulimancy was widely practiced (Andree 1906:143–65) in North America and has been reported from Asia, India, and Europe. There are other divinatory rituals that also involve the use of impersonal chance-like devices in arriving at decisions, for example, the ancient Chinese divination by cracks in burnt tortoise shells. One hundred and twenty-five different figures formed by these cracks were distinguished for oracular purposes (see Plath 1862:819–27). All manner of objects and events have been used in divination.[7] Some arrangements are perhaps not obviously chance-like, but prove to be so when analyzed, as for instance Azande divination (Evans-Pritchard 1937). The basic divinatory equipment associated with the Azande "poison oracle" consists of poison, probably strychnine, and fowls. The Azande have little control over the potency of the poison they administer to the fowls since they do not make their own poison, and not all fowls have the same tolerance for this poison. The Azande ask questions of the poison oracle and base decisions on whether the fowls live or die. They have no way of knowing in advance what the outcome will be.[8]

The heuristic analysis given here is potentially relevant to all situations in which human beings base their decisions on the outcome of chance mechanisms. It is obvious, however, that light would be shed on the actual workability of these procedures only in terms of a thorough-going investigation of the problems men face within the societal context in which these problems occur. Certainly the apparent irrelevance of such techniques is no guarantee of their inutility. On the contrary, if shoulder-blade augury, for example, has any worth as a viable part of the life-supporting hunt, then it is because it is in essence a very crude way of randomizing human behavior under conditions where avoiding fixed patterns of activity may be an advantage. The difficulty of providing an empirical test for this hypothesis points to the fact that it is an open question.

Years ago Tylor (1924:80) noted that "the art of divination and games of chance are so similar in principle that the very same instrument passes from one use to the other." Tylor's observation is acute. However, it would appear that the relationship in "principle" is not between divination and games of chance,

---

[7] It is interesting to reflect upon the difficulties social scientists face in trying to predict the behavior of people who themselves sometimes use chance devices in deciding what to do.

[8] Incidentally, their manner of framing questions—they use complex conditionals—so as to obtain as many definitive answers while sacrificing as few fowls as possible, would do credit to a logician.

but between divination and games of strategy. It is only very recently that the distinction between games of chance and games of strategy has been drawn clearly. We are indebted to von Neumann and Morgenstern (1947:143–65) for clarifying this. It is beyond the scope of this paper to discuss the theory of games of strategy, but it is worth pointing out that this theory makes evident how some classes of interactional problems can be solved optimally by means of a "mixed" or "statistical" strategy. In order to employ a statistical strategy it is necessary to have, adapt, or invent a suitable chance mechanism. Its being "suitable" is critical, for unless the chance device will generate appropriate odds for the problem at hand, then its potential advantage may be lost. It should go without saying that no one assumes that preliterate magicians are in any position to get the most out of their crude chance-like devices. Nevertheless, it is possible that through a long process of creative trial and error some societies have arrived at some approximate solutions for recurring problems.

SUMMARY

It is the object of this paper to suggest a new interpretation of some aspects of divination. It should be emphasized that this interpretation is offered as a supplement to existing theories of magic and not as a replacement. An examination of many magical practices suggests that the utility of some of these techniques needs to be reassessed. It seems safe to assume that human beings require a functional equivalent to a table of random numbers if they are to avoid unwitting regularities in their behavior which can be utilized by adversaries. Only an extremely thorough study of the detailed structure of problems will enable scientists to determine to what degree some very ancient devices are effective.

BIBLIOGRAPHY

Andree, R.
   1906 *Scapulimantia*. Boas Anniversary Volume. New York: G. E. Stechert.
Evans-Pritchard, E. E.
   1937 *Witchcraft, Oracles and Magic Among the Azande*. Oxford: Clarendon Press.
Moore, O. K., and S. B. Anderson
   1954a "Modern Logic and Tasks for Experiments on Problem Solving Behavior." *Journal of Psychology*, 38: 151–60.
   1954b "Search Behavior in Individual and Group Problem Solving." *American Sociological Review*, 19: 702–14.
Plath, J. J.
   1862 *Die Religion und der Cultus der alten Chinesen, Part 1*. Abhandlungen der Bayerischen Akademie. München: Verlag der K. Akademie. Akademie.
Speck, F. G.
   1935 *Naskapi*. Norman: University of Oklahoma Press.
Tylor, E. B.
   1924 *Primitive Culture*, Vol. 1. New York: Brentano's.
Von Neumann, J., and O. Morgenstern
   1947 *Theory of Games and Economic Behavior*. Princeton: Princeton University Press.
Yule, G., and M. G. Kendall
   1948 *An Introduction to the Theory of Statistics*. London: C. Griffin.

7 THE POTLATCH SYSTEM
OF THE SOUTHERN KWAKIUTL:
A NEW PERSPECTIVE[1]

Stuart Piddocke

THIS PAPER is, first, an attempt to reconstruct the potlatch system of Southern Kwatkiutl society around the last decade of
the eighteenth century, i.e. at the beginning of direct contact with
Occidental civilization; and, second, an argument that in aboriginal times the potlatch had a very real pro-survival or subsistence function, serving to counter the effects of varying resource
productivity by promoting exchanges of food from those groups
enjoying a temporary surplus to those groups suffering a temporary deficit.[2] In making this reconstruction, I find myself forced
by the data to depart from the orthodox portrait of the Kwakiutl

Reprinted from *Southwestern Journal of Anthropology*, Vol. 21 (1965),
pp. 244–64, by permission of the author and publisher.

[1] This inquiry into the ecological relationships of the Kwakiutl potlatch was
first started in 1959–60 as part of a seminar on Northwest Coast cultures
conducted at the University of British Columbia by Dr. Wayne Suttles
and Dr. A. P. Vayda, who must be regarded as the joint inspirers of
this paper and for whom its first version was written. A second version
was read in the late fall of 1960 at the London School of Economics
seminar on anthropological theory conducted by Professor Raymond Firth,
whose criticism has greatly benefited both this paper in particular and
my own thinking in general. Reference to this unpublished second version
is also made in a 1961 paper by Dr. Vayda; and the preparation and
publication of this final version is therefore in the nature of a somewhat
belated fulfillment of a scholastic obligation.

[2] Compare Suttles (1960:296–305), where he shows how the Coast Salish
potlatch, status rivalry, subsistence activities, variations in production
within the Coast Salish resources, and their system of exchanges between
affinal relatives were all linked together as parts of a single socioeconomic system.

potlatch and to develop another based on data rather neglected in the literature. At the same time, there is no need to reject the orthodox picture as at least an approximately accurate description of *later* Kwakiutl potlatching, because the later form can be deduced from the proposed model of the aboriginal potlatch when certain actual historical processes, i.e. the events of the contact period, are fed in as conditions disturbing the original state of equilibrium specified in the model. Therefore, although this paper is not intended as a reconstruction of Kwakiutl history, it does provide an explanation for some of the responses that actually occurred in the historic period.

In particular, I wish to present evidence for the following propositions:

(a) The Kwakiutl have been commonly described as having a "fantastic surplus economy" distinguished by a great abundance of food and other natural resources further maximized by efficient methods of exploiting and storing the various products; this great abundance, preserved in summer, fed the people throughout the winter, during which season an abundance of leisure time enabled the people to develop their extraordinary potlatches and winter ceremonials (Codere 1950:4–5, 14, 63–64, 68, 126; Ford 1941:8). What I hope to show is that, however true such a picture of abundance may have been for the Kwakiutl as a whole, it was less than true for the various individual local groups. For these latter, scarcity of food was an ever-present threat, depending on the varying productivity of sea and land; and without the distribution of food from wealthier local groups to poorer ones, the latter would often have died of hunger.

(b) The potlatch was in aboriginal times confined to the chiefs or headmen of the various localized kin-groups or numayms that made up the tribes or winter-village groups, and hence the series of potlatches between the various chiefs were in effect exchanges of food and wealth between tribes and numayms. Through this exchange system, the effects of variations in productivity were minimized, and a level of subsistence was maintained for the entire population.

(c) In this system food could be exchanged for wealth objects, such as blankets, slaves, and canoes; and wealth objects exchanged in turn for increased prestige.

(d) The desire for prestige and the status rivalry between chiefs directly motivated potlatching and so indirectly motivated the people to continue the system of exchanges; and the continuation of these practices ensured the survival of the population.

Kwakiutl history may be divided into four periods: the Aboriginal or Pre-Contact period, extending from the indefinite past to 1792; the Early Contact period, 1792 to 1849; the Potlatch period, 1849 to the early 1920's; and the Post-Potlatch period, from the early 1920's to the present. What I have here separated as the Aboriginal and Early Contact periods corresponds to the Pre-Potlatch period distinguished by Codere (1961:434); the two later divisions follow Codere exactly. In 1792, European civilization, in the persons of Captain Vancouver and his expedition, first made direct contact with the Kwakiutl at the place known as "Cheslakee's Village" (Vancouver 1801:268–73).[3] European influence thenceforward slowly but steadily increased until in 1849 the Hudson's Bay Company established their trading post of Fort Rupert (Dawson 1887:66), and shortly thereafter the four Kwakiutl tribes later to be known as the Fort Rupert tribes settled hard by the post. This marks the appearance in Kwakiutl country of a direct non-traditional source of wealth, as contrasted with indirect trade through Nootka or relatively inconstant trade with trading ships. And with this new source of wealth there came changes in Kwakiutl society, notably an intensification of status rivalry and an increase in the frequency and volume of potlatching, so much so that the potlatch became the predominant Kwakiutl institution. This Potlatch period ended in the early 1920's when the beginning of an economic depression for the Kwakiutl coincided with the first notable successes in the Government's campaign to stop the Indians from potlatching.

SUBSISTENCE

Sea-fishing, river-fishing, berry picking, and the hunting of land and sea animals were the chief subsistence activities. Reviewing the list of the fish, animals, and plants eaten, one gets at first glance an impression of abundance: salmon, salmon-spawn, herring, herring-spawn, eulachen or candle-fish (notable for its oil), halibut, cod, perch, flounder, kelp-fish, devil fish, sea-slugs, barnacles, and winkles; seals, porpoises, and the occasional beach-stranded whale; mountain goats; elderberries, salalberries, wild

---

[3] Identified by Dawson (1887:72) with the Nimkish village of Whulk, at the mouth of the Nimkish River.

currants, huckleberries, salmon-berries, viburnum berries, dogwood berries, gooseberries, and crabapples; clover roots, cinquefoil roots, sea-milkwort, bracken roots, fern-roots, erythronium roots, lupine roots, wild carrots, and lily-bulbs; eel-grass and some sea-weeds. Of these, some would be eaten in summer, and the rest preserved for use in winter (Boas 1921:173–514).

This impression of abundance is, however, not sustained by further examination. For instance, the various roots and berries did not grow everywhere. Good crabapples could be picked in only two places; elsewhere they were "rotten." Viburnum berries could be picked only at the end of summer at the head of Knight Inlet (Boas 1921:213, 216). And berries and roots, generally, could be picked only in season.

Similar restrictions governed the supply of fish. The several varieties of salmon ran only at certain seasons of the year and did not spawn in every stream. Herring did not spawn everywhere. The eulachen ran in spring (Boas 1921:198), and, according to Curtis (1915:22–23), in three streams only, namely those on Kingcome River, at the head of Knight Inlet, and at the head of Rivers Inlet; furthermore, "this fish cannot be taken for its oil above tidal water." Curtis (1915:24–25) also informs us that only the following groups specialized in halibut fishing (though others might fish for halibut also, their fishing was only occasional): four tribes of Quatsino, two tribes (one now extinct) at Cape Scott, the Newettee of Hope Island, the Goasila of Smith Inlet, the Naqoaqtoq of Seymour Inlet, and the Owikeno of Rivers Inlet; the principal halibut banks were near Hope Island, Galiano Island, the Gordon group, and certain islands of the larger inlets. Flounders had to be caught in calm weather, when the tide was coming in (Boas 1921:413). Winkles were collected only when they spawned (Boas 1921:509). Kelp-fish were not caught in large numbers, and there was in any one catch usually only enough for a family (Boas 1921:397, 400, 405, 408). Of this apparent abundance of products, only a few were staples; the rest were additions, very welcome and very necessary to the Kwakiutl, but still only supplementary to the main diet. These staples were salmon, herring, eulachen, berries, and, to a somewhat lesser extent, goats, seals, and porpoises.

The Kwakiutl quarreled and fought amongst themselves over rights to hunting grounds, fishing stations on rivers, use of fish weirs and traps, and berrying grounds; trespassing was a frequent cause for conflict (Boas 1921:1345–48; Curtis 1915:22). Wars were waged "to take the land away from people" (Boas 1935:60, 66–67).

Starvation was no stranger to the Kwakiutl. Stories of starvation were more numerous among the tribes living on the islands in Queen Charlotte and Johnstone Straits, but all experienced hunger. Reasons given for such starvation included prolonged periods of bad weather which prevented hunting and fishing, and the failure of fish runs. The tales emphasized the especial dependence of the people on the salmon (Boas 1935:24). People would eat fern-roots when they were hungry and lacking in other food or when they had to camp for a long time in bad weather. The lupine root when eaten caused dizziness and sleepiness; yet it would be eaten in spring "when the tribes are hungry" before the eulachen arrived in Knight Inlet (Boas 1921:196, 198). As we would expect in such circumstances, they wasted very little of what food there was; for instance, recipes are given for salmon tails and roasted salmon backbone (Boas 1921:329).

This evidence can only lead, I think, to the conclusion that the abundance of the resources of the Kwakiutl has been somewhat overestimated and its significance misinterpreted. It was great enough to support a population larger than the usual size reported for hunting and gathering societies; but this population lived sufficiently close to the margins of subsistence so that variations in productivity which fell below normal could threaten parts of the population with famine and death from starvation.

Thus the evidence in the ethnographic record. It describes the localization of Kwakiutl subsistence resources and indicates—but does not document—variations in productivity. Further evidence for variation, however, is to be found in fisheries statistics concerning production of salmon and herring.

Herring

Statistics on herring show great variations, some spawning grounds apparently not being continuously used. Times of spawning vary from place to place. Changes in population abundance, says Outram (1956:7; 1957:7; cf. also 1958), are due primarily to variations in environmental conditions which causes variations in the "relative strengths of the contributing year classes" rather than to inadequate spawning or over- or under-fishing.

The Kwakiutl ate both herring and herring-spawn, and caught both at the spawning grounds. Besides the variation from year to year in the absolute number of herring spawn deposited (measured in miles of spawn at some standard intensity of deposition), the intensity of spawn varied from ground to ground, and we might expect this to have some effect on the catch made by Kwakiutl.

Salmon

Considerable year-to-year variation is likewise shown in the statistics on the packs of canned sockeye and other salmon taken at Rivers Inlet from 1882 to 1954 (Cobb 1921:172–74; Godfrey 1958a:333; cf. also Hoar 1951, for a general survey of variations in abundances of pink salmon on the British Columbia coast). These variations in salmon packs are traced to variations in the actual size of the salmon populations, variations which are in turn due to several causes. Notable among these causes are variable water levels and temperatures in the spawning streams, variations in the permeability of the stream beds, occasional extreme floods, variable temperatures and salinity in the ocean, and the variable freshwater runoffs and the action of tides, currents, winds, and deep-water upwelling in the estaurine and inshore waters that are the habitat of the young salmon for weeks or perhaps months before they reach the open seas (Godfrey 1958b; Neave 1953, 1958; Rostlund 1952:16; Wickett 1958). These causes are likely to have operated in previous centuries as well as in the present, and therefore indicate the existence of variations before statistics began to be kept on the fish population.

Rostlund (1952:16–17) has suggested that Indian fishing, before the advent of commercial fishing, helped to maintain the optimum salmon population by preventing over-crowding of the salmon streams. This may have been so, and it is a possibility to be taken into account when evaluating the productivity of subsistence resources for the Kwakiutl. But the effect of the Indian fishing would nevertheless not eliminate variations due to the causes enumerated above.

In addition to the variation in actual numbers of fish and game available for food, we must take into consideration the effects of the weather in hindering or preventing hunting and fishing expeditions. This has already been referred to as one of the reasons for starvation among the Kwakiutl.

The evidence is, I think, sufficient. For the various local groups of the Kwakiutl, scarcity of food was an ever-present threat, depending on the varying production of sea and land. Oftentimes it fell out that a local group would have died of starvation if it had not acquired food from other groups. The remainder of this paper will now be devoted to showing how the exchange system of the Kwakiutl ensured a continual movement of food from those groups enjoying a temporary abundance to those groups suffering privation, and so contributed to the survival of the whole population involved in the exchanged system.

SOCIAL UNITS

The basic unit of Kwakiutl society was the numaym, which may be summarily described as a named group associated mythologically with a traditional place of origin; it owned property consisting of fishing locations, hunting territory, and one or more houses in winter villages; and it was headed by a chief or headman descended, at least in theory, in the most senior genealogical line from a founding ancestor.[4] The members of the numaym consisted of people related, sometimes closely, sometimes distantly, usually patrilineally, but often through their mothers or wives, to the chief. There would at any time probably be a number of visitors dwelling with the people of the numaym, and some of the members of the numaym would also likely be away visiting. The numaym was in pre-contact times the potlatching unit, resource-exploiting unit, and the unit of social control.[5]

---

[4] Succession to the chief's position could apparently go to a woman, if she were a chief's eldest child and on condition that she resided in her father's numaym. We can perhaps best describe the succession as one of primogeniture with a patrilineal bias and a residence qualification. Since marriage seems to have been generally virilocal, at least for persons of high status, the residence qualification would tend to have ruled out most daughters, barring uxorilocal exceptions (which, of course, occurred). See also the section on rank, below.

[5] The whole question of the nature of the Kwakiutl numaym is still a thorny one. This brief sketch, based on Boas (1889:832; 1897:332–38;

The next larger unit of Kwakiutl society was the tribe. This was composed of a number of numayms which shared a common winter village site. In summer the villages dispersed and the various numayms departed for their fishing stations. At these summer grounds, groups living in separate winter villages would meet. This seasonal migration was an important feature of Kwakiutl life, and it involved both inter-tribal meetings and some sharing of access to resources (Curtis 1915:21–23, 108; Dawson 1887:64, 72).

CHIEFTAINSHIP

The position of the chief or numaym head among the Kwakiutl was described by the people themselves as "the office of giving potlatches among the tribes" (Boas 1925:91, 105), an expression which points out the position of the chief as representative of his numaym and his special task of potlatch giving. In former times, potlatching was a chiefly prerogative. Dawson (1887:79) has a significant passage on this point:

> Mr. George Blenkinsop, who has been for many years among the Kwakiool, informs me that the custom [of the potlatch] was formerly almost entirely confined to the recognized chiefs, but that of late years it has extended to the people generally, and become very much commoner than before. The Rev. A. J. Hall bears testimony to the same effect. With the chiefs, it was a means of acquiring and maintaining prestige and power. It is still so regarded, but has spread to all classes of the community and become the recognized mode of attaining social rank and respect.

By the time Boas was making his studies of the Fort Rupert Kwakiutl and collecting and editing George Hunt's texts, the potlatch was no longer a chiefly prerogative alone, and it had also, perhaps, been modified with respect to the job it was performing in society. This change seems to have been due to the advent of European traders, bringing sources of wealth beyond those tra-

---

1920:112ff.; 1921:795ff.; 1925:57–58, 91, 101; 1935:173), Curtis (1915:28, 132), and Ford (1941:15) should be considered still only approximate and provisional and should also be considered in relation to the portrait of Kwakiutl ranking (see below).

ditionally provided for by Kwakiutl culture, and to the decline of population, which led to some groups having more "seats" (see below) than members (cf. Codere 1961; Drucker 1955:121–22; Wike 1952:98–99).

The chief was the custodian or manager of the resources of the numaym. As such, it was his duty to perform the necessary rituals concerning the exploitation of these resources at the appropriate season. In this position, he received a certain portion (sometimes called "tribute" in the texts) of the fish, seals, goats, etc., caught by the men. His wife similarly received a portion of the berries and roots collected by the women. With this supply the chief could hold potlatches (though not always without further assistance) and could pay for the carving of totem poles, the construction of canoes, and the building of a new house (Boas 1921:1333–40; 1925:311ff., 331; Curtis 1915:28).[6]

RANK

Three status levels have been distinguished among the Kwakiutl and are termed in the literature "nobles," "commoners," and "slaves." But the distinctions between them are not of the same sort. Slaves were not, writes Boas (1897:338), strictly part of the numaym but were, rather, captives taken in war or people obtained by purchase; they might change ownership like any other piece of property, being, for instance, given away as marriage gifts (Boas 1921:856, 865–66, 881), presented to guests as a potlatch (Boas 1921:1027), or used as part of the purchase price of a copper (Boas 1921:1024). Indeed, according to one ancient account, a woman-slave was once killed and eaten in the cannibal

---

[6] It should be noted that the term "chief" in the literature denotes sometimes simply "numaym head" and at other times "numaym head and other high ranking nobles," but it is not always clear which usage is intended. That there is a distinction between the "numaym head" and the other "chiefs" seems to be indicated by the tenor of the various relevant texts. However, it does not matter much for my argument if nobles other than the headmen occasionally gave inter-numaym or even inter-tribal potlatches, as it is clear they gave them on behalf of their numayms. Nor would such other nobles constitute a very great part of the "nobility" as a whole.

dance (Boas 1921:1017). Marriages between free persons and slaves were possible, but they were considered disgraceful; and the stigma of having had slaves among one's ancestors descended to the children and grandchildren of the marriage, and beyond (Boas 1921:1094ff., 1104ff.). Not even the accumulation (in later, post-contact times) of wealth and of names could remove it.

The distinction between "nobles" and "commoners" is of a different kind than that between free persons and slaves. Codere (1957:474–75) has summed it up in the following words:

> "Commoner" in Kwakiutl refers to a person who at the moment of speaking is either without a potlatch position, chief's position, or standing place—all these being interchangeable but "noble" terms—or applies to one who has low rank which is nevertheless a "standing place" or position. The man referred to at that moment might have passed on his position just the moment before, or he might just the next moment be a successor to a position. "Commoners" in Kwakiutl society cannot be considered a class, for they have no continuous or special function; they have no identity, continuity, or homogeneity as a group, and no distinguishing culture or subculture. Individuals can at will become commoners by retirement from potlatch positions, and they customarily did so; individuals are raised from a common to a noble position at the will of others; individuals chose to consider "common" the lower positions of noble social rank; brothers and sisters of the same parents were given positions greatly varying in social rank and the younger ones might receive a position so lowly as to be "common."

These potlatch positions, or "seats" as Boas (1897:338) called them, were ranked in serial order, the chief of the numaym occupying the position of highest rank. Boas described these seats as each having associated with a tradition of origin ("which almost always concerns the acquisition of a manitou"), certain crests, and certain privileges which the holder of the seat may enjoy; the rank was recognized in the order of seating the holders at potlatches, whence the position with its privileges came to be referred to as a "seat." Curtis (1915:137–38) describes the properties of the seat as including "names, crests, special ceremonial privileges, and territorial rights as to fishing and gathering vegetal food."

Succession to rank was by succession to the name and crest

and complex of associated privileges, which of course also included its ranking. According to Curtis (1915:139), this succession was

> ordinarily reckoned directly through the male line from father to eldest son; but a childless man may transfer his rank to a younger brother by adopting him as a son. More commonly, if he has a daughter his seat goes to her eldest son, or to her in trust for her infant or expected son. Less important names, along with ceremonial privileges, are regularly given to the son-in-law as a part of the dowry, in trust for his children; in fact, the acquisition of titles and privileges for children yet unborn is the most important consideration in arranging a union. But the principal name and rank never thus pass out of the direct succession unless there is no direct male heir. If a man dies while his eldest son is too young for man's responsibilities, the seat may be given in trust to an elder sister of the boy, or to an uncle.

Though Boas in his earlier work (1897:338–40) does not mention this distinction between names and positions which could go out of the numayn and those which could not, he does recognize it in his later paper (1920:121) reviewing Kwakiutl social organization. This distinction is also repeatedly affirmed by the Kwakiutl themselves in the texts collected by Boas (1921:786–87, 824, 231; 1925:91, 101, 105), that only those names acquired from one's father-in-law can be given to one's son-in-law, and that certain names and positions, including that of headchief of the numaym, cannot be given away or go out of the numaym, daughters therefore inheriting when sons are not available. The distinction was sharper in principle than in practice, for, as might be expected, a few exceptions to the rule also did occur.

The numaym may be seen, then, not only as a kinship unit (as it was described earlier) but also as a collection of ranked positions, their incumbents, and persons related to these incumbents. As Codere (1957:479) has put it:

> A numaym is a lineage group consisting of a series of ranked social positions, plus children and adults who do not have one of the ranked positions but who may receive one as a relative of someone who has one to pass on to or who may have held one and retired from it.

The numayms within a tribe were also ranked in serial order, the head of the highest-ranking numaym being reckoned the head chief of the tribe or village. This seems also to have been true in aboriginal times. There is no evidence, however, that the villages or tribal groups were ranked prior to European contact; the ranking of villages is a later nineteenth century development (cf. Codere 1961:445).

Thus far in this paper we have examined subsistence, the basic units, chieftainship, and rank, demonstrated the first of the four propositions of this paper, and laid the foundation for demonstrating the remaining three. If in aboriginal times only chiefs potlatched (the chiefs being the numaym headmen and possibly one or two other leading men in each numaym as well), and if chiefs were supported in their potlatching by their numayms and potlatched on behalf of their numayms, then potlatches could only be between different numayms and were in effect exchanges of gifts between these numayms. The evidence for the first part of the antecedent in this proposition has been given in the section on "Chieftainship," and the second part of the antecedent implicitly supported there also. The numaym has been described and its resource-exploiting function noted. Kwakiutl ranking and its relation to the numayn have also been described, and something of its importance to the social structure suggested. What remains to be described is the system of exchanges, the conversions between food, wealth, and prestige, and the motivating factor of "status rivalry." These come to a focus in the institution of the potlatch, and to this we must now turn.

THE POTLATCH

What may be called the orthodox[7] view of the Kwakiutl potlatch is based largely on the summary and analysis given by Helen Codere in *Fighting with Property* (1950:63–80), following in turn the interpretation given by Boas in his early study of Kwakiutl social organization and "secret societies" (1897:341–

---

[7] It has, for instance, been followed by Herskovits (1952:165, 225, 306) in his now classic work on economic anthropology, and by Bohannan in his recent textbook (1963:253–59).

58). As Codere has herself admitted (1950:89), however, her reconstruction does not apply to the *aboriginal* potlatch but to the potlatch of the later contact period. Between the aboriginal potlatch and the potlatch of Codere's reconstruction there are several very important differences.

The first point of difference concerns Codere's setting the potlatch "in the context of a fantastic surplus economy" (1950:63). There seems no valid reason to doubt the appearance among the Kwakiutl in the last quarter of the nineteenth century of a great surplus beyond the needs of subsistence. But in aboriginal times such a surplus did not exist. Earlier in this paper I assembled evidence to indicate that the "fantastic surpluses" of the Kwakiutl have been overestimated, and that they were much closer to the margins of survival than has commonly been thought. The appearance of great wealth and "surpluses above any conceivable need" in later, post-contact times was probably due (a) to the drastic population decline from smallpox, venereal diseases, etc., ensuring that the productivity of sea and land, variable or not, was more than ample for the survivors' needs; and (b) to the increase in wealth coming from the sale of sea-otter furs to the fur traders and, later, to other non-traditional sources of wealth made possible by the contact situation. In aboriginal times, no such source of wealth was available, and it may also be presumed that the population was then at the limit of subsistence. Hence the threat of starvation, and in turn a very real pro-subsistence function for potlatch exchanges.

Secondly, Codere's account emphasizes not merely the giving away of gifts in the potlatch and the consequent accrual of honor to the giver, but also the obligation on the recipient to give a return potlatch or else lose prestige. She particularly writes (1950:68–69):

> The property received by a man in a potlatch was no free and wanton gift. He was not at liberty to refuse it, even though accepting it obligated him to make a return at another potlatch not only of the original amount but of twice as much, if this return was made, as was usual, in a period of about a year. This gave potlatching its forced loan and investment aspects, since a man was alternately debtor and creditor for amounts that were increasing at a geometric rate.

This passage links the obligatory nature of the return potlatch to the institution of borrowing-and-lending-at-interest. Following Boas (1897:341), Codere sees borrowing-and-lending-at-interest as an integral, indeed essential, part of potlatching, and a consequent continuous increase in the size of potlatch gifts as therefore also integrally part of the whole system.

This interpretation has, however, been vigorously denied by Curtis (1915:143–44) whose account has been curiously neglected in the study of the Kwakiutl potlatch:[8]

> It has been said of the potlatch that "the underlying principle is that of the interest-bearing investment of property." This is impossible. A Kwakiutl would subject himself to ridicule by demanding interest when he received a gift in requital of one of like amount made by him. Not infrequently at a potlatch a guest calls attention to the fact that he is not receiving as much as he in his last potlatch gave to the present host; and he refuses to accept anything less than the proper amount. Even this action is likened to "cutting off one's own head," and results in loss of prestige; for the exhibition of greed for property is not the part of a chief; on the contrary he must show his utter disregard for it. But to demand interest on a potlatch gift is unheard of. Furthermore, a man can never receive through the potlatch as much as he disburses, for the simple reason that many to whom he gives will die before they have a potlatch, and others are too poor to return what he gives them. Thus, only a chief of great wealth can make a distribution in which all the tribes participate and every person receives something; but all except a very few of these members of other tribes will never hold an intertribal potlatch, and consequently the man who gives presents to them cannot possibly receive any return for them. As to those who die, it may be said that theoretically a man's heir assumes his obligations, but he cannot be forced to do so, and if they far exceed the credits he is likely to repudiate them.
>
> The potlatch and the lending of property at interest are two

---

[8] It is very odd that though Codere in *Fighting with Property* (1950) relies very heavily on Curtis' accounts of Kwakiutl warfare, she makes absolutely no reference to Curtis' description of the potlatch, even though it is in the same volume as the war histories.

According to his book, Curtis gathered his data intermittently between 1910 and 1914 and was assisted by George Hunt; his inquiry was also facilitated by Boas' earlier work, especially *Social Organization and Secret Societies* (1897). Curtis' book contains Kwakiutl material which cannot be found in any other published source.

entirely distinct proceedings. Property distributed in a potlatch is freely given, bears no interest, cannot be collected on demand, and need not be repaid at all if the one who received it does not for any reason wish to requite the gift. When the recipient holds a potlatch he may return an equal amount or a slightly larger amount, or a smaller amount with perhaps the promise to give more at a future time.

The feeling at the bottom of the potlatch is one of pride rather than greed. Occasionally men have tried to accumulate wealth by means of the potlatch and of lending at interest, but the peculiar economic system has always engulfed them, simply because a man can never draw out all his credits and keep the property thus acquired. Before his debtors will pay, he must first call the people together and inaugurate a potlatch, thus ensuring an immediate redistribution.

This is a very different picture of the potlatch system. The practice of borrowing-and-lending-at-interest is both clearly distinct from and subordinated to the potlatch proper. The appearance of its being part of the potlatching is clearly due to the fact that debts were paid and could be called in only in connection with potlatching, often (Curtis 1915:144) only on the day of the potlatch itself.

The whole tone of the potlatch is different in Curtis' account— "one of pride rather than greed." This picture is much more consistent with data provided by Codere (1956:334ff.) on the "amiable side" of Kwakiutl potlatching and by Boas himself (1925: 249) in texts published at a later date, indicating that a chief should not be too proud or arrogant. The inability of creditors to enforce their claims unless they were intending to be put on a potlatch—in which case their claims would be reinforced by public opinion—is in perfect accord with the lack of developed institutions of social control among the Kwakiutl. This institution of borrowing-and-lending-at-interest was, furthermore, by no means a universal Northwest Coast institution, apparently being confined to the Southern Kwakiutl (Barnett 1938:349ff.; Olson 1940:173).

Curtis' report of potlatch gifts as not increasing in size but remaining about the same is, ironically, supported by Codere's own analysis of aboriginal potlatches (1950:90–94; 1961:446), where she notes that during the one hundred twenty years previous to 1849 the potlatches recorded in the texts involved relatively small distributions and showed no tendency to increase in size.

Finally, Curtis' account is more consistent with Dawson's report, already quoted in the section on chieftainship, that formerly only chiefs potlatched. In aboriginal times only chiefs would be able to assemble the wealth with which to hold a potlatch. For most people in the numaym the importance of having a position of rank would be in the receiving of gifts at potlatch distributions, not in having to validate these positions by potlatch giving—note Curtis' remark that many if not most of the persons receiving gifts in a potlatch, especially an intertribal one, would not be able to give potlatches in return.

For these reasons, the viewpoint followed in this paper in reconstructing the aboriginal potlatch is Curtis' rather than Boas' and Codere's.

Thirdly, we must also raise the doubts about the aboriginal existence of the sacrifice potlatch, an institution which looms large in all the accounts of our authorities (Boas, Codere, *and* Curtis) on the post-contact potlatch. The sacrifice potlatch and the grease feast are not mentioned in Kwakiutl mythology, nor does their presence in aboriginal times seem indicated by any other evidence. Concerning the destruction of property in the context of public assemblies or feasts Boas (1935:68), in summing up, Kwakiutl culture as reflected in mythology, has only the following to say:

> In myths the destruction of property occurs only in connection with the cannibal ceremony when the cannibal devours his own slaves or is given slaves to eat. Canoe breaking during a potlatch occurs in a tale on which the person who breaks canoes owned by others makes them whole again by his magical powers. A man pushes a copper under a mountain during a feast.

No sacrifice potlatch or grease feast here!

The destruction of property in aboriginal times is, however, clearly indicated in connection with the dead or dying. For example, food is burnt and so sent to a spirit in order to persuade him to spare the life of the dying child; spoons must be burnt by a woman visiting the ghost-country in order that the spirits of the dead may receive the gifts; and when a man has died, bundles of dried salmon, along with oil, fishing hooks, clothing and his canoe, are burnt to provide him with travelling provisions

(Boas 1921:705–11, 1329). What we have, then, in historic times is a spread of the idea of the destruction of property from a funeral context to a context of potlatching and active status rivalry, with the idea of honoring the dead perhaps providing the semantic link between the two contexts, and the new wealth consequent upon contact providing the means. This would be part of the religious changes suggested by Wike (1952) as having taken place on the Northwest Coast during the nineteenth century, namely a transfer of interest and concern from practices linked with the dead to a more secular manipulation of wealth and prestige.

How, then, may we describe the potlatch of aboriginal or precontact times, taking into consideration the points debated above?

The Kwakiutl potlatch, during those early times, may be described as the giving by a numaym, represented by its chief or headman, of a feast and presents to other numayms and their chiefs, often from other villages. At these distributions the more generous the host was, the more prestige he received; and if his generosity was not matched by the guests when they gave their potlatches, the host and his numaym increased in prestige at the expense of the guests. Hence there was a competitive element necessarily present in the potlatch.

Potlatches were held on several occasions: following or during funerals, by the deceased's successor when he entered formally into his new position; when a man wished to make a public announcement of his successor; whenever a name was changed or a person took on a new status in the community, as when a boy attained puberty or a girl first menstruated; when a marriage was contracted, and at several points thereafter during the marriage cycle; during the winter ceremonials, when dances were given; when persons were initiated into the "secret societies" or dance-fraternities; at "house-warmings," given when one's new house had been completed; when a copper was sold or bought; whenever a man, having accumulated a lot of property, wished to do something for the honor of himself and his numaym; when a man wished to humiliate his rivals and elevate his rank at their expense; and, sometimes, when persons on ill terms with one another decided to make peace (Boas 1921:691; 1925:135–357; Curtis

1915:142; Ford 1941:17, 19–23, 31, 36ff., 49, 169, 184–85, 218ff.).[9] Potlatching, that is to say, was not so much a special social event (though such purely potlatch events did occur) as an aspect or accompaniment of many social happenings.

At these potlatchings a great many people would be present, and these spectators would act as witnesses to the changes of status thus announced and to whatever other transactions also went on. Such memorable events therefore served the function of marking and validating changes in social status; in fact, Barnett (1938) saw in this task the especial function and underlying principle of the potlatch. In the old days, a numaym member who did not himself have sufficient wealth to hold a potlatch (and most numaym members would be in such a predicament) would give such wealth as he did have to the chief of his numaym, and the latter would put on the potlatch for him (Drucker 1955:125, 129).

In potlatching, a chief was assisted by the members of his numaym, who gave food, blankets, and other property in amounts dependent upon their means. They did not expect him to return to them what they had given him, but they would receive recognition of their services in intangible but no less important returns (Boas 1921:1340–44; Drucker 1955:124–25, 129). This was in addition to the wealth received by the chief as "tribute"; and if he still did not have as much as he wanted, he could obtain it by borrowing from his friends and relatives in other numayms or calling in what was owed him.

Blankets, as already intimated, were not the only gifts given in the potlatches. The guests were heavily feasted, the food being formally reckoned as worth a hundred blankets (Boas 1925:205); and the food they did not eat they would take home with them (Boas 1935:38) or their hosts take them afterwards, often with the very feast dishes as well (Boas 1921:768, 775). Canoes might be given away with or instead of blankets. "The potlatch which took place upon the occasion of the marriage payment by the bride's family a few years after the wedding invariably

---

[9] Many of the occasions named here would be more important in the lives of nobles and their immediate relatives rather than in the lives of commoners. Potlatching was a responsibility of aristocrats.

involved the distribution of such household articles as provisions, wooden boxes, mats, blankets . . ." (Ford 1941:19). At another form of the potlatch, known as the "grease feast," boxes of eula-chen oil were given away.

Potlatches were given by one numaym to other numayms, or by one tribe to other tribes. In the light of the data presented on subsistence, the utility of intertribal distributions of food and wealth will be readily obvious. But the utility of distributions be-tween the various numayms *within* a single tribe may not be obvious at first glance. However, the numaym and not the tribe was the land-owning, resource-exploiting unit, and in summer the various numayms of the tribe dispersed to different places. It might easily happen, therefore, that some of the numayms within the tribe had a more fruitful year than did the others; and in such circumstances, distributions of food and wealth between the numayms even within the same tribe would be advantageous to all.

The potlatch had no one essential function, but several. It redistributed food and wealth. It validated changes in social status. It converted the wealth given by the host into prestige for the host and rank for his numaym, and so provided motivation for keeping up the cycle of exchanges. The potlatch was, in fact, the linch-pin of the entire system.

BUYING AND SELLING

But blankets, canoes, and boxes cannot be eaten. A starving numaym would find it very awkward if it could not convert into food the wealth it had received in potlatches. I have shown how, through the potlatch, wealth could be converted into prestige. Could food be exchanged for wealth, so that a starving numaym could sell blankets for the food it needed in order to subsist, and a wealthy numaym sell food in return for the blankets necessary to potlatch?

The answer is yes. In preparing to give a potlatch, the host, if he did not have sufficient food to feed his guests, could buy it with blankets (Boas 1897:342). I have already noted that food given in a potlatch was reckoned as being worth one hun-dred blankets. In a short summary of accounts of buying and selling in the texts which he collected, Boas (1935:67) wrote:

When a man catches many herrings at his beach, he sells them for slaves and becomes a rich man. People go out in canoes and buy food from another tribe. A chief goes out and buys many cherries from the neighbouring tribe. Starving people pay for food with dressed elkskins, slaves, canoes, and even their daughters.

CONCLUSIONS

In the beginning of this paper I set forth four propositions linking (a) variable productivity of food sources, (b) potlatch exchanges, (c) interconvertibility of food, wealth, and prestige, and (d) status rivalry among the Kwakiutl. The rest of the paper has been devoted to presenting the evidence in support of these propositions. It remains simply to explain the picture of aboriginal Kwakiutl society that results.

Let us first consider a simplified system made up of only two numayms, A and B. This simplification is not wholly artificial, since the total Kwakiutl potlatch exchange system may be considered as being made up of combinations of such overlapping pairs. Let our pair, furthermore, start out evenly balanced in resources, food supply, wealth, and prestige. Both, however, are pressing in numbers upon the margins of their resources, so that a poor harvest for either one would result in its going hungry and, if the poor harvests continue, in eventual starvation, certain diminution, and possible extinction. Since the initial amount of wealth possessed by each is the same, at the end of a potlatch cycle each numaym has still about the same amount of wealth as it began with, and the prestige of the two numayms also remains alike.

Let A suffer a severe failure in food supply. To feed themselves, the members of A sell blankets to B in exchange for food. This increment of wealth enables B either to hold potlatches more frequently or to give bigger gifts in their potlatches. And B does so, giving wealth to A in batches larger than before and so gaining increased prestige in return. Thus through the potlatch A recovers its wealth in return for granting more prestige to B. With this wealth A can either hold a return potlatch and regain its prestige by giving equally large gifts or use the wealth to purchase more food. If A uses some of this wealth to purchase more food, it will not be able to give a return potlatch of generosity equal to

B's potlatch, and the increment in B's prestige will be more firmly established. If, sometime later, B suffers a deficiency in food supply, it can buy food from A, and this cycle will be repeated with the roles reversed.

Two consequences stand out from the above model: (a) if a numaym continually suffers from a failure of food supply, it will not be able to respond in potlatching with gifts of value equal to what it has received, and its prestige will steadily decline. Because the potlatch-system is also tied in with other aspects of society, such as marriage and war,[10] such a steady decline of prestige would probably have the effect of forcing the numaym in time out of the system entirely as an independent unit: it would either literally die out, or it would become a permanent dependency of its wealthy partner. (b) There will be, over time, a steady increment in the absolute size of potlatch gifts, regardless of which partner suffers food deficiencies. In fact, the more frequent such deficiencies are, the greater the rate of incrementation is likely to be. This does not, however, necessarily entail an increase in the number of actual wealth objects; tally sticks, such as the Kwakiutl did in fact use (e.g. Boas 1897:352), would serve the purpose adequately.

The institution of borrowing and lending can be seen as another way of acquiring blankets with which, in times of economic distress, to maintain one's level of potlatch giving and so maintain one's prestige.

This system would be more efficient the more units were involved. With many numayms selling food, the increment in wealth received by them would be for each much smaller than that if only one numaym was the seller, and the temptation to increase potlatch gifts would be correspondingly reduced. Consequently, with many numayms in the system, the rate of increase in sizes of potlatch gifts would be reduced. Further, the chances of many

---

[10] Codere (1950) has shown how in historic times warfare declined as potlatching increased. We may further add that comparisons of the war histories and the marriage accounts suggest a tendency for the groups with which a given numaym warred not to be those with which it intermarried; war and marriage were alternate means of gaining new crests. Establishing new marriage links would also have had the effect of increasing the number of relatives, both affines and kinsfolk, with whom oneself and one's children and other relatives could visit.

numayms all suffering deficient harvests simultaneously would be considerably less than the chances for two numayms being thus afflicted together.

If the food deficiences be *short-term, intermittent,* and *not sustained,* the relative ranking of the numayms involved will over the long-run remain constant, whether or not one numaym is given to suffering more deficiencies than another. If the deficiencies be *long-term and sustained,* however, as pointed out above, the numaym so marked out will be forced in the long run out of the system.

However, even a long-term run of bad luck, with continually deficient food supply and declining prestige, may be offset if the wealthier partner in its turn suffers a long-term deficiency while the food supply of the poorer improves, provided of course that the poorer numaym's run of misfortune has not been so prolonged as to drive it out of the system altogether. In such circumstances the *long-term* relative ranking of the numayms will oscillate about a constant level.

The model presupposes, therefore, an overall balance of resource productivity among the numayms involved in the system. No numaym, or at most only a few, suffers from long-term, sustained resource deficiencies which would take it out of the system: variations in resources tend to be short-term and intermittent. All groups are pressing on their resources, so that times of low productivity menace their existence; but the population/resource ratio for each is substantially the same. Indeed, we may suspect that a rough equality in population/resource ratios between numayms is necessary for this system to work.

This system, coping successfully with variable productivity and by its exchanges of food and wealth enabling a larger population to live in the Southern Kwakiutl country than would otherwise have lived there, is nevertheless vulnerable to the following:

(a) A change in the pattern of resource exploitation such that some numayms increase their food production consistently relative to the remainder: This change will change their population/resource ratio, enable them to sell more food for more wealth, and so, as has already been explained, by increased potlatching gain more prestige than can be matched by poorer numayms. Such a resource discrepancy may occur through some numayms decreasing their food production, through some increasing theirs, or

through population decline in some numayms and not in others so
that the former no longer press so closely on their resources.
Changes in food production could in turn be due either to changes
in the natural environment beyond human control or intent, or to
changes in techniques of resource exploitation.

(b) The entry into the system of a new, non-traditional source
of wealth: The general effect of this factor would be to promote
more frequent potlatches and bigger potlatch gifts, and to permit
persons other than the traditional chiefs to engage in potlatching.
This in turn would promote an increase in competitive or rivalrous potlatching. Exchanges would become less between numayms
and more between prestige-seeking individuals. The balance between food, wealth, and prestige would, I think, become more
precarious, but, provided the effects were distributed evenly over
the whole system, the system would still survive, though at a
higher level of activity. Destruction of wealth, if adopted, would
serve to take some of this new wealth out of the system and so
serve to inhibit the increase in the velocity of circulation. And,
finally, if the influx were only for a short time, the system could
probably survive it without much change.

But if the influx of wealth were unevenly distributed among the
numayms, benefiting some more than others, not only would
potlatch rivalry be accentuated, but some groups would rapidly
gain an ascendancy over the others, and the balance of the system
would be upset. The groups having lost prestige would in one way
or another eventually be forced out of the system. And through
the decline in the number of potlatching social units, the system
itself would become increasingly unstable. This instability would
be further heightened by the increase in potlatching rivalry and by
a concurrent increasing individualization of potlatching. The end
result would, in time, be to destroy the system beyond recovery.

(c) A general decline in population, with the consequence that
the population no longer presses on the margins of its resources,
and the threat of starvation resulting from reduced harvests is
removed: Assuming that the amount of wealth in the total system
remains constant, this change would both free more wealth from
food-purchasing for use in potlatching and increase the per capita
wealth among the Kwakiutl. Frequency and size of potlatches
would increase, and with this increased wealth the chances of
more persons being engaged in it would also be increased. The
effects of population decline would therefore be similar to those
of the influx of new wealth.

In post-contact times we find the latter two changes taking place
together and in marked degree, viz., an influx of new wealth, first
from the fur-trade and later from other non-traditional sources,
and a drastic decline in population, both prolonged for about a

hundred years. The result was as would be expected if the construction proposed in this paper is correct: an increase in the size and frequency of potlatches, a general spread of potlatching to most persons in the Kwakiutl communities, an increase in rivalrous potlatches with a concomitant individualizing of potlatches, and the appearance of the "fantastic surplus economy" so marked in the later ethnographic record.

BIBLIOGRAPHY

Barnett, H. G.
  1938 "The Nature of the Potlatch." *American Anthropologist,* 40: 349–58.
Boas, Franz
  1889 "First General Report on the Indians of British Columbia." *Report of the British Association for the Advancement of Science:* 801–93.
  1897 "The Social Organization and the Secret Societies of the Kwakiutl Indians." *Report of the U. S. National Museum for 1895:* 311–738.
  1920 "The Social Organization of the Kwakiutl." *American Anthropologist,* 22: 111–26.
  1921 *Ethnology of the Kwakiutl.* Bureau of American Ethnology, 35th Annual Report (1913–1914): 41–1581.
  1925 *Contributions to the Ethnology of the Kwakiutl.* New York: Columbia University Press.
  1935 *Kwakiutl Culture as Reflected in Mythology.* American Folklore Society, Memoir 28.
Bohannan, Paul
  1963 *Social Anthropology.* New York: Holt, Rinehart & Winston.
Cobb, John N.
  1921 "Pacific Salmon Fisheries," Third Edition, Appendix I. *U. S. Bureau of Fisheries: Report of U. S. Commission of Fisheries for the Fiscal Year 1921.*
Codere, Helen S.
  1950 *Fighting with Property.* American Ethnological Society, Monograph 18.
  1956 "The Amiable Side of Kwakiutl Life: The Potlatch and the Play-Potlatch." *American Anthropologist,* 58: 334–51.
  1957 "Kwakiutl Society: Rank without Class." *American Anthropologist,* 59: 473–86.
  1961 "Kwakiutl," in E. H. Spicer (ed.), *Perspectives in American Indian Culture Change.* Chicago: University of Chicago Press.
Curtis, Edward S.
  1915 *The North American Indian, Volume X. The Kwakiutl.* Norwood (Mass.): The Plimpton Press.

Dawson, George M.
1887 "Notes and Observations on the Kwakiool People. . . ." *Transactions of the Royal Society of Canada,* Sect. ii.
Drucker, Philip
1955 *Indians of the Northwest Coast.* New York: McGraw-Hill, for The American Museum of Natural History.
Ford, Clellan S.
1941 *Smoke from Their Fires.* New Haven: Yale University Press, for the Institute of Human Relations.
Godfrey, H.
1958a "A Comparison of Sockeye Salmon Catches at Rivers Inlet and Skeena River, B.C., with Particular Reference to Age at Maturity." *Journal of the Fisheries Research Board of Canada,* 15: 331–54.
1958b "Comparisons of the Index of Return for Several Stocks of British Columbia Salmon to Study Variations in Survival." *Journal of the Fisheries Research Board of Canada,* 15: 891–908.
Herskovits, Melville J.
1952 *Economic Anthropology.* New York: Knopf.
Hoar, W. S.
1951 "The Chum and Pink Salmon Fisheries of British Columbia 1917–1947." *Fisheries Research Board of Canada,* Bulletin 90.
Neave, Ferris
1953 "Principles Affecting the Size of Pink and Chum Salmon Populations in British Columbia." *Journal of the Fisheries Research Board of Canada,* 9: 450–91.
1958 "Stream Ecology and Production of Anadromous Fish," in P. A. Larkin (ed.), *The Investigation of Fish-Power Problems—A Symposium Held at the University of British Columbia April 28 & 30, 1957.* Vancouver: U. B. C. Institute of Fisheries.
Olson, Ronald L.
1940 "The Social Organization of the Haisla of British Columbia." *Anthropological Records,* 2: 169–200.
Outram, D. H.
1956 *Amount of Herring Spawn Deposited in British Columbia Coastal Waters in 1956.* Fisheries Research Board of Canada, Pacific Biological Station, Nanaimo, B.C., Circular 42.
1957 *Extent of Herring Spawning in British Columbia in 1957.* Fisheries Research Board of Canada, Pacific Biological Station, Nanaimo, B.C., Circular 46.
1958 *The 1958 Herring Spawn Deposition in British Columbia Coastal Waters.* Fisheries Research Board of Canada, Pacific Biological Station, Nanaimo, B.C., Circular 50.
Rostlund, Erhard
1952 *Freshwater Fish and Fishing in Native North America.* University of California Publications in Geography 9.
Suttles, Wayne
1960 "Affinal Ties, Subsistence, and Prestige among the Coast Salish." *American Anthropologist,* 62: 296–305.

Vancouver, George
  1801 *A Voyage of Discovery to the North Pacific Ocean* . . . , *Vol. 2.*
    London: John Stockdale.
Vayda, Andrew P.
  1961 "A Re-Examination of Northwest Coast Economic Systems." *Transactions of the New York Academy of Sciences,* Series II, 23: 618–24.
Wickett, W. P.
  1958 Review of Certain Environmental Factors Affecting the Production of Pink and Chum Salmon." *Journal of the Fisheries Research Board of Canada,* 15: 1103–26.
Wike, Joyce
  1952 "The Role of the Dead in Northwest Coast Culture," in Sol Tax (ed.), *Indian Tribes of Aboriginal America: Selected Papers of the XXIXth International Congress of Americanists.* Chicago: University of Chicago Press.

8 CAMEL PASTORALISM IN NORTH ARABIA AND THE MINIMAL CAMPING UNIT[1]

Louise E. Sweet

TRADITIONAL ACCOUNTS of the north Arabian Bedouin tribes have emphasized the fluctuation between tribal unity and disunity, intertribal conflict, and internal feuding. They have thereby given a confusing and contradictory picture of a desert pastoral society at once cohesive and divisive, aristocratic and equalitarian, communalistic and intensely individualistic. More recently an attempt has been made to characterize this polarity of Arab Bedouin society in more rigorous terms: it shows "the potentiality for massive aggregation of agnatic units, on one hand, and atomistic individualism on the other." It is said to lack stable or corporate segmentary organization below the level of the tribe, although segmentation processes along agnatic lines, ordered by genealogical relationships and ideology, form its basic structural design (Murphy and Kasdan 1959:21).

I should like to propose here that recognition of a relatively

Pp. 129–52 of *Man, Culture, and Animals: The Role of Animals in Human Ecological Adjustments*, A. Leeds and A. P. Vayda, eds., Publication No. 78 of the American Association for the Advancement of Science, 1965. Reprinted by permission of the author and publisher (copyright 1965 by the American Association for the Advancement of Science).
[1] The writer would like to express appreciation to Grace L. Wood Moore for suggestions improving earlier versions of this paper, and to Anthony Leeds for stimulating and careful criticisms leading to the final version.
Field notes gathered from interviews with Bedouin tribesmen and others were taken in Kuwait in 1958–1959, in the course of field research supported by a grant from the Social Science Research Council. The writer's gratitude is also owed to the Kuwait Oil Company for providing opportunities to interview men of pastoral background and to travel widely in Kuwait, and to the hospitality of the State of Kuwait.

stable social unit smaller than the tribe may help to dispel some of the confusion over the internal structure and cohesion of Bedouin tribal society, and may clarify the nature of minimal camping units in relation to other units of the tribe. This smaller unit, the tribal section, governs a number of aspects of the techniques and economics of camel pastoralism in north Arabia, and it shows features of corporate structure and process in relation to the control of productive resources. Control and protection of resources is vested in the section and administered through a redistribution system. The section is flexible in size and internal organization in response to ecological conditions and is corporately organized for nomadic grazing movement as well as for the defense of its herds and their aggrandizement by predation. This is in contradiction to the statement that in Bedouin society "there are no lineages in the sense of bounded groups having a continuing and cohesive base in corporate rights and duties" (Murphy and Kasdan 1959:24).

Attention to the empirical data that are available on the techniques and economics of camel pastoralism in north Arabia, rather than merely to the logic of kinship, blood feud, and parallel cousin marriage, requires notice of this structure and of its relation to the camel as the strategic resource of the Bedouin tribes.

I shall deal first with the camel, its capacities and requirements, its role in Bedouin economy, and then shall endeavor to show how adaptation to these factors is related to the organization of the societies dependent upon this animal and to the corporate structure of the tribal section. (See Appendix, section 1.)

ECOLOGY AND CAMELS

The steppes and desert of north Arabia have been occupied for some three thousand years by camel pastoralist societies. From time to time they have overrun the agricultural societies on the northern rim of their range or have given rise to oasis-based kingdoms to the south. Within the arid regions in which their culture developed, however, the Bedouin camel-breeding tribes have maintained a distinctive pattern and a dominant position over other societies and settlements in their territories by virtue of their ability to exploit the grazing ranges into which other local economies cannot spread, and by virtue of their fighting strength, mobility, and control of communication routes. The camel is their basic resource and tool for dominance. The Bedouin tribes of camel-breeding specialists, such as the Rwala, Shammar, and Mutair, are to be distinguished from the non-Bedouin peoples in the same region who use the camel for transport and labor, but whose economies are based upon shepherd pastoralism, agriculture, commerce, or specialized services and crafts. (See Appendix, section 2.) The northern tribes are also to be distinguished from camel breeders of south and southeastern Arabia, whose herds are smaller and whose usages are somewhat different. The discussion here will be confined primarily to the better-known northern tribes, particularly the Rwala, the Shammar tribes of the Nefud, and the Mutair.

The camel is the largest of the domesticated animals of Arabia. Its range and scale of uses, its specific adaptations to desert conditions, and its limitations are the foundations of Bedouin culture. As a source of food it provides both meat and milk, but for the Bedouin the camel is more significant as a milk producer. In the desert and steppe environments of north Arabia few other food resources are available. Game (gazelle, lizards, birds), plants (truffles, the semh seed), and locusts are sporadically utilized, but they are seasonal in availability, difficult to procure, and sparse in yield. The camel herds provide a more stable food supply. But camels mature slowly and reproduce slowly as compared with other domestic dairy and meat animals such as sheep and goats. A female camel is bred for the first time in her sixth year, and then only once in two years produces a single offspring. If this offspring is a male cub, it is more often butchered than kept, in order to conserve the mother's milk for human use (Johnstone 1961:294). Milking camels are the heart of the herd and are never sold. The female gives milk for 11 to 15 months, and it is this unique lactation period that makes camels the only dependable year-round source of food. The yield per animal, however, is small, varying from 1 to 7 liters per day according to season and pasturage (Musil 1928b:88–89). In order to meet subsistence needs in milk, minimum herd size must therefore be maintained and the herd must be managed so that both pregnant and lactating females are available to ensure a continuous supply; hence there is strong pressure to increase herd size.

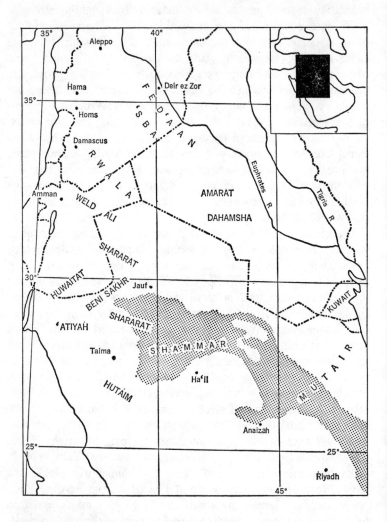

*BEDOUIN TRIBES OF NORTH ARABIA The stippled area in-
dicates the Nefud, the chief grazing area of the Shammar Bedouin*

The literature on the Bedouin provides no clear information
on the minimal number of animals required to support a family.
There is apparently great variation in wealth in camels, but
there are also many facets of interdependence and customary
means of supporting the poorest folk. One example may suggest
a median figure. My Dosiri Bedouin informant in Kuwait in

1959 regarded his family as relatively secure and well off with about 18 female camels, half of which were pregnant and half giving milk. In addition to these, his family had at least two strong baggage camels for transporting the tent and equipment and bringing water, as well as a few riding camels. He felt his family to be well enough supplied with milking camels to be able to lend some to kinsmen who had no fresh animals. The British estimates of tribal herd strengths about 1917 are based on allowing 20 camels as an average figure per tent (Great Britain, Admiralty 1917:77). Subsistence needs satisfied from the milking camels are, however, only one aspect of the use of camels by the Bedouin. Nor is milk their only food.

Although camels also provide meat, this is rarely, if ever, a part of the daily Bedouin diet, but rather is a feature of the ceremony of hospitality and of sacrifices on such special occasions as the return of successful raiding parties or the fulfillment of vows. There is no way to gauge the possible frequency of such contexts in which a camel would be butchered for a feast. Musil notes that usually the only meat eaten by the Rwala Bedouin is camel meat, but it is a luxury (1928b:96).

The transport uses of camels—for riding, carrying domestic equipment, and fetching water—are probably of as great general significance as the food uses, since these uses and capacities of the camel enable the Bedouin to penetrate grazing ranges inaccessible to small-animal breeders, to migrate over greater distances, and to mobilize mounted warrior parties. The diversified uses of camels are reflected in differences between milking, baggage, and fine riding types as well as between breeds distinctive in color and build and characteristic of different tribes and regions of Arabia. Mention should also be made of the use of hair and hides for tents and especially the largest water bags, and of the fat.

Camels are more commonly used for meat in Egypt, throughout the north Arabian oasis towns, and in the urban centers of the Levant. Moreover, the work capacity of the camel to carry freight, 150 to 300 kilograms per animal (Musil 1928a:453), and to pull plows or irrigation apparatus is utilized extensively in commercial and agricultural activities of other Arabian societies. Hence among the Bedouin breeding or acquiring camels for sale exerts additional pressure to maximize the herds. Exchanging camels (males and old or barren females) in the oasis town markets or selling them to the itinerant merchants moving among the tribes is as important as predatory tactics in obtaining supplies of arms, grain foods and condiments, domestic hardware, and textiles. It should be noted here that camel pastoralism in north Arabia appears to have developed long after the rise of the ancient oriental civilizations (Mikesell 1955), and therefore has operated in continuous contact with complex, inter-regionally supplied economies in which money and market systems of exchange only recently developed. This contact cannot be ignored as an influence on Bedouin camel breeding and herd building, as well as on Bedouin social structure. However, there is no clear evidence that the tribesmen buy or sell camels among themselves at all.

For the Bedouin the camel is thus a multipurpose resource for food and other materials, a valuable commodity for exchange, a means of heavy transport, and a fast-moving durable mount for defensive and offensive movement. In combination, these features are superior to those of any other animal in Arabia and render the Bedouin superior to or independent of non-Bedouin societies in the same region at strategic points of interaction with them.

The capacity of camels to tolerate extremes of heat and lack of water, to thrive on desert plants beyond the capacities of other domestic animals, and to cover distances in the course of nomadic grazing supports Bedouin life in the outer ranges of the ecological niche of desert pastoralism. But the climate and rainfall regime of north Arabia and the geographical distribution of permanent watering points enforce an annual migration pattern which, after winter in the interior desert, converges upon summer camping places in the vicinity of settled areas. The range of a pastoral society in north Arabia thus includes winter pastures, permanent watering points for summer, and access to an urban market. These are the basic features of the tribal territory, and it is the relatively stable dominance over such a territory, with its other inhabitants, over time by a group of genealogically related agnatic segments which identifies the Bedouin tribe. The Rwala tribal territory, for example, extends from the vicinity of Damascus, their summer camping zone, to the southeast between the Wadi Sirhan and the Anaizah highland, and into the sand desert of the Nefud, south of Jauf oasis, a distance of some 800 kilometers (Raswan 1947:5).

The great size of tribal territories and the long nomadic grazing treks are features of camel pastoralism. Müller says the normal migration range of the camel tribes is about 600 kilometers and in some years may reach 700 or 800 (1931:97). Such extensive ranges seem to be required because of sparse and sporadic distribution of vegetation and the variable rainfall patterns—the cyclic patterns of years of drought and years of abundance, and the annual variation within one tribal grazing zone.

Desert vegetation provides three categories of plants on which the herds depend for forage: annual grasses and plants, xerophytic surface perennial shrubs, and perennials which survive the dry, hot months by root and bulb adaptations. The Bedouin rainfall and plant lore recorded by Musil and others indicates that the full growth cycle of these plants, providing the most abundant pasturage through the year, requires a sequence of good rains from early October until the final storms that may occur in mid-April or May. The failure of the early rains in any area, especially those of November, affects the later development of plants, especially the annuals, and spells trouble for the herds. An abundant growth of the annual plants, particularly from March to mid-April, is especially necessary for the kinds of pasturage that will result in abundance of milk from the camels. If the autumn and winter rains fail or are meager for two or three years running, then the growth of annuals will fail altogether (Musil 1928b:8–16). In such years of extreme drought affecting a whole tribal area, the tribe must move into better-favored areas. Such an emergency emigration may be accomplished by peaceable agreement with allied tribes (Dickson 1949:46) or by threat or use of force against others.

The number of camels which the north Arabian tribal territories can carry in view of the pasturage and rainfall variation is not known in any systematic or accurate fashion. The few figures available are scarcely more than estimates. One that is given for the Rwala is perhaps suggestive: in the 1930's (1936?) they were said to number 35,000 persons in 7000 tents, and to own some 350,000 camels (Raswan 1947:36). This was a year of extreme drought, and the Rwala lost many camels before they successfully threatened and negotiated their way into the territory of a neighboring tribe for the season. Montagne has characterized the north Arabian area as "overpopulated" and says there is intense competition for pasturage (1947:23). But such competition and temporary tribal emigration seem rather to be features of the drought-end years of a rainfall cycle. (See Appendix, section 3.) Though camels are bred in many other parts of Arabia, the north Arabian steppes and deserts are the optimum breeding areas, if the location there of the greatest herds and the most powerful Bedouin societies is an adequate measure.

Within a tribal territory the rainfall pattern varies each year in such a way that areas of good pasturage one year may be barren the next. A sector occupied by some agnatic segments or families of a Bedouin tribe may be more favored than that of other segments or families. Though it is logical to suppose that freedom of access to adequate pasturage is a condition of tribal life, how this is regulated within the tribal structure of north Arabian Bedouin society has not been fully understood. It is not patently deducible, for there are at least two possible modes: (1) independent movement of the minimal property-holding and camel-herding units of extended or joint families, and (2) co-ordinated and cooperative movement of larger units composed of a number of genealogically related families. Determining which mode is operative requires a clearer understanding of the structure of Bedouin society than is now available. The discussion below of the significance of the tribal section as a corporate unit may contribute to the solution of this problem.

FISSIONING IN THE SOCIAL ORDER AND ECOLOGY: THE CAMPING UNIT

Security depends on striving to maintain and increase the size of the herds that support any given social unit, in order to counteract any hazards of the habitat (drought, disease, accident) and other factors that may tend to reduce the herds below the survival limits for man. These limits, however, are set not only by the subsistence and domestic transport use of camels by the Bedouin, but also by their exchange value for equipment and supplementary foods (chiefly dates and wheat) taken into the desert, and their military use for offense and defense. A "surplus" of camels is required above subsistence needs. When the slow breeding rate of the camels, failure of pasturage, or loss by theft and raid threatens the security of a unit, its members have recourse to certain actions which are to a considerable extent formalized in Bedouin society. First, they may secure replacement or increase by predation upon the herds of others. The institutionalization of raiding other Bedouin tribes for camels, with its elaboration of tactics, etiquette, division of spoils, celebration in sacrifice and poetry and song, strikes one as an elaborate "take-away" ceremony comparable to the "give-away" feasts of the northwest coast Indians of North America. Raiding, too, results in the reciprocal distribution of economic goods between societies (Sweet 1965). Predation against non-Bedouin tribes is equally widespread and is prevented only by the payment of tribute or protection fee, often also in camels. Secondly, in times of poor pasturage a Bedouin unit may move with its herds to a more fortunate area. As we have seen, tribal emigration takes place under conditions of widespread drought, but localized droughts may have the same effect upon smaller segments of the society. It would seem that the asserted freedom of minimal lineage groups, families, or even siblings to split from their kinsmen and nomadize by themselves or to join, through the custom of establishing "neighbor" relations, other sections or tribes than their own, is a means of adapting to unfavorable habitat conditions for grazing in local areas, at least temporarily. Thirdly, persons or families who have lost their herds entirely or who have never succeeded in acquiring enough camels to support themselves may join other more fortunate families in various client or free servant roles. Fourthly, new grazing territory or well points may be seized. There is as yet no evidence of such seizure by a unit smaller than the tribe. Finally, Bedouin may partly or completely abandon specialized camel breeding by moving out of the ecological niche in which it flourishes and becoming sedentary or diversifying their economy with sheepherding. Such a process has taken place among Shammar tribes who moved in the nineteenth century across the Euphrates to the Jazira region of Syria.

A pastoral society of atomistically fissioning lineages, uncommitted to any scale of corporate organization or structure other than the tribe, accords well with the mobility required under desert conditions. Such kin groups, however, are vulnerable to predation or competition for pasturage from analogous units which are larger. This implies competition within the tribal structure and territory which does not seem to accord with other facts. Within the Bedouin tribal territory the grazing areas are systematically exploited, herds are managed, and camels or other wealth are distributed within structures which encompass a number of minimal lineages, and which also have means of acting upon or bringing pressure to bear upon vengeance unit operations within their organizations at times of crisis. These are the tribal sections (*fakhd*). Their functions are economic as well as political; in evolutionary perspective, it seems likely that they could well be classed as petty chiefdoms (cf. Sahlins 1961:327) rather than as segments of "tribal" societies. Musil regularly refers to these units as "clans."

For the exploitation of its territory a Bedouin tribe is divided into a number of segments or sections, the residence units of the peoples of the tribe. Through the annual regime of nomadic movement, each section moves in systematic relation to analogous sections. Dickson says that the Mutair sections set out from their summer camps on the wells, which are "jealously treasured possessions" of the sections (1949:46), one after the other. A serial order of migration is implied, each section separated from the others; in orderly fashion they occupy the pasture areas. The migration proceeds rather slowly, especially in years of abundant pasturage, and the distances between sections apparently allow enough time for the growth of annual plants in the pasture areas, in the course of a few rains, to recover. There is probably a fanlike dispersal of the Mutair sections rather than a rigid serial order of march; Dickson provides very little detail. Musil's accounts of the Rwala indicate quite clearly a parallel movement of sections across the tribal territory (1928b:165 et passim). Constant communication between the chiefs of sections circulates information on the conditions for grazing and sources for water. A similar regular movement of sections is implied for the Shammar tribes of the Nejd (Montagne 1932:71–72). The cyclic movement of the sections thus appears to have a close relation to the variations of the habitat within the tribal range.

Control over and defense of the camel herds is a concern of the whole section. Individual "ownership" of camels has been emphasized to the point of obscuring the operation of social control,

vested in the office of the chief and administered through a redistributive system. (See Appendix, section 4.) As a group of
genealogically related lineages, a section brands its camels with a
common sign. Of the Shammar, Montagne says, "Each section is
an association which defends in common its camels, each marked
with the same brand" (1932:71). Musil describes the special
section herd of the Rwala group with whom he traveled (that of
the tribal chief), and seems to imply that other Rwala sections
also maintained such herds of white camels, built up from animals selected from raid booty as well as by natural increase.
(They are not the total herd of the section, but a selected group
under the trusteeship of the chief.) These herds are sources of
pride and prestige for the whole section and are guarded by
outstanding young men selected from the members of the section
lineages (Musil 1928b:335–36). The herds of a section thus
include two categories, the sectional herd and those of varying
size and composition which belong to individuals and families. It
is unfortunate that no more is known of the distribution of
camels within Bedouin economy.

In their position as the dominant power groups of the north
Arabian steppes, Bedouin groups also own or control through
tribute relations a portion of the products of oasis cultivators.
Among the Shammar, at least, the ownership of date palm
gardens in oasis settlements is vested in the section; the agreed
tribute portion of the harvest is transmitted to the section chief,
who then distributes it among the kin groups of his section
(Montagne 1932:71). Among the Rwala a distinction must be
made between garden properties in oases owned by chiefly
families and the protection tribute paid to the tribe (and probably
section) by agricultural settlements or subordinate tribes. In
either case, however, the tenant of tributary contributions are
subject to distribution among the tribesmen by the chief.

This redistributive role of the section chief is a marked feature
of Bedouin society. It functions not only with respect to the obligations of hospitality and the distribution of valuable goods received from outside the section structure, but also in calling upon
the collectivity to support the individual. Thus the section chief
might call together the prominent men of his unit and assess each
man, in proportion to his herds, camels to replace those that a fellow section member had lost in a raid or for other reasons (au-

thor's field notes, Dosiri informant, Kuwait, 1959). The chief is expected to see that every needy family has at least the minimum requirement in camels for keeping up with the section. While the section is nomadizing during the winter and spring, selection of grazing areas and of camping places is made in the chief's tent with the collaboration of the leading men of the unit. The chief's tent serves as a collecting point of information of all kinds, but particularly that which bears upon the grazing conditions and security lying ahead of the line of migration. Travelers, couriers from other chiefs, members of independently roving bands of the Salubba peoples, and scouts sent out by the section chief seek him out or are brought to him to report their observations. Although the decision to move and where to move is signaled by the chief, an occasion when he must demonstrate his astuteness, the group may, as one incident in Musil's accounts indicates, override the chief's decision (1928a:203–4). His authority is by no means despotic, and his status is maintained largely by his demonstrated ability in the economics of herd management, as well as by his generosity, and his success in leading the unit on major predatory raids.

Smith has noted that the "tribe" on the march moves with all the precautions of war (1885:55). Presumably he was referring to the nomadic trek of the section during the winter grazing season. Pasturage scouts and guards move ahead of the group and are organized to defend the other section members and its herds as they move in a body together. In the camp, security and pasturage conditions dictate the camp pattern. Among both the Mutair and the Rwala the tent clusters of kin groups are more or less compactly placed, depending in part upon the terrain and the likelihood of raiders. When a season of consistently good rains has brought forth abundant vegetation, the family and lineage components of the section may pitch their tents close together, since the herds may all be grazed nearby. But in a year of poor and scanty distribution of vegetation, some dispersal of the section according to its subunits is enforced, so that the grazing herds may range over a wider territory. When predators are expected and a more compact encampment is established, the clustering of tents in kin units, with their couched camels, at 200- to 400-yard intervals makes for maximum security and mobilization, as Dickson says of the Mutair. At such a time a balance between the greater mobility of small units and the greater security in gathering numbers of such units together is achieved. Though the raiders may make off with peripheral herds, it is more difficult to pillage the whole camp before resistance can be mobilized. The Shammar likewise order their camp settlements in kin units, and often the whole is surrounded by the tents and animals of nonmembers (clients, herdsmen, merchants, blacksmiths) moving under the protection of the clan section (Montagne 1932:72–73).

One of the confusing aspects of earlier accounts of Bedouin society is the lack of distinction among raiding, warfare, and vengeance action. If these activities are distinguished, the function of the tribal section in organized raiding operations emerges more clearly. And the raid itself appears as an institutionalized means of increasing or restoring the herds of the section, or ensuring the "surplus" necessary for maintaining regional dominance. Elaborate rules govern the prosecution of raids between Bedouin tribes, all of whom stand in some degree of kinship relation to one another in the ideology of common genealogical descent. The more closely two mutually raiding tribes are considered to be related to each other, the more the rules restrict taking advantage of prime conditions for attack. The major objective of raids is the capture of camels, particularly adult females. Other property in tents and desirable furnishings may be seized in rare instances of complete rout of the defenders; but even in such cases a raided group will not be completely wiped out or pillaged. The men defending will flee rather than fight when the odds are clearly against them, and women and children must be left with sufficient camels to get them to their nearest kinsmen in neighboring sections. Various rules of restitution also protect the camels and property of persons living with the raided section who are not members of that kin group.

Though raiding relations are formally declared between *tribes,* the organization of raids takes place in the tribal sections, and the raids are necessarily directed at sections of other tribes. The taking and retaking of camels through raiding seems then to serve as a means of circulating or distributing a scarce resource over a wide area (Sweet 1965).

The ancient pattern of northward drift of the camel pastoralist societies out of the less favorable ecological setting of southern and central Arabia and into the better-watered steppes of north

Arabia, and the probable southern origin of camel breeding in such less favorable areas (Mikesell 1955), suggest on the one hand that the raiding complex is an adaptive feature. It offsets the slow reproductive rate of camels, in an area where large herds are an economic and political advantage and where in fact ecological conditions make large herds possible. On the other hand, it may be that the raider's preference for adult female camels simply by-passes losses due to the localized effects of habitat hazards as well as other factors. That is, in the prolonged and difficult work of breeding and raising camels in a desert environment subject to cyclic periods of drought, the acquisition of an adult female camel suitable for breeding saves five or six years of labor.

The sizes of tribal sections vary widely among the Rwala, Mutair, and Nefud Shammar. This variation probably reflects to a considerable extent ecological differences among the tribal territories which are significant for breeding camels. Of the three Bedouin groups, the Mutair territory lies farthest south and east, and their sections range in size from 20 tents to 200, though most fall between 50 and 100 (Dickson 1949:564–66). To the west and slightly north of the Mutair, the Shammar tribes of the Nefud range in section units that average between 200 and 300 tents each (Montagne 1932:73). The Rwala Bedouin, the most powerful of the north Arabian tribes and representative of the Anaizah group, move in sections that range from 150 to 800 tents, most of them numbering between 300 and 500 (Great Britain, Admiralty 1917:50). About 1917 the observation was made that the Shammar tribes were not so rich in camels as the tribes of the Anaizah group, but that they must have possessed on the average 20 to 30 camels to a tent, or, having 4000 tents, a total of at least 80,000 animals (ibid.:77).

A few general features of the internal organization of a tribal section should be mentioned. The agnatic lineages of a section are ranked relatively to each other; that is, the office of section chief is vested in a chiefly lineage as distinct from non-chiefly lineages. Such hereditary rights in an office may, as Montagne notes, be held through eight to ten generations and then be lost to a rising rival lineage (1932:70). At any one time, however, the lineages of a section are ranked, and the larger the section, the more internal segments, each also ranked, it may contain.

("Fissioning agnatic segments," "prominent families," "subsections" are terms common in the literature that seem to refer to such ranked internal segments of a section; at present the single ranking distinction between chiefly lineages and others is all that can be made, but the possibility of further ranking mechanisms should be considered.) These kin groups who move together and camp together in the section are "fixed lineages" in the sense of the term proposed by Bacon and are to be distinguished from the "sliding lineage" or the egocentric vengeance unit (*khamsa*): the two do not necessarily coincide (Bacon 1958:123–34).

At this point there is a regrettable gap in the descriptive data needed to relate this lineage structure to the actual camping units and economic activities. There are few detailed descriptions of the composition of particular tent clusters in a camp or of their herds and herding. One can only say that the members of a "fixed lineage" within the section camp together and comprise one or more extended families. The family cluster of tents within it (*ahl*), together with its nonmember dependents, if any, is the minimum or "real" herding unit. The kinsmen of this cluster are likely to be "the descendants of one grandfather" (author's field notes, Dosiri informant, Kuwait, 1959). This will give several possible combinations of brothers, fathers and sons, uncles and nephews as heads of families, forming a camping unit of close kinsmen for which parallel cousin marriage would be an advantageous means of intensifying internal cohesion.

There is clearly unequal distribution of wealth in camels among Bedouin families, in terms of ownership, but kinship obligations tend to equalize to some extent the access to the camels or to their products. All writers on the Bedouin distinguish between the majority of "ordinary" poor tribesmen and the minority of wealthy, most but not all of whom are of chiefly lineages. Apart from this there is very little to indicate how, except from good fortune in the natural increase in herds and in raiding, one man may become more wealthy in camels than another. Good fortune is transitory, however, and Western observers have also remarked upon the "fatalism" with which a man may face loss of his wealth through raids. Only the chiefs, whether of tribe, section, or subsection, display their economic power in slightly larger tents and finer equipment.

Besides the core of member patrilineages and their family components, a tribal section includes other persons or families. There are likely to be fellow tribesmen from other sections; there may be refugee families or individuals of other tribes. As fellow Bedouin, these are members of the *'aṣiil* or caste of noble tribes, the camel-breeding specialists, who dominate the north Arabian desert. The greater the reputation and power of a section and its chief, the more likely it is to attract such reinforcements. There are also individuals or families from the non-noble or subordinate tribes; the men of this category are usually the herdsmen of the camels. There are also the blacksmith families, the slaves, and the Salubba guides and hunters, the lowest caste of Arabian desert society. Under optimum conditions in north Arabia, such as Musil saw among the Rwala, the tribal section is a mobile petty chiefdom, heterogeneous in composition, and ranked in structure, but organized around a central core of genealogically related patrilineages. It may number five hundred tents and some twenty-five hundred or more people, and control and depend upon more than ten thousand camels.

Everywhere, however, in accounts of the society or in contact with the people themselves, the "individualism" of the Bedouin is noted. When a man has acquired camels, a tent, and a wife, he is not obliged to remain with his father's or brother's or uncle's cluster—an attitude which he expresses assertively—but may independently move with others. A poor man who has no camels seeks a wealthier man and works for him as a herdsman. Each year he receives an animal or two as part of his compensation, and he expects, after seven or eight years of good fortune, to be independent (author's field notes, Dosiri informant, Kuwait, 1959). Such data tend to reinforce the impression of economic "individualism" in Bedouin society. A minor lineage chief within a section, disgruntled with the section chief's treatment of him in the distribution of largess or the collection of tax camels, may remove his kin group from the section temporarily. Such fissioning has been emphasized as a major trait of Bedouin social process, and less attention has been given to data which just as clearly underline the cohesion of Bedouin social units within the key structure of the tribal section. Even after so critical an event as murder, membership in the section is retained by the violator and his kinsmen, and there are customary means of return to it after exile in a distant tribe as fugitives from vengeance. A quarrel at the wells resulting in homicide may split such a small body of kinsmen, the *khamsa* or vengeance unit of the murderer, from the section and send it into refuge with another tribe until the blood price can be arranged. Once it has been settled, however, the kinsmen are welcomed back with feasting and celebration. "For do they not return who might have been lost?" (Musil 1928a:489–93).

SUMMARY

The size, strength, mobility, endurance, and lactating capacity of the camels provide the subsistence base for Bedouin society; for many families, milk may be the only food for several months of the year. In the north Arabian steppes and deserts where conditions for specialized camel breeding are at their optimum, the herds are larger than elsewhere in Arabia and the camping units tend to be correspondingly larger.

The extremes of desert life and dependence upon the camel enforce mobility of the social units, of which the smallest and most mobile is the extended or joint family and its herds. This unit, however, is also the most insecure because of factors tending to deplete the herd: the slow reproductive rate of camels in the face of environmental hazards, the need for supplies produced outside the pastoral economy for which camels must be exchanged, and the threat of raid. Hence three other units of organization within the tribal boundary are functionally significant: the section, composed of a core of ranked lineages; the separate or "fixed" lineages themselves; and the "sliding lineage" or egocentric vengeance unit (*khamsa*). The section appears to be the maximum unit governing the maintenance of herds in the subregions of the tribal grazing range, and also to be the minimum unit for security against predatory raiders and for the effective mobilization of retaliatory measures to gain animals and to keep the size of the group's herds at maximum. Conditions which demand the dominance of the larger-scale units of organization over the lesser and more atomistic include not only protection from and aggrandizement by predation, but adjustment to such fortuitous hazards as the habitat presents. Likewise, intersectional relations and the relations to other societies, their markets and governments, foster this dominance and the dependence of the smaller units upon the larger. It can be said, then, that the effective minimal camping unit of Bedouin society is the tribal section. The variability of desert grazing conditions, however, demands flexibility in social arrangements; hence fissioning into lineages and families serves as a means of meeting threatening conditions, and it is ideologically emphasized throughout Bedouin society.

APPENDIX

1. *Sources*

Ethnographic and ecological data in this paper are based primarily upon the works of H. R. P. Dickson, Doughty, Müller, Montagne, and Musil cited in the references. In all cases, the writers were in Arabia at times and under circumstances of political upheaval. Only Doughty and Musil actually lived and moved with Bedouin groups for any length of time; Müller and Montagne were involved in forwarding the policies of the French mandate government in Syria after the first World War, and Dickson was similarly engaged as a British political resident stationed at Kuwait. At these times the "normal" flow of economic life was obscured by pressures and activities of the Great Powers. Musil's journeys, spanning the period from 1900 to 1915, likewise reflect the overlay of political tensions developing in the rivalry between the Shammar Rashidi emirate and the rising Saud hegemony.

None of the sources on the Bedouin provide the intensive descriptive and analytic detail needed today for a well developed essay of this type. The culling of anecdotes and of interpretations of poems, and the collating of diary-recorded observations provided the data used here, an awkward and uncertain procedure at best.

2. *"Bedouin"*

In the use of the term "Bedouin" I have followed Musil (1928b:45) and, so far as I know, the usage of the *'aṣiil* tribesmen themselves. It designates the tribes who are engaged predominantly in camel breeding and who, in particular, share a common ideology of descent expressed in the traditional tribal genealogies. Two great genealogical plans group Arabian tribes respectively as the descendants of *Ishmael* ("North") or of *Yoktan* ("South"). To what extent these genealogies reflect historical connections would be a matter of lengthy dispute with those historians who accept this interpretation as their major import. Peters (1960) has, on the other hand, demonstrated clearly their immediate political and ecological significance for the Bedouin tribes of Libya. In north Arabia, tribes with genealogies, whose members "know their ancestors," as an Utaibi told me in Kuwait, are *'aṣiil* or noble. These are the tribes with which the present paper is concerned. North Arabian desert society is not, however, homogeneous. The steppes and deserts are inhabited by oasis dwellers, small-animal breeders, and a number of pariah or ignoble tribes, peoples who may or may not breed camels exclusively. The Awaazim, Hutaim, and Shararat are among the latter. The blacksmith caste and the Salubba hunters are also to be found in the region, living among or in the tribal territories of the noble tribes. The *control* of wells, pasturage territories, caravan routes, minor settlements is held largely by the Bedouin tribes. This does not exclude others from passage or use, provided the customary arrangements have been made with the dominant tribes, through their chiefs.

Relations between the Bedouin tribes and others are clear and explicit along general lines. The former do not intermarry with the latter, and in particular would not allow their women to do so. Intermarriage between Bedouin tribes is not uncommon, however, especially between chiefly lineages. Moreover, many of the non-noble tribes are "clients" or "serfs" of the Bedouin tribes, or pay tribute to them. Such subordinate tribes are frequently sheep and goat breeders, and some may be engaged in managing properties in flocks of sheep for the Bedouin.

3. *Rains, Vegetation, and Grazing*

Buxton (1923) is the only source I am aware of for an ecological study of desert life from the biologist's point of view which applies to north Arabia. This supplements and confirms the water and plant lore of the Bedouin, which is most extensively recorded in Musil's several books, together with his own observations.

The plant life of the desert is of two major kinds, annuals and perennials. During the rainy season, from early October until

May, depending upon the abundance of rains through the fall sequence, green forage is available for the animals, and water in pools, crevices, wells, or at shallow depth is available for man. With green, lush growth camels need not be watered for as long as 30 days. When the rains cease and heat and aridity dry the annuals to straw and hay and the perennials lose their sappiness, the return to permanent watering places takes place. Camels, as well as other animals, subsist on the dried forage in summer, but require water once every three days or oftener, depending on the heat.

The distribution of vegetation in "areas" is known only for Kuwait (V. Dickson 1955) and from a few remarks in Musil. The latter mentions that the sand desert area of the Nefud means to the Shammar, in fact, the vegetation area of the *raza* shrub, a good source of forage for camels as well as fuel for the Bedouin (Musil 1928c:19). Philby, incidentally, has said that the northeastern parts of the Rub' al Khali desert have vegetation areas recognized, named, and exploited by the Murra Bedouin sections (1933:131). Musil's accounts of his exploratory journeys, apart from the Rwala section which often served as his base, list the grazing plants found in various areas, and the lack of them because of failure of rains in a local area over a number of years. There are very few passages in his books which suggest or state that there is *competition* for pasturage between groups whether tribal or subtribal. Rather, the first concern of the migrating group is to locate the best pasturage and water resources ahead of them. Scouts are sent ahead to do so, information is collected from all travelers, and word is sent to other groups. The intense interest of pastoralists in vegetation and water conditions was impressed upon the writer in her contacts with Bedouin in Kuwait. After every trip made to some out-lying sector of Kuwait, her informants inquired as to what plants she had seen, how widely and high they grew, if water was standing in pools, if animals were drinking from pools.

The general body of literature on the Arabian pastoralists suggests that, rather than competition leading to conflict, a kind of squatter's rights process takes place: once a good pasture area has been located and settled on by one group, others seek elsewhere, unless the abundance is sufficient for all. But the sectional movement of migration, parallel or serial relative to others, seems to reduce considerably any random searching. Sections *seem* to have customary lines of movement, favorite sites, which however vary over years with the sporadic distribution of rain. Any pasturage seems to be left before it has been eaten out or trampled down completely. Both Müller and V. Dickson suggest explicitly that the camps so move in order to conserve the plants for the future (Müller 1931:97; V. Dickson 1955:116). Dickson also says that pastures left for two weeks or so recover; that is, the annuals especially continue to sprout and develop, if the sequence of rains keeps up through the season. In some areas where reeds grow heavily in the vicinity of brackish swamps, the Bedouin may burn them off in summer to improve the fresh growth for pasturage in the following winter (Musil 1928a:337).

4. *Herd Management and Ownership*

Apart from the section herd, camels are clearly held by individuals. Whether the concept of ownership is as fully developed as that of "private ownership" in our sense may be seriously doubted. I have given in the text the general information I have found which indicates that the "herds" carrying the brand of a large kin group, the clan or section, are or may be regarded as communal property in no small sense. Their defense is certainly a concern of the whole section. Men rally to defend the whole herd. In management, inheritance, and other respects, however, camels are held in herds in the name of the head of a household; a man of an extended family which owns twenty camels speaks of them as "our camels," but in referring to a kin cluster of two brothers and their uncle, he will say each man has his camels. These herds, whether small or large, are kept together when couched at night before the owner's tent, and if the "owner" is wealthy in animals they are under the care of a herdsman who is responsible only for those particular animals. However, the herdsmen appear chiefly to lead their particular animals out to graze and to return them to the family tent cluster; in the grazing range, the animals of several owners move or mix together. The location of pasturage is a whole section concern. I think the problem is not one of apparent conflicting principles which must be solved by deciding that the section herds are either communally or privately owned. Both these relations to camels can operate, and grazing and security conditions, death of a family head, maturing or marriage of a son are among the varying conditions which call for the operation of one or the other relationship to ensure the consistent and continuous management of the animals. A man who is "wealthy in camels" is the trustee of a herd in the interest of those who are attached to him as kinsmen, clients, servants, slaves, and so on. But this is a hypothesis for the substantiation of which much more information is necessary. This is an area of great weakness in our knowledge of Bedouin economy.

BIBLIOGRAPHY

Bacon, E.

1958 *Obok: A Study of Social Structure in Eurasia.* Viking Fund Publication in Anthropology No. 25. New York: Wenner-Gren Foundation.

Buxton, P. A.

1923 *Animal Life in Deserts.* London: Edward Arnold.

Dickson, H. R. P.

1949 *The Arab of the Desert.* London: Allen & Unwin.

Dickson, V.

1955 *The Wildflowers of Kuwait and Bahrein.* London: Allen & Unwin.

Doughty, C. M.

1937 *Travels in Arabia Deserta.* New York: Random House.

Great Britain, Admiralty

1917 *A Handbook of Arabia. I. General.* London: His Majesty's Stationers' Office.

Johnstone, T. M.

1961 "Some Characteristics of the Dosiri Dialect of Arabic as Spoken in Kuwait." *Bulletin of the School of Oriental and African Studies, University of London,* 24: 249–97.

Mikesell, M. K.

1955 "Notes on the Dispersal of the Dromedary." *Southwestern Journal of Anthropology,* 11: 231–45.

Montagne, R.

1932 "Notes sur la vie sociale et politique de l'Arabie du Nord: Les Semmar du Neğd." *Revue études islamiques,* 6: 61–79.

Müller, V.

1931 *En Syrie avec les Bédouins.* Paris: E. Leroux.

Murphy, R. F., and L. Kasdan

1959 "The Structure of Parallel Cousin Marriage." *American Anthropologist,* 61: 17–29.

Musil, A.
   1928a *Arabia Deserta*. New York: American Geographical Society.
   1928b *Manners and Customs of the Rwala Bedouins*. New York:
   American Geographical Society.
   1928c *Northern Neğd; A Topographical Itinerary*. New York: American
   Geographical Society.

Peters, E.
   1960 "The Proliferation of Segments in the Lineage of the Bedouin
   of Cyrenaica." *Journal of the Royal Anthropological Institute,* 90:
   29–53.

Philby, H St. J. B.
   1933 *The Empty Quarter*. New York: Holt.

Raswan, C.
   1947 *Black Tents of Arabia*. New York: Creative Age.

Sahlins, M. D.
   1961 "The Segmentary Lineage: An Organization of Predatory Expansion." *American Anthropologist,* 63: 322–45.

Smith, W. R.
   1885 *Kinship and Marriage in Early Arabia*. Cambridge, England:
   University Press.

Sweet, L. E.
   1965 "Camel Raiding of North Arabian Bedouin: A Mechanism of Ecological Adaptation." *American Anthropologist,* 67: 1132–50.

9 RITUAL REGULATION OF ENVIRONMENTAL RELATIONS AMONG A NEW GUINEA PEOPLE[1]

Roy A. Rappaport

MOST FUNCTIONAL studies of religious behavior in anthropology have as an analytic goal the elucidation of events, processes, or relationships occurring within a social unit of some sort. The social unit is not always well defined, but in some cases it appears to be a church, that is, a group of people who entertain similar beliefs about the universe, or a congregation, a group of people who participate together in the performance of religious rituals. There have been exceptions. Thus Vayda, Leeds, and Smith (1961) and O. K. Moore (1957) have clearly perceived that the functions of religious ritual are not necessarily confined within the boundaries of a congregation or even a church. By and large, however, I believe that the following statement by Homans (1941:172) represents fairly the dominant line

Reprinted from *Ethnology,* Vol. 6 (1967), pp. 17–30, by permission of the author and publisher. The last two footnotes were prepared by the author after publication of the original article and are being published for the first time here.

[1] The field work upon which this paper is based was supported by a grant from the National Science Foundation, under which Professor A. P. Vayda was principal investigator. Personal support was received by the author from the National Institutes of Health. Earlier versions of this paper were presented at the 1964 annual meeting of the American Anthropological Association in Detroit, and before a Columbia University seminar on Ecological Systems and Cultural Evolution. I have received valuable suggestions from Alexander Alland, Jacques Barrau, William Clarke, Paul Collins, C. Glen King, Marvin Harris, Margaret Mead, M. J. Meggitt, Ann Rappaport, John Street, Marjorie Whiting, Cherry Vayda, A. P. Vayda and many others, but I take full responsibility for the analysis presented herewith.

of anthropological thought concerning the functions of religious ritual:

> Ritual actions do not produce a practical result on the external world—that is one of the reasons why we call them ritual. But to make this statement is not to say that ritual has no function. Its function is not related to the world external to the society but to the internal constitution of the society. It gives the members of the society confidence, it dispels their anxieties, it disciplines their social organization.

No argument will be raised here against the sociological and psychological functions imputed by Homans, and many others before him, to ritual. They seem to me to be plausible. Nevertheless, in some cases at least, ritual does produce, in Homans' terms, "a practical result on the world" external not only to the social unit composed of those who participate together in ritual performances but also to the larger unit composed of those who entertain similar beliefs concerning the universe. The material presented here will show that the ritual cycles of the Tsembaga, and of other local territorial groups of Maring speakers living in the New Guinea interior, play an important part in regulating the relationships of these groups with both the non-human components of their immediate environments and the human components of their less immediate environments, that is, with other similar territorial groups. To be more specific, this regulation helps to maintain the biotic communities existing within their territories, redistributes land among people and people over land, and limits the frequency of fighting. In the absence of authoritative political statuses or offices, the ritual cycle likewise provides a means for mobilizing allies when warfare may be undertaken. It also provides a mechanism for redistributing local pig surpluses in the form of pork throughout a large regional population while helping to assure the local population of a supply of pork when its members are most in need of high quality protein.

Religious ritual may be defined, for the purposes of this paper, as the prescribed performance of conventionalized acts manifestly directed toward the involvement of nonempirical or supernatural agencies in the affairs of the actors. While this definition relies upon the formal characteristics of the performances and upon the motives for undertaking them, attention will be focused upon the empirical effects of ritual performances and sequences of ritual performances. The religious rituals to be discussed are regarded as neither more nor less than part of the behavioral repertoire employed by an aggregate of organisms in adjusting to its environment.

The data upon which this paper is based were collected during fourteen months of field work among the Tsembaga, one of about twenty local groups of Maring speakers living in the Simbai and Jimi Valleys of the Bismarck Range in the Territory of New Guinea. The size of Maring local groups varies from a little over 100 to 900. The Tsembaga, who in 1963 numbered 204 persons, are located on the south wall of the Simbai Valley. The country in which they live differs from the true highlands in being lower, generally more rugged, and more heavily forested. Tsembaga territory rises, within a total surface area of 3.2 square miles, from an elevation of 2,200 feet at the Simbai river to 7,200 feet at the ridge crest. Gardens are cut in the secondary forests up to between 5,000 and 5,400 feet, above which the area remains in primary forest. Rainfall reaches 150 inches per year.

The Tsembaga have come into contact with the outside world only recently; the first government patrol to penetrate their territory arrived in 1954. They were considered uncontrolled by the Australian government until 1962, and they remain unmissionized to this day.

The 204 Tsembaga are distributed among five putatively patrilineal clans, which are, in turn, organized into more inclusive groupings on two hierarchical levels below that of the total local group.[2] Internal political structure is highly egalitarian. There are no hereditary or elected chiefs, nor are there even "big men" who can regularly coerce or command the support of their clansmen or co-residents in economic or forceful enterprises.

It is convenient to regard the Tsembaga as a population in the ecological sense, that is, as one of the components of a system of trophic exchanges taking place within a bounded area. Tsembaga territory and the biotic community existing upon it

---

[2] The social organization of the Tsembaga will be described in detail elsewhere.

may be conveniently viewed as an ecosystem. While it would be permissible arbitrarily to designate the Tsembaga as a population and their territory with its biota as an ecosystem, there are also nonarbitrary reasons for doing so. An ecosystem is a system of material exchanges, and the Tsembaga maintain against other human groups exclusive access to the resources within their territorial borders. Conversely, it is from this territory alone that the Tsembaga ordinarily derive all of their foodstuffs and most of the other materials they require for survival. Less anthropocentrically, it may be justified to regard Tsembaga territory with its biota as an ecosystem in view of the rather localized nature of cyclical material exchanges in tropical rainforests.

As they are involved with the nonhuman biotic community within their territory in a set of trophic exchanges, so do they participate in other material relationships with other human groups external to their territory. Genetic materials are exchanged with other groups, and certain crucial items, such as stone axes, were in past obtained from the outside. Furthermore, in the area occupied by the Maring speakers, more than one local group is usually involved in any process, either peaceful or warlike, through which people are redistributed over land and land redistributed among people.

The concept of the ecosystem, though it provides a convenient frame for the analysis of interspecific trophic exchanges taking place within limited geographical areas, does not comfortably accommodate intraspecific exchanges taking place over wider geographic areas. Some sort of geographic population model would be more useful for the analysis of the relationship of the local ecological population to the larger regional population of which it is a part, but we lack even a set of appropriate terms for such a model. Suffice it here to note that the relations of the Tsembaga to the total of other local human populations in their vicinity are similar to the relations of local aggregates of other animals to the totality of their species occupying broader and more or less continuous regions. This larger, more inclusive aggregate may resemble what geneticists mean by the term population, that is, an aggregate of interbreeding organisms persisting through an indefinite number of generations and either living or capable of living in isolation from similar aggregates of the same species. This is the unit which survives through long periods of time while its local ecological (*sensu stricto*) sub-units, the units more or less independently involved in interspecific trophic exchanges such as the Tsembaga, are ephemeral.

Since it has been asserted that the ritual cycles of the Tsembaga regulate relationships within what may be regarded as a complex system, it is necessary, before proceeding to the ritual cycle itself, to describe briefly, and where possible in quantitative terms, some aspects of the place of the Tsembaga in this system.

The Tsembaga are bush-fallowing horticulturalists. Staples include a range of root crops, taro (*Colocasia*) and sweet potatoes being most important, yams and manioc less so. In addition, a great variety of greens are raised, some of which are rich in protein. Sugar cane and some tree crops, particularly *Pandanus conoideus,* are also important.

All gardens are mixed, many of them containing all of the major root crops and many greens. Two named garden types are, however, distinguished by the crops which predominate in them. "Taro-yam gardens" were found to produce, on the basis of daily harvest records kept on entire gardens for close to one year, about 5,300,000 calories[3] per acre during their harvesting lives of 18 to 24 months; 85 per cent of their yield is harvested between 24 and 76 weeks after planting. "Sugar-sweet potato gardens" produce about 4,600,000 calories per acre during their harvesting lives, 91 per cent being taken between 24 and 76 weeks after planting. I estimated that approximately 310,000 calories per acre is expended on cutting, fencing, planting, maintaining, harvesting, and walking to and from taro-yam gardens. Sugar-sweet potato gardens required an expenditure of approximately 290,000 calories per acre.[4] These energy ratios, ap-

---

[3] Because the length of time in the field precluded the possibility of maintaining harvest records on single gardens from planting through abandonment, figures were based, in the case of both "taro-yam" and "sugar-sweet potato" gardens, on three separate gardens planted in successive years. Conversions from the gross weight to the caloric value of yields were made by reference to the literature. The sources used are listed in Rappaport (1966: Appendix VIII).

[4] Rough time and motion studies of each of the tasks involved in making, maintaining, harvesting, and walking to and from gardens were undertaken. Conversion to energy expenditure values was accomplished by

proximately 17:1 on taro-yam gardens and 16:1 on sugar-sweet potato gardens, compare favorably with figures reported for swidden cultivation in other regions.[5]

Intake is high in comparison with the reported dietaries of other New Guinea populations. On the basis of daily consumption records kept for ten months on four households numbering in total sixteen persons, I estimated the average daily intake of adult males to be approximately 2,600 calories, and that of adult females to be around 2,200 calories. It may be mentioned here that the Tsembaga are small and short statured. Adult males average 101 pounds in weight and approximately 58.5 inches in height; the corresponding averages for adult females are 85 pounds and 54.5 inches.[6]

Although 99 per cent by weight of the food consumed is vegetable, the protein intake is high by New Guinea standards. The daily protein consumption of adult males from vegetable sources was estimated to be between 43 and 55 grams, of adult females 36 to 48 grams. Even with an adjustment for vegetable sources, these values are slightly in excess of the recently published WHO/FAO daily requirements (Food and Agriculture Organization of the United Nations 1964). The same is true of the younger age categories, although soft and discolored hair, a symptom of protein deficiency, was noted in a few children. The WHO/FAO protein requirements do not include a large "margin for safety" or allowance for stress; and, although no clinical assessments were undertaken, it may be suggested that the Tsembaga achieve nitrogen balance at a low level. In other words, their protein intake is probably marginal.

Measurements of all gardens made during 1962 and of some

---

reference to energy expenditure tables prepared by Hipsley and Kirk (1965:43) on the basis of gas exchange measurements made during the performance of garden tasks by the Chimbu people of the New Guinea highlands.

[5] Marvin Harris, in an unpublished paper, estimates the ratio of energy return to energy input on Dyak (Borneo) rice swiddens at 10:1. His estimates of energy ratios on Tepotzlan (Mesi-America) swiddens range from 13:1 on poor land to 29:1 on the best land.

[6] Heights may be inaccurate. Many men wear their hair in large coiffures hardened with pandanus grease, and it was necessary in some instances to estimate the location of the top of the skull.

gardens made during 1963 indicate that, to support the human population, between .15 and .19 acres are put into cultivation per capita per year. Fallows range from 8 to 45 years. The area in secondary forest comprises approximately 1,000 acres, only 30 to 50 of which are in cultivation at any time. Assuming calories to be the limiting factor, and assuming an unchanging population structure, the territory could support—with no reduction in lengths of fallow and without cutting into the virgin forest from which the Tsembaga extract many important items—between 290 and 397 people if the pig poulation remained minimal. The size of the pig herd, however, fluctuates widely. Taking Maring pig husbandry procedures into consideration, I have estimated the human carrying capacity of the Tsembaga territory at between 270 and 320 people.

Because the timing of the ritual cycle is bound up with the demography of the pig herd, the place of the pig in Tsembaga adaptation must be examined.

First, being omnivorous, pigs keep residential areas free of garbage and human feces. Second, limited numbers of pigs rooting in secondary growth may help to hasten the development of that growth. The Tsembaga usually permit pigs to enter their gardens one and a half to two years after planting, by which time second-growth trees are well established there. The Tsembaga practice selective weeding; from the time the garden is planted, herbaceous species are removed, but tree species are allowed to remain. By the time cropping is discontinued and the pigs are let in, some of the trees in the garden are already ten to fifteen feet tall. These well-established trees are relatively impervious to damage by the pigs, which, in rooting for seeds and remaining tubers, eliminate many seeds and seedlings that, if allowed to develop, would provide some competition for the established trees. Moreover, in some Maring-speaking areas swiddens are planted twice, although this is not the case with the Tsembaga. After the first crop is almost exhausted, pigs are penned in the garden, where their rooting eliminates weeds and softens the ground, making the task of planting for a second time easier. The pigs, in other words, are used as cultivating machines.

Small numbers of pigs are easy to keep. They run free during the day and return home at night to receive their ration of garbage and substandard tubers, particularly sweet potatoes. Supplying the latter requires little extra work, for the substandard tubers are taken from the ground in the course of harvesting the daily ration for humans. Daily consumption records kept over a period of some months show that the ration of tubers received by the pigs approximates in weight that consumed by adult humans, i.e., a little less than three pounds per day per pig.

If the pig herd grows large, however, the substandard tubers incidentally obtained in the course of harvesting for human needs become insufficient, and it becomes necessary to harvest especially for pigs. In other words, people must work for the pigs and perhaps even supply them with food fit for human consumption. Thus, as Vayda, Leeds, and Smith (1961:71) have pointed out, there can be too many pigs for a given community.

This also holds true of the sanitary and cultivating services rendered by pigs. A small number of pigs is sufficient to keep residential areas clean, to suppress superfluous seedlings in abandoned gardens, and to soften the soil in gardens scheduled for second plantings. A larger herd, on the other hand, may be troublesome; the larger the number of pigs, the greater the possibility of their invasion of producing gardens, with concomitant damage not only to crops and young secondary growth but also to the relations between the pig owners and garden owners.

All male pigs are castrated at approximately three months of age, for boars, people say, are dangerous and do not grow as large as barrows. Pregnancies, therefore, are always the result of unions of domestic sows with feral males. Fecundity is thus only a fraction of its potential. During one twelve-month period only fourteen litters resulted out of a potential 99 or more pregnancies. Farrowing generally takes place in the forest, and mortality of the young is high. Only 32 of the offspring of the abovementioned fourteen pregnancies were alive six months after birth. This number is barely sufficient to replace the number of adult animals which would have died or been killed during most years without pig festivals.

The Tsembaga almost never kill domestic pigs outside of ritual contexts. In ordinary times, when there is no pig festival in progress, these rituals are almost always associated with misfortunes or emergencies, notably warfare, illness, injury, or death. Rules state not only the contexts in which pigs are to be ritually slaughtered, but also who may partake of the flesh of the sacrificial animals. During warfare it is only the men participating in the fighting who eat the pork. In cases of illness or injury, it is only the victim and certain near relatives, particularly his co-resident agnates and spouses, who do so.

It is reasonable to assume that misfortune and emergency are likely to induce in the organisms experiencing them a complex of physiological changes known collectively as "stress." Physiological stress reactions occur not only in organisms which are infected with disease or traumatized, but also in those experiencing rage or fear (Houssay et al. 1955:1096), or even prolonged anxiety (National Research Council 1963:53). One important aspect of stress is the increased catabolization of protein (Houssay et al. 1955:451; National Research Council 1963:49), with a net loss of nitrogen from the tissues (Houssay et al. 1955:450). This is a serious matter for organisms with a marginal protein intake. Antibody production is low (Berg 1948:311), healing is slow (Large and Johnson 1948:352), and a variety of symptoms of a serious nature are likely to develop (Lund and Levenson 1948:349; Zintel 1964:1043). The status of a protein-depleted animal, however, may be significantly improved in a relatively short period of time by the intake of high quality protein, and high protein diets are therefore routinely prescribed for surgical patients and those suffering from infectious diseases (Burton 1959:231; Lund and Levenson 1948:350; Elman 1951:85ff.; Zintel 1964:1043ff.).

It is precisely when they are undergoing physiological stress that the Tsembaga kill and consume their pigs, and it should be noted that they limit the consumption to those likely to be experiencing stress most profoundly.[7] The Tsembaga, of course, know nothing of physiological stress. Native theories of the etiology and treatment of disease and injury implicate various categories of spirits to whom sacrifices must be made. Nevertheless, the behavior which is appropriate in terms of native understandings is also appropriate to the actual situation confronting the actors.

We may now outline in the barest of terms the Tsembaga

---

[7] The possible significance of pork consumption by protein-short people during periods of physiological stress was unknown to me while I was in the field. I did not, therefore, investigate this matter in full detail. Georgeda Bick and Cherry Vayda, who visited the Maring area in 1966, have investigated the circumstances surrounding pork consumption further, and will publish their more detailed materials elsewhere.

ritual cycle. Space does not permit a description of its ideological correlates. It must suffice to note that Tsembaga do not necessarily perceive all of the empirical effects which the anthropologist sees to flow from their ritual behavior. Such empirical consequences as they may perceive, moreover, are not central to their rationalizations of the performances. The Tsembaga say that they perform the rituals in order to rearrange their relationships with the supernatural world. We may only reiterate here that behavior undertaken in reference to their "cognized environment"—an environment which includes as very important elements the spirits of ancestors—seems appropriate in their "operational environment," the material environment specified by the anthropologist through operations of observation, including measurement.

Since the rituals are arranged in a cycle, description may commence at any point. The operation of the cycle becomes clearest if we begin with the rituals performed during warfare. Opponents in all cases occupy adjacent territories, in almost all cases on the same valley wall. After hostilities have broken out, each side performs certain rituals which place the opposing side in the formal category of "enemy." A number of taboos prevail while hostilities continue. These include prohibitions on sexual intercourse and on the ingestion of certain things—food prepared by women, food grown on the lower portion of the territory, marsupials, eels, and, while actually on the fighting ground, any liquid whatsoever.

One ritual practice associated with fighting which may have some physiological consequences deserves mention. Immediately before proceeding to the fighting ground, the warriors eat heavily salted pig fat. The ingestion of salt, coupled with the taboo on drinking, has the effect of shortening the fighting day, particularly since the Maring prefer to fight only on bright sunny days. When everyone gets unbearably thirsty, according to informants, fighting is broken off.

There may formerly have been other effects if the native salt contained sodium (the production of salt was discontinued some years previous to the field work, and no samples were obtained). The Maring diet seems to be deficient in sodium. The ingestion of large amounts of sodium just prior to fighting would have permitted the warriors to sweat normally without a lowering of blood volume and consequent weakness during the course of the fighting. The pork belly ingested with the salt would have provided them with a new burst of energy two hours or so after the commencement of the engagement. After fighting was finished for the day, lean pork was consumed, offsetting, at least to some extent, the nitrogen loss associated with the stressful fighting (personal communications from F. Dunn, W. Macfarlane, and J. Sabine, 1965).

Fighting could continue sporadically for weeks. Occasionally it terminated in the rout of one of the antagonistic groups, whose survivors would take refuge with kinsmen elsewhere. In such instances, the victors would lay waste their opponents' groves and gardens, slaughter their pigs, and burn their houses. They would not, however, immediately annex the territory of the vanquished. The Maring say that they never take over the territory of an enemy for, even if it has been abandoned, the spirits of their ancestors remain to guard it against interlopers. Most fights, however, terminated in truces between the antagonists.

With the termination of hostilities a group which has not been driven off its territory performs a ritual called "planting the *rumbim.*" Every man puts his hand on the ritual plant, *rumbim* (*Cordyline fruticosa* (L.), A. Chev; *C. terminalis*, Kunth), as it is planted in the ground. The ancestors are addressed, in effect, as follows:

> We thank you for helping us in the fight and permitting us to remain on our territory. We place our souls in this *rumbim* as we plant it on our ground. We ask you to care for this *rumbim*. We will kill pigs for you now, but they are few. In the future, when we have many pigs, we shall again give you pork and uproot the *rumbim* and stage a *kaiko* (pig festival). But until there are sufficent pigs to repay you the *rumbim* will remain in the ground.

This ritual is accompanied by the wholesale slaughter of pigs. Only juveniles remain alive. All adult and adolescent animals are killed, cooked, and dedicated to the ancestors. Some are consumed by the local group, but most are distributed to allies who assisted in the fight.

Some of the taboos which the group suffered during the time of fighting are abrogated by this ritual. Sexual intercourse is now permitted, liquids may be taken at any time, and food from any part of the territory may be eaten. But the group is still in debt to its allies and ancestors. People say it is still the time of the *bamp ku,* or "fighting stones," which are actual objects used in the rituals associated with warfare. Although the fighting ceases when *rumbim* is planted, the concomitant obligations, debts to allies and ancestors, remain outstanding; and the fighting stones may not be put away until these obligations are fulfilled. The time of the fighting stones is a time of debt and danger which lasts until the *rumbim* is uprooted and a pig festival (*kaiko*) is staged.

Certain taboos persist during the time of the fighting stones. Marsupials, regarded as the pigs of the ancestors of the high ground, may not be trapped until the debt to their masters has been repaid. Eels, the "pigs of the ancestors of the low ground," may neither be caught nor consumed. Prohibitions on all intercourse with the enemy come into force. One may not touch, talk to, or even look at a member of the enemy group, nor set foot on enemy ground. Even more important, a group may not attack another group while its ritual plant remains in the ground, for it has not yet fully rewarded its ancestors and allies for their assistance in the last fight. Until the debts to them have been paid, further assistance from them will not be forthcoming. A kind of "truce of god" thus prevails until the *rumbim* is uprooted and a *kaiko* completed.

To uproot the *rumbim* requires sufficient pigs. How many pigs are sufficient, and how long does it take to acquire them? The Tsembaga say that, if a place is "good," this can take as little as five years; but if a place is "bad," it may require ten years or longer. A bad place is one in which misfortunes are frequent and where, therefore, ritual demands for the killing of pigs arise frequently. A good place is one where such demands are infrequent. In a good place, the increase of the pig herd exceeds the ongoing ritual demands, and the herd grows rapidly. Sooner or later the substandard tubers incidentally obtained while harvesting become insufficient to feed the herd, and additional acreage must be put into production specifically for the pigs.

The work involved in caring for a large pig herd can be extremely burdensome. The Tsembaga herd just prior to the pig festival of 1962–63, when it numbered 169 animals, was receiving 54 per cent of all of the sweet potatoes and 82 per cent of all of the manioc harvested. These comprised 35.9 per cent by weight of all root crops harvested. This figure is consistent with the difference between the amount of land under cultivation just previous to the pig festival, when the herd was at maximum size, and that immediately afterwards, when the pig herd was at minimum size. The former was 36.1 per cent in excess of the latter.

I have estimated, on the basis of acreage yield and energy expenditure figures, that about 45,000 calories per year are expended in caring for one pig 120–150 pounds in size. It is upon women that most of the burden of pig keeping falls. If, from a woman's daily intake of about 2,200 calories, 950 calories are allowed for basal metabolism, a woman has only 1,250 calories a day available for all her activities, which include gardening for her family, child care, and cooking, as well as tending pigs. It is clear that no woman can feed many pigs; only a few had as many as four in their care at the commencement of the festival; and it is not surprising that agitation to uproot the *rumbim* and stage the *kaiko* starts with the wives of the owners of large numbers of pigs.

A large herd is not only burdensome as far as energy expenditure is concerned; it becomes increasingly a nuisance as it expands. The more numerous pigs become, the more frequently are gardens invaded by them. Such events result in serious disturbances of local tranquillity. The garden owner often shoots, or attempts to shoot, the offending pig; and the pig owner commonly retorts by shooting, or attempting to shoot, either the garden owner, his wife, or one of his pigs. As more and more such events occur, the settlement, nucleated when the herd was small, disperses as people try to put as much distance as possible between their pigs and other people's gardens and between their gardens and other people's pigs. Occasionally this reaches its logical conclusion, and people begin to leave the territory, taking up residence with kinsmen in other local populations.

The number of pigs sufficient to become intolerable to the Tsembaga was below the capacity of the territory to carry pigs. I have estimated that, if the size and structure of the human population remained constant at the 1962–1963 level, a pig population of 140 to 240 animals averaging 100 to 150 pounds in size could be maintained perpetually by the Tsembaga without necessarily inducing environmental degradation. Since the size of the herd fluctuates, even higher cyclical maxima could be achieved. The level of toleration, however, is likely always to be below the carrying capacity, since the destructive capacity of the pigs is dependent upon the population density of both people and pigs, rather than upon population size. The denser the human population, the fewer pigs will be required to disrupt social life. If the carrying capacity is exceeded, it is likely to be exceeded by people and not by pigs.

The *kaiko* or pig festival, which commences with the planting of stakes at the boundary and the uprooting of the *rumbim,* is thus triggered by either the additional work attendant upon feeding pigs or the destructive capacity of the pigs themselves. It may be said, then, that there are sufficient pigs to stage the *kaiko* when the relationship of pigs to people changes from one of mutualism to one of parasitism or competition.

A short time prior to the uprooting of the *rumbim,* stakes are planted at the boundary. If the enemy has continued to occupy its territory, the stakes are planted at the boundary which existed before the fight. If, on the other hand, the enemy has abandoned its territory, the victors may plant their stakes at a new boundary which encompasses areas previously occupied by the enemy. The Maring say, to be sure, that they never take land belonging to an enemy, but this land is regarded as vacant, since no *rumbim* was planted on it after the last fight. We may state here a rule of land redistribution in terms of the ritual cycle: *If one of a pair of antagonistic groups is able to uproot its rumbim before its opponents can plant their rumbim, it may occupy the latter's territory.*

Not only have the vanquished abandoned their territory; it is assumed that it has also been abandoned by their ancestors as well. The surviving members of the erstwhile enemy group have by this time resided with other groups for a number of years, and most if not all of them have already had occasion to sacrifice pigs to their ancestors at their new residences. In so doing they have invited these spirits to settle at the new locations of the living, where they will in the future receive sacrifices. Ancestors of vanquished groups thus relinquish their guardianship over the territory, making it available to victorious groups. Meanwhile, the *de facto* membership of the living in the groups with which they have taken refuge is converted eventually into *de jure* membership. Sooner or later the groups with which they have taken up residence will have occasion to plant *rumbim,* and the refugees, as co-residents, will participate, thus ritually validating their connection to the new territory and the new group. A rule of population redistribution may thus be stated in terms of ritual cycles: *A man becomes a member of a territorial group by participating with it in the planting of rumbim.*

The uprooting of the *rumbim* follows shortly after the planting of stakes at the boundary. On this particular occasion the Tsembaga killed 32 pigs out of their herd of 169. Much of the pork was distributed to allies and affines outside of the local group.

The taboo on trapping marsupials was also terminated at this time. Information is lacking concerning the population dynamics of the local marsupials, but it may well be that the taboo which had prevailed since the last fight—that against taking them in traps—had conserved a fauna which might otherwise have become extinct.

The *kaiko* continues for about a year, during which period friendly groups are entertained from time to time. The guests receive presents of vegetable foods, and the hosts and male guests dance together throughout the night.

These events may be regarded as analogous to aspects of the social behavior of many nonhuman animals. First of all, they include massed epigamic, or courtship, displays (Wynne-Edwards 1962:17). Young women are presented with samples of the eligible males of local groups with which they may not otherwise have had the opportunity to become familiar. The context, moreover, permits the young women to discriminate amongst this sample in terms of both endurance (signaled by how vigorously and how long a man dances) and wealth (signaled by the richness of a man's shell and feather finery).

More importantly, the massed dancing at these events may be regarded as epideictic display, communicating to the participants information concerning the size or density of the group (Wynne-Edwards 1962:16). In many species such displays take place as a prelude to actions which adjust group size or density, and such is the case among the Maring. The massed dancing of the visitors at a *kaiko* entertainment communicates to the hosts, while the *rumbim* truce is still in force, information concerning the amount of support they may expect from the visitors in the bellicose enterprises that they are likely to embark upon soon after the termination of the pig festival.

Among the Maring there are no chiefs or other political authorities capable of commanding the support of a body of followers, and the decision to assist another group in warfare rests with each individual male. Allies are not recruited by appealing for help to other local groups as such. Rather, each member of the groups primarily involved in the hostilities appeals to his cognatic and affinal kinsmen in other local groups. These men, in turn, urge other of their co-residents and kinsmen to "help them fight." The channels through which invitations to dance are extended are precisely those through which appeals for military support are issued. The invitations go not from group to group, but from kinsman to kinsman, the recipients of invitations urging their co-residents to "help them dance."

Invitations to dance do more than exercise the channels through which allies are recruited; they provide a means for judging their effectiveness. Dancing and fighting are regarded as in some sense equivalent. This equivalence is expressed in the similarity of some pre-fight or pre-dance rituals, and the Maring say that those who come to dance come to fight. The size of a visiting dancing contingent is consequently taken as a measure of the size of the contingent of warriors whose assistance may be expected in the next round of warfare.

In the morning the dancing ground turns into a trading ground. The items most frequently exchanged include axes, bird plumes, shell ornaments, an occasional baby pig, and, in former times, native salt. The *kaiko* thus facilitates trade by providing a market-like setting in which large numbers of traders can assemble. It likewise facilitates the movement of two critical items, salt and axes, by creating a demand for the bird plumes which may be exchanged for them.

The *kaiko* concludes with major pig sacrifices. On this particular occasion the Tsembaga butchered 105 adult and adolescent pigs, leaving only 60 juveniles and neonates alive. The survival of an additional fifteen adolescents and adults was only temporary, for they were scheduled as imminent victims. The pork yielded by the Tsembaga slaughter was estimated to weigh between 7,000 and 8,500 pounds, of which between 4,500 and 6,000 pounds were distributed to members of other local groups in 163 separate presentations. An estimated 2,000 to 3,000 people in seventeen local groups were the beneficiaries of the redistribution. The presentations, it should be mentioned, were not confined to pork. Sixteen Tsembaga men presented bridewealth or childwealth, consisting largely of axes and shells, to their affines at this time.

The *kaiko* terminates on the day of the pig slaughter with the public presentation of salted pig belly to allies of the last fight. Presentations are made through the window in a high ceremonial fence built specially for the occasion at one end of the dance ground. The name of each honored man is announced to the assembled multitude as he charges to the window to receive his hero's portion. The fence is then ritually torn down, and the fighting stones are put away. The pig festival and the ritual cycle have been completed, demonstrating, it may be suggested, the ecological and economic competence of the local population. The local population would now be free, if it were not for the presence of the government, to attack its enemy again, secure in the knowledge that the assistance of allies and ancestors would be forthcoming because they have received pork and the obligations to them have been fulfilled.

Usually fighting did break out again very soon after the completion of the ritual cycle. If peace still prevailed when the ceremonial fence had rotted completely—a process said to take about three years, a little longer than the length of time required to raise a pig to maximum size—*rumbim* was planted as if there had been a fight, and all adult and adolescent pigs were killed. When the pig herd was large enough so that the *rumbim* could be uprooted, peace could be made with former enemies if they were also able to dig out their *rumbim*. To put this in formal terms: *If a pair of antagonistic groups proceeds through two ritual cycles without resumption of hostilities their enmity may be terminated.*[8]

---

[8] After this article had gone to press in *Ethnology*, where it was originally published, I learned from A. P. Vayda, who spent the summer of 1966 in the Maring area, that he received somewhat different accounts of peace-making mechanisms, both from informants in other Maring local groups and from the Tsembaga man who had supplied me with the only full account which I was able to obtain (details of his account were, however, corroborated by information obtained from other Tsembaga

The relations of the Tsembaga with their environment have been analyzed as a complex composed of two subsystems. What may be called the "local subsystem" has been derived from the relations of the Tsembaga with the nonhuman components of their immediate or territorial environment. It corresponds to the ecosystem in which the Tsembaga participate. A second subsystem, one which corresponds to the larger regional population of which the Tsembaga are one of the constituent units and which may be designated as the "regional subsystem," has been derived from the relations of the Tsembaga with neighboring local populations similar to themselves.

It has been argued that rituals, arranged in repetitive sequences, regulate relations both within each of the subsystems and within the larger complex system as a whole. The timing of the ritual cycle is largely dependent upon changes in the states of the components of the local subsystem. But the *kaiko,* which is the culmination of the ritual cycle, does more than reverse changes which have taken place within the local subsystem. Its occurrence also affects relations among the components of the regional subsystem. During its performance, obligations to other local popula-

---

men). According to Vayda's account, when the ceremonial fence had rotted away completely, some, but not all, adult and adolescent pigs were slain and offered to certain ancestral spirits to insure the health and fecundity of the remaining pigs, and no *rumbim* was planted. When the herds of the erstwhile antagonists again reached maximum size peace could be made.

It is important to note here that the other rituals treated in this paper were either observed by me or described by a number of informants who had participated in them, but none of either Vayda's informants or mine had ever participated in peace-making procedures, for none had taken place during the adult life of any of them. They were only reporting what they remembered from their childhood or what they had heard from their fathers or grandfathers. It is likely, therefore, that none of the informants are particularly well-versed in the details of the procedure. However, it is also important to note that all of the informants are in basic agreement upon what is in the present context the most important aspect of peace-making: that the rituals were not performed until pig herds of the erstwhile antagonists had reached maximum size. The rule which I have proposed would seem to stand if it is understood that the second ritual cycle of the sequence may differ from the first in that *rumbim* might not be planted, and if it is understood that the truce may not be sanctified during the second cycle of the sequence.

tions are fulfilled, support for future military enterprises is rallied, and land from which enemies have earlier been driven is occupied. Its completion, furthermore, permits the local population to initiate warfare again. Conversely, warfare is terminated by rituals which preclude the reinitiation of warfare until the state of the local subsystem is again such that a *kaiko* may be staged and completed. Ritual among the Tsembaga and other Maring, in short, operates as both transducer, "translating" changes in the state of one subsystem into information which can effect changes in a second subsystem, and homeostat, maintaining a number of variables which in sum comprise the total system within ranges of viability. To repeat an earlier assertion, the operation of ritual among the Tsembaga and other Maring helps to maintain an undegraded environment, limits fighting to frequencies which do not endanger the existence of the regional population, adjusts man-land ratios, facilitates trade, distributes local surpluses of pig throughout the regional population in the form of pork, and assures people of high quality protein when they are most in need of it.

Religious rituals and the supernatural orders toward which they are directed cannot be assumed *a priori* to be mere epiphenomena. Ritual may, and doubtless frequently does, do nothing more than validate and intensify the relationships which integrate the social unit, or symbolize the relationships which bind the social unit to its environment. But the interpretation of such presumably *sapiens*-specific phenomena as religious ritual within a framework which will also accommodate the behavior of other species shows, I think, that religious ritual may do much more than symbolize, validate, and intensify relationships. Indeed, it would not be improper to refer to the Tsembaga and the other entities with which they share their territory as a "ritually regulated ecosystem," and to the Tsembaga and their human neighbors as a "ritually regulated population."

BIBLIOGRAPHY

Berg, C.
  1948 "Protein Deficiency and Its Relation to Nutritional Anemia, Hypoproteinemia, Nutritional Edema, and Resistance to Infection," in M. Sahyun (ed.), *Protein and Amino Acids in Nutrition*. New York: Reinhold.
Burton, B. T. (ed.)
  1959 *The Heinz Handbook of Nutrition*. New York: McGraw-Hill.
Elman, Robert
  1951 *Surgical Care*. New York: Appleton-Century-Crofts.
FAO
  1964 *Protein: At the Heart of the World Food Problem*. World Food Problems No. 5. Rome: Food and Agriculture Organization of the United Nations.
Hipsley, Eben, and Nancy Kirk
  1965 *Studies of the Dietary Intake and the Expenditure of Energy by New Guineans*. South Pacific Commission, Technical Paper No. 147. Noumea.
Homans, G. C.
  1941 "Anxiety and Ritual: The Theories of Malinowski and Radcliffe-Brown." *American Anthropologist*, 43: 164–72.
Houssay, B. A., et al.
  1955 *Human Physiology*, Second Edition. New York: McGraw-Hill.
Large, A., and C. G. Johnson
  1948 "Proteins as Related to Burns," in M. Sahyun (ed.), *Proteins and Amino Acids in Nutrition*. New York: Reinhold.
Lund, C. G., and S. M. Levenson
  1948 "Protein Nutrition in Surgical Patients," in M. Sahyun (ed.), *Proteins and Amino Acids in Nutrition*. New York: Reinhold.
Moore, O. K.
  1957 "Divination—a New Perspective." *American Anthropologist*, 59: 69–74.

National Research Council
    1963 "Evaluation of Protein Quality." National Academy of Sciences
    —National Research Council Publication 1100. Washington.
Rappaport, R. A.
    1966 *Ritual in the Ecology of a New Guinea People.* Unpublished Doc-
    toral Dissertation, Columbia University [published as *Pigs for the An-
    cestors: Ritual in the Ecology of a New Guinea People,* New Haven:
    Yale University Press, 1968].
Vayda, A. P., A. Leeds, and D. B. Smith
    1961 "The Place of Pigs in Melanesian Subsistence," in V. E. Garfield
    (ed.), *Proceedings of the 1961 Annual Spring Meeting of the Ameri-
    can Ethnological Society.* Seattle: University of Washington Press.
Wynne-Edwards, V. C.
    1962 *Animal Dispersion in Relation to Social Behaviour.* Edinburgh
    and London: Oliver and Boyd.
Zintel, H. A.
    1964 "Nutrition in the Care of the Surgical Patient," in M. G. Wohl
    and R. S. Goodhart (eds.), *Modern Nutrition in Health and Disease,*
    Third Edition. Philadelphia: Lee and Febiger.

10 EXPANSION AND WARFARE AMONG SWIDDEN AGRICULTURALISTS[1]

Andrew P. Vayda

I N SPITE OF the growing recognition that "ecological factors always affect cultural patterning and social organization" (Forde 1948:9), these factors have tended to be slighted in investigations of primitive warfare. Even Julian Steward, an anthropologist who has contributed notably to ecological studies, has interpreted what he calls "bloodthirsty primitive patterns of warfare" as being means of release for pent-up aggressions rather than being expressions of competition for resources or being in some other way ecologically determined (Steward 1958:207–8).

While Steward has tried to support his interpretation by reference to the Tupinamba Indians of the tropical forest in Brazil, Murphy (1957) has recently made an analysis along similar lines with special reference to another Brazilian Indian group, the Mundurucú. Murphy has described the warfare of these people as a "safety-valve institution" (p. 1032), has denied that it had

Reprinted from *American Anthropologist*, Vol. 63 (1961), pp. 346–58, by permission of the publisher.

[1] An earlier version of this paper was presented at the Northwest Anthropological Conference at Portland State College in Portland, Oregon, on April 18, 1959. Helpful comments on one or another of my preliminary drafts were received from Paul Bohannan, Robert Carneiro, Harold Conklin, Gertrude Dole, Ronald Dore, Marvin Harris, Edmund Leach, Anthony Leeds, Frederick Lehman, Lorenz Löffler, Robert Murphy, Raoul Naroll, Marshall Sahlins, David Smith, Wayne Suttles, Eric Wolf, and my students in a seminar on warfare at the University of British Columbia. Not all of these persons agree with my interpretations and point of view. To the Social Science Research Council I am indebted for a grant-in-aid that enabled me to do research in England on Borneo warfare.

territorial conquest as a goal (p. 1027), or that it was due in any appreciable degree to the "pressure of external circumstances" (p. 1028), and has concluded that warfare in general is "an especially effective means of promoting social cohesion in that it provides an occasion upon which the members of the society unite and submerge their factional differences in the vigorous pursuit of a common purpose" (p. 1034). Rather similarly, Wedgwood (1930:33) has interpreted Melanesian warfare as serving the "double purpose of enabling people to give expression to anger caused by a disturbance of the internal harmony, and of strengthening or reaffirming the ties which hold them together." While Wedgwood herself has not explicitly denied the operation of ecological factors, Wright (1942:71–73), drawing upon her discussion, has concluded that primitive warfare "functions primarily" to maintain the solidarity of the social group and that many of the Melanesians fought "without economic or political objectives or consequences."

It may of course be argued that a group's survival and prosperity depend *inter alia* upon the group's solidarity (White 1959:103) and therefore anything that maintains or promotes solidarity does indirectly have economic or ecological consequences. However, we know that the solidarity of peoples throughout the world has been achieved by many means other than warfare. It has been achieved through ceremonies, through games—through a very large variety of customs (White 1959: 215). Therefore it seems doubtful that the solidarity of any particular people should be attainable only through warfare, which is a means having such maladaptive or dysfunctional effects as the loss of life, the considerable diversion of time and effort from productive activities, etc. On the assumption that culture tends to be adaptive in the sense of providing people with the means of adjustment to the geographical environment and to the other basic conditions of life (Murdock 1959:131), we should expect warfare to serve people in more ways than merely through providing them with solidarity or cohesion and we should expect, furthermore, that the other functions of warfare will tend to offset the maladaptive consequences of fighting. In other words, we have grounds for expecting the primitive hostilities of the types discussed by Steward, Murphy, Wedgwood, and Wright to have more direct ecological functions or consequences than those deriving from the attainment of social solidarity.[2]

In saying this, I do not mean to say that wherever warfare exists it must be useful. Obviously we must allow for the possibility that a people whose survival and/or increase has been promoted by warfare in the past will go on fighting even if, under changed conditions, warfare no longer functions for them as it had. At the same time we may regard it of some heuristic value to argue that wherever warfare exists it is likely to have been useful or adaptive (in the sense of being more advantageous than disadvantageous) at some time in the course of its development. My interpretations in this paper have been made with this proposition in mind.

The procedure in this paper will be to consider some ecological factors that may affect warfare in social and environmental settings similar to those in which the warfare of the Tupinamba, the Mundurucú, and some of the Melanesians was carried on. Two models of warlike expansion will be presented. This will be done with special reference to the Maoris of New Zealand and the Ibans of Sarawak. It must be emphasized that the models to be presented are models of expansion. For populations that are not expanding, other models would be appropriate and we would have to consider such possible functions of warfare as the adjustment of male-female ratios through the occasional capture of women and children (Oberg 1955:473–74; Zegwaard 1959: 1036), the spacing out of relatively stable populations within finite territories (Suttles 1961), and the prevention of population increase so great as to lead to an over-exploitation and deterioration of resources (Allan 1949:26; Cook 1946).

---

[2] Some brief remarks upon my use of such terms as "consequences," "effects," "results," etc. may be in order here. It should be understood that in using the terms I do not have in mind one-way linear cause-to-effect sequences. I think it is necessary to recognize that there are "feedbacks" from effects to causes, that the adaptiveness of an effect—its contribution to the survival and well-being and perhaps also the increase of people—favors the continuation and spread of the motives and actions leading to the effect. The same ecological phenomena may be both consequences and determinants. With special reference to the study of the "causes" of war, I have discussed more fully in another place (Vayda 1959) the circular relations between effects and causes.

I

Although such warriors of Oceania and the South American tropical forest as have been discussed by Steward and the other authors cited above have gained fame largely for being head-hunters or cannibals or torturers, it is something else about them that seems particularly significant to me. This is the fact that most of them practice slash-and-burn or swidden agriculture, a system of cultivation which may be defined, in Conklin's (1954:133) words, as "always involving the impermanent agricultural use of plots produced by the cutting back and burning off of vegetative cover." In various discussions of Maori warfare (e.g., Vayda 1956; 1960), I have already given some consideration to ways in which the practice of swidden agriculture may influence the practice of war. In some parts of New Zealand, the Maoris were swidden agriculturalists (N. H. Taylor 1958:76; R. Taylor 1870: 494), and, like other primitive swiddeners equipped with only wooden and stone tools (Drucker and Heizer 1960:39–40; Goodenough 1956:174–75), they found it very much harder to clear primary forest (true rain forest in the case of New Zealand) than to clear second growth. In light of this, I have argued that Maori groups needing more land may have preferred getting previously used land from other groups, by force if necessary, rather than expanding into the virgin rain forest. If the time and effort required for clearing virgin land were considerably more than were necessary for the operations of both conquest and the preparation of previously used land for cultivation, it follows that territorial conquests, such as some of those recorded in Maori traditional history, would have added more efficiently to the prosperity of particular groups than would peaceful dispersion.

While this argument, first published in 1956, still seems acceptable to me, it can now be amplified somewhat by considering some features of social organization.

Maori population was organized into nonunilineal nonexogamous descent groups (Davenport 1959; Firth 1957). In late 18th century New Zealand there were 100,000 to 300,000 Maoris distributed among roughly 40 tribes or *iwi,* most of which were subdivided into numerous subtribes or *hapu*. The members of a hapu were consanguineal relatives who could trace their descent from a common ancestor several generations back; the members of each of the related hapu constituting a tribe could trace their descent back to a single ancestor of all the tribesmen. The average Maori village community may be very roughly estimated to have contained a few hundred people. A village community was ordinarily regarded as belonging to a single hapu, and marriages between members of a hapu were frequent and were considered desirable. It was from small beginnings in an early settlement period that the 18th century population of 100,000 to 300,000 Maoris had developed. In the course of population growth, the descent groups, both hapu and iwi, had proliferated.

It must be conceded that the increase in population and in the number of descent groups could have taken place peacefully while tribes or subtribes were able to expand into virgin land adjoining areas already under their exploitation. However, sooner or later there would have been groups whose territory adjoined only the territory of other groups rather than any virgin land suitable for agriculture. If *these* groups were to expand their holdings without abandoning any of their own land and without taking over that of other groups, they would have had to colonize new land separated and possibly quite distant from their existing territory. In such new land, the position of the colonists could be extremely insecure because in Maori society only the closer categories of kinsmen could be relied upon fairly consistently for cooperation in the tasks of subsistence and defense. The colonists would need help for clearing the land, a task characteristically performed among the Maoris by working bees called *ohu,* comprised sometimes of more than forty men (Best 1925:101–2; Buck 1949: 378; Firth 1929:219–20). But at the time when the colonists would most need this help, their close kin might be far away, busy with agricultural labors in the home territory. Neighbors of the colonists would be distant kin or nonkin and not likely to want to give aid. If somehow the colonists would nevertheless manage to perform the clearing operations, they would be making what Goodenough (1956:175) has termed a "significant capital gain," and the cleared land would be an attractive prize for the colonists' nonkin or distant kin neighbors whose own numbers might be increasing. The colonists would lack the manpower and would have no nearby close kin to appeal to for defense of their new territory.

This whole chain of events is hypothetical. Let us consider now another possibility: expansion by means of taking over the territory of other groups. We know that conquests involving displacement of the vanquished foe from their territory did in fact occur in pre-European New Zealand (Vayda 1956), although we do not know exactly how they occurred. The process could have taken place among the kinship-organized, genealogy-conscious Maoris very much as it did among the Tiv of West Africa. The latter people cultivate yams and other crops in savanna country in Northern Nigeria, and their recognized technique for the expansion of land holdings was, as described by Bohannan (1954: 5), a simple one:

> . . . always, when you make new farms, clear land towards that man whose land bounds yours, but who is most distantly related to you. When he objects, you are thus assured of the largest possible supporting group in any litigation, argument, or fight which may develop, since all the people who are more closely related to you than to him will come to your aid instead of his.
>
> Thus, to ensure the support of one's entire minimal segment [corresponding to the Maori hapu], one expands one's holdings against the territory of the companion minimal segment. To ensure the support of both these minimal segments, one expands against the territory of a genealogically more distant lineage.

The expansion of the Tiv in all directions was still going on during Bohannan's term of field work. Unfortunately the student of Maori culture does not have the same opportunities for observing the process of expansion as Bohannan had. Yet there are indications that the process among the Maoris not only could have been but actually *was* similar in some significant respects. The influence of considerations of genealogical proximity in determining to whom aid would be given is shown, for example, in Polack's eye-witness account of fighting between two hapu of the Nga Puhi tribe in 1837. Polack (1838:42) mentions that the Hokianga natives, arriving after the hostilities had begun, were sorely puzzled which of the two parties to join, as they were *equally* related to both of them.[3] Consistent with a Tiv-like process of expansion are the Maori conditions described summarily by Firth (1929:371) as follows:

> The general position seems to have been that the various major *hapu* of the tribe safeguarded their lands very carefully against one another, that trespassers or food poachers were severely punished or even killed, and that warfare, involving considerable loss of life, not infrequently arose among them from disputes about land. At the same time the *hapu* would unite to protect the interests of any one of them against forces from outside the tribe.

A process of territorial expansion with the support of the more closely related people or groups against the less closely related and the unrelated would have obviated the hypothetical problems that have previously been described for Maori colonists in virgin territory. The process must be envisaged as involving something like a chain reaction. The expansion of group A into the contiguous territory of group B might lead group B to expand into the contiguous territory of group C—and so forth until finally there would be a displacement of a group having territory contiguous to virgin land. If members of this last group were to settle in the virgin territory, they might do this without having to give up having neighbors who were close kin, i.e., neighbors who could be called upon for aid in subsistence and defense.

It should not be inferred from this discussion that every permanent enlargement of a particular group's territorial holdings would have led ultimately to an expansion into virgin territory somewhere in New Zealand. The chain reaction in the redistribution of population upon the land might stop short of this if there were heavy loss of life in the hostilities attendant upon attempts at expansion. For example, group A might kill so many members of group B in the process of taking over some of the latter's land that the land remaining to group B could sustain its surviving members and, moreover, group B might be too weak to become

---

[3] L. Bohannan (1958:46) refers to a parallel contretemps among the Tiv: "MbaDigam . . . being equally related to the warring segments MbaGishi and MbaTyende, could come to the help of neither without repudiating its relationship with the other. MbaDigam took the only possible course—peacemaking."

the successful aggressor against some other group. The evidence on battle mortality which I have marshalled elsewhere (Vayda 1960) suggests that something like this did happen sometimes, although at other times the chain reaction ended only with the occupation and exploiting of previously unexploited or underexploited land.

We have here then our first model of warfare among swidden agriculturalists, and it is a model in which warfare has such direct ecological functions or consequences as the expansion of population and an increase in the extent of the environment being exploited.

It is reasonable to ask how closely this model approximates warfare among various other swiddening people. Unfortunately the question is not answerable on the basis of the data that I have found it possible to examine. No doubt there are some groups on whom no more than sparse data are available anywhere and therefore no definite answer about them can ever be given. However, with regard to the Tupinamba referred to by Steward, even the limited facts at my disposal make it seem unwarranted to conclude that the warfare of these Brazilian Indians had no ecological functions or consequences. We know that the population of the Tupinamba was increasing (Fernandes 1952:64), that their various tribes and local communities were often at war with one another (Métraux 1948:119), that their hostilities could lead to displacements of the vanquished from their lands (Fernandes 1952:60–63), and that the Tupinamba seem to have dispersed over a large area from a common center and to have ended their movements only in the second half of the 16th century (Métraux 1948:97). All of these facts are congruent with my first model of warlike expansion and may be congruent also with other models in which warfare has direct ecological functions or consequences.

II

One other model will be described: a model in which there is relative intratribal peace as a contrast to the recurrent intratribal as well as extratribal hostilities that characterize the first model. This second model will be discussed with special reference to the Ibans of Sarawak.

We cannot say that there was no intratribal warfare at all among the Ibans, for there are a few scattered references (e.g., Brooke 1866:I, 145–46) to hostilities between neighboring and closely related Iban villages. It seems to have been more common and more characteristic, however, for members of one Iban tribe to fight either against members of other Iban tribes or against non-Ibans. Freeman (1955a:53) has recently defined what a tribe was among the Ibans:

> The tribe, we may say, is a diffuse territorial grouping dispersed along the banks of a major river and its diverging tributaries. Formerly, it was a grouping whose members did not take one another's heads, but with pacification and the abandonment of head-hunting, tribal boundaries have become blurred. The tribe is still a predominantly endogamous group however, and is intricately reticulated by ties of bilateral kinship. A tribe is perhaps best described then, as an interlocking aggregation of kindreds, and in the widest sense all its members are kith and kin, of common, albeit remote ancestry.

It should be noted that the reasons for the Ibans having little intratribal warfare may have been ecological as well as social. Distances between the village communities of the Ibans may have been shorter than between the village communities of other primitive swiddeners such as the Maoris. Freeman (1955a:27; 1955b:8) says that Iban long-house communities are encountered about once in every two or three miles throughout the Baleh region of Sarawak and that sometimes, although not often, they are found even within hailing distance of one another. My impression, set forth in somewhat more detail elsewhere (Vayda 1960), is that the distances in miles between Maori villages usually were very much greater.

It is necessary to take into account not only the distances in miles but also pheric distances, i.e., distances measured by the time required for covering them (Andrzejewski 1954:191). Freeman (1955b:8) mentions that all Iban communities are situated on the banks of rivers or streams navigable by dugout canoes. The Maoris, on the other hand, lived in a habitat characterized by a rough topography and an often impenetrable rain forest and their canoe traveling was severely limited by difficult portages and turbulent waters. It seems very likely that pheric distances between Iban communities tended to be shorter than between the Maori villages.

In any case, regardless of whether or not it was due at least partly to ecological factors, there seems to have been considerable intervillage mobility among the Ibans. Their communities were, and apparently still are, linked together by what Leach (1948: 92) has called "innumerable ties of affinal kinship at all social levels." Freeman (1958) has described in detail how the small autonomous family groups occupying individual apartments in the Iban long-houses can lose members, female as well as male, both through their marriage into other families and through their departure to set up their own autonomous domestic units. It should be remarked also that the incentives of material profit and social prestige stimulate Iban young men to try to spend at least six months of every year in making journeys, sometimes inland for the collection of gutta-percha and other jungle produce, sometimes seawards, sometimes even to distant parts of the Indies. Going on expeditions, including ones for headhunting in former days, is said to be the greatest and most consuming interest that Iban young men find in life (Freeman 1955b:74–75; cf. Anonymous 1885:114).

Not only individuals but also the family groups themselves, called *bilek* families by Freeman, were mobile. Freeman (1955a: 32) states that a bilek family, as an autonomous unit, might join any of the various long-house communities where kith or kin were already members. He goes on to say:

> . . . *bilek-families* often set off, either singly, or in twos or threes, to attach themselves to some long-house, the situation of which they considered especially advantageous. Provided certain essential ritual formalities had been observed, a *bilek-family* was free to leave one longhouse, and join another, whenever it desired. Such independent movement was frequently resorted to, and when a whole community decided to shift to a new territory, it was seldom, if ever, that all its *bilek-families* remained together. Although the majority usually continued their old association, almost always some would detach themselves, and disperse to separate destinations (Freeman 1955a:32–33).

One further fact that remains to be underscored in this account of the mobility of the Ibans is that not only was there apparently considerable movement between Iban communities but also there were periodical shiftings of the very community sites. Freeman (1955b:32ff.) describes in detail the abandoning of settlements by the Ibans.

The point of this discussion of Iban mobility and of ecological and social factors promoting it is the implication that there were effective nonwarlike ways and means whereby population could be moved about or redistributed within the total territory of each Iban tribe. It seems likely that there need have been no very serious intratribal conflicts over land as long as substantial cultivable land was available somewhere within the tribal area. When population pressure was felt locally, there were other parts to which some Ibans could move.

This, however, suggests that an important condition of peace within the tribe was precisely this availability of cultivable land somewhere within the tribal territory. It follows that if the original tribal territory was relatively small and the population was increasing, then peace within the tribe could require an enlargement of territory, by means of war against other tribes if necessary. We have here then our second model of warfare and expansion among swidden agriculturalists: intratribal peace and mobility plus wars of territorial conquest against other tribes.

Available facts about the Ibans fit this model. That their population was expanding is indicated by Charles Brooke, who wrote as follows in the 1860's:

> To offer one instance of the multiplying process, I will mention the upper Batang Lupar river, which has now a population of eighteen or twenty thousand souls residing on it, and has emitted a supply, about fifty years ago, to a neighbouring stream (a tributary of Rejang), from which a population has now increased to from ten to twelve thousand souls, without the aid of any intermixture from other directions. Many other instances might be adduced of a similar nature, which have come under my immediate observation (Brooke 1866:II, 336).

According to Hose and McDougall (1912:188), Iban settlements before the 19th century were practically confined to the rivers of the southern part of Sarawak. The basin of the great Rejang River was inhabited at this time by the Kayans, Kenyahs, Punans, Ukits, and other non-Iban tribes, and, says Freeman (1955b:11), there were probably no Ibans living north of the southern watershed of the Rejang basin (cf. Richards 1949:79ff.; 1958:126). Today, according to Freeman, there are more than 114,000 Ibans settled in areas north of this line. These people constitute more than one-fifth of the total population of Sarawak and more than three-fifths of the entire Iban population of the country. They had driven the other people away (cf. Freeman 1955b:25–26 note).

Some further comments about mobility in connection with the second model are in order. It has to be noted that for the Ibans there was very considerable mobility outside as well as within the tribal territories. "Before the advancing Iban," says Freeman (1955b:25), "there lay thousands of square miles of deserted, or extremely sparsely populated, rain-forest. On their head-hunting forays Iban bands had penetrated into the remote head-waters of the Rejang, Kayan, Mahakam, and Kapuas rivers, and the vast extent of the territories which extended before their tribe was well enough known." The accessibility of these extra-tribal regions, both because of strictly geographical factors and also because of their not being densely populated, provides a contrast to conditions found in such areas of highland swiddening as Northern Luzon, central New Guinea, and the Naga Hills of Assam. In these latter areas, and to some extent also in such areas as New Zealand (see the discussion in Sharp 1956:130), mountain ridges are barriers to mobility, and, furthermore, as soon as the valleys between the ridges have become thickly settled, there can be demographic barriers to mobility as well. "Mountain province groups in Northern Luzon," writes Conklin (1959), "could not retreat or advance over hundreds of miles in any direction, because in the next valley, on all sides, lived potential or actual enemies." Iban warfare had something of a pioneering character. The young men, whose agriculture activities could be confined to felling the jungle during one or two months of the year, forged far ahead of the main body of settlers. In doing this, they learned about the land and drove from it the other tribes that had some claim to it. It may be that considerable mobility outside as well as within the tribal territories is a requirement of the kind of warlike expansion that the Ibans exemplify.

A few additional points about the ecological setting of warlike expansion as described in my second model can be made. We sometimes find in the anthropological literature (e.g., Fathauer 1954:117; Murphy 1957:1027, 1028) statements implying that in order to show significant economic, ecological, or demographic influences upon warfare it is necessary to show that the warring people exist within a given territory in numbers either almost as great as, or as great as, or possibly even greater than the numbers that the territory can continue to support under a given system of exploitation. In contrast to these statements, we have Birdsell's (1957:54) observation, made in a discussion of generalized hunting and collecting populations, that it is untenable to assume that a native population would begin to colonize adjacent favorable and unspoiled territories only when its existing territories attain a maximum carrying capacity. According to Birdsell, "even among horticultural peoples the environmental stimuli of a slowly reducing food supply *per capita* begin to exert important pressures for escape from the approaching equilibrium at considerably lower levels." Our Iban case is instructive because it shows the warlike extension of territory as a means whereby a group can *avoid* experiencing any very great privations due to the pressure of population upon available resources. Iban men, in their head-hunting forays during what for them was the agricultural slack season, were pioneering some areas which might not be "needed" or even brought into agricultural use by the growing Iban population until years later. This very pioneering may have been an important precondition for relative peace within each Iban tribe and for its having a mobile labor force for exploiting the environment, for it would be a factor tending to obviate those situations of potential conflict in which some Iban tribesmen had enough land for their needs while others did not.

Inasmuch as an estimate based upon a recent census (Noakes 1950:17) gives a mean population density of less than twelve people per square mile for all of Sarawak, it may of course still be asked why the Ibans in the last century, when their numbers were smaller than now, should have taken land claimed by other tribes. If Iban population was increasing, then why did it not spread peacefully into virgin territory not claimed by anybody? In answer to this, it must be noted that some land is better suited than other land for exploitation by a people with given techniques and a given organization. Thus it may be the case that for swidden agriculturalists in the humid tropics in general it is advantageous to farm in second-growth land rather than in primary forests, which, at least in the humid tropics, may be almost as difficult to clear with iron tools as with wooden and stone ones (Goodenough 1956:174–75; cf. Conklin 1954:137, 140). This may have been true of the Ibans, notwithstanding that Freeman (1955b:111, 115, 117–18) attributes a preference for virgin forest to them. This preference is also something that may have promoted peace within the Iban tribes—by virtue of stimulating the younger and hardier people to settle the more recently pioneered areas and not to vie unduly for land in the old areas. It should be noted also that for the younger and hardier people the virgin forest may have seemed more attractive because of the greater possibilities there for the collection of jungle produce. However, as Freeman (1955b:22, 113, 120ff.) himself makes clear, the preference for virgin forest was neither so general nor so intense among the Ibans as to induce them to allow second growth to revert to climax vegetation. Leach (1950:89), writing of Sarawak, has stated that in "most normal circumstances the total amount of virgin jungle cleared in any one year is almost infinitesimal," and it seems warranted to conclude that the relative ease of clearing second growth may well have been a factor in the Ibans taking previously farmed land from other groups at times rather than expanding into virgin territory.

However, much of the land that the Ibans took from other groups was only very sparsely inhabited and no doubt some of it had not been previously cultivated or else had been allowed to revert to climax vegetation. It seems likely that its riverine location made even such land more suitable for Iban use than virgin territory elsewhere would have been. Throughout most of Sarawak, as in many other parts of the humid tropics, human occupation has taken the form of ribbon development along the banks of the rivers, which, for the Ibans, were important, not only for getting to the rice fields (Hose and McDougall 1912:131) and probably for facilitating movement between communities of the same tribe so as to enable people to cooperate more effectively in military undertakings, but also for providing access to trade goods. By using the rivers for taking rice, gutta-percha, and other products to the Chinese and Malay traders (or by being on the rivers so that the traders could come to them), the natives of the interior could get not only the treasured brassware and ceramics (Freeman 1955b:76–77) but also guns (Cunynghame 1892:77; Grant 1885:117; Maxwell 1881:87) and the bars of European iron and steel from which were fashioned essential agricultural and fishing implements (chopping knives, fish spears, etc.) and the swords and spears used in fighting (Hose and McDougall 1912:193ff.; Low 1848:158, 209–11). It may be suggested that the readier the access to trade goods the more efficient would be the economic and military system and, furthermore, that by spreading aggressively along the rivers as Iban population was increasing, the Ibans were probably maintaining the conditions (including the relatively ready access to trade goods and the facility of intercommunity cooperation) under which further increase in numbers remained feasible for them.

We see then that the type of warfare exemplified by the Ibans, as well as the other type described with special reference to the Maoris, may have important ecological functions or effects. Conclusions about the "primary functions" of warfare among any swiddening people are likely to be premature until substantial data on the populations and environments in question have been examined in the light of such models as I have presented in this paper and in the light of other models as well.

BIBLIOGRAPHY

Allan, William
1949 *Studies in African Land Usage in Northern Rhodesia.* Rhodes-Livingstone Papers No. 15. Cape Town: Rhodes-Livingstone Institute.
Andrzejewski, Stanislaw
1954 *Military Organization and Society.* London: Routledge.
Anonymous ("An Occasional Correspondent")
1885 "Trusan." *Sarawak Gazette,* 15: 113–15.
Best, Elsdon
1925 *Maori Agriculture.* Dominion Museum Bulletin No. 9. Wellington: Dominion Museum.
Birdsell, Joseph B.
1957 "Some Population Problems Involving Pleistocene Man." *Cold Spring Harbor Symposia on Quantitative Biology,* 22: 47–68.
Bohannan, Laura
1958 "Political Aspects of Tiv Social Organization," in John Middleton and David Tait (eds.), *Tribes Without Rulers.* London: Routledge.
Bohannan, Paul
1954 "The Migration and Expansion of the Tiv." *Africa,* 24: 2–16.
Brooke, Charles
1866 *Ten Years in Sarawak.* 2 vols. London: Tinsley Brothers.
Buck, Peter H. (Te Rangi Hiroa)
1949 *The Coming of the Maori.* Wellington: Whitcombe and Tombs.
Conklin, Harold C.
1954 "An Ethnoecological Approach to Shifting Agriculture." *Transactions of the New York Academy of Sciences,* 2d. ser., 17: 133–42.
1959 Personal Communication.
Cook, S. F.
1946 "Human Sacrifices and Warfare as Factors in the Demography of Pre-colonial Mexico." *Human Biology,* 18: 81–100.
Cunynghame, P. F.
1892 "Trusan [Report for February 1892]." *Sarawak Gazette,* 22: 77.

Davenport, William
  1959 "Nonunilinear Descent and Descent Groups." *American Anthropologist*, 61: 557–72.
Drucker, Philip, and Robert F. Heizer
  1960 "A Study of the Milpa System of La Venta Island and Its Archaeological Implications." *Southwestern Journal of Anthropology*, 16: 36–45.
Fathauer, George H.
  1954 "The Structure and Causation of Mohave Warfare." *Southwestern Journal of Anthropology*, 10: 97–118.
Fernandes, Florestan
  1952 "A função social da guerra na sociedade tupinambá." *Revista do Museu Paulista*, n.s., 6: 1–425.
Firth, Raymond
  1929 *Primitive Economics of the New Zealand Maori*. London: Routledge.
  1957 "A Note on Descent Groups in Polynesia." *Man*, 57: 4–8.
Forde, Daryll
  1948 "The Integration of Anthropological Studies." *Journal of the Royal Anthropological Institute*, 78: 1–10.
Freeman, J. D.
  1955a *Report on the Iban of Sarawak*, Vol. 1. Kuching: Sarawak Government Printing Office.
  1955b *Iban Agriculture: A Report on the Shifting Cultivation of Hill Rice by the Iban of Sarawak*. Colonial Research Studies No. 18. London: Her Majesty's Stationery Office.
  1958 "The Family System of the Iban of Borneo," in Jack Goody (ed.), *The Developmental Cycle in Domestic Groups*. Cambridge Papers in Social Anthropology, No. 1. Cambridge: University Press.
Goodenough, Ward H.
  1956 "Malayo-Polynesian Land Tenure [reply to Charles O. Frake]." *American Anthropologist*, 58: 173–76.
Grant, C. T. C.
  1885 "A Tour Amongst the Dyaks of Sarawak." *Sarawak Gazette*, 15: passim.
Hose, Charles, and William McDougall
  1912 *The Pagan Tribes of Borneo*, Vol. 1. London: Macmillan.
Leach, E. R.
  1948 "Some Features of Social Structure Among Sarawak Pagans." *Man*, 48: 91–92.
  1950 *Social Science Research in Sarawak: A Report on the Possibilities of a Social Economic Survey of Sarawak*. Colonial Research Studies, No. 1. London: His Majesty's Stationery Office.
Low, Hugh
  1848 *Sarawak; Its Inhabitants and Productions*. London: Bentley.
Maxwell, F. R. O.
  1881 Letter, dated Simanggang, 15th September, 1881, to His Highness The Rajah of Sarawak. *Sarawak Gazette*, 11: 85–87.

Métraux, Alfred
  1948 "The Tupinamba," in Julian Steward (ed.), *Handbook of South American Indians*, Vol. 3. Bureau of American Ethnology Bulletin No. 143. Washington: Government Printing Office.
Murdock, George Peter
  1959 "Evolution in Social Organization," in *Evolution and Anthropology: A Centennial Appraisal*. Washington: Anthropological Society of Washington.
Murphy, Robert F.
  1957 "Intergroup Hostility and Social Cohesion." *American Anthropologist*, 59: 1018–35.
Noakes, J. L.
  1950 "A Report on the 1947 Population Census [Sarawak and Brunei]." Kuching: Government Printer.
Oberg, Kalervo
  1955 "Types of Social Structure Among the Lowland Tribes of South and Central America." *American Anthropologist*, 57: 472–87.
Polack, J. S.
  1838 *New Zealand*, Vol. 2. London: Bentley.
Richards, A. J. N.
  1949 "The Migrations of the Ibans and Their Poetry." *Sarawak Museum Journal*, 5: 77–87.
  1958 "Sea Dayaks—Ibans." *Sarawak Gazette*, 84: 125–29.
Sharp, Andrew
  1956 *Ancient Voyagers in the Pacific*. Polynesian Society Memoir No. 32. Wellington: Polynesian Society.
Steward, Julian H.
  1958 "Problems of Cultural Evolution." *Evolution*, 12: 206–10.
Suttles, Wayne
  1961 "Subhuman and Human Fighting." *Antropologica*, n.s., 3: 148–63.
Taylor, N. H.
  1958 "Proceedings of the New Zealand Archaeological Society: 7—Soil Science and New Zealand Prehistory." *New Zealand Science Review*, 16: 71–79.
Taylor, Richard
  1870 *Te ika a Maui; or New Zealand and Its Inhabitants*. London: Macintosh.
Vayda, A. P.
  1956 "Maori Conquests in Relation to the New Zealand Environment." *Journal of the Polynesian Society*, 65: 204–11.
  1959 "The Study of the 'Causes' of War." Paper Read at the 58th Annual Meeting of the American Anthropological Association in Mexico City, December 1959 [revised version in press, *Ethnohistory*, 1969].
  1960 *Maori Warfare*. Wellington: Polynesian Society.
Wedgwood, Camilla H.
  1930 "Some Aspects of Warfare in Melanesia." *Oceania*, 1: 5–33.

White, Leslie A.
  1959 *The Evolution of Culture: The Development of Civilization to the Fall of Rome.* New York: McGraw-Hill.
Wright, Quincy
  1942 *A Study of War,* Vol. 1. Chicago: University of Chicago Press.
Zegwaard, Rev. Gerard A.
  1959 "Headhunting Practices of the Asmat of Netherlands New Guinea." *American Anthropologist,* 61: 1020–41.

11 AN ETHNOECOLOGICAL
APPROACH TO SHIFTING
AGRICULTURE

Harold C. Conklin

M ETHODS OF shifting cultivation, while unfamiliar to many
of us living in temperate latitudes, are typical of vast areas
in the tropics. Such methods account for approximately one-third
of the total land area used for agricultural purposes in Southeast
Asia today (Dobby 1950:349). In some countries, including the
Philippines, it has been estimated that shifting cultivation produces food for up to 10 per cent of the total population (Pelzer
1945:29). In these regions the economy of large segments of the
upland population is based solely on such means. Nevertheless,
shifting agriculture is still only inadequately understood. It is
often categorically condemned as primitive, wasteful, or illegal,
with little or no regard for such pertinent local variables as
population density, available land area, climate, or native agricultural knowledge. For most areas, detailed field reports against
which such statements might be tested are totally lacking. There
is a definite need for ascertaining what are the real facts about
shifting agriculture.

In this paper, I shall attempt to throw some light on the nature
of such methods of upland farming and to draw our attention to
certain important problems in this area of research. First we shall
review some of the more frequent statements made by writers on
the subject. Then we shall examine the pertinent ethnographic
data for a specific culture, emphasizing not only the local environmental conditions and their apparent modification, but es-

Reprinted from *Transactions of the New York Academy of Sciences,*
2nd ser., Vol. 17 (1954), pp. 133–42, by permission of the author and
publisher.

pecially the determination of how these conditions and modifications are culturally interpreted.

For our purposes we may consider shifting cultivation, also known by such designations as field-forest rotation (Pelzer 1945:17) or slash-and-burn agriculture, as always involving the impermanent agricultural use of plots produced by the cutting back and burning off of vegetative cover. We shall call such a field a *swidden*. This term, like its by-forms *swithen* or *swivven,* is an old dialect word from northern England (Northumberland, Yorkshire, Lancashire, and elsewhere) meaning "burned clearing" or "to burn, sweal, or singe, as heather" (Halliwell-Phillips 1847:838; Wright 1904:881–82). It has been revived recently, and in an ethnographic description, by a Swedish anthropologist (Izikowitz 1951:7). There are many vernacular terms for swidden, but few are widely known or used in the literature except in reference to limited geographical regions: *kaingin* (*caiñgin*) in the Philippines, *ladang* in Indonesia, *taungya* in Burma, and terms such as *djum* in India, *chitemene* in parts of Africa, and *milpa* in Central America (see Pelzer 1945:16).

Swidden agriculture, of course, involves more than is stated in our minimal definition, but before we attempt greater precision, let us examine some of the characteristics which various authors have attributed to it. The following list is not intended to be complete, but does include the most frequent and problematic statements and assumptions I have encountered.

(1) Swidden farming is a haphazard procedure involving an almost negligible minimum of labor output. It is basically simple and uncomplicated.

(2) Usually, and preferably, swiddens are cleared in virgin forest (rather than in areas of secondary growth). Tremendous loss of valuable timber results.

(3) Swidden fires escape beyond cut-over plots and destroy vast forest areas. One author states that from 20 to more than 100 times the swidden area itself are often gutted by such fires (Cook 1921:313).

(4) Swidden techniques are everywhere the same. Such features as the lack of weeding and the use of a single inventory of tools are practically universal.

(5) Stoloniferous grasses such as "notorious *Imperata*"

(Gourou 1953:18) are abhorred as totally useless pests by all groups whose basic economy is swidden agriculture.

(6) Swiddens are planted with a single (predominant) crop. Any given swidden can thus be said to be a rice or a maize or a millet field or the like. Hence, it is possible to gauge the productivity of a swidden by ascertaining the harvest yield of a single crop.

(7) Furthermore, it is possible to gauge the efficiency (i.e., relative to some other method of agriculture) of a given swidden economy in terms of its one-crop yield per unit of area cultivated (Hutton 1949:26).

(8) Swiddens are abandoned when the main crop is in. "The harvest ends the series of agricultural operations" (Gourou 1953:28).

(9) There is no crop rotation in swidden agriculture. Instead, soil fertility is maintained only by the rotational use of the plots themselves. The duration of the rotational cycles can be determined by the time interval between successive clearings of the same plot.

(10) Not only is fertility lost, but destructive erosion and permanent loss of forest cover result from reclearing a once-used swidden after less than a universally specifiable minimum number of years of fallowing (set by some authors at twenty-five years) (Gourou 1953:31). It is claimed that "dangerous" consequences of more rapid rotation often result from native ignorance.

On these and many other points there is frequently an over-all assumption that the standards of efficiency in terms of agricultural economy in the United States or Western Europe are attainable and desirable among any group of swidden farmers.

FIELD OBSERVATIONS

From November 1952 until January 1954 I lived with the Yāgaw Hanunóo of southeastern Mindoro Island in the Philippines. The Hanunóo, numbering approximately 6,000, are pagan mountaineers who occupy about 800 square kilometers of forest and grass-covered hinterland, and whose primary economic activity is swidden agriculture (Conklin 1953:1–3). I was able to observe and participate in more than a full annual cycle of agricultural activities. Since most of my efforts during this time were directed toward an ethnographic analysis of the relation between Hanunóo culture and the natural environment (Conklin 1954), I was drawn toward an increasingly closer examination of Hanunóo concepts of the ecology of the Yāgaw area and of Hanunóo methods of swidden farming.

The following brief statements summarize the preliminary results of my investigation of Hanunóo swidden agriculture. Except where otherwise noted, these remarks apply specifically to the Hanunóo on the upper eastern slopes of Mt. Yāgaw (Map). The six settlements in this area comprise an unstratified, unsegmented, neighborhood-like community, which has a total of 128 inhabitants. The average population density for the entire Hanunóo territory is ten per square kilometer, but in the more heavily settled areas, such as Yāgaw, there are from twenty-five to thirty-five persons per square kilometer.

The Hanunóo do not have a general term for swidden or for swidden cultivation, but do employ a set of terms distinguishing developmental stages of potential, actual, or used swidden areas. These are based on changes—natural or artificial—in the vegetational cover. Swidden activities are best outlined by taking these stages in sequence, indicating the significant human activities and plant changes occurring at each:

First year.—(1) Activities resulting in a slashed clearing, a *gāmasun* (January–February): Possible swidden locations are discussed within the settlement group. Final decision depends on location augury, dreams, the local omens, as well as an intimate knowledge of the local forms of vegetation. The cultivator marks his plot with bamboo stakes and, using a large bolo, cuts down the underbrush and small saplings. Men and women participate in this initial clearing, family units making up the usual work teams. The average size of a Hanunóo swidden is two-fifths of a hectare. This area averages about one hectare of cultivated swidden cleared each year for every eight people. The total area of productive swidden land in a given area, however, is always several times that of the most recently cleared fields, because of intercropping. As shown in the Map, 48 new swiddens (numbered serially for each settlement) were cleared in the Yāgaw area in 1953. Of these only four were cut partly from virgin forest (amounting to less than 10 per cent of the total area cleared).

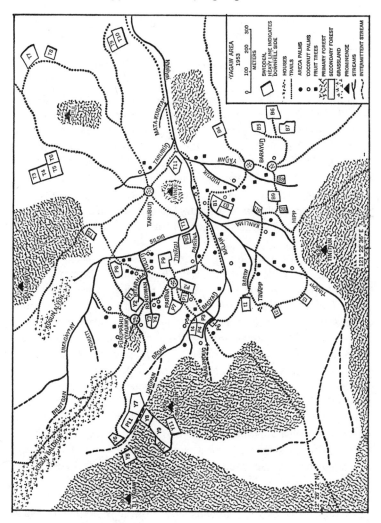

Map of Yāgaw Area, Mindoro. (Sources: field data and U. S. Coast and Geodetic Survey, 1935.)

Second-growth forest areas are preferred because the clearing of primary forest requires much more manpower for a given area, and demands a longer drying period before burning can take place than can profitably be allotted to such tasks.

(2) Activities resulting in a cut clearing, a *buklid* (February–March): Using the same bolos and a few single-bladed axes, men begin the more arduous task of felling large trees. Women continue to clear undergrowth and begin planting root crops (such as taro) which can survive the intense heat of swidden burning. Instead of being felled, a number of larger trees are pollarded, not only to remove unwanted shade branches, but also to provide firewood and promote seeding of other trees in the first fallow year. Smaller branches and cut underbrush are spread over the whole area so that complete burning will occur and exposed patches of earth will be protected from the dry season sun. These cutting, trimming, and drying activities may take more than a month, especially in a primary forest clearing. Group labor parties, repaid with feasts of rice, are usually needed to finish this stage.

(3) Activities resulting in a burned clearing, a *tūtud* (March–April–May): While the field dries, the Hanunóo farmer removes cut timber suitable for fence building or other construction purposes and clears a 4-meter-wide safety path around the entire clearing to prevent the fire from escaping into surrounding forest or fallow swidden areas. Firing starts at the upward and windward margins. A steep hectare of dry, second-growth vegetation will burn up in an hour or less, depending on the wind. While secondary burning is being completed, men begin fencing the entire swidden to prevent wild and domestic mammals (especially the zebu) from getting at young crop plants. Constant guarding against daytime animal marauders is facilitated by the construction of scarecrows of straw, windblown dangling objects, and small field houses from which children can jerk lines leading to distant parts of the swidden.

(4) Activities resulting in, and necessary for the maintenance of, a planted swidden, a *tanman* (May through October): Maize is planted soon after the swidden is burned. The main rice planting comes at the end of the dry season, in May or early June. It is an important social and religious event and involves special spirit offerings, large work parties in gala attire, feasting, and the participation of men, women, and children. Men make the seed holes (*ca.* 5 cm. deep and 25 cm. apart) with two-meter long, pointed dibbles. Women and children follow, dropping a small handful of prepared seed (often from a mixture containing

small quantities of pigeon pea, cucumber, melon, and sorghum seeds as well as rice). The Yāgaw average for planted rice seed is 40 gantas (1⅗ cavans) per hectare. Other important swidden crops are planted less ceremoniously (e.g., sweet potatoes, in August), as are many secondary (i.e., nonstaple) crops. During the rice growing season, other swidden activities include: completion of fences, continued guarding against destructive animals and birds, constant thinning and weeding (the entire swidden area being cleaned of weeds, shoots, and noncultivated vines at least three times), building of granaries, and the almost continuous planting and harvesting of other crops in both new and old swiddens (see discussion of intercropping below).

(5) Activities resulting in a riceless field, a *dayamihan* (October–November): The most important harvest in a new swidden is that of short-growing-season maize (in July and August). This is usually performed (including minor magical rites) by the cultivator himself, with only one or two helpers. The main rice harvest, in late October and early November, involves elaborate arrangements for group labor, feasts, magical rites, and religious offerings. It is the most important agricultural event of the year. Harvesting rice is done by hand (usually without knives) by men, women, and older children. The normal yield in rice ranges from 25 to 40 times the volume of the seed planted. One hectare of swidden land may give more than 30 cavans of unhusked rice. After threshing, drying, hulling, cooking, and other preparations, a settlement-wide celebration is held, after which the rigid observance of many rice-connected taboos, such as that which forbids one to eat new rice from another's swidden, are removed.

(6) Activities resulting in a cleaned swidden, a *lūmun bag?ūhan* (November–December): After gleaning, all rice stalks are cut, piled, and burned. Group labor, with compensatory rice feasts, are necessary to finish this task in less than two months. Other cultigens, especially leguminous crops and sweet potatoes, are now the focus of attention.

Dry season swiddens, always cut in second-growth areas, are cleared in September and October, planted in early November, and harvested unceremoniously in February, March, and April. They are usually small and are planted with corn and root crops only, never with rice. Some dry-season crops (including maize, certain beans, and sugar cane) are planted in main swiddens a few weeks before the rice harvest.

After the first year.—(7) Activities resulting in a recleaned (used, but still productive) swidden, a *lūmun dāʔan:* Fruit trees, and other perennial cultivates planted in new swiddens continue to provide edible food products if the plot is systematically weeded and cleaned. By interplanting cultigens other than the principal grain staples, the Hanunóo practice a kind of limited crop rotation. Such intercropping results in successive harvests of different primary and secondary crops for at least two years, frequently extended to five or six years, especially where the cultivation of banana plants is continued. The many leguminous crops so interplanted incidentally return significant amounts of nitrogen to the soil (Wernstedt 1954:65). Single-crop swiddens are nonexistent. Up to 40 separate crops have been observed growing in one Hanunóo swidden at the same time (cf. Anderson 1952:84; Merrill 1907:179–80; Hester 1953:288–92; Segawa 1953:49–66). One informant drew a map of an "ideal" swidden containing 48 basic kinds of plants (over 250 subsumed specific types) including: forty-one cultigen crop foods (including varieties of rice, sweet potatoes, yams, taro, maize, squash, sugar cane, and beans); one non-cultigen food plant (papaya); and six non-food cultigens, namely: tobacco, for chewing with betel, areca, and lime; betel vine, for leaves used in the betel chew; cotton, for spinning and weaving into garments; indigo for dyeing cotton yarn; derris, for its fish-stupefying roots; and vetiver, for its scented roots (sachet).

Once productive cultivates give out—but usually not for two or three years after the main rice harvest—fallowing begins. After five years, fallow second-growth forest (*talun*) types are readily distinguishable by their predominant plant forms. The most common types are either some kind of tree or bamboo. Bamboo second growth is preferred for swidden making, because it dries uniformly and burns quickly and completely. If not recleared, of course, *talun* eventually reverts to primary forest (*pūruʔ*). Swidden areas are not recut before at least five years of fallowing—after the last cultigens give out—and this period is extended preferably to more than ten. In 1953, most Yāgaw swiddens had been fallowed for more than eight years. The Yāgaw area is in a rain belt and thus fallowing usually means the growth of replacement forest and a continuing natural refertilization of the land.

In areas where there is a long dry season—aided by frequent burning for hunting purposes—tough grasses tend to dominate the replacement vegetation. Without artificial manuring and draft animals, productive swidden cultivation then becomes difficult. Damper areas seem more suited to continue swidden making. Despite an apparently long history of occupation by swidden farmers—there are more than a dozen groves of coconut palms in the area (see Map)—the Yāgaw region today includes very little grassland. And *kūgun* (*Imperata* spp.), the predominant grass, is highly valued for livestock pasturage and especially for roof thatching. It is a persistent weed, but in other respects it is an important economic necessity.

Swidden activities require from 500 to 1000+ hours of work per year on the part of the average adult Hanunóo. In addition to swiddens, houseyard gardens are kept for experimentation with new cultigens, and for the individual cultivation of medicinal, ritual, aromatic, and ornamental plants.

The Hanunóo recognize innumerable natural and artificial factors as variables affecting swidden agriculture. Ecologically speaking, climatic factors, while closely observed, can be modified least by the Hanunóo. Edaphic factors, though not practically amenable to artificial change, can be dealt with in a more concrete manner. A study of Hanunóo soil classification and associated ideas regarding suitability for various crops—other variables being equal—checked well with the results of a chemical analysis of soil samples. Ten basic and thirty derivative soil and mineral categories are distinguished by the Hanunóo farmer. He may now know of the minute degree of lime disintegration and low pH value of *nāpunāpuʔ*, but he does know that certain beans and sugar cane (considered "high lime" crops, technically) will not thrive in such soil as they will in *baragʔan* (which has a higher lime content and pH value). Effects on soil quality of erosion, exposure, and over-swiddening are well understood. They are topics of frequent discussion, and preventive measures are often taken. Biotic factors are most subject to control and experimentation by the Hanunóo, and are of the greatest concern to them. More than 450 animal types and over 1,600 plant types are distinguished. The floral component is the more significant, especially in regard to swidden agriculture. Of some 1,500 "useful" plant types over 430 are cultigens (most of which are swidden-grown), ex-

isting only by virtue of the conscious domestication of the Hanunóo. Partly as a result of this intensified interest in plant
domestication and detailed knowledge of minute differences in
vegetative structures, Hanunóo plant categories outnumber, by
more than 400 types, the taxonomic species into which the same
local flora is grouped by systematic botanists. (For full details, see
Conklin 1954.)

CONCLUSIONS

Much of the foregoing is fragmentary and perhaps more suggestive than conclusive. There is certainly a need for continued
research in other areas (see, for example, Leach 1949) and for
field observations covering greater periods of time. However, by
using what recent ethnographic materials are available, we may
tentatively rephrase the statements made earlier, so that a more
accurate picture of swidden agriculture will emerge. Most of the
changes we shall make indicate that the swidden farmer sometimes knows more about the interrelations of local cultural and
natural phenomena than ethnocentric temperate zone writers
realize.

(1) Swidden farming follows a locally-determined, well-defined
pattern and requires constant attention throughout most of the
year. Hard physical labor is involved, but a large labor force is
not required.

(2) Where possible, swidden making in second-growth forest
areas (rather than in primary forests) is usually preferred.

(3) Swidden fires are often controlled by firebreaks surrounding the plot to be burned. Accidents happen, but greater damage
may result from hunting methods employing fire in an area having
a long dry season than from swidden clearing per se.

(4) Many details of swidden technique differ from area to
area, and with changing conditions. Weeding is assiduously accomplished in some regions. Fencing is considered requisite if
domestic cattle are kept, less so where such animals are rare.
Wooden hand implements are very simple and are used only
once. Metal cutting implements and harvesting equipment, however, vary greatly from region to region.

(5) Even the most noxious weeds, in one context, may serve
the local economy admirably in another. *Imperata*, if dominant,

restricts swidden opportunities, but its total loss causes similar hardships for those depending on it for pasture and thatch.

(6) Swiddens are rarely planted with single or even with only a few crops. Hence, the productivity of a swidden can be determined only partially by an estimate of the harvest yield of any one crop.

(7) It appears that the efficiency of swidden farming can be ascertained—relative to some other type of economy—only by taking into account the total yield per unit of labor, not per unit of area (Hutton 1949; Leach 1949).

(8) Because of intercropping, the harvest of one main swidden crop may serve only to allow one or more other crops to mature in turn. Plantings and harvests overlap usually for more than a full year, and frequently continue for several years.

(9) Swidden intercropping, especially if wet season cereals are alternated with dry season leguminous crops, amounts to a type of crop rotation, even if on a limited scale. Cycles of field "rotation" cannot be meaningfully assessed by merely determining the number of years which lapse between dates of successive clearings. The agricultural use of the swidden plot following initial clearing may have continued for one, several, or many years.

(10) It is difficult to set a minimum period of fallowing as necessary for the continued, productive use of swidden land by reclearing. Many variables are at work. A reasonable limit seems to be somewhere between eight and fifteen years, depending on the total ecology of the local situation. Swidden farmers are usually well aware of these limitations.

BIBLIOGRAPHY

Anderson, E.
1952 *Plants, Man, and Life*. Boston: Little Brown.
Conklin, H. C.
1953 *Hanunóo-English Vocabulary*. University of California Publications in Linguistics, No. 9. Berkeley: University of California Press.
1954 *The Relations of Hanunóo Culture to the Plant World*. Ph.D. Dissertation in Anthropology, Yale University, New Haven, Connecticut.
Cook, O. F.
1921 "Milpa Agriculture: A Primitive Tropical System," in *Annual Report of the Smithsonian Institution for 1919*. Washington: Government Printing Office.
Dobby, E. H. G.
1950 *Southeast Asia*. London: University of London Press.
Gourou, P.
1953 *The Tropical World: Its Social and Economic Conditions and Its Future Status*. New York: Longmans Green.
Halliwell-Phillips, J. O.
1847 *A Dictionary of Archaic and Provincial Words . . . from the Fourteenth Century*. London: J. R. Smith.
Hester, J. A., Jr.
1953 "Agriculture, Economy, and Population Densities of the Maya." *Carnegie Institute Yearbook*, No. 52: 288–92. Washington, D.C.
Hutton, J. H.
1949 "A Brief Comparison Between the Economics of Dry and Irrigated Cultivation in the Naga Hills and Some Effects of a Change from the Former to the Latter." *Advancement of Science*, 6: 26.
Izikowitz, K. G.
1951 *Lamet: Hill Peasants in French Indochina*. Etnologiska Studier, 17. Göteborg, Sweden.
Leach, E. R.
1949 "Some Aspects of Dry Rice Cultivation in North Burma and British Borneo." *Advancement of Science*, 6: 26–28.

Merrill, E. D.
 1907 "The Ascent of Mount Halcon, Mindoro." *Philippine Journal of Science*, 2: 179–203.
Pelzer, K. J.
 1945 *Pioneer Settlement in the Asiatic Tropics.* American Geographic Society, Special Publication No. 29. New York: Institute of Pacific Relations.
Segawa, K.
 1953 "The Means of Subsistence Among the Formosan Aborigines." *Japanese Journal of Ethnology*, 18: 49–66.
Wernstedt, F. L.
 1954 "The Role of Corn in the Agricultural Economy of Negros Oriental." *Silliman Journal*, 1(1): 59–67.
Wright, J. (ed.)
 1904 *The English Dialect Dictionary*, Vol. 5. London: H. Frowde.

12 MAN AGAINST HIS ENVIRONMENT: A GAME THEORETIC FRAMEWORK

Peter R. Gould

WITHOUT CATALOGING the many and various definitions of human geography by professional geographers over the past few decades, it is safe to say that most have included the words *Man* and *Environment*. Traditionally, geographers have had a deep intellectual curiosity and concern for the face of the earth and the way it provides, in a larger sense, a home for mankind. Much of what we see upon the surface of the earth is the work of Man, and is the result of a variety of decisions that men have made as individuals or groups. Unfortunately, we have all too often lacked, or failed to consider, conceptual frameworks of theory in which to examine Man's relationship to his environment, the manner in which he weighs the alternatives presented, and the rationality of his choices once they have been made. Underlining a belief that such theoretical structures are desirable, and that they sometimes enable us to see old and oft-examined things with new eyes, this paper attempts to draw the attention of geographers to the Theory of Games as a conceptual framework and tool of research in human geography.[1] Upon its initial

Reprinted from *Annals of the Association of American Geographers*, Vol. 53 (1963), pp. 290–97, by permission of the author and publisher.
[1] References to Game Theory in geographic literature are almost non-existent. What few references there are usually appear as peripheral points to a larger discussion on linear-programming solutions, for example: Garrison 1959:480–81. It should be noted, parenthetically, that much of the mathematics used in Game Theory is the same as that used in linear programming, and one of the hopeful things about the new ways of looking at old problems is that a common mathematics underlies many of the same theoretical structures. In terms of efficiency, a key made from a little modern algebra may often open many doors.

and formal appearance in 1944,[2] a reviewer stated: "Posterity may regard this . . . as one of the major scientific achievements of the first half of the twentieth century," and although the social sciences have been relatively slow in considering the Theory of Games, compared to the widespread application of all forms of decision theory throughout engineering, business, and statistics, its increasing use in our sister disciplines of economics, anthropology, and sociology indicates a sure trend, fulfilling the extravagant praise heaped upon it at an earlier date.

The Theory of Games, despite its immediate connotation of amusements of a frivolous kind, is an imposing structure dealing, in essence, with the question of making rational decisions in the face of uncertain conditions by choosing certain strategies to outwit an opponent, or, at the very least, to maintain a position superior to others. Of course, we do not have to think in terms of two opponents sitting over a chessboard; we may, as geographers, think in terms of competition for locations whose value depends upon the locational choices of others;[3] or, perhaps more usefully, in terms of man choosing certain strategies to overcome or outwit his environment. A good example of the latter is a Jamaican fishing village,[4] where the captains of the fishing canoes can set all their fishing pots close to the shore, all of them out to sea, or set a proportion in each area. Those canoes setting pots close to the shore have few pot losses, but the quality of the fish is poor so that the market price is low, particulary when the deep-water pots have a good day and drive the price of poor fish down still further. On the other hand, those who set their pots out to sea catch much better fish, but every now and then a current runs in an unpredictable fashion, battering the pots and sinking the floats, so that pot losses are higher. Thus, the village has three choices, to set all the pots in, all the pots out, or some in and some out, while the environment has two strategies, current or no-current. Game Theory has successfully predicted the best choice of strate-

---

[2] The basic work, now revised, is von Neumann and Morgenstern 1953. Excellent introductions are Williams 1954 and Rapoport 1961, while a complete critique and survey is Luce and Raiffa 1958.

[3] Garrison 1959, reviewing Koopmans and Beckmann 1957.

[4] Davenport 1960; an excellent case study drawn from detailed anthropological field work which provided the basis for assigning actual monetary values to the various choices presented to the village as a whole.

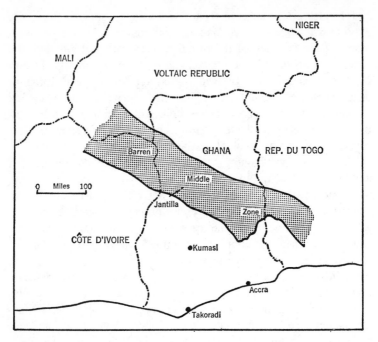

Figure 1 The Barren Middle Zone of Ghana of low population density and extreme variability of rainfall

gies and the proportion each should be used, a proportion very close to that arrived at by the villagers over a long period of trial and error.

Man continually finds himself in situations where a number of different choices or stategies may be available to wrest a living from his environment. Indeed, without soaring to those stratospheric heights of philosophical, or even metaphysical, discussion, to which all discourse in the social and physical sciences ultimately leads, let it be said that to be Man rather than Animal is, in part, to be able to recognize a variety of alternatives, and in a *rational* manner, reasoning from those little rocks of knowledge that stick up above the vast sea of uncertainty, choose strategies to win the basic struggle for survival. The perception that alternatives exist, and the recognition that their specific value, or utility, for a given time and place may depend upon an unpredictable environment, about which Man has only highly probabilistic notions based upon past experience, is clearly central to any discussion of man–environment relationships within a game theoretic framework. Thus, growing concomitantly with, and, indeed, embedded in, the Theory of Games, is a theory of utility intuitively raised, axiomatically treated, and experimentally tested in the real world.[5]

The Barren Middle Zone of Ghana (Fig. 1), a belt which, for environmental and historical reasons, has a very low population density, has one of the severest agricultural climates in West Africa (Manshard 1961:225), with heavy precipitation followed by the extreme aridity of the Harmatten, which sweeps south from the Sahara. A further problem is that the high degree of variability of the precipitation makes it difficult for the farmers to plan effectively (Walker 1957:37, map).

Let us assume that the farmers of Jantilla, a small village in Western Ghana, may use the land to grow the following crops, each with different degrees of resistance to dry conditions, as their main staple food: yams, cassava, maize, millet, and hill rice (Manshard 1961:226–29; see also Poleman 1961). In Game Theory terms the cultivation of these crops represents five strategies. In the same terms, and to simplify this initial example, let us make the somewhat unrealistic assumption that the environment has only two strategies; dry years and wet years. These strategies may be put into matrix form (Fig. 2), called the payoff

			ENVIRONMENT	
			MOISTURE CHOICES	
			Wet Years	Dry Years
		Yams	82	11
FARMERS	CROP	Maize	61	49
OF	CHOICES	Cassava	12	38
JANTILLA		Millet	43	32
		Hill rice	30	71

Figure 2 Payoff matrix for two-person-five-strategy-zero-sum game; crop choices against moisture choices

[5] The barbarous treatment of utility theory by those who fail, or refuse, to see the difference between a man declaring a preference because of the supposedly existing greater utility, rather than assigning a higher utility to a man's preference after it has been declared, did much damage at one time in the field of economics. The latter must always be kept in mind to avoid confusion; see Luce and Raiffa 1958:22.

matrix, and represent a two-person-five-strategy-zero-sum game, in which the values in the boxes represent the average yields of the crops under varying conditions, perhaps in calorific or other nutritional terms. For example, if the farmers of Jantilla choose to grow only yams, they will obtain a yield of eighty-two under wet year conditions, but the yield will drop to eleven if the environment does its worst. It should be noted that the values in the boxes have been chosen simply to provide an example of Game Theory, but this, in turn, emphasizes the close relationship of these methods

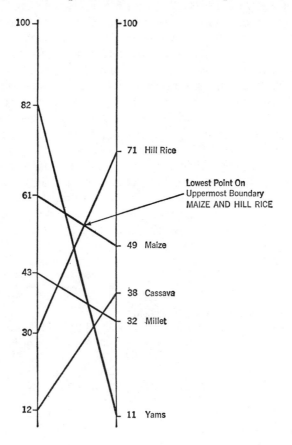

Figure 3 Graphical solution to assign critical pair of strategies in two-person-five-strategy-zero-sum game

to direct field work, for only in this way can we obtain these critical subcensus data. In a very real sense, our tools are out-running our efforts to gather the necessary materials. We might also note, parenthetically, that extreme accuracy of data, while always desirable, is not essential in order to use Game Theory as a tool, since it can be shown that payoff matrices subjected to a fairly high degree of random shock by injecting random error terms still give useful approximations and insights upon solution.[6]

A payoff matrix in which one opponent has only two strategies can always be reduced to a two-by-two game which is the solution for the complete game, in this case a five-by-two. We may, if time is no object, and we like dull, tedious work, take every pair of rows in turn and solve them for the maximum payoff to the farmers; but, fortunately, we also have a graphical solution which will point to the critical pair at once (Fig. 3). If we draw two scales from zero to one hundred, plot the values of each of the farmer's strategies on alternate axes, and connect the points, then the lowest point on the uppermost boundary will indicate which crops the farmers should grow to maximize their chances of filling their bellies.[7] Now we can take this pair of strategies, maize and hill rice (Fig. 4), and by calculating the difference be-

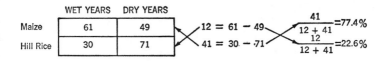

Figure 4 Solution of two-by-two payoff matrix to achieve most efficient choice of crop proportions

tween each pair of values and assigning it, regardless of sign, to the alternate strategy, we find the proportion each strategy should be used. Thus, maize should be grown 77.4 per cent of the time

---

[6] In linear-programming terms this would follow from the notion that the boundary conditions would have to change quite drastically, in most cases, in order for there to be a change in the mini—max point which would alter, in turn, the choice of strategies (see Fig. 3).

[7] This is simply the graphical solution to the basic linear-programming problem. The values, and the resulting slopes, have been deliberately exaggerated for the purposes of illustration.

and hill rice 22.6 per cent of the time, and if this is done the
farmers can assure themselves the maximum return or payoff
over the long run of fifty-four.

These proportions immediately raise the question as to how
the solution should be interpreted. Should the farmers plant
maize 77.4 per cent of the years and hill rice for the remaining 22.6 per cent, mixing the years in a random fashion;[8] or,
should they plant these proportions each year? As Game Theory
provides a conceptual framework for problems where choices
are made repeatedly, rather than those involving choices of the
unique, once-in-history variety, the cold-blooded answer is that
over the long haul it makes no difference. However, when men have
experienced famine and have looked into the glazed eyes of their
swollen-bellied children, the long run view becomes somewhat
meaningless. Thus, we may conclude that the farmers will hold
strongly to the short-term view and will plant the proportions
each year since the truly catastrophic case of hill rice and wet
year could not then occur.

It is interesting to note, simply as an aside, that solving this
two-by-two matrix vertically tells us that over the long run we
may expect dry years 58.5 per cent of the time (Fig. 5); if we

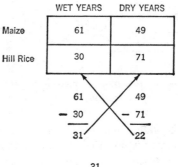

*Figure 5 Vertical solution of two-by-two payoff matrix to yield
proportion of dry years expected*

---

[8] For a discussion on the necessity of a random mix of strategies, see
Braithwaite 1955:236–39.

assume the environment to be a totally vindictive opposing player trying to minimize the farmers' returns.

The solution of this little game raises some interesting questions for the geographer. Does the land-use pattern approach the ideal? And if not, why not? If the land-use pattern does not approach the ideal, does this imply a conscious departure on the part of the people, or does their less-than-ideal use of the land reflect only the best estimate they can make with the knowledge available to them, rather than any degree of irrationality? Do the farmers display rational behavior in our Western sense of the term despite all the warnings of the anthropologists about the illusory concept of economic man in Africa? If one were in an advisory position, would this help to make decisions regarding the improvement of agricultural practices? If the solution exceeds the basic calorific requirements of the people, is it worth gambling and decreasing the proportion of one or both crops to achieve a better variety of foods—if this is desired by the people? How far can they gamble and decrease these proportions if inexpensive, but efficient, storage facilities are available, either to hold the surpluses of one year to allay the belt-tightening "hungry season" of the next, or to sell in the markets of the south when prices are high? Thus, the usefulness of the tool is not so much the solving of the basic problem, but the host of questions it raises for further research.

A further example from Ghana will make this clear (Fig. 6). For centuries the people living south of the great Niger arc have raised cattle and have driven them along the old cattle trails to the markets of Ghana (Gould 1961:137). The driving of cattle is a chancy business because, while Man can overcome cattle diseases such as rinderpest with modern veterinary medicines, he cannot yet predict the very dry years in this area of high rainfall variability through which the cattle have to be driven to market. Let us assume that the northern cattle traders of the Voltaic Republic, Mali, and Niger have the choice of selling their cattle in five markets: Ouagadougou, Navrongo, Tamale, Prang, and Kumasi. Each market thus represents a strategy and the traders may choose any one, or a mixture, of these in which to sell their animals. Let us further assume that Nature, or the environment, also has five strategies ranging from years with intensely dry conditions to unusually wet years. Thus, the strate-

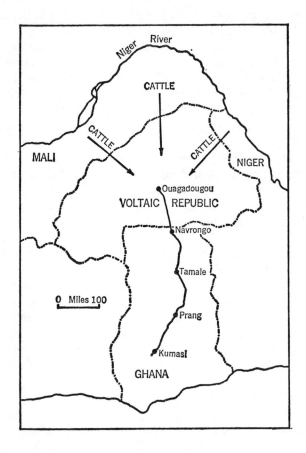

Figure 6   Areas of cattle production and main route to traditional cattle markets

gies available to the cattle traders and the environment form a two-person-five-by-five-zero-sum game and may be represented by a five-by-five matrix which indicates, for example, the average price of an animal in various markets under different conditions (Fig. 7). The matrix indicates that a trader may gamble upon the season being a very wet one, in which case he would drive all his animals to Kumasi; but, if he guessed wrong, and the season was a less than average one, cattle would die or lose a great deal of weight on the way and he would get much less in Kumasi than if

		ENVIRONMENT				
		AVAILABLE MOISTURE CHOICES				
		Very Wet	Above Average	Average	Below Average	Intense Drought
CATTLE TRADERS'	Ouagadougou	15	20	30	40	50
MARKETS	Navrongo	20	15	15	20	5
	Tamale	40	30	20	15	10
	Prang	60	50	40	20	15
	Kumasi	80	70	40	25	10

Figure 7 Payoff matrix in two-person-five-by-five-zero-sum game; market choices against available moisture choices

he had sold them in another market such as Ouagadougou.[9] This, of course, is a deliberate simplification, for we are not taking into account the possibility of varying demands, the question of alternative local supplies at some of the markets, nor the probability of Ghanaian consumers substituting one source of protein for another, for example, fresh fish from the coast or dried Niger perch (Garlick n.d.:19). It might be possible to gather data to fill payoff matrices for other suppliers, but the situation would become much more difficult since we would be in the realm of non-zero-sum games that are, both conceptually and computationally, much more complex.[10]

Given the above strategies, what are the best markets the cattle traders can choose, and what are the best proportions?— "best" in the sense that over the long run the traders selling

---

[9] It has been suggested by Professor William Garrison that this problem might be readily handled in a practical sense by a standard linear-programming approach; a suggestion that would confirm Luce's and Raiffa's evocative comment on the Theory of Games that ". . . one can often discover a natural linear programming problem lurking in the background" (Luce and Raiffa 1958:18).

[10] Zero-sum games are so called because upon choosing a particular strategy one competitor's gain (+) becomes the opponent's loss (−), the gain and loss summing to zero. Non-zero-sum games are those cases where an alteration in strategic choice *may* raise or lower the payoff for both players. Two-person-non-zero-sum games can be handled using the notion of imaginary side payments. *N*-person-non-zero-sum games may best be described as computationally miserable.

CATTLE TRADERS'   ENVIRONMENT
MARKETS   AVAILABLE MOISTURE CHOICES

						1	2	3	4	. . .	59	60	Total
Ouagadougou	15	20	30	40	50	15	65	115*	165*	. . .	2,060	2,110*	32
Navrongo	20	15	15	20	5	20	25	30	40	. . .	870	875	0
Tamale	40	30	20	15	10	40	50	60	70	. . .	2,045	2,055	0
Prang	60	50	40	20	15	60	75	90	105	. . .	1,875	1,890	0
Kumasi	80	70	40	25	10	80*	90*	100	110	. . .	2,065	2,075	28
	15*	20	30	40	50								
	95	90	70	65	60*								
	175	160	110	90	70*								
	. .	. .	. .	. .	. .								
	2,190	2,250	1,880	1,845	1,830								
			etc.										

Ouagadougou	32	$\frac{32}{60} = 53.4\%$
Kumasi	28	$\frac{28}{60} = 46.6\%$

Figure 8 Solution by iteration of payoff matrix

certain proportions of their cattle in these markets will get the maximum payoff. The solution of a five-by-five matrix in a zero-sum game is not as easy as the case where one opponent has two, or even three, choices. We do have, however, ways of choosing the strategies and *estimating* the proportions that should be used, the estimation being based upon a relatively simple iteration which converges upon the solution and which may be carried to any degree of required accuracy (Fig. 8). In the above example, the iteration has been carried out sixty times, and by counting the number of asterisks in each row of a market,

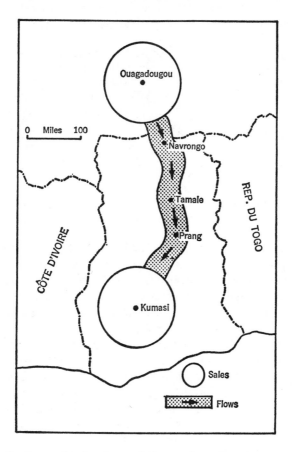

Figure 9 Proportional sales and flows of cattle prior to road improvements and trucking

which mark the maximum figure in each column of the estimating process, we can calculate that the traders should sell thirty-two sixtieths, or 53.4 per cent, of their cattle in Ouagadougou and then drive the remainder right through Navrongo, Tamale, and Prang to the Kumasi market (Fig. 9).

Let us pose the question, now, of what might happen if a really strong transportation link were forged between Tamale and Navrongo, such as the remaking and tarring of a road, so that upon arrival at the Voltaic–Ghanaian border cattle would no longer have to make their way on the hoof, but could be driven in trucks to the southern markets arriving in much better condition even in the very driest of seasons (Fig. 10). The payoff

		ENVIRONMENT				
		AVAILABLE MOISTURE CHOICES				
		Very Wet	Above Average	Average	Below Average	Intense Drought
CATTLE TRADERS'	Ouagadougou	15	20	30	40	50
MARKETS	Navrongo	20	15	15	20	5
	Tamale	80	80	70	70	80
	Prang	100	100	90	80	70
	Kumasi	130	130	120	90	60

Figure 10 New payoff matrix indicating price changes in markets as a result of new road link between Tamale and Navrongo

matrix would obviously change, and we might expect very much higher prices to prevail in Tamale, Prang, and Kumasi for the fat, sleek animals, rather than the bags-of-bones that often stumbled into these markets in former years. Again, the payoff matrix can be solved using the iterative method 160 times on this occasion (Fig. 11), to produce completely different choices and proportions from the previous example. Now it is no longer worthwhile for the traders to sell cattle in the Ouagadougou or Navrongo markets, but sell instead 62.5 per cent in Tamale, 25 per cent in Prang, and 12.5 per cent in Kumasi. Thus, an improved road link, a visible sign on the landscape of a technological improvement, changes Man's perception and evaluation of the same choices available to him before, and as a result changes the patterns of flows and sales (Fig. 12). Now the flow has increased over the northern portion of the route, and it has

ENVIRONMENT
AVAILABLE MOISTURE CHOICES

CATTLE TRADERS' MARKETS	15	20	30	40	50	1	2	3	4	...	160	Total
Ouagadougou	15	20	30	40	50	50	100	150	190	.	.	0
Navrongo	20	15	15	20	5	5	10	15	35	.	.	0
Tamale	80	80	70	70	80	80*	160*	240*	310*	.	.	100
Prang	100	100	90	80	70	70	140	210	290	.	.	40
Kumasi	130	130	120	90	60	60	120	180	270	.	.	20
	130	130	120	90	60*							
	210	210	190	160	140*		etc.			.		

$$\text{Tamale} \quad \frac{100}{160} = 62.5\%$$

$$\text{Prang} \quad \frac{40}{160} = 25.0\%$$

$$\text{Kumasi} \quad \frac{20}{160} = 12.5\%$$

Figure 11 Solution by iteration of new payoff matrix

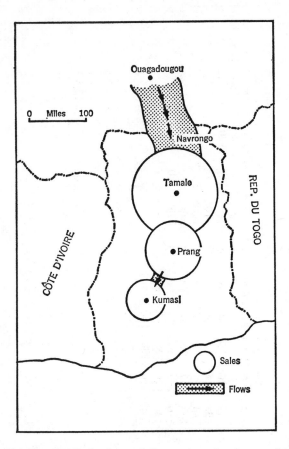

*Figure 12   Proportional sales and flows of cattle after road improve-
ments and trucking*

become desirable to sell portions of the herds in the Tamale and
Prang markets, the increases at these markets coming from former
sales at Ouagadougou and Kumasi. Again, solving the payoff
matrix points up some interesting questions for the geographer.
First, it raises the whole question of estimating the effects of
improving a transportation link—what will the flows be before
and after? Can we obtain payoff values from one part of West
Africa and use them to estimate changes of flows in other parts?
Secondly, the question, again: how close does the behavior of the

cattle traders approach that required to obtain the maximum pay-off over the long run? Thirdly, what would be the effect of increasing the speed of communication so that cattle traders who started early in the season could inform others on the trail to the north about the conditions they find? And, finally, we should note the way an improved transportation link in effect extends the influence of one or more markets over others as the effect of distance is broken down allowing the demands of one center to impinge upon another.

By taking two examples from the traditional economy of Ghana, this paper has tried to point out the possible utility of the Theory of Games as a tool of research and as a conceptual framework in human and economic geography. That such frameworks are needed is evident, for without these broad conceptual constructions in which to place our facts and observations it becomes an almost impossible task to raise and tackle, in a meaningful and lasting fashion, questions of Man's equilibrium with his environment, his perceptions and judgments about it, and the rules by which he reacts at different points in time and space? The work of Man is all around us upon the face of our earth, and is the result of men perceiving a variety of alternatives, subsequently limiting the range of choices according to their idea of what is useful and good, and *deciding* upon certain strategies to gain those ends. Thus, the whole body of decision theory, of which the Theory of Games is but one part, has an increasingly important role to play. Perhaps, in the same way that information theory has illuminated old problems of central-place structure, linear-programming solutions have helped our understanding of shifting flows and boundaries, and the theory of queues is throwing light upon problems ranging from those of the Ice Age to those of livestock production, the Theory of Games may also have a role to play.

Braithwaite, R. B.
  1955 *Scientific Explanation: A Study of the Function of Theory,
  Probability, and Law in Science.* Cambridge: The University Press.
Davenport, W.
  1960 *Jamaican Fishing: A Game Theory Analysis.* Yale University
  Publications in Anthropology, No. 59. New Haven: Yale University
  Press.
Garlick, P.
  No Date "The French Trade de Nouveau." Economic Bulletin of the
  Department of Economics, University of Ghana (mimeographed).
Garrison, W. L.
  1959 "Spatial Structure of the Economy, II." *Annals of the Association
  of American Geographers,* 49: 471–82.
Gould, P. R.
  1961 *The Development of the Transportation Pattern in Ghana.* North-
  western University Studies in Geography, No. 5. Evanston: North-
  western University Press.
Koopmans, T. C., and M. Beckmann
  1957 "Assignment Problems and the Location of Economic Activities."
  Econometrica, 25: 53–76.
Luce, R. D., and H. Raiffa
  1958 *Games and Decisions.* New York: John Wiley.
Manshard, W.
  1961 "Land Use Patterns and Agricultural Migration in Central Ghana."
  Tijdschrift voor Economische en Sociale Geografie, 9: 225–30.
Poleman, T. T.
  1961 *The Food Economies of Urban Middle Africa.* Stanford: Food
  Research Institute.
Rapoport, A.
  1961 *Fights, Games and Debates.* Ann Arbor: University of Michigan
  Press.

Von Neumann, J., and O. Morgenstern
1953 *Theory of Games and Economic Behavior.* Princeton: Princeton University Press.
Walker, H. O.
1957 "Weather and Climate of Ghana." Ghana Meteorological Department, Departmental Note No. 5. Accra (mimeographed).
Williams, J. D.
1954 *The Compleat Stratygyst.* New York: McGraw-Hill.

13 COMPUTERS AND THE EVALUATION OF RESOURCE MANAGEMENT STRATEGIES

Kenneth E. F. Watt

As more insight into the nature of ecological systems accumulated in the last two decades, it has become increasingly apparent that problems of managing renewable natural resources could not be solved by conventional mathematical means. During the same period, mathematicians and computer program designers, unaware of the problems in resource management, have been developing tools singularly appropriate for the solution of these problems, but for entirely different purposes. In this paper we shall explain why problems of systems management in agriculture, forestry, fisheries, wildlife management, and epidemiology contain characteristics prohibiting their solution using classical mathematical optimization techniques. Then we shall show why application of large memory, high speed computers, used in conjunction with modern programing aids and dynamic programing, make solution of such problems feasible.

THE IMMEDIACY OF THE PROBLEM

Until the last few decades, there has been no need for sophisticated operations research type studies of techniques of managing resources. As recently as the early nineteenth century, for example, the only problem in connection with buffalo and sperm whales was how to catch more. There were about forty million buffalo in North America, being killed at the rate of two or more million a year (Roe 1951), and sperm whales were being killed by the New England whaling fleet at the rate of about 4300 a

Reprinted from *American Scientist,* Vol. 52 (1964), pp. 408–18, by permission of the author and publisher.

year (Hohman 1928). Similarly with agriculture, since the continent was still being opened up, and man was not pressing hard enough on his resources for competition from insects to be critical. Trees and fresh water seemed to be inexhaustible.

However, in 1963, the world looks very different. Most intelligent people concede that even the most plentiful resources can be depleted through over-exploitation, and that pest control is critical. For example, by 1910 the world catch of sperm whales had been driven down to one hundred and fifty-five (Clarke 1954), and by 1888, there were about one hundred and fifty buffalo left in the U.S. (Roe 1951). Other resources such as fresh water, sardines, and salmon are watched with apprehension, and insect pests are the object of extremely sophisticated research. Particularly if we use trees for gasoline, the worldwide annual growth of wood will be exploited as fast as it becomes available. A recent critical study predicts that timber shortages will cause a revolution in construction techniques in the U.S. by the year 2000 (Lansberg, Fischman, Fisher 1963). The margin for error in long-term resource management planning is vanishing rapidly.

CHARACTERISTICS OF THE PROBLEMS

Problems in resource management are typically identical in structure to those the mathematician calls "extremum" problems. That is, we are confronted with a complicated system which must be manipulated so that some variable of commercial interest is made to take a maximum or minimum possible value, subject to various constraints which restrict our ability to control the system, or set economic feasibility limits on the controls we can apply. Examples are a fishery, in which the yield of edible tissue must be maximized, or a forest, in which we wish to maximize the yield of useful lumber by minimizing the depredations of insect pests, and the effects of fire, disease, and wasteful inter-tree competition.

Many difficulties are encountered in the attempt to describe such systems mathematically and manipulate the mathematical models to find the values of independent variables that yield the "extremum" value of the dependent variable (e.g., maximum yield of fish or trees, or minimum survival of insect pests).

Different types of resource management strategies have fundamentally different types of effect in space and time, and this renders difficult comparative evaluation of long-term effectiveness.

We will illustrate the different types of effects various management strategies can have by considering four basic types of strategy available for managing animal populations.

The first and oldest technique is to effect an ecological change in the population itself. That is, we change the open season on deer, stock pheasant chicks, kill insects with insecticides, change the minimum legal length limit on game fish or the international numerical quota on whales. Examples of newer techniques are electrified barriers to kill downstream-migrating lamprey larvae, and sex attractants to lure male moths to their doom or "jam the radar" of the powerful sex scents the females emit. Basically, all these techniques are similar, in that their effects do not persist indefinitely and do not disperse or magnify with the passage of time. Rather, they are compensated for by animal populations, because, if we remove members of a population, this only diminishes the intensity of the struggle for existence among the remainder who have resultant increased survival and reproductive rates. This is why insect pests are still with us, despite decades of treatment by a battery of powerful chemicals.

A second level of sophistication is represented by the attempt to change the numbers of some other organism which attacks the pest, game, or food species of concern. We may seek to exterminate the mountain lions which kill deer, or introduce a wasplike parasite into an orchard to kill a caterpillar. Aircraft may be used to spray a virus, bacterium or fungus over vast tracts of forest in order to kill a pest insect. These techniques differ from the first group because, in successful cases, their effects may spread in space and build up in time for twenty years or more (Smith 1959). Also, if a pathogen, parasite or predator effect declines, it may flare up again if the pest undergoes rapid population buildup.

An entirely new Pandora's box opened up with the spectacular control of the Florida screw worm by the mass release of radiation-sterilized males. Generalization of this notion led to a host of new ideas about genetic manipulation of populations. Another example is the planting of splake, or speckled-trout X lake-trout crosses, in order to produce a fast-growing fish whose habits make it less vulnerable to lamprey predation. A more sophisticated notion is to release foreign races of Gypsy moths in America, in order to introduce reproductive difficulties of various types into the population (Downes 1959).

Perhaps the most sophisticated control techniques of all have to do with environmental modification. Of course, fertilization of the land, ponds, lakes and arms of the sea is a venerable idea (Cooper and Steven 1948). However, there are some very new techniques of this class. One is to grow plants specially to provide pollen for the adult stages of wasps that parasitize phytophagous larvae, thus increasing the carrying capacity of the environment for the parasites (Townes 1958). Another idea is supported by recent research in population dynamics. Pests are most likely to build up to catastrophic densities where there are large, even-aged stands of trees of the same species, or only two similar species (Morris 1963). Therefore, we can militate against pandemics by appropriate checkerboard logging operations, or by mixed-tree species plantings in orchards.

The availability of all these types of control renders strategy evaluation very difficult, because we have to compare procedures that are very different with respect to the frequency with which they are used, the conditions under which they are applied, the type of effect they produce, and the speed with which they produce it. Also, the economics of the different procedures is very different. Some methods are cheap, but take a long time to build up to maximum effect, and hence are best used as preventive rather than emergency measures; some methods produce spectacular but transitory results, but are sufficiently expensive and have enough undesirable side effects to be used only in emergencies. Particularly if we plan to use mixtures of such techniques, comparative evaluation is very complex. For example, in forestry it is feasible to withhold application of insecticides until a pandemic pest condition must be treated if foliage is to be saved. However, biological control agents could not be released in adequate numbers fast enough or cheaply enough over, say, 10,000 square miles to be of use in this "emergency, save the foliage" type of control. Parasites and predators should ideally be released years in advance of a pest crisis, in order to take economic advantage of their self-spreading feature. This means that a sensible economic comparison is between preventive applications of some kinds of control versus emergency, short-term applications of other types of control. The implication for simulation studies is that we must compare, for various types of control, the cumulative sums of control costs and losses due to noncontrol over long periods of time, since the different strategies of timing of application do not allow for comparison on a short-term basis. Therefore, we need a mathematical model that simulates events over a sequence of many years.

Perhaps the single feature of natural resource management strategy evaluation that introduces the greatest analytic complexity is the fact that an event at a particular place may be the result of some prior event at *another* place.

Four examples from different fields illustrate this point. Spruce budworm populations do not build up at all points in a large area simultaneously. Rather, initial population buildup develops at certain epicenters, then high densities radiate out from these epicenters in wave-like fashion (Elliott 1960). Other authors have shown that the epicenters for insect pest outbreaks can only develop at certain positions on the surface of the earth, and the location of these sites is determined by the interaction of topographic, site and meteorological factors (Wellington 1954a and 1954b). Similarly, population fluctuations in fur-bearers are not in phase over wide areas, but show wave-like effects radiating out from epicenters (Butler 1953). Catches of sardines off the coast of California in a given year are in part dependent upon the number of sardines spawned off the coast of Mexico two years previously, which, in turn, depends on behavior of the California current (Sette 1960). Epidemics in human populations often show a characteristic pattern of migration from endemic focal points to distant points on the earth's surface. Bubonic plague, in particular, has repeatedly shown this pattern of slowly spreading from Oriental focal points to proceed wave-like over parts of Africa, the Middle East, Europe, the British Isles and North America (Creighton 1891; Link 1955).

Therefore, in all these cases we are dealing with a complex historical process in which movement through space must be considered as well as the passage of events through time. Such processes could be simulated using conventional mathematical procedures if only one such type of process occurred at one time, and there were no other complications. However, several processes are changing through time, not all in phase at any position in space, and there are several other complications, as we shall explain hereinafter. Therefore, the only feasible way to mimic such processes is to have separate models to mimic each point in space, or each square or cube in a two- or three-dimensional grid, respectively. The sheer bookkeeping effort involved in computing with such a conceptual system is out of the question unless we use an automatic bookkeeping system, such as FORTRAN or ALGOL (pseudoalgebraic computer programing languages) make available to us.

MATHEMATICAL PROBLEMS

However, the magnitude of the bookkeeping effort required in such problems only constitutes the beginning of our difficulties. Several other mathematical problems are raised by the following characteristics of biological systems.

(1) A complex ecological system (lake, forest, ocean, or farming area) is under the influence of a great many independent variables, all of which are liable to interact in subtle and important causal pathways.

(2) These independent variables may only be important if they operate at a certain time. For example, an egg predator or parasite has no effect once the host species has reached the larval stage; wind and ocean currents are critical at certain larval stages in the lives of fish and insects, but not at subsequent stages (Sette 1943). Therefore, problems of synchronization should be considered in structuring models for use in evaluating resource management strategies.

(3) The same independent variable may enter several different causal pathways in a complex ecological system, and the end effects of some of these pathways may tend to cancel each other. For example, increase in temperature speeds development of a host, therefore diminishing the period in which it is vulnerable to parasitism; however, the parasites are made to search more rapidly by the same temperature increase.

(4) Inequational constraints must be built into the strategy evaluation model for biological as well as economic reasons. All biological entities are subject to restrictions of the following type: the organism can eat an amount of food per unit time up to, but

not exceeding, a certain maximum; increasing hunger increases the perceptual field within which a predator will attack prey up to, but not exceeding, a certain maximum. Economic constraints arise because we cannot control a problem in a resource at a cost that exceeds the economic return from the resource, or apply control measures to such an extent that economically undesirable side effects result.

(5) Large-scale biological mechanisms often exhibit cumulative effects, lags, and thresholds. Consider the case of animals eating perennial plants. The leaves of the plant compete for sunshine, so, up to a certain threshold level, consumption of the leaves by animals only reduces interleaf competition, and no permanent harm to the plant is done. However, consumption of leaves above this threshold level by animals exerts a deleterious effect on the plants which cumulates from year to year, and which reveals its true extent only some years after irreversible damage has been done (Belyea 1952). That is, we have a lag, as well as a cumulative effect.

(6) A most difficult problem in evaluating resource management strategies is created by the number of strategies available for evaluation. For example, an insect pest can be controlled, in principle, by different insecticides, pathogens, parasites, and predators, or by sex attractants, genetic modification of the population, or ecological modification of the pest's environment. Each possible strategy can be applied at one or many times, at any feasible level of application, or in any combination with one of the other strategies. Consider the problem of managing the world stock of whales. What is the best way to distribute effort over species and lengths in order to ensure a maximum sustained catch? Clearly, some technique is needed for quickly eliminating that large proportion of the strategies in any situation which are sufficiently suboptimal to be unworthy of further consideration.

(7) Many resource management problems are very complex because they contain meteorological, technological, and economic components.

THE POWER OF COMPUTER SIMULATION

We simulate a phenomenon whenever it is cheaper than studying the phenomenon itself, or infeasible for some other reason to study nature directly. Recently, scientists in many fields have discovered the potential of mathematical experimentation using large digital computers in conjunction with the new pseudoalgebraic languages FORTRAN and ALGOL. These languages in effect constitute a new and very powerful type of mathematics that incorporates the features of many different branches of mathematics. They can describe functions, simulate logical processes, or describe matrix operations, through subscript notation. This last feature means that the computer can work with maps of populations on which a row X column grid has been superimposed. It is relatively easy to program the machine to simulate dispersal from one square to adjacent squares and whole maps can be printed on magnetic tape in a matter of seconds, or fractions a second. Computers have many features that make them ideally preadapted for solution of large-scale problems in resource management. Tables of weather data for half a century can be stored in a fast-access memory (access time in the 2–10 msec range) and brought out for computing on each year's simulation in turn. Enormously complex relations between animals and the plants they eat, and their predators, parasites and pathogens can be simulated easily on a machine that does additions in 2–10 msec.

We shall illustrate typical present applications of computer simulation studies to resource management with three cases. The aim in discussing these examples is not only to illustrate the capability of computer simulation for solving ultra-complex problems in resource management. Also, I wish to show that this new way of problem solving has the most profound implications for the character, organization, financing, and allocation of resources in science as a whole, and the education of scientists. In each of the three cases to be mentioned briefly, the following points will be noticed.

(1) Research has been done on whole problems, not on isolated fragments of problems. The four following points are corollaries of this one.

(2) Unlike much scientific work, in which an effort is made to strip a phenomenon down to bare essentials, these simulation studies attempt to mimic reality in detail, and therefore are massively complex. Complexity is not an issue with a machine that adds in 2 msec, can remember any one of 32,000 10-digit

numbers in a similar time, and output data at 75,000 characters per second.

(3) All three studies are extremely interdisciplinary. The mathematical models used draw on data from economic studies, legal considerations, and meteorology, biology, engineering, irrigation, and other fields.

(4) An immediate implication of the preceding point is that simulation studies are typically the outcome of a long period of work by an enthusiastic, tightly organized team within which there is a very high degree of cooperation and a real esprit de corps.

(5) Since the models used are realistic, they consider movement of entities through space, as well as changing conditions through time. Thus, the fundamental character of the mathematical models used is dynamic in a spatial as well as a temporal sense.

(6) The people who construct the computer programs think and write about them in terms of computer languages, such as FORTRAN. In fact, the complexity of many of the models, due to their dynamic character, constraints, and immensely complex interacting systems would make description of the systems difficult or impossible in any other mathematical language. This point may have the implication that FORTRAN or ALGOL will become the Esperanto or Interlingua of science.

We will now consider three examples.

The first study was conducted by a team consisting of a lawyer, biostatisticians, and economists at the University of Washington, on salmon gear limitation in Northern Washington waters (Royce, Bevan, Crutchfield, Paulik, and Fletcher 1963). The role of the legal member was to determine if it is constitutional for the federal government and the State of Washington to restrict the number of operators exploiting a common property resource, if this was done in the operator's interests. He concluded it probably was. Therefore, the object of the simulation study was to determine the biological and economic effects of restricting the number of units of gear fished. An IBM 709 was programed to simulate, in detail, the inland movements of sockeye, pink, silver, and chum salmon into the State of Washington and British Columbia waters. The four fish species were treated separately, as were four different categories of gear. The model mimics the behavior of the salmon with respect to all the waters they swim through, and the passage times. The spatial distribution of the gear, the length of time it is set, and all economic factors related to value of the catch, the operating cost, and profit for each type of gear in each place were in the model. One thousand separate equations were included in the computer program. It was shown that the fishery would be more profitable if the number of units of gear were restricted. An idea of the nature of the results is indicated by the following specific conclusion. "For example, when the sockeye run was increased to four times the standardized level to give a total run of approximately 17,000,000 fish in convention waters and the gear intensity (the amount of gear) was reduced to one-half of the present level, the fishery managed to harvest 77.9 per cent of the run."

The second study was conducted by the Harvard Water Program (Maass 1962). The team is a large group that, between 1955 and 1960, included about 50 people. Information from politics, economics, mathematics, statistics, power plant engineering, and other fields was built into the computer program, which, as in the preceding case, was written in FORTRAN. An IBM 704 computer was used. The problem posed in the simulation study was as follows. "Given: (1) a certain combination of reservoirs, power plants, and irrigation-diversion and distribution facilities; (2) target levels of irrigation and energy outputs; (3) specified allocations of reservoir capacity for active, dead, and flood storage; (4) a representative series of monthly runoff values, and 6-hr flows for flood months; and (5) a specified operating procedure—then by routing the available flows through the reservoirs, power plants and irrigation systems for an extended period of years, such as fifty, determine the physical outputs and the magnitude of the net benefits created." The computer simulated the behavior of some two hundred and fifty variables, and arrived at the optimal operating values for five reservoirs, irrigation and energy target values, power-plant capacities, and flood-control storage.

The third study was conducted by the Statistical Research Service, Canadian Department of Forestry, using data from many entomologists, foresters, and economists in the Canadian Government, and in collaboration with mathematicians at the RAND Corporation in Santa Monica (Watt 1964). The object was to find out how best to control an insect pest in 10,000 square miles of balsam forest. The program was written in FORTRAN and run on an IBM 7090. Included in the simulation program were data on weather conditions over a thirty-five year period, and equations describing the population growth of an insect pest, and its inter-relationships with the trees, parasites and pathogens. The operating costs of any strategy selected were computed, as were the losses due to lost tree growth and tree mortality. Spread and buildup of parasites and disease were simulated. The 10,000 square miles were treated as six hundred and twenty-five 4 mile $\times$ 4 mile squares, for each of which all computations were performed separately. Maps showing the distribution of pests, parasites, and incidence of disease were printed on magnetic tape, along with updated financial statements on timber losses and operating costs of controls at the end of each year. Physiological parameters describing the pests, parasites, and epidemiology of the pathogens were included. The results have shed considerable light on the whole matter of pest control.

Thus we see that a powerful new tool is available for solving scientific problems in resource management of the utmost complexity. It is to be hoped that widespread use of the tool will cause many breakthroughs. However, there is a very real problem. Most scientific workers in resource management simply lack the background necessary in mathematics, statistics, and computing to exploit the new tool. Herein lies an enormous challenge for a new, interdisciplinary type of education. Traditionally, mathematics courses or science courses with considerable mathematical content have emphasized problem solution. The great complexity of the systems analysis required in resource management strategy evaluation studies is creating a need for greater emphasis on problem formulation and systems description.

In order to particularize the type of education needed, we must look rather carefully at the most recent trends in management of extremely complex systems. Whether we are talking about optimization of a space shot trajectory, flight path selection for an airline, routing of forms in an insurance company, the productivity of California deer herds, sardines, German forests, or blue whales in the Antarctic waters, we have certain fundamental problems in all cases. One of the most pressing of these is the plethora of strategies that are typically available for consideration.

To this point, I have given the impression that this problem is solved by the availability of high speed modern computers. A moment's reflection will show that this is not true.

We have mentioned that resource management problems are dynamic. This implies that we are dealing with complex historical processes. Therefore, an action taken now has an effect on the future state of the system, which in turn will determine the decision which is optimal at a later time. An implication of this remark is that we are not interested in evaluating strategies on a "one-shot" basis, but rather we must compare the effects of various sequences of policies. To put the matter differently, policy *A* may be better than policy *B* now, but from the standpoint of the whole history of the system, *A* may *only* be optimal now if it is followed by *B* next time. Also, policy *A* may be optimal at time three in a sequence of times, but it may be grossly suboptimal at time seventeen if it has not been used before. Consider, for example, insect pest control in a forest. If a parasite with the appropriate egg complement, searching ability, and intraspecific competition coefficient is released sufficiently early in development of a pest outbreak, releasing parasites may be the optimal policy. However, if we postpone action until the pest is in a pandemic state, we will not be able to get out enough parasites at reasonable cost to control the outbreak. In this case, insecticides would be called for to save the foliage on an emergency basis. Clearly, a specific policy may not be optimal at all times; some policies are optimal at certain stages in the history of a resource, and other policies are optimal at other times.

The best policy to follow policy *A* itself may not be *A*, but *B*, because *A* may be too expensive to apply repeatedly, or it may not be permissible to apply *A* repeatedly for some other reason.

Hence, we are forced into comparative evaluation of the optimality of sequences of operations over time, not the optimality of "one-shot" action. Consider the implications of this for the number of strategies to be tested, and the volume of computation required. Suppose we wish to explore the consequences of all possible combinations of *M* factors at *N* levels each over *t* times. At the first time, we would simulate *MN* experiments. For each of these, at the second time, there would be *MN* experiments. Proceeding in a simple trial and error fashion, there would be

$(MN)^t$ sequences to compare with respect to their economic return, or "payoff." For two alternative courses of action tested at two levels each, for a sequence of four times, this number is

$$(2\times2)^4=256$$

For three alternative procedures, at three levels each, over four times, the number is

$$(3\times3)^4=6561$$

Clearly, this matter quickly gets out of hand, and for more realistic values, such as $M=N=10$ and $t=50$, we are beyond the range of the largest computers possible in principle.

Happily, Richard Bellman, a mathematician of the RAND Corporation, saw this problem on the horizon some years ago, and presented us with a solution (Bellman, 1957, 1961; Bellman and Dreyfus 1962). The solution depends on a very powerful principle: the optimality principle. This states, "An optimal policy has the property that whatever the initial state and initial decision are, the remaining decisions must constitute an optimal policy with regard to the state resulting from the first decision." This means that, at each time, we compute the states resulting from all possible combinations of policies and levels, and select the optimal one. *Only* this one is used as the input datum for the next time interval computation. The computational implication of this principle is that, at each of the t times, instead of considering MN cases for each of the MN cases at the previous time, we only consider MN cases for the *optimal* case at the previous point in time. The impossible computing load of MN^t cases has become MNt cases, a far more reasonable number!

Matters such as these are dealt with in a new branch of mathematics called dynamic programing, which is one of a whole new group of mathematical disciplines included under the general heading of operations research. Here is the terrible point however: to my knowledge, no foresters, biologists, botanists, zoologists, epidemiologists, entomologists, fisheries biologists, range managers, or agronomists anywhere in the world are exposed to these subjects as part of their required university training program; yet these subjects, like FORTRAN, are obviously of enormous potential value in resource management, which is how a lot of these people earn a living. May I respectfully submit that this is a problem worthy of serious consideration by the academic community. Clearly, there is urgent need for a complete revitalization of teaching programs in resource management, so that relevant new trends are included in the curricula.

BIBLIOGRAPHY

Bellman, R.
  1957 *Dynamic Programming.* Princeton: Princeton University Press.
  1961 *Adaptive Control Processes.* Princeton: Princeton University Press.
Bellman, R., and S. E. Dreyfus
  1962 *Applied Dynamic Programming.* Princeton: Princeton University Press.
Belyea, R. M.
  1952 "Death and Deterioration of Balsam Fir Weakened by Spruce Budworm Defoliation in Ontario." *Journal of Forestry,* 50: 729–38.
Butler, L.
  1953 "The Nature of Cycles in Populations of Canadian Mammals." *Canadian Journal of Zoology,* 31: 242–62.
Clarke, R.
  1954 "Open Boat Whaling in the Azores: The History and Present Methods of a Relic Industry." *Discovery Reports,* 26: 283–354.
Cooper, L. H. N., and G. A. Steven
  1948 "An Experiment in Marine Fish Cultivation." *Nature,* 161: 631–33.
Creighton, C.
  1891 *A History of Epidemics in Britain from A.D. 664 to the Extinction of Plague.* Cambridge: The University Press.
Downes, J. A.
  1959 "The Gypsy Moth and Some Possibilities of the Control of Insects by Genetical Means." *Canadian Entomologist,* 91: 661–70.
Elliott, K. R.
  1960 "A History of Recent Infestations of the Spruce Budworm in Northern Ontario, and an Estimate of Resultant Timber Losses." *Forestry Chronicle,* 36: 61–82.
Hohman, E. P.
  1928 *The American Whaleman.* New York: Longmans Green.
Lansberg, H. H., L. L. Fischman, and J. L. Fisher
  1963 *Resources in America's Future: Patterns of Requirements and Availabilities, 1960–2000.* Baltimore: Johns Hopkins Press.

Link, V. B.
1955 *A History of Plague in the United States of America.* U. S. Public Health Monograph No. 26.

Maass, A. (ed.)
1962 *Design of Water-Resource Systems. New Techniques for Relating Economic Objectives, Engineering Analysis, and Governmental Planning.* Cambridge: Harvard University Press.

Morris, R. F. (ed.)
1963 *The Dynamics of Epidemic Spruce Budworm Populations.* Memoirs of the Entomological Society of Canada No. 31. Ottawa.

Roe, F. G.
1951 *The North American Buffalo.* Toronto: University of Toronto Press.

Royce, W. F., D. E. Bevan, J. A. Crutchfield, G. J. Paulik, and R. F. Fletcher
1963 *Salmon Gear Limitation in Northern Washington Waters.* University of Washington Publication in Fisheries, New Series, Vol. II, No. 1. Seattle: University of Washington.

Sette, O. E.
1943 "Biology of the Atlantic Mackerel (*Scomber scombus*) of North America." *U. S. Department of the Interior, Fish and Wildlife Service, Fishery Bulletin,* 50: 149–237.
1960 "The Long Term Historical Record of Meteorological, Oceanographic, and Biological Data." *California Cooperative Oceanic Fisheries Investigation Reports,* 7: 181–94.

Smith, R. W.
1959 "Status in Ontario of *Collyria calcitrator* (Crav.) (Hymenoptera: Ichneumonidae) and of *Pediobius beneficius* (Gahan.) (Hymenoptera: Eulophidae) as Parasites of the European Wheat Stem Sawfly, Cephus pygmaeus (L.) (Hymenoptera: Cephidae)." *Canadian Entomologist* 91: 697–700.

Townes, H.
1958 "Some Biological Characteristics of the Ichneumonidae (Hymenoptera) in Relation to Biological Control." *Journal of Economic Entomology,* 51: 650–52.

Watt, K. E. F.
1964 "The Use of Mathematics and Computers to Determine Optimal Strategy and Tactics for a Given Insect Pest Control Problem." *Canadian Entomologist,* 96: 202–20.

Wellington, W. G.
1954a "Atmospheric Circulation Processes and Insect Ecology." *Canadian Entomologist,* 86: 312–33.
1954b "Weather and Climate in Forest Entomology." *Meteorological Monographs,* 2 (8): 11–18.

14 CULTURAL INFLUENCES ON POPULATION: A COMPARISON OF TWO TUPÍ TRIBES

Charles Wagley

CONTACT WITH European civilization has had a varied effect upon the population trends of native societies. Frequently conquest warfare, slavery, bad labor conditions, disruption of aboriginal subsistence methods, and above all foreign disease have brought a rapid population decline which has led in many cases to the total disappearance of aboriginal groups as distinct ethnic units. In other instances, native groups have made an adjustment to the new circumstances. After an initial epoch of sharp decline in population, a few native groups have not only regained their former population level but actually increased in number several times fold. The depopulation of many Melanesian Islands, the decimation of the coastal Tupí speaking peoples of Brazil, and the rapid disintegration of the aboriginal groups of the Antilles are well known examples of sharp population decline following European contact from which the groups never recovered. The multiplication of the Navajo during the last century and the population growth of the Polynesian Island of Tikopia after European contact are examples of recovery and expansion (cf. Firth 1939:39–49).

In many cases, these differences in population trend following European contact may be explained in terms of the nature of contact with Europeans to which the different native groups have been subjected. Epidemics have varied in frequency and in intensity among native groups and the systematic exploitation of native peoples through slavery and other forms of enforced labor

Reprinted from *Revista do Museu Paulista,* new series, Vol. 5 (1951), pp. 95–104, by permission of the author and publisher.

has taken heavier toll upon native population in some areas than in others. On the other hand, introduced crops, domesticated animals, new instruments, and new techniques have sometimes raised the aboriginal subsistence level and made possible an expansion of population.

Yet, the causes of such different trends in population among native groups after European contact cannot always be sought in the contact situation alone. The variables which allowed one group to absorb the shock of new disease and other disrupting accompaniments of European contact and to revive, or which led to quasi—or total extinction of a people may also be found in the culture and the society of peoples concerned. Each culture has a population policy—an implicit or explicit set of cultural values relating to population size. The social structure of each society is closely inter-related with a specific population level. A modification of the external environment, such as that brought about by contact with Europeans, generally calls for change both in cultural values as well as in social structure. In addition to environment, technology, and other material factors, cultural values and social structure act also to determine population size and demographic trends in face of modified external circumstances. A rapid decrease in population due to new disease or an increase in population resulting from an increased food supply calls for adjustments in population policy (implicit or explicit) and in social structure. It is the purpose of the present paper to examine the relationship between these social and cultural factors and the population trends following European contact of two Tupí speaking tribes of Brazil.

The two Tupí speaking tribes in question are the Tenetehara of northeastern Brazil and the Tapirapé of central Brazil.[1] After more than 300 years of contact with Luso-Brazilians the Tenetehara in 1945 still numbered some 2000 people—not much, if at all, less than the aboriginal population. On the other hand, by 1947 the Tapirapé with less than forty years of sporadic and peaceful contact with Luso-Brazilians had been reduced to less than one hundred people, the remnant of an aboriginal population

---

[1] Basic descriptions of the Tapirapé and the Tenetehara have been published elsewhere: Wagley and Galvão 1948a, 1948b, and 1949; Baldus 1937, 1944–49, 1948b, 1949b, Ms. Only directly pertinent descriptive data are present in this paper.

which must have numbered more than one thousand. While the Tenetehara still maintained a functioning social system and continued as a distinct ethnic group, Tapirapé society was in 1947 almost totally disorganized and the Tapirapé as a distinct people were clearly on the road to extinction.[2]

A partial answer to this very different reaction to Luso-Brazilian contact may be found in the nature of the acculturation process which each has experienced. Although the first decades of Tenetehara relations with Europeans were marked by slave raids, massacres, and epidemics, the protection of the Jesuits during more than one century (1653–1759) seems to have given the Tenetehara time to make adjustments in their culture and society to changing external circumstances. The missionaries were able to prevent the movement of colonists into Tenetehara territory; and after the expulsion of the Jesuits in 1759, the increased importation of African slaves into Maranhão eased the pressure for Indian slaves. Close relations with the missionaries, and later with the civil authorities and the rural Luso-Brazilian population, presented the Tenetehara with new culture patterns, new attitudes which either replaced aboriginal elements or were incorporated in their culture as alternative patterns. The missionaries urged larger families in order to have numerous innocents to baptize. Warfare was prohibited in the area.[3] The Tenetehara learned that children might be useful in collecting babassu nuts for sale to

---

[2] Cf. Wagley (1940) and Baldus (1945 vol. 103, 1948b, 1949b), for discussion of Tapirapé depopulation and disorganization. Baldus (1948b: 137–38), who found the village called Tampiitáua inhabited by 130 individuals in 1935, and only 62 in 1947, mentions that during this lapse of time several inhabitants had emigrated to another Tapirapé village very far from Tampiitáua, but that their number seems to be lower than the number of those who came from there to Tampiitáua. According to information received by this author, the other village is smaller than Tampiitáua, so that in 1947 the whole tribe probably counted less than a hundred members. In the same year, shortly after Baldus' visit, the Tapirapé were attacked by Kayapó Indians and lost several individuals.

[3] There are no indications that the Tenetehara shared the warfare-cannibalism complex of the Tupinambá, but the lower reaches of the Mearim-Grajaú-Pindaré River system and the Island of Maranhão at its mouth were inhabited by Tupinambá groups (Métraux 1948:95ff.; see also Fernandes 1949).

Luso-Brazilians. Steel instruments and new plants (such as rice, bananas, lemons, etc.) made agriculture more productive. The sale of babassu nuts, copaiba oil, and other forest products brought the Tenetehara imported products. Although Tenetehara culture and society were modified, the aboriginal and the borrowed elements slowly combined to form a new culture and a new social system which at least met the minimum requirements for survival.

The Tapirapé, on the other hand, have had only intermittent contact with Luso-Brazilians. Since about 1911, the Tapirapé have had occasional contact with Luso-Brazilians. A few Tapirapé have visited Luso-Brazilian settlements and missionary stations on the Araguaya River and a few Luso-Brazilians have visited Tapirapé villages. Tapirapé contact with Luso-Brazilians has been limited to relatively short periods and to small groups of people. They have acquired a few axes, hoes, some salt, cloth, beads, and other material objects from their occasional visitors but, on the whole, their culture was little modified by borrowed patterns and elements from Luso-Brazilians. Yet the presence of Luso-Brazilians brought about a crucial modification in their environment. With the arrival of Luso-Brazilians in the area, the Tapirapé were subjected to a series of foreign diseases. If the memory of older Tapirapé informants may be trusted, foreign disease (common colds, measles, and smallpox) came at first via the neighboring Karajá sometime before their first meeting with Luso-Brazilians. Since about 1911 to 1914, however foreign disease acquired directly from Luso-Brazilians, has steadily decimated the Tapirapé. Unlike the Tenetehara, before the Tapirapé were presented with a broad segment of Luso-Brazilians culture, which might have provided them with alternative patterns and values with which they might have made adjustments to their new circumstances, they have been practically wiped out.

Still, the difference in population trends after Luso-Brazilian contact of these two tribes cannot be explained entirely in terms of the differences in the contact continuum. The first fifty years of contact between the Tenetehara and Europeans were more violent than anything the Tapirapé have experienced. In the early 17th century organized slave raiding parties penetrated into Tenetehara territory and armed forces such as the one led by Bento Maciel Parente in 1616 made war upon the Tenetehara.

Epidemics, which raged in the early 17th century among the Indian populations of northeast Brazil, certainly reached the Tenetehara. From time to time smallpox, measles, and other diseases have taken a heavy toll among these Indians. The impact of the dominant culture upon the Tenetehara was more intense than it has been upon the Tapirapé. In addition to differences in the nature of the contact continuum, factors inherent in the society and the culture of the two tribes were responsible for the reaction of these societies to Luso-Brazilian contact and for the population trends which followed. Since the Tenetehara and the Tapirapé have historically related cultures sharing many patterns and institutions common to most Tupí speaking tribes, a comparison of the two societies and cultures should allow us to determine the variables responsible for their contrasting reactions.

The subsistence methods of the tribes were in aboriginal times basically similar. Both were tropical forest horticulturalists depending upon hunting, fishing, and forest fruits to supplement their diet. For fishing, the Tenetehara had an advantage, since their villages were normally situated near rivers and streams while the Tapirapé villages were located inland many kilometers from the river. In hunting, the Tapirapé had the advantage of nearby open plains country where hunting was more productive than in the tropical forest. Neither tribe had a land problem: the nearest village of the Karajá, who were Tapirapé neighbors, was at least two hundred kilometers away and the Timbira neighbors of the Tenetehara were savanna people offering no competition for forest land. Both tribes during aboriginal times had sufficient territory to move their villages every five or six years when suitable garden sites near their villages had been used up by the slash-and-burn system of horticulture. The two tribes inhabited similar physical environments and they had approximately the same technological equipment to cope with it. Their technology and their subsistence methods must have limited the maximum population of any one village and there are indications that approximately two hundred people was the average village size for both groups. On the other hand, a lack of territory evidently did not enforce a limitation on the number of villages for the tribe. Yet while the Tapirapé tell of only five villages in aboriginal times many times that number are reported by early observers for the Tenetehara. Although specific data are not available, it seems that in aboriginal times Tapirapé population was relatively small and stable while the Tenetehara population was at least twice as large and probably expanding.

This difference in population level between the two tribes in aboriginal times was related to the population policies held by the two groups as well as to differences in social structure of the groups concerned. These cultural values relating to population level are explicit in attitudes toward family size and in positive actions to limit families. Among the Tenetehara infanticide is indicated only in the case of the birth of twins, since they are believed to be the result of sexual relations between the mother and a dangerous supernatural, and in the case of infants with certain supernaturally caused abnormalities. Since there is a low incidence of twins and since in several known cases "abnormal" children have been allowed to live, infanticide has had little or no effect upon Tenetehara population trends. The Tenetehara tell of one or two formulas thought to produce abortion. The long taboos imposed on both parents during the pregnancy of the mother and during the early infancy of the child are a source of irritation and discomfort which would seem to tend to discourage large families. But, in general, there is little planned effort among the Tenetehara to limit family size. Men seem proud of several children; women are eager to bear children and they will leave a husband whom they believe to be sterile.

In contrast, the Tapirapé value small families. They take specific steps to limit their families and have explicit ideas as to maximum family size. Not only do the Tapirapé bury twins at birth as do the Tenetehara (and for similar reasons) but they believe that a woman should not have more than three live children.[4] In addition, the three children of a woman should not be of the same sex. In other words, if a woman has two living daughters and her third child is also a girl, it is usually buried at birth. Similarly, if she has two male children and her third is a male, infanticide is in order. Furthermore, all men who have

---

[4] Baldus (1949 vol. 123, p. 55) was told the same regarding the limitation of number of children of the Tapirapé family, but the contrary in relation to twins. According to information given to him by these Indians, the Tapirapé appreciate twins and, therefore, husband and wife eat twin or double bananas, i.e., with two fruits in the same peel.

sexual relations with a woman during her pregnancy are considered fathers to her child. More than two co-fathers leads to complications. All co-fathers are expected to observe taboos on sexual relations and on the eating of certain meats during the pregnancy of the woman and the early infancy of the child. If there are three, four, or more co-fathers one of them is certain to break these taboos thus endangering the health of the infant; consequently the woman is urged to bury the child.[5]

On an overt level, the Tapirapé justify these checks on population by saying, "We do not want thin children" or "They would be hungry." They enlarge upon such statements by adding that it is difficult for a father to supply a large family with meat from hunting. In aboriginal times, manioc was plentiful and no one lacked the tubers with which to manufacture flour but meat was especially scarce during the rainy season when the forest is partially flooded and the paths to the savanna country are impassable. In addition, a complex set of food taboos make the job of supplying meat for a family more difficult. Children before adolescence are allowed to eat only specific meats and women are prohibited others. When a Tapirapé says, "I am hungry," he generally means by implication: "hungry for meat." Although empirical data are not available, it is my impression that meat is (and was in the past) just as scarce in Tenetehara villages, and during the rainy season fish are extremely difficult to catch. The Tenetehara, with roughly the same food supply as the Tapirapé, do not feel called upon to impose drastic limitations upon the family size. Population control among the Tapirapé seems not to result from a direct limitation imposed by food supply but from culturally derived values. In other words, although family limitation among the Tapirapé has a basis in subsistence, it does not derive from a minimum starvation situation. Family limitation seems to be related to a desire for a specific food, which the

---

[5] Genealogies indicated that these rules are adhered to almost without exception. In 1939, during my residence in a Tapirapé village, one woman hesitated in allowing her third male child to be buried. Less than a month after its birth, she appeared one day without the infant and announced that he had died of a cold. Another woman whose child had four fathers allowed the child to live only to have it die of an intestinal disorder. The villagers took a definite "I-told-you-so" attitude.

organism needs but which is also selected by Tapirapé culture as particularly desirable.

This population policy of the Tapirapé with its explicit concept of maximum family size and the use of infanticide to limit the number of children must have maintained Tapirapé population in aboriginal times on a stable level. Even then, the balance between a stable and a declining population must have been a delicate one. With an increase in the death-rate from new disease for which the people did not have an acquired immunity, this delicate equilibrium was thrown off balance. After Luso-Brazilian contact, the population declined rapidly. Tapirapé concepts of population limitation remained unchanged in face of modified circumstances and families were not large enough to replace the adult population. The less rigid population policy of the Tenetehara was conducive to a large population during aboriginal times and it made the Tenetehara less vulnerable than the Tapirapé to modifications in the external environment. Without doubt numerous Tenetehara died from new diseases, from war, and from slavery after contact with Luso-Brazilians, but their desire for large families must have allowed them to replace their population in at least sufficient numbers to survive until they were able to adjust to the new circumstances.

Secondly, differences in social structure between the two tribes were also important in determining aboriginal population size as well as population trends after Luso-Brazilian contact. An extended family based upon at least temporary matrilocal residence and a widely extended bilateral kin group were basic social groupings of both the Tapirapé and the Tenetehara in aboriginal times. Tenetehara social structure was in fact limited to the extended family and the bilateral kin group. The Tapirapé, on the other hand, also had two other sets of social groups which were lacking in Tenetehara society. First, there were patrilineal ceremonial moieties limited to men. Each moiety was divided into three age-grades—boys, young men or warriors, and older men. Second, both men and women among the Tapirapé belonged to one of eight "Feast Groups" which were non-exogamous. Membership in these "Feast Groups" was patrilineal for men and matrilineal for women, although these rules were often modified by the personal desires of a parent. Both Tapirapé men's moieties and age grades and the "Feast Groups" were basic to all ceremonials and important in economic production and distribution. The masked dances with impersonation of forest spirits performed by the men during the dry season were a function of the men's moieties. The "Feast Groups" met at intervals during the dry seasons at their traditional stations in the central plaza for ceremonial meals. At such times, as Herbert Baldus (1937:88ff.) has shown, these "Feast Groups" functioned as a mechanism for food distribution in a season when more food was available than a family would normally consume. The "Feast Groups" sometimes formed to collect honey and to hunt. The age grades of the men's moieties also frequently acted together economically; they organized work parties for clearing of large garden sites and they went out on large cooperative hunts after herds of wild pigs.

In aboriginal Tapirapé society ceremonial life and many important cooperative subsistence activities were based upon this balanced set of associations. A Tapirapé village in order to assure adequate representation in the various age grades of the men's moieties as well as in the "Feast Groups" by necessity had to consist of about 200 people or more. A small village of fifty to a hundred people, for example, would not have provided sufficient numbers of males of the proper ages to allow the age graded moieties to carry out their ceremonials nor to organize their cooperative subsistence activities. Tapirapé village organization was therefore not conducive to a process of "splitting off" of groups from one village to form another. The size of Tapirapé villages was limited by their technological equipment within their tropical forest environment, yet the social structure made the formation of numerous small villages difficult. In contrast, the less formalized social structure of the Tenetehara allowed for villages of varying size within the limits of their ecological adjustment. Extended family groups easily might break off from a larger village to form a new settlement fully able to carry out the cooperative economic activities and even ceremonials of the society. This process is constantly occurring in contemporary Tenetehara society. When tensions arise between extended families, one group simply splits off from the parent village to join another or to form a separate village without serious effects on the ceremonial or economic system. Tenetehara social structure offered a favorable condition for an expanding population.

Tapirapé social structure seems also to have been more vulnerable to disorganization in face of a rapid change in population size. Rapid depopulation after Luso-Brazilian contact among the Tapirapé seriously affected the normal functioning of their highly segmented and balanced social structure. By 1940, the lack of men had thrown the system of reciprocal and competitive activities of the men's age-graded moieties out of balance. There were not enough men of the "older" age-grade of either moiety nor of the young men "warrior" age-grade of one moiety to form functioning units to reciprocate in cooperative garden clearing and to participate in group hunts. Several of the "Feast Groups" had been disbanded for lack of numbers. Ceremonials in 1940 had not been abandoned but they were performed in an attenuated and disheartened manner. There was little motivation to accumulate the meat, the forest fruits, and the garden products which important ceremonials require among the Tapirapé.

Ceremonials and cooperative economic activities in Tenetehara society are organized by extended family and kin groups. Lack of numbers, of course, creates difficulties in carrying out ceremonials and in organizing economic activities but it does not have the effect of disorganizing the society. Cooperation of large extended families in gardening and in collecting babassu nuts and copaiba oil is still the general pattern among the Tenetehara. Tenetehara social structure was malleable to change. Adjustment to new circumstances after Luso-Brazilian contact must have been easier for the Tenetehara than for the Tapirapé.

This brief comparison of the cultural values and of aspects of social structure of the Tenetehara and of the Tapirapé in terms of their effect upon population size and on population trends after Luso-Brazilian contact suggests several general hypotheses. First, the available information concerning the population size of these two tribes in aboriginal times indicates that the Tenetehara were much more numerous than the Tapirapé. Yet both tribes were tropical forest peoples with roughly similar technological equipment. It seems to the writer that this difference in population size between the two tribes was functionally related to ideological values and to social structure and not to differences in technology and environment. In other words, such differences in population can hardly be interpreted strictly in Malthusian terms. While population potentials are certainly limited by food supply, the level of technology, the application of medical knowledge, and other material factors, social institutions and culturally derived values are influential in determining trends in population size within the limits set by such "natural" factors.

Second, the social structure and the cultural values of any society are functionally related to a given population level. With change in population size, both the cultural values regarding population size and social structure must be adjusted. The Tapirapé concept of family size remained unchanged in face of modified conditions (i.e., higher death-rate caused by foreign disease) with the result that the adult population was no longer replaced by births. A rapidly declining population disrupted Tapirapé socio-ceremonial organization and affected the internal system of production and distribution. The Tenetehara with a more malleable social structure than that of the Tapirapé were able to survive the initial impact of Luso-Brazilian contact until the protection of the Jesuits allowed them to make necessary adjustments to the new circumstances.

Finally, this comparison between the Tapirapé and the Tenetehara calls to mind other primitive societies whose social structure must have been functionally related to population level and to demographic trends in face of European civilization. In Brazil, the Ramkokamekra (Eastern Timbira) with their complex moiety system and the Apinayé with their *kiye* marriage classes, to mention only two examples, had social systems comparable to that of the Tapirapé. Such social structures depended upon a balanced representation of population in each of the numerous social units. A sudden decline of population might easily throw such highly segmented societies out of balance, so to speak. Without sufficient representation in one or more of these social units, reciprocal socio-ceremonial affairs become impossible or may be carried out in a highly attenuated manner. Again, the social structure of the Karajá of the Araguaya River is based essentially upon extended family and kinship ties and lacks the highly segmented social units which cross cut villages and even family groups. Like that of the Tenetehara, Karajá social structure would seem to be less vulnerable to change in population size and more conducive to population growth. In addition to technological equipment and subsistence methods, social structure and cultural values also influence strongly the final adjustment of each society to its environment. Differences in social structure and of value systems between societies must be taken into account in studies of population size and of population trends in any natural area, such as the tropical forest of South America.

BIBLIOGRAPHY

Baldus, H.
1937 *Ensaios de Etnologia Brasileira.* São Paulo: Companhia Editora Nacional.
1944–49 "Os Tapirapé, tribo tupi no Brasil Central." *Revista do Arquivo Municipal,* 96–105, 107–24, 127. São Paulo.
1948b "Tribos da bacia do Araguaia e o Servico de Protecão aos Indios." *Revista do Museu Paulista,* 137–68. São Paulo.
1949b "Akkulturation im Araguaya-Gebiet." *Anthropos,* 41–44: 889–91.
1952 "Caracterização da cultura tapirapé," in Sol Tax (ed.), *Indian Tribes of Aboriginal America: Selected Papers of the 29th International Congress of Americanists.* Chicago: University of Chicago Press.
Fernandes, F.
1949 "A análise funcionalista da guerra: possibilidade de aplicacão à sociedade tupinambá." *Revista do Museu Paulista,* n.s., 3: 7–128. São Paulo.
Firth, Raymond
1939 *A Primitive Polynesian Economy.* London: Routledge.
Métraux, A.
1948 "The Tupinamba," in J. Steward (ed.), *Handbook of South American Indians,* Vol. 3. Bureau of American Ethology Bulletin, No. 143. Washington: U. S. Govt. Printing Office.
Wagley, Charles
1940 "The Effects of Depopulation upon Social Organization as Illustrated by the Tapirapé Indians." *Transactions of the New York Academy of Sciences,* 2nd ser., 3(1): 12–16. New York.
1943 *Tapirapé Shamanism.* Boletim do Museu Nacional, Antropologia, No. 3. Rio de Janeiro.
Wagley, Charles, and Galvão, Eduardo
1948a "The Tapirapé," in J. Steward (ed.), *Handbook of South American Indians,* Vol. 3. Bureau of American Ethnology Bulletin, No. 143. Washington: U. S. Govt. Printing Office.
1948b "The Tenetehara," ibidem.
1949 *The Tenetehara Indians of Brazil, a Culture in Transition.* New York: Columbia University Press.

Part II | ORIGINS AND DEVELOPMENT

15 THE ECOLOGY OF EARLY FOOD
PRODUCTION IN MESOPOTAMIA

Kent V. Flannery

G REATER MESOPOTAMIA—broadly defined here as the whole
area drained by the tributaries of the Shatt-al-Arab—has
long been the scene of popular interest and scholarly research.
In recent years attention has been drawn to the fact that this was
one of the few areas in the world where agriculture and animal
husbandry seem to have arisen autonomously. A number of
excellent cultural-historical reconstructions of the way food production began in the Near East are already available (Braidwood and Howe 1962; Perrot 1962), but most of these reconstructions do not deal directly with some of the ecological
questions most commonly asked by the interested nonspecialist.
This article examines some of those questions.

THE ENVIRONMENT

From the standpoint of agriculture and grazing potential, the
area under consideration includes four main environmental
zones: the alluvial plain of Mesopotamia proper, the steppe-
land of Assyria, the woodland belt of the Zagros Mountains, and
the edge of the high central plateau of Iran (see Figs. 1 and
2). The first three of these zones have already been described by
Hatt (1959); I have added the high plateau, although it is not
actually drained by the Shatt-al-Arab system, because its mineral
resources figured prominently in the early village period.

Reprinted from *Science,* Vol. 147 (1965), pp. 1247–56 (copyright 1965
by the American Association for the Advancement of Science) by permission of the author and publisher.

1) *The central plateau of Iran.* Central Iran is an interior drainage basin at altitudes of 900 to 1500 meters, with annual rainfall as low as 100 to 230 millimeters. The basin is filled with sierozem and desert soils, overlain in places by shallow brackish lakes surrounded by salt-crusted flatland. Rugged mountains jut unexpectedly from the plain, some of them ore-bearing; there are veins of copper just east of the prehistoric site of Tepe Sialk, and one of the world's major turquoise sources lies in the northeast corner of the plateau near Meshed. Both turquoise and copper were traded as far away as the Assyrian steppe zone by 6500 B.C. (Hole et al. 1965).

Herds of gazelle (*Gazella subgutturosa*) and wild ass (*Equus hemionus*) would have been available to hunters in the area, but without irrigation the high plateau is very marginal agricultural land; the only source of hope for the early farmer would have been the alluvial aprons of mountain soil produced where streams break through the Zagros to enter the salt lake basins. Despite the uncertain rainfall, some of these "oasis" locations appear to have been permanently settled by 5500 B.C., especially those near copper sources.

2) *The oak-pistachio woodland belt.* The Zagros Mountains break away from the eastern edge of the high plateau and descend in tiers toward the Tigris-Euphrates basin. In places the mountains form parallel ridges which are separated by long, narrow, synclinal or anticlinal valleys, frequently poor in surface water; in other areas there are irregular mountain masses bordering wide flat valleys. Acting as aquifers, these porous mountain masses may trap tremendous quantities of winter snow or rain and release it through springs, which in turn feed permanent poplar-bordered streams. At elevations of 600 to 1350 meters there are alluvial valleys of chernozem, chestnut, brown, or reddish-brown soils, with alpine meadows scattered through the surrounding peaks. Summers are warm and dry, winters cool and wet; depending on altitude and topography, the annual rainfall varies from 250 to 1000 millimeters, and hillsides have varying densities of oak, maple, juniper, hawthorn, pistachio, and wild pear. On well-watered slopes grow hard-grained annual grasses like wild emmer wheat (*Triticum dicoccoides*), barley (*Hordeum spontaneum*), and oats (*Avena fatua*).

Much of the area is too rugged for large-scale agriculture, but

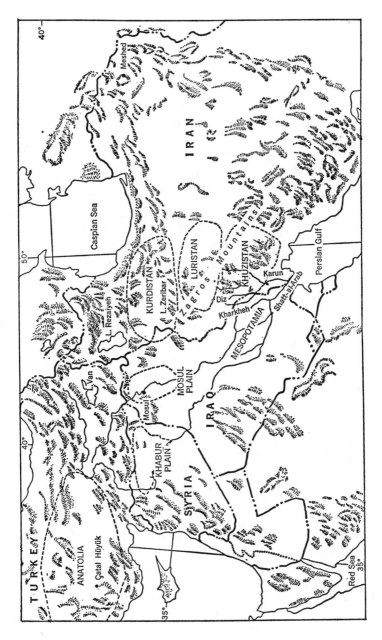

Figure 1   Map of Greater Mesopotamia and adjacent areas today

even the narrower and drier valleys have been used for sheep or goat grazing since at least 8500 B.C.; broad valleys with annual rainfall in excess of 300 millimeters have been farmed for at least the same length of time.

3) *The Assyrian steppe.* The Zagros Mountains fall away through a series of foothills and eventually level off onto a steppe region of great natural winter grassland at elevations of 150 to 300 meters; these plains have reddish-brown or brown prairie soils of high fertility. Here the mountain streams have collected into larger rivers like the Tigris, Kharkheh, Diz, and Karun, which flow into the area through erosional valleys and have wide, farmable floodplains. Hot and dry in the summer, the Assyrian steppe is transformed by 250 to 380 millimeters of winter rain into meadows of Bermuda grass, canary grass, and wild narcissus. Herds of gazelle, wild ass, and wild cattle once roamed the plain, and the rivers had carp and catfish. The Assyrian steppe is oil country, and one of its most widely traded commodities in prehistoric time was bitumen or natural asphalt, used for cementing flint tools into their handles.

Some parts of the steppe, too salty for effective agriculture, are used for winter grazing. Other areas are real breadbaskets for winter wheat (like the upper Khabur plain; the area near Mosul, Iraq; or the Khuzistan plain of southwest Iran), and the density of prehistoric villages in these regions is staggering. Adams' comments (1962) on northern Khuzistan—that the adequate rainfall, underlying gravels, and consequent good drainage in this zone facilitated the crucial transition from dry farming to irrigation—may apply to other favored parts of the steppes.

4) *Southern Mesopotamia.* Below 150 meters the Assyrian steppe gives way to the lower drainage of the Tigris, Euphrates, and Karun, as they flow together and empty into the Persian Gulf. Here the annual rainfall is under 250 millimeters (an amount usually inadequate for dry farming) and the grassland is replaced by two kinds of biotopes: alluvial desert and blowing sand dunes on higher ground, and reed-bordered swamps in the low-lying areas. The delta area is a subsiding geosyncline, slowly settling and filling with river alluvium, across which the big rivers run between their own natural levees, flooding and changing courses periodically (Lees and Falcon 1952). Contrary to what was once believed, the area has never been under the waters of the Persian Gulf (at least not since the Pliocene), and in pre-

historic times it must have looked much as it does today. It was in this environmental zone that urban life, civilization, and writing began, about 3000 B.C. When permanent settlement began here is undetermined, but villages dating back to 5500 B.C. are known even in the bleak area west of the Euphrates. Surely these villages must have followed the old swamps and watercourses, beyond which agriculture would have been impossible and grazing difficult.

THE LOCAL CLIMATIC SEQUENCE

The possibility that the environment in the Near East might have been different during the beginnings of agriculture has intrigued archeologists for generations. The few prehistoric pollen

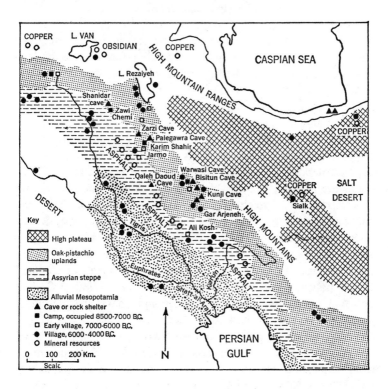

Figure 2 Map of Greater Mesopotamia, showing environmental zones, mineral resources, and archeological sites. Only sites mentioned in the text are labeled

sequences we have suggest that, although some climatic fluctuations did occur, they were not on a scale capable of creating or destroying the complex of plants and animals that were eventually domesticated. The facts we have are too few to permit us to say dogmatically that climatic change played *no* role, but it appears that the problem is cultural rather than climatic; the inescapable conclusion is that agriculture began in an area where, then as now, only about 10 percent of the land surface is suitable for dry farming (Cressey 1960:158–60).

One pollen sequence comes from Lake Zeribar in the wooded mountains of western Iran, at an altitude of about 1200 meters. Studies by van Zeist and Wright (1963) show that during the late Pleistocene the area was steppe, characterized by the sagebrush-like *Artemisia,* which implies a cool dry climate. About 11,000 B.C., at the end of the Pleistocene, the area became warmer and the vegetation made the transition to savanna, with scattered oaks and pistachios. The savanna thickened to oak forest about 3500 B.C., either through increased precipitation or through lowered temperature. Cereal-type pollen (possibly wild wheat and barley?) is present throughout the entire sequence, so climatic fluctuation would seem not to have been a determining factor in the beginning of agriculture there.

Six hundred meters lower, in the Zagros Mountains of Iraq, a slightly conflicting pollen story is available from human occupational debris in Shanidar Cave. More striking climatic fluctuations are implied, one of which Solecki (1963) interprets as the "shock stimulus" which triggered the beginnings of food production. Actually, however, the late-Pleistocene to early-Recent pollen sequence from Shanidar is not in much conflict with that from Lake Zeribar: at about 10,000 B.C. a "relatively cool climate" changed to "a warmer one similar to the present climate." Cereal pollen is known at least as early as 14,000 B.C., and potential animal domesticates (sheep and goat) are present in the cave debris even at 40,000 B.C.

Neither of these pollen sequences supports the age-old myth that the Near East was once lush and well watered, then suffered from desiccation. Nor do any of the inferred climatic fluctuations imply the sudden, overnight appearance of wheat, barley, sheep, or goats. I do not feel qualified to evaluate the "shock stimulus" theory, but I suspect that, although drastic climatic change explains why certain plants and animals become extinct, it does not explain how or why cultures change.

PRE-AGRICULTURAL SUBSISTENCE PATTERN

Scattered caves, rock shelters, and open-air sites have given us only hints of how man lived in this part of the world before domestication of plants and animals. All appearances are that his way of life conformed to a flexible, "broad-spectrum" collecting pattern, keyed to the seasonal aspects of the wild resources of each environmental zone, with perhaps a certain amount of seasonal migration from zone to zone. The less mobile members of society appear to have collected such resources as snails, turtles, freshwater clams and crabs, and the seeds of wild annuals and perennials, while more mobile members pursued wild ungulates by special techniques, according to the species involved. Although cave remains include fish, birds, and small mammals, the bulk of the meat diet—often more than 90 percent (see, for example, Perkins 1964)—came from ungulates, like the wild sheep, goat, ox, pig, wild ass, gazelle, and deer. Note that the first four were early domesticates.

Hunting patterns were influenced by the topography of the region. In the steep, rugged rockslide area around Shanidar Cave, wild goat (*Capra hircus*) was the animal most frequently taken. The goat, a resident of the limestone crags, is difficult to hunt by means of drives; it is best pursued by small groups of agile men who know their country well and are equipped with light projectiles. Rock-shelters or caves overlooking broad, flat valleys are usually rich in the bones of the wild ass, a plains-dwelling animal which could best have been hunted by drives or surrounds, then dispatched with a larger weapon, like a thrusting spear. Gazelles and hares are also creatures of the flat valley, while the wild sheep of the Near East (*Ovis orientalis*) frequent rolling, round-top hills and are hunted today by ambush in the brushy stream-canyons where they hide during the noon hours. Some of the smaller rock-shelters excavated in the Zagros Mountains seem to have been stations or overlooks used mainly for hunting or butchering a single species of ungulate, or two species at most.[1]

In recent years the oak-pistachio uplands, in the 400- to 1000-millimeter rainfall belt at altitudes of 450 to 900 meters, have been singled out as an "optimum" zone which includes all the potential domesticates (Braidwood, Howe, et al. 1960). Actually, topography is a much more important ecological factor for wild sheep and goats than either altitude or rainfall; sheep range down to sea level along the Caspian Sea, and up to 2700 meters in the Zagros Mountains, if rolling mountain meadows are available. Goats reach sea level on the foothills flanking the Persian Gulf, and are as much at home on the last rugged sandstone hills separating southwest Iran from southern Mesopotamia (180 meters above sea level) as they are on the 3000-meter crags of the northern Zagros. Pigs range over a wide area, from sea level to timberline, and if we knew more about the ecological requirements of wild cattle we might find their range equally broad.[2] The crucial factor for hunters of wild ungulates, or early herders of semiwild ungulates, would have been the ability to move from upland to lowland as seasonal pasture was available, a pattern known as "transhumance."

Let me give one example. Khuzistan, the Iranian arm of the Assyrian steppe, is lush winter grassland from December to April while many of the mountains to the east are covered with snow. Through late spring and summer the steppe becomes blisteringly hot and dry, while melting snow on the mountains gives rise to good spring and summer grassland. The Persian herder classifies the steppe as *quishlaq* (winter pasture) and the mountains as

---

[1] The foregoing discussion is based in part on published studies of faunas from the sites of Shanidar Cave and Zawi Chemi (Perkins 1964), Zarzi Cave, and Palegawra Cave, all in Iraq (for a summary, see Braidwood, Howe, et al. 1960:169–70), and Bisitun Cave in Iran (see Coon 1951). It is based, also, on personal examination of unpublished faunal collections from Karim Shahir in Iraq (Braidwood, Howe, et al. 1960) and from the following Iranian sites: Qaleh Daoud Cave (see Hole 1962), Warwasi Rock Shelter (see Braidwood and Howe 1962:135) and Kunji Cave and Gar Arjeneh Rock Shelter (F. Hole and K. Flannery, unpublished data).

[2] For a good summary of the differences in ecology between sheep and goat, see Perkins 1959. Perkins explains the skeletal differences, especially differences in metapodial length, which reflect the somewhat different habitats occupied by *Ovis* and *Capra*.

yehlaq (summer pasture), and he moves his herd from one to the other as the season demands. Prehistoric hunters may have followed game over the same route; and as for prehistoric herders, Adams (1962) reminds us: "It is, in fact, erroneous to consider the upper plains as a zone of occupance distinct from the surrounding uplands. Both together constitute a single natural ecosystem, whose seasonal alternation of resources provides as strong an inducement to migratory stockbreeding as to intensive, settled agriculture."

The wild plants of southwestern Asia have much the same seasonal aspect. MacNeish's work (1964) in the New World has shown that a long period of intensive plant collecting preceded agriculture there; archeologists have long assumed that this was the case in the Near East, but preserved plant remains were not available to tell us which specific plants were used in the preagricultural era. New light was thrown on the problem in 1963 by a collection of some 10,000 carbonized seeds from basal levels at the site of Ali Kosh in lowland southwestern Iran.[3] The area, a part of the Assyrian steppe, lies outside the range of wild wheat and barley, but locally available plants were intensively collected; the most common were wild alfalfa (*Medicago*) and the tiny-seeded wild legumes *Astragalus* and *Trigonella,* as well as fruits like the wild caper (*Capparis*), used today mainly as a condiment. These data indicate that intensive plant collecting may have been the pattern everywhere in southwest Asia, not merely at the altitude where wild wheat grows best. Moreover, the fact that *Astragalus* and *Trigonella* occur in the mountains as well as the lowlands suggests that prehistoric collectors could have harvested one crop on the Assyrian steppe in March, moved up to 600 meters for a harvest in April or May, and arrived at 1500 meters for another harvest in June or July. Somewhere between 600 and 1200 meters these migrant collectors could have harvested the seeds of the annual grasses ancestral to domestic wheat, barley, and oats. These cereals, which are dependent on annual rainfall of 400 to 750 millimeters, do not range down to the Assyrian steppe today, although they are available over a surprisingly wide area; according to

---

[3] The plants were identified by Dr. Hans Helbaek of the Danish National Museum (see Hole et al. 1965:106).

Helbaek (1960a), wild barley "grows in the mountain forest, on the coastal plain, in the shade of rock outcrops in semidesert areas, and as a weed in the fields of every conceivable cultivated crop" from Morocco to Turkestan.

Other plants useful to the collector—and eventually, in some cases, to the primitive cultivator—were ryegrass (*Lolium*), *Aegilops* grass, wild flax (*Linum bienne*), and large-seeded wild legumes like lentil, vetch, vetchling, chick pea, and *Prosopis* (a relative of mesquite). The lowlands had dates; the foothills had acorns, almonds, and pistachios; and the northern mountains had grapes, apples, and pears.

Most of the important species occurred in more than one zone, and their months of availability were slightly different at different altitudes—key factors from the standpoint of human ecology. An incredibly varied fare was available to the hunter-collector who knew which plants and animals were available in each season in each environmental zone; which niche or "microenvironment" the species was concentrated in, such as hillside, cliff, or stream plain; which species could be stored best, and which it was most practical to hunt or collect. From 40,000 to 10,000 B.C., man worked out a pattern for exploiting the natural resources of this part of the world, and I suspect that this pre-agricultural pattern had more to do with the beginning of food production than any climatic "shock stimulus."

BEGINNINGS OF FOOD PRODUCTION

Leslie White (1959:283–84) reminds us that "we are not to think of the origin of agriculture as due to the chance discovery that seeds thrown away from a meal subsequently sprouted. Mankind knew all this and more for tens of thousands of years before cultivation of plants began." The cultivation of plants required no new facts or knowledge, but was simply a new kind of relationship between man and the plants with which he was most familiar.

One striking aspect of the late pre-agricultural pattern in the Greater Mesopotamian area as the trading of obsidian from its source in central and eastern Turkey to cave sites in the central Zagros, such as Zarzi and Shanidar (Braidwood, Howe, et al. 1960; Solecki 1963). Natural asphalt was traded in the opposite direction, up from the tar pits of the Assyrian steppe to camp-sites in the mountains, wherever flints had to be hafted. By 7000 B.C., handfuls of emmer wheat from the oak-pistachio belt had reached the lowland steppe of Khuzistan (Hole et al. 1965). Typical of the prehistoric Near Easterner was this penchant for moving commodities from niche to niche within environmental zones, and even from zone to zone.

It has been argued that the last millennia of the pre-agricultural era were a time of "settling in" to one's area, of increasing intensification and regionalization of the exploitation of natural resources (Braidwood, Howe, et al. 1960:180). This is indeed reflected in the flint tools, but such "regional specialization" may not be the essential trend which led to food production. From the standpoint of human ecology, the single most important factor may have been the establishment of the above-mentioned pattern of interchange of resources between groups exploiting contrasting environmental situations—a kind of primitive redistribution system. It was this pattern that set the stage for the removal of certain key species of edible grasses from the niches in which they were indigenous, and their transferral to niches to which they were foreign.

With the wisdom of hindsight we can see that, when the first seeds had been planted, the trend from "food collecting" to "food producing" was under way. But from an ecological standpoint the important point is not that man *planted* wheat but that he (i) moved it to niches to which it was not adapted, (ii) removed certain pressures of natural selection, which allowed more deviants from the normal phenotype to survive, and (iii) eventually se-lected for characters not beneficial under conditions of natural selection.

All that the "settling in" process did for the prehistoric collector was to teach him that wild wheat grew from seeds that fell to the ground in July, sprouted on the mountain talus in February, and would be available to him in usable form if he arrived for a harvest in May. His access to those mature seeds put him in a good position to bargain with the goat-hunters in the mountain meadow above him. He may have viewed the first planting of seeds merely as the transfer of a useful wild grass from a niche that was hard to reach—like the talus below a limestone cliff—to an accessible niche, like the disturbed soil around his camp on a nearby stream terrace. Happily for man, wild wheat and barley both grow well on disturbed soils; they will sprout on the back-dirt pile of an archeological excavation, and they probably did equally well on the midden outside a prehistoric camp (Helbaek 1960a). It is obvious from the rapid spread of agriculture in the Mesopotamian area that they grew as readily on the midden outside the forager's winter camp at 180 meters as they did in his summer camp at 900 meters, in the "optimum" zone.

Viewed in these terms the advent of cultivation may have been a rather undramatic event, and the concept of "incipient cultivation" (Braidwood, Howe, et al. 1960) becomes rather hard to define. Was it a fumbling attempt at cultivation, or only the intensification of an already existent system of interregional exchange?

BIOLOGICAL OBSTACLES TO
EARLY FOOD PRODUCTION

The transfer of species from habitat to habitat made the products of all zones available to all people; but it was a process not without difficulty, since some of the plant and animal species involved had not yet developed the most tractable or productive phenotypes, from man's point of view.

Some of the biological obstacles faced by early agriculturalists were as follows.

1) The difficulty of harvesting wild, brittle-rachis grains. One adaptive mechanism for seed dispersal in wild wheat and barley is a brittle rachis or axis which holds the seeds together in the mature head of grain. When a dry, ripe head of wild barley is struck by a twig or a gust of wind, the rachis disintegrates and the seeds are spread far and wide.[4] The disadvantages of this mechanism for the prehistoric collector are obvious: the slightest tug on the stem of the plant or the slightest blow with a flint sickle might send the seeds scattering in every direction.

2) The difficulty of removing the grain from its husk. Even after a successful harvest, the prehistoric collector's troubles were

---

[4] This, and all subsequent discussion of the ecology of the early cereals, is based on personal communications from Hans Helbaek or on Dr. Helbaek's articles (1960a, 1960b, 1963).

not over. Primitive grains like emmer or einkorn wheat have a tough husk, or glume, which holds each kernel in a stubborn grip long after the brittle rachis has disintegrated. Even vigorous threshing will usually not release these primitive grains from the glume so that they can be eaten.

3) The difficulty of farming in the niche to which the grain was adapted. Both wild wheat and barley are grasses of hillsides and slopes, and they usually do not occur on the flat stream floodplains, where it would have been most convenient for prehistoric man to farm. The deep alluvial soils in the valley centers, prime areas from an agricultural standpoint, were already occupied by competing grasses and wild legumes.

Research on archeological grain remains by Danish botanist Hans Helbaek has shown us some of the ways in which early farmers either consciously or unconsciously overcame these three obstacles.

1) Selection for tough-rachis grains. Within the gene pool of wild wheat and barley were variants whose rachis was tough enough so that it did not shatter on contact. Normally these variants would have left few descendents, because of the inadequacy of their seed-dispersal mechanism. When man harvested with sickles or flails, however, he automatically selected *for* the tough-rachis grains because their heads stayed intact despite the rough treatment of the harvest. When seeds from the harvest were planted, the next generation of plants contained an abnormally high proportion of tough-rachis individuals, and each successive generation reinforced the trend.

2) The development of techniques for removing the seeds from their glumes. Sometimes before 7000 B.C. man discovered that by roasting the grain he had collected he could render the glumes so dry and brittle that they could be crushed by abrasion; roasting, moreover, killed the wheat or barley germ so that it would not sprout, and the grain could be stored even through the winter rainy season. Many of the preceramic villages excavated throughout the Near East contain clay ovens appropriate for roasting grain in this manner, and nearly all seem to have stone grinding slabs of one kind or another on which the dry grain could be abraded out of its glume. Further grinding resulted in "groats," or coarse grits of grain which could be

cooked up into a mush or gruel. (By and large, the tough-glumed primitive grains were unsuitable for bread-making.)

3) Actual genetic change in the grain species themselves, resulting in new strains. Because early cultivated grain was somewhat shielded by man from the natural selection pressures to which uncultivated grain was subjected, the chance that random mutants would survive was much greater. One of the first mutations that occurred, apparently, was a change from the standard adhering-glume kernel to a "naked" kernel which could be easily freed by

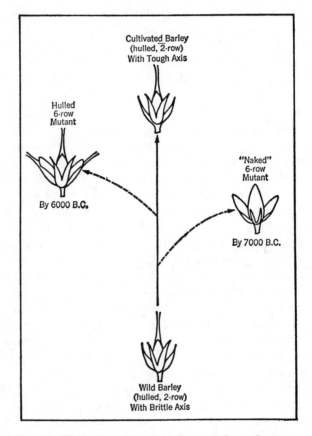

Figure 3 Simplified diagrams of barley spikelets, showing some of the changes which took place after domestication. Data courtesy of Helbaek (see text)

threshing. According to Stubbe (1959), a single gene controls the difference between "hulled" and "naked" barley, and when a mutation took place at that locus, sometime before 7000 B.C., free-threshing barley was born. A second genetic change was that which transformed standard wild barley (*Hordeum spontaneum*), which has only two fertile kernel rows, into mutant barley with six fertile rows (*Hordeum hexastichum*). Helbaek, who has actually produced the six-row mutant in his laboratory by subjecting wild two-row barley to x-rays (Helbaek 1960b), feels that ecological factors probably determined the early distribution of these two strains: two-row barley is adapted to the fairly late (April and May) rainfall of the cool Zagros Mountain uplands, while mutant six-row barley may be more successfully adapted to much drier spring weather and the irrigation farming of the Mesopotamian plain (Helbaek 1960a). Archeological remains tend to support this. The two-row form seems to be the only one known so far from the highlands before 5000 B.C., while six-row barley is known from lowland Khuzistan by 6000 B.C.; the two-row strain does not seem to have caught on in the lowlands, possibly because it was poorly adapted to the climate there. Present data, in fact, suggest that although the cool uplands probably contributed the original ancestor (two-row hulled barley) it may have been the lowland ecology which stabilized the important "naked" and "six-row" strains (see Fig. 3).

Another important early genetic change was polyploidy, an actual increase in the chromosome number, which produced new strains of wheat. Wild emmer wheat (*Triticum dicoccoides*) is tetraploid—that is, it contains 4×7 chromosomes and has tough glumes enclosing the kernels. A native annual grass of well-watered mountains, it prefers the 400- to 750-millimeter rainfall zone, from Palestine and Syria to the Zagros Mountains of Iran and Iraq. By 6000 B.C., however, on the Anatolian plateau of central Turkey, a mutant had been produced which was free-threshing: this was hexaploid wheat (*Triticum aestivum*), with 6×7 chromosomes. Such polyploid strains, together with irrigation, were instrumental in the spread of free-threshing wheat throughout southwest Asia.

Mutations and changes in gene frequency also played a role in the establishment of races of domestic animals, and once again there were biological obstacles to be overcome by early herders.

Some of the adaptive and nonadaptive changes which took place were as follows.

1) A change in the sex and age ratios within the captive population. If early herds of domesticated sheep or goats were small, as we assume they were, how did the animals avoid being eaten during the winter and survive until the spring lambing season? Work by Charles A. Reed (1960) and Dexter Perkins (1964) on archeological bones from early villages in Kurdistan suggests that some kind of conservation may have been practiced. Perkins notes that the proportion of immature sheep relative to adult sheep at Zawi Chemi, Iraq, was far higher than that in any normal wild herd, an observation from which he infers domestication (see also Dyson 1953). Evidently the young animals were eaten, while the older breeding stock was saved. The practice was much the same at the village of Jarmo, where Reed noted a high proportion of butchered young males, as if the females were being held back for breeding. Such practices would have resulted in an abnormally high proportion of adult females in the herd, and consequently in milk surpluses in late winter and early spring. Although wild sheep and goats produce very little milk in comparison to today's domestic breeds, such seasonal surpluses may eventually have been exploited by early herders. Today, milk, yogurt, and cheese are part of the whole trading complex of southwest Asian pastoralists.

2) Changes leading to wool production. Wild sheep (*Ovis orientalis*) have a coat like a deer or gazelle, and are no woolier than the latter. Microscopic examination of their skin reveals two kinds of follicles: "primaries," or hair follicles which produce the visible coat, and "secondaries," which produce the hidden, wooly underfur. In the skin of wild *Ovis* the secondary follicles lie intermingled with the primaries in groups of three to five. After domestication, genetic changes moved the secondaries out to the side, away from the primaries, and greatly increased their numbers; while wild strains of sheep or goat may have a ratio of only two to four secondaries for each primary, the ratio may be as high as seven to one in fine Merino sheep. The wool of the domestic sheep grows from these dense clusters of secondary follicles (Ryder 1958). Wool may already have been spun as early as 6000 B.C. at Çatal Hüyük in Anatolia (Mellaart 1964).

Both "hairy" and "wooly" sheep were known by 3000 B.C. in Mesopotamia (Hilzheimer 1941), and the now-famous Dead Sea Scrolls, dating to the time of Christ, have been shown by Ryder (1958) to have been written on parchment made both from hairy and from wooly sheep (see Fig. 4).

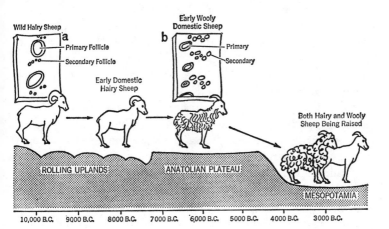

Figure 4 Simplified diagram showing some of the steps in the evolution of domestic sheep. (a) Section, as seen through a microscope, of skin of wild sheep, showing the arrangement of primary (hair) and secondary (wool) follicles; (b) section, similarly enlarged, of skin of domestic sheep, showing the changed relationship and the change in the size of follicles that accompanied the development of wool. [After Ryder 1958; see text.]

3) Nonadaptive genetic changes, such as the twisted horns of domestic goats. One of the most interesting (if poorly understood) changes which followed domestication was one affecting the horns of the goat (*Capra hircus*). The wild goat of the Near East has scimitar-shaped horns whose bony cores are quadrangular or diamond-shaped in cross section near the skull. Sites dating from 8500 to 7000 B.C. are known where goat domestication is inferred from the ratio of immature animals to adult animals, but no changes in the cross section of the horn during this period are noted. By 6500 B.C., from the Jordan Valley to the Zagros Mountains, there are scattered occurrences of goats whose horn

cores show a flattening of the medial surface, and thus a triangular or almond-shaped cross section. By 6000 B.C. in the Mesopotamian area, from the Assyrian steppe to the oak-pistachio woodlands, a new type of horn core makes its appearance: the core is medially flattened in section, and it also shows signs of a corkscrew twist like that of the modern domestic goat in southwest Asia. The irregular geographic distribution of the trait suggests that it was strongest in the Iran-Iraq area, occurring only sporadically elsewhere before 4500 B.C.; even at 3500 B.C. not all sites in the Palestinian area show goats of a uniformly "twisted horn" type (Reed 1960). Possibly its rapid spread in the Zagros was due to transhumant herding (see Fig. 5).

4) The problem of pig domestication. One of the questions most frequently asked is why the pig was domesticated at 6000 B.C. in some parts of the Near East, like the Zagros Mountain valleys (Reed 1961:32), but was apparently never domesticated in prehistoric time in other areas, such as the Khuzistan steppe (Hole et al. 1965). The most common answer is that this was the result of religious or dietary laws; but in fact, the reasons may be ecological. According to Krader (1955:315), "the disappearance of the pig from Central Asia is not the clear-cut case of religious determination that might be supposed. The pig is not a species suitable to pastoral nomadism . . . it is nomadism with its mastery of the steppe ecology and movements of herds and herdsmen which is the decisive factor in the disappearance of pigs from this part of the world." Figure 5 shows the sites where domestic pigs are known either to have been, or not to have been, present in the Mesopotamian area between 6000 and 5000 B.C. Since pigs seem to be incompatible with transhumant herding, the areas where they do *not* occur may be those where there was greatest reliance on seasonal movement of flocks.

EFFECTS ON HUMAN LIFE
AND CULTURAL ECOLOGY

In the past it has been customary to treat each of the Mesopotamian environmental zones as if it were a "cultural and natural area"—a region characterized by a certain flora and fauna and exploited by a certain group of inhabitants who knew it particu-

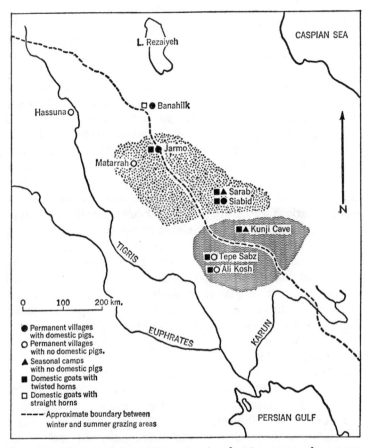

Figure 5   Map of Greater Mesopotamia, showing areas where trans-humance is believed to have been of importance in prehistoric times. Ceramic objects from sites in the stippled area (Jarmo, Sarab, Matarrah) all have one set of traits; those from sites in the hachured area (Kunji, Ali Kosh, Tepe Sabz) all have another set. The rapid spread of the twisted-horn goat in both areas suggests that flocks may have been moved from one elevation to another seasonally; so does the almost complete absence of the domestic pig, an animal unsuitable for transhumant herding. In the summer grazing area (northeast of the dashed line), many sites appear to be seasonal shepherds' camps in caves or on valley floors. These camps seem to have stronger ties, from the standpoint of ceramic objects, with sites in the adjacent winter grazing area (southwest of the dashed line) than with other sites in their own environmental zone (see text).

larly well.[5] There are hints that such a situation obtained in Palestine, for there Perrot (1962:162) has distinguished two archeological traditions, one adapted to the moist Mediterranean side of the mountains, the other adapted to the arid eastern foothills.

In 1956 Fredrik Barth pointed out that the "cultural and natural area" concept did not fit northern Pakistan, and there are a considerable number of data to suggest that it does not fit the Mesopotamian area at 6000 B.C. either. Barth showed that a single valley system might be occupied by three distinct ethnic groups, each of which occupied only a portion of the total resources, leaving the rest open for other groups to exploit. The first group consists of sedentary agriculturalists who practice intensive irrigation agriculture on the river floodplain, growing two crops a year and never moving to a higher elevation. A second group raises one crop a year in this same floodplain area, but its members also migrate annually with their flocks up through five seasonal campsites to high mountain meadows. Still a third group is made up of pastoral nomads who are assimilated into the society of the intensive agriculturalists as a special "herder caste," contributing milk and meat in exchange for grain; they are permitted to use prime grazing land not needed by the sedentary farmers (Barth 1956).

At 6000 B.C. there are striking contrasts between archeological sites in the oak-pistachio belt and the Assyrian steppe of the Greater Mesopotamian area which suggest Barth's model. Jarmo, at an elevation of 750 meters in the oak woodlands, was a village of permanent, mud-walled houses with courtyards and ovens; Tepe Sarab, at an elevation of 1260 meters, has no obvious houses, and only the kind of ashy refuse beds that might occur around a tent camp. The pottery objects at the two sites are nearly identical, but Jarmo has goats, sheep, and even domestic pigs, along with two strains of wheat and one of barley, whereas Tepe Sarab has only goats and sheep, and no grinding stones suggestive of local agriculture. The ages of the domestic goats show that Tepe Sarab was occupied in late winter or early spring. In this case we suspect that the camp at 1260 meters

---

[5] For the origins of the "cultural and natural area" hypothesis, see Kroeber 1939.

may have been occupied by seasonal herders who obtained their grain from more permanent farming villages at 750 meters (Braidwood and Howe 1962; Flannery 1962; Reed 1963).

From the Assyrian steppe of Khuzistan, southwestern Iran, come further data of the same type. From 7000 to 6500 B.C. at the site of Ali Kosh, goat grazing and tiny amounts of agriculture supplemented the collection of wild legumes; from 6500 to 6000 B.C. the growing of wheat and barley greatly increased at the expense of wild plants. At 6000 B.C. a striking expansion of sheep and goat grazing occurred, and amounts of wild wheat and wild barley lessened, while the pod-bearing perennial *Prosopis* came to the fore (Hole et al. 1965). We doubt that this was a simple case of abandonment of agriculture; *Prosopis,* Helbaek reminds us, is intimately associated with herding peoples in southwest Asia, and the increase in domestic sheep and goats suggests that this was a time when, in conformity with Barth's ecological model, Ali Kosh became primarily a "herding village" coexisting in a symbiotic framework with "farming villages" in adjacent areas.

Finally, we have the occurrences of typical Khuzistan pottery at a shepherds' camp in Kunji Cave, 1200 meters up, in the mountains of western Iran.[6] This part of Luristan seems to have stronger cultural ties with lowland Khuzistan than with other mountain areas in the same environmental zone, suggesting that at 6000 B.C. some valleys in Luristan were summer grazing land for herds that wintered in Khuzistan.

SUMMARY AND SPECULATION

The food-producing revolution in southwestern Asia is here viewed not as the brilliant invention of one group or the product of a single environmental zone, but as the result of a long process of changing ecological relationships between groups of men (living at varying altitudes and in different environmental settings) and the locally available plants and animals which they had been exploiting on a shifting, seasonal basis. In the course of making available to all groups the natural resources of every environmental zone, man had to remove from their natural con-

---

[6] F. Hole (of Rice University) and I made a test excavation of Kunji Cave in 1963; the data have not been published.

texts a number of hard-grained grasses and several species of ungulates. These species, as well as obsidian and native copper, were transported far from the biotopes or "niches" in which they had been at home. Shielded from natural selection by man, these small breeding populations underwent genetic change in the environment to which they had been transplanted, and favorable changes were emphasized by the practices of the early planter or herder.

Successful cultivation seems to have intensified exchanges of natural resources and cultivars between groups, and there are hints that the diversity of environments made village specialization in certain commodities the best means of adapting to the area. We have suggestive evidence (Hole et al. 1965) that by 4000 B.C. the redistributive economy had produced regional temple-and-market towns which regulated the produce of a symbiotic network of agriculturists engaged in intensive irrigation, transhumant herders, and perhaps even traders who dealt in obsidian, copper, salt, asphalt, fish, and regional fruits.[7]

---

[7] Much of the research leading to discoveries mentioned in this article was made possible by National Science Foundation grants to R. J. Braidwood of the University of Chicago (1959–60) and Frank Hole of Rice University (1963). Hans Helbaek, Frank Hole, and James Neely made suggestions which led to the formulation of many of the ideas presented. I thank Nancy H. Flannery for the original preparation of Figs. 2–5.

BIBLIOGRAPHY

Adams, R. M.
  1962 "Agriculture and Urban Life in Early Southwestern Iran." *Science,*
  136: 109–22.
Barth, F.
  1956 "Ecologic Relationships of Ethnic Groups in Swat, North Pakistan." *American Anthropologist, 58:* 1079–89.
Braidwood, R. J., and B. Howe
  1962 "Southwestern Asia Beyond the Lands of the Mediterranean
  Littoral," in R. J. Braidwood and G. R. Willey (eds.), *Courses
  Toward Urban Life.* Chicago: Aldine.
Braidwood, R. J., and G. R. Willey (eds.)
  1962 *Courses Toward Urban Life.* Chicago: Aldine.
Braidwood, R. J., B. Howe, et al.
  1960 *Prehistoric Investigations in Iraqi Kurdistan.* Oriental Institute
  "Studies in Ancient Oriental Civilization," No. 31. Chicago: University
  of Chicago Press.
Brothwell, D., and E. Higgs
  1963 *Science in Archaeology.* London: Thames and Hudson.
Coon, C. S.
  1951 *Cave Explorations in Iran in 1949.* Philadelphia: University of
  Pennsylvania Museum.
Cressey, G. B.
  1960 *Crossroads: Land and Life in Southwest Asia.* New York: Lippincott.
Dyson, R. H., Jr.
  1953 "Archaeology and the Domestication of Animals in the Old
  World." *American Anthropologist, 55:* 661–73.
Flannery, K. V.
  1962 "Early Village Farming in Southwestern Asia," in V. E. Garfield
  (ed.), *Proceedings of the 1961 Annual Spring Meeting of the American Ethnological Society.* Seattle: University of Washington Press.
Hatt, R. T.
  1959 *The Mammals of Iraq.* University of Michigan Museum of Zoology
  Miscellaneous Publications, No. 106. Ann Arbor.

Helbaek, H.
  1960a "Paleo-ethnobotany of the Near East and Europe," in R. J.
    Braidwood, B. Howe, et al. *Prehistoric Investigations in Iraqi Kurdi-
    stan.* Oriental Institute "Studies in Ancient Oriental Civilization,"
    No. 31. Chicago: University of Chicago Press.
  1960b "Ecological Effects of Irrigation in Ancient Mesopotamia." *Iraq,*
    22: 186–96.
  1963 "Paleoethnobotany," in D. Brothwell and E. Higgs (eds.), *Science
    in Archaeology.* London: Thames and Hudson.
Hilzheimer, M.
  1941 *Animal Remains from Tel Asmar.* Oriental Institute "Studies in
    Ancient Oriental Civilization," No. 20. Chicago: University of Chicago
    Press.
Hole, F.
  1962 "Archaeological Survey and Excavation in Iran, 1961." *Science,*
    137: 524–26.
Hole, F., K. Flannery, and J. Neely
  1965 "Early Agriculture and Animal Husbandry in Deh Luran, Iran."
    Current Anthropology, 6: 105–6.
Krader, L.
  1955 "Ecology of Central Asian Pastoralism." *Southwestern Journal
    of Anthropology,* 11: 301–26.
Kroeber, A. L.
  1939 *Cultural and Natural Areas of Native North America.* University
    of California Publications in American Archaeology and Ethnology,
    Vol. 38.
Lees, G. M., and N. L. Falcon
  1952 "The Geographical History of the Mesopotamian Plains." *Geo-
    graphical Journal,* 118: 24–39.
MacNeish, R. S.
  1964 "Ancient Mesoamerican Civilization." *Science,* 143: 531–37.
Mellaart, J.
  1964 "A Neolithic City in Turkey." *Scientific American,* 210(4): 94–
    104.
Perkins, D., Jr.
  1959 "The Post-cranial Skeleton of the Caprinae: Comparative Anatomy
    and Changes Under Domestication." Unpublished Ph.D. Thesis, Har-
    vard University.
  1964 "Prehistoric Fauna from Shanidar, Iraq." *Science,* 144: 1565–66.
Perrot, J.
  1962 "Palestine-Syria-Cilicia," in R. J. Braidwood and G. R. Willey
    (eds.), *Courses Toward Urban Life.* Chicago: Aldine.
Reed, C. A.
  1960 "A Review of the Archaeological Evidence on Animal Domestica-
    tion in the Prehistoric Near East," in R. J. Braidwood, B. Howe, et
    al., *Prehistoric Investigations in Iraqi Kurdistan.* Oriental Institute

"Studies in Ancient Oriental Civilization," No. 31. Chicago: University of Chicago Press.

1961 "Osteological Evidences for Prehistoric Domestication in Southwestern Asia." *Zeitschrift für Tierzüchtung und Züchtungsbiologie* (Journal of Animal Breeding and Genetics), 76: 31–38.

1963 "Osteo-archaeology," in D. Brothwell and E. Higgs (eds.), *Science in Archaeology.* London: Thames and Hudson.

Ryder, M. L.

1958 "Follicle Arrangement in Skin from Wild Sheep, Primitive Domestic Sheep and in Parchment." *Nature,* 182: 781–83.

Solecki, R. S.

1963 "Prehistory in Shanidar Valley, Northern Iraq." *Science,* 139: 179–93.

Stubbe, H.

1959 "Considerations on the Genetical and Evolutionary Aspects of Some Mutants of Hordeum, Glycine, Lycopersicon and Antirrhinum." *Cold Spring Harbor Symposia on Quantitative Biology,* 24: 31–40.

Van Zeist, W., and H. E. Wright, Jr.

1963 "Preliminary Pollen Studies at Lake Zeribar, Zagros Mountains, Southwestern Iran." *Science,* 140: 65–67.

White, L. A.

1959 *The Evolution of Culture.* New York: McGraw-Hill.

16 SICKLE-CELL TRAIT IN HUMAN BIOLOGICAL AND CULTURAL EVOLUTION[1]

Stephen L. Wiesenfeld

MEDICAL ANTHROPOLOGY has been moving increasingly into central areas of anthropological theory. Alland (1966) has demonstrated some of the ways in which medical anthropology may serve "as a major link between physical and cultural anthropology, particularly in the areas of biological and cultural evolution." The purpose of this article is to examine the relationship between the sickle-cell trait, malaria, and agriculture in east and west Africa so as to derive hypotheses regarding concomitant human biological and cultural evolution.

Malarial infection, both natural and experimental, and mortality from such infection are consistently lower in individuals having the sickle-cell trait (Allison 1954a, 1961; Motulsky 1964). The normal population has reduced fertility rates as compared to the "sickler" population in endemic areas (Archibald 1956b; Rucknagel and Neel 1961). Also, the distribution of the sickle-cell trait in tropical Africa parallels that of subtertian malaria (Allison 1954a; Livingstone 1958), so it is reasonable to believe that malaria is the selective agent producing high frequencies of the

Reprinted from *Science,* Vol. 157 (1967), pp. 1134–40 (copyright 1967 by the American Association for the Advancement of Science) by permission of the author and publisher. The author has revised a few sentences for the present volume and has added footnote[5].

[1] I thank N. L. Petrakis, P. Mustacchi, S. L. Washburn, J. N. Anderson, and F. L. Dunn for aid and helpful criticism. The research reported in this article was supported in part by U. S. Public Health Service fellowship grant 5T5 GM 43-05 and in part by U. S. Public Health Service grant FR-00122 for computing services at San Francisco Medical Center, University of California. The research was also supported in part by PHS research grant CA 05485-07.

sickle-cell trait in the area of sub-Saharan Africa stretching from the east coast to Gambia on the west coast. Livingstone (1958) proposed that malaria in west Africa became hyperendemic when large tracts of tropical rain forest were reclaimed for agriculture, by multiplying the number of breeding places for the *Anopheles gambiae* species complex, which contains major vectors of hyperendemic malaria.[2]

Two important areas in the interaction of the sickle-cell trait, malaria, and agriculture have not been examined previously. First, not all agricultural systems have the same effect on the development of malaria and of high frequencies of the sickle-cell trait. The data presented here show that agricultural systems do differ in this respect, with one, the Malaysian agricultural system (Murdock 1959),[3] having a greater effect than any other. Second, the effects of changes in the frequency of an adaptive gene on the incidence of the disease selecting for it have not been fully examined. Computer models were developed to determine the nature of the interaction of the sickle-cell trait and malaria, and it was found that increasing frequencies of the sickle-cell trait cause reductions in malaria parasitism by reducing the number of people in a population capable of undergoing intense parasitism and of infecting mosquitoes. Both of these arguments are critical to the hypothesis that the development and differentiation of the Malaysian agricultural system is intimately bound to changes in the gene pools of populations using this agricultural system. The action of high frequencies of the sickle-cell trait is to reduce the environmental limitation of malarial parasitism on these populations, thus allowing more human energy to flow into the development and maintenance of the Malaysian agricultural system. A number of lines of evidence are presented here to support the hypothesis.

---

[2] What has been called *Anopheles gambiae* is now thought to be a complex of five or more sibling species (Davidson 1964). Two of these species (*A. melas* and *A. merus*) are saltwater breeders and three unnamed species are freshwater breeders. The relative role of each species in producing endemic malaria has not been evaluated (Russell et al. 1963). This group of species is referred to in this article as the *A. gambiae* species complex.

[3] The term *Malaysian agricultural complex* is Murdock's. I have adopted Murdock's scheme for the origin and development of this complex.

METHODS AND MATERIALS

Data, for the communities of this survey, on the degree of dependence on agriculture, the type of crop regime, and the manner of crop production were obtained from the "World Ethnographic Survey," a continuing series in *Ethnology*. Each community was scored from 0 to 9 according to the reported degree of its dependence on agriculture (0, dependence 0 to 5 percent; 1, 6 to 15 percent; 2, 16 to 25 percent; 3, 26 to 35 percent; 4, 36 to 45 percent; 5, 46 to 55 percent; 6, 56 to 65 percent; 7, 66 to 75 percent; 8, 76 to 85 percent; and 9, 86 to 100 percent).

Data on the frequency of the sickle-cell trait for various tribes in west and east Africa were used only if the sample size was considered adequate. Otherwise, data were used only if confirming studies had been made, in which case the results were pooled.

The mathematical models relating hyperendemic malaria and the sickle-cell gene frequency were set up on the basis of a Fortran IV program and run on the IBM 1401 computer.

AGRICULTURE AND THE SICKLE-CELL TRAIT

Data from 60 communities in east and west Africa met our criteria; they are plotted in Fig. 1, according to the percentage of individuals with the sickle-cell trait in the community. Data for tribes with agricultural dependence scores of 3 and below were combined, as were those for tribes with scores of 8 and 9.

The 50th percentile (median), the 25th percentile, and the 75th percentile found for each degree of dependence on agriculture show that a greater dependence on agriculture is associated with a higher frequency of the sickle-cell trait. The 25th and 75th percentiles represent the amount of variation around the median. Tribes are ranked either I, II, III, or IV according to which region of Fig. 1 they occupy. The sample of communities having less than 35-percent dependence on agriculture is too small to be considered significant, but communities falling in this region probably have very low frequencies of the sickle-cell trait. There

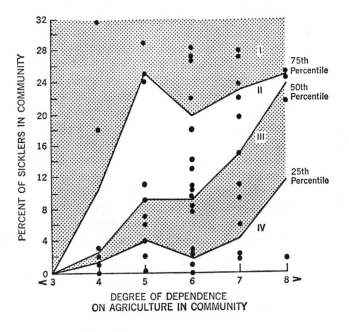

Figure 1 Relationship between percentage of individuals with sickle-cell trait and degree of dependence on agriculture, in 60 communities.

is a trend toward stabilization of the median from 46- to 65-percent dependence on agriculture, but the widest variations in the trait frequencies are found here. Cultures with greater than 66-percent dependence on agriculture show a marked increase in the frequencies of the sickle-cell trait, with a reduction in the amount of variation around the median.

For any degree of dependence on agriculture there is a wide variation in the frequencies of the sickle-cell trait in various communities, indicating that different relevant variables may differentiate cultures in ranks III and IV from those in ranks I and II. Table 1 shows the distribution of the crop complexes among the four ranks of Fig. 1. Fifty-three of the cultures for which data were available were classified according to their main crop, but this classification does not mean that members of one crop complex may not have crops from another. Cereals, representing crops found in the Sudanic agricultural complex, have a wide distribution but are associated mainly with low frequencies of the sickle-cell trait. Root and tree crops from the Malaysian agricultural complex are associated almost exclusively with higher frequencies of the sickle-cell trait. A more revealing analysis of the relationship between crop regime and frequency of the sickle-cell trait is shown in Table 2. Cereals show wide variation but, for the most part, are associated with low frequencies of the trait. The eight communities in the 25- to 29-percent sickler group do not conform to the normal distribution that would be expected on the basis of data in Table 1. Most of these communities are in east Africa and are societies practicing intensive irrigation of crops. Root and tree crops are clearly associated with very high frequencies of the trait.

Also, note that communities with root and tree crops tend to have a greater economic dependence on agriculture than communities using cereals (Fig. 2).

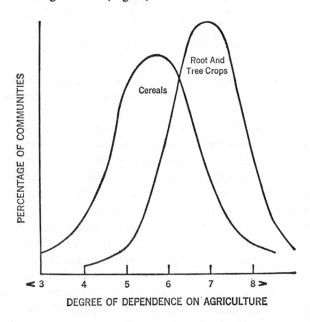

Figure 2   Normal distribution of the degrees of dependence on agriculture in communities using cereals and in those using root and tree crops.

MALAYSIAN AGRICULTURAL COMPLEX

According to Murdock (1959), the predominant root crops in east and west Africa are yams and taro and not the Guinea yam as has been suggested by Livingstone (1958:551) and Chevalier (1946). The Guinea yam does not have the status of a staple in either of the areas considered. The main tree crops are bananas and coconuts. These root and tree crops all belong to what Murdock calls the Malaysian agricultural complex that was introduced into Madagascar and the coast of east Africa from certain parts of southeast Asia a few centuries before Christ.

The ancient Malayo-Polynesian-speaking Mongoloid peoples of the coastal areas of southeast Asia were excellent sailors who carried their culture eastward into the islands of the Pacific and westward to Madagascar (Linton 1958:45). The Malagasy are Mongoloid peoples found on Madagascar who speak a language of the Malayo-Polynesian stock which is very closely related to the language of the Ma'anyan of southeast Borneo (Dahl 1951). These people once occupied a coastal position and were great navigators. Southeast Borneo lies along the Sabaean Lane, a water route of great antiquity connecting Indonesia, Malaya, the Philippines, southeast China, and India. Dyen (1953) has applied lexicostatistical methods to Dahl's work and estimates that the separation of the Malagasy from the Ma'anyan occurred at least 1900 years ago.

It is believed that the Ma'anyan brought with them from Borneo swidden agricultural techniques, dry rice, and root and tree crops. The sweet potato also appears to have been introduced at this time. Evidently the wet-rice or paddy-rice cultivation prominent on the mainland of southeast Asia and established on Java and Sumatra around the beginning of the Christian era had not yet been introduced into Borneo. Wet rice appears never to have been adopted by the Ma'anyans, who were, in succeeding centuries of the Christian era, displaced from their original coastal position into the adjacent interior of the island by tribes practicing paddy-rice cultivation (Murdock 1959).

The Azanians on the coast of east Africa adopted parts of the Malaysian agricultural complex during the first century of the

Christian era, according to early written evidence (Schoff 1912). Taro (*Colocasia antiquorum*), yams (*Dioscorea alata, D. bulbifera, D. esculenta*), bananas, and coconuts are still prominent in this area (Burkill 1953). These Cushites of Azania carried the agricultural complex west into the interior of Africa and southwest into Uganda (Murdock 1959:210).

A solid band of tribes located in what is called the "yam belt" runs across sub-Saharan Africa from the east to the west coast. In all these tribes the Malaysian agricultural complex figures importantly (Murdock 1959). Prior to the spread of this complex the Sudanic agricultural complex, with many cereal crops, predominated over native agriculture in sub-Saharan Africa (Murdock 1959). Communities practicing agriculture with the Sudanic set of crops were limited to the fringes of the tropical rain forest, because these crops were poorly suited to the rain-forest environment. Also, these communities never attained a high degree of dependence on agriculture in their economies (see Fig. 2). Throughout the "yam belt" there is evidence of the recent development of the Malaysian agricultural complex, which is well suited to the tropical forest environment, and of the recent penetration of the tropical rain forest by Negroid peoples using this complex; this penetration caused the displacement of hunting and gathering pygmy peoples (Seligman and Seligman 1932; Vavilov 1949). It is estimated that the occupation and displacement occurred within the last 2000 years.

Although the crops of the Sudanic complex play only minor roles in the societies under consideration, their planting and harvesting are attended by elaborate ritual, indicating great antiquity.

Table 1. The number of communities in each rank, according to crop (see Fig. 1).

Crop	Rank			
	IV	III	II	I
Cereals	15	13	8	7
Root and tree crops	0	1	3	6

In west Africa the Sudanic complex is more important in the north, where it appears to have arrived at an early date. Also, a number of crops were probably domesticated originally in west Africa, among them the Guinea yams and the oil palm (Chevalier

1952). However, the Malaysian complex is of great importance in the south, where the tropical forest predominates. Wet rice is cultivated in many parts of west Africa; it appears to have been introduced by Arabs around A.D. 1500 (Paulme 1954).

Murdock also believes that the Malaysian complex was an important factor in the large expansion of the Bantu peoples through much of tropical Africa, and in the development of forest states in west Africa, due to the suitability of the crops for the tropical forest environment. As noted above, slash-and-burn cultivation is conducive to the development of breeding places for the *Anopheles gambiae* species complex, and thus to the development of intense malaria parasitism. With the shift from use of the tropical forest for hunting and gathering to swidden cultivation, there was a change in the nature of breeding places available to various species of mosquitoes and therefore a shift from *A. funestus* to *A. gambiae* as the major vector of malaria. This shift is significant because the behavior of the species comprising the *A. gambiae* species complex is much more conducive to the development of hyperendemic malaria.

Livingstone (1958) noted a north-south gradient in the frequencies of the sickle-cell trait, with greater frequencies in the south. All along the "yam belt," expecially in the central Sudan and in Nigeria, there is a north-south gradient in the distribution of Malaysian crops (Murdock 1959), paralleling the gradient of the sickle-cell trait. Figure 3 shows the distribution of the Malaysian agricultural complex and the distribution of sickle-cell-trait frequencies higher than 5 percent. There is a striking overlap of these areas.

Table 2. Relationship between crop regime and frequency of the sickle-cell trait in 53 communities.

	Percentage of individuals with sickle-cell trait						
	0–4	5–9	10–14	15–19	20–24	25–29	30 and up
Cereals	19	9	5	2	0	8*	0
Root and tree crops	0	0	0	1	6	2	1

* These communities practice extensive irrigation and have high malarial parasitism (see text).

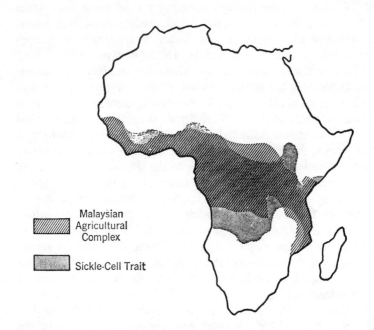

Figure 3   Distribution of the Malaysian agricultural complex and distribution of sickle-cell-trait frequencies higher than 5 percent.

The relationship between agriculture and malaria was noted over a century ago when outbreaks of malaria followed irrigation work (Baker et al. 1847). Angel (1966) has demonstrated that in the eastern Mediterranean during prehistoric times porotic hyperostosis, or a thickening of the spongy marrow space of the skull due to sicklemia or one of the thalassemias, is associated frequently with early farmers who lived in marshy areas in Greece, but rarely with paleolithic hunters. The frequency of the disease also appears to have decreased in areas where farming methods improved.

GENES AND SOCIOECONOMIC ADAPTATIONS

The introduction of the Malaysian food complexes into sub-Saharan Africa brought about major changes in human ecological niches. Introduction of the crops allowed Negroes to penetrate the tropical rain forest and allowed their populations to increase to new equilibrium levels, making this band across the continent, especially in west Africa, the most densely populated part of Africa. As Geertz (1963) has demonstrated in Indonesia, a population adopting a new agricultural system which provides a greater and more certain food supply not only undergoes expansion but also tends to involute. More people are centered in one area, and people tend to move less, due to vastly increased needs of husbandry to keep the agricultural system yielding at maximum capacity. Malaria increases in such a situation, for infected individuals remain constantly close to uninfected individuals and the probability of transmission by mosquito increases.

The new agricultural system allows expansion and involution of the population and, at the same time, is the ultimate cause of an increase in malaria parasitism. The population growth puts increased pressure on the agricultural system for greater food production, but the parasitism takes its toll through mortality and morbidity, thus reducing the total energy available for agricultural production. The sickle cell presents a biological solution to a cultural problem by providing many members of the population with genetic immunity, thereby allowing more human energy to flow into agricultural production to meet the demands of an increasing population.

These concepts may be formulated into a principle regarding the interaction of biology and culture in man. Where a socioeconomic adaptation causes a change in the environment, the frequency of a gene will change in proportion to the survival value the gene confers on the carriers in the new ecosystem. Increasing frequencies of an adaptive gene remove environmental limitations and allow further development of the socioeconomic adaptation. The environmental conditions crucial to the transmission of malaria are also crucial to the economy, but the sickle-cell trait removes a limitation for agricultural development and maintenance by reducing the number of people capable of undergoing intense parasitism and of infecting mosquitoes. The gene frequency and the socioeconomic adaptation continue to develop in a stepwise fashion until either the limit of the gene frequency or the limit of the socioeconomic adaptation is reached.

Evidence to support the hypothesis is found in Table 2 and Fig. 2, which show that societies with the greatest dependence on agriculture have the highest frequencies of the sickle-cell trait.

MATHEMATICAL MODELS: CONCEPTS

It has been possible to develop mathematical simulations relating the dynamics of the sickle-cell trait to the dynamics of hyperendemic malaria. The models show that an increase in the sickle-cell trait reduces the intensity of malaria parasitism by reducing the number of people capable of undergoing intense parasitism and of infecting mosquitoes. The models are offered as evidence that the sickle-cell trait removes an environmental limitation on the development of the Malaysian agricultural complex in Africa. The model presented is believed to be valid for hyperendemic malaria in sub-Saharan Africa. The variables used reflect basic epidemiologic determinants of malarial transmission and are taken from actual field studies. Before considering the models we should consider certain factors of the epidemiology of malaria.

Malaria is a three-factor disease, with mosquitoes and mammals serving as hosts, and is a disease caused by infection with one of the four malaria parasites; however, only two of them, *Plasmodium falciparum* and *P. ovale,* are important in areas where the sickle-cell trait is found. *Plasmodium falciparum* is usually associated with stable, hyperendemic malaria, while *P. vivax* and *P. ovale* are dominant in areas with unstable, epidemic malaria with marked seasonal variations. Stable malaria, as found in sub-Saharan Africa, is associated with the following characteristics. The mosquito, usually from the *Anopheles gambiae* species complex, bites man frequently, and its probability of survival through the period of development of the parasite in its salivary gland is good. An infective mosquito with a long life span is a greater epidemiologic hazard than a short-lived counterpart. The high longevity of the mosquito in sub-Saharan Africa is due mainly to the humid and stable climatic conditions.

The main vectors for malaria in sub-Saharan Africa are the species of the *Anopheles gambiae* complex and *A. funestus.* The *A. gambiae* species complex is mainly associated with agricultural societies and hyperendemic malaria, while *A. funestus* is associated with areas of unchanged tropical rain forest, hunting and gathering cultures, and lower levels of endemic malaria. This difference in ecological niche is due solely to a difference in the breeding places of the various species, as noted above. The fresh-water breeders of the *A. gambiae* species complex will multiply in many types of water but prefer open, sunlit pools of the type created in the tropical rain forest when slash-and-burn agriculture is practiced. *Anopheles funestus* is found in swamps with heavy vegetation, in vegetated river edges, and in other bodies of water that are not in direct sunlight (Wilson 1949). Such breeding places are found most readily in the unchanged tropical forest. It is possible to use these mosquitoes as "ecological labels" for different human socioeconomic adaptations, a concept introduced by Audy (1954).

Figure 4 shows the relationship between the sporozoite rate (or the proportion of mosquitoes, in a population of mosquitoes, with malaria parasites in their salivary glands) and the selective advantage of the sickle-cell trait in seven African communities. The sporozoite rate is a good index of the amount of malaria in an area where it is endemic because the sporozoite rate depends (i) on the number of infected people in a population capable of producing infection in a mosquito, (ii) on the frequency with

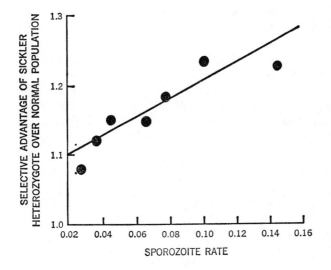

Figure 4   Relationship between the intensity of endemic malaria (the sporozoite rate) and the selective advantage of the sickler heterozygote over the normal population (see Appendix).

which a mosquito will bite men, (iii) on the time it takes the malaria parasite to develop within the mosquito, and (iv) on the mortality rate of the mosquitoes (see Appendix, Eq. 3). The selective advantage of the population with the sickle-cell trait is determined according to Livingstone (1964:435), and in Africa is represented as some value greater than 1, because 1 is taken as the selective advantage of the population lacking the sickle-cell trait. The greater the selective advantage of the sickler, the more the sicklers will contribute to the composition of future generations. The basic prerequisite for determining the selective advantage of the heterozygote is that the frequency of the sickle-cell gene be in equilibrium with the amount of malaria in the area being considered.

The best-fitting straight line was determined (see Appendix, Eq. 1). The selective advantage of the heterozygote clearly tends to increase as the amount of malaria in an area increases.

MATHEMATICAL MODELS: RESULTS

Figures 5 and 6 are mathematical simulations of various epidemiological conditions and show the dynamics of endemic malaria in response to the presence of the sickle-cell trait in the population.

One more epidemiological concept must be introduced before the models are discussed. This is the basic reproduction rate, or the number of human infections produced by an earlier human infection (see Appendix, Eq. 5). If one case of malaria gives rise to two other cases at a later date, then the basic reproduction rate is 2. The basic reproduction rate is directly proportional to the sporozoite rate and serves as a very good index of the intensity of malaria. If the basic reproduction rate ever falls below 1.0, malaria will not continue to be transmitted in the community, so 1.0 represents the critical value for the continuance of malaria. If the basic reproduction rate "continuously exceeds this critical value, malaria will persist but its epidemiological characteristics will be largely determined by the biting habit and longevity of the mosquito" (MacDonald 1957:39–40).

The logic of these models may be presented with a minimum of mathematics. The frequency of the sickle-cell gene in a population is assumed to be initially very low, and the longevity of the mosquito and its man-biting habit are taken to be high. For a given sporozoite rate in a particular area it is possible to determine what the selective advantage of the sickler population is, according to the relationship shown in Fig. 4 and in Eq. 1 of the Appendix. For each generation the frequency of the sickle-cell trait is determined for the next generation on the basis of the selective advantage of the sickler (Appendix, Eq. 2). Given this new frequency of the gene, it is possible to see by what degree the population capable of being infected is reduced, hence the value for the basic reproduction rate of malaria for that generation may be determined (Appendix, Eq. 6). Since the basic reproduction rate is directly proportional to the sporozoite rate and the sporozoite rate is directly proportional to the selective advantage of the sickler heterozygote, it is possible to derive an expression relating the selective advantage to the basic reproduction rate (Appendix, Eq. 7), and a new value for the selective advantage is found, which is used in determining the frequency of the gene in the next generation. These three steps—determining (i) the new gene frequency, (ii) the new basic reproduction rate, and (iii) the new selective advantage of the heterozygote—are followed for each generation.

Comparison of the corresponding curves of the top and bottom graphs of Fig. 5 shows that an increase in the frequency of the sickle-cell gene causes a reduction in the basic reproduction rate of hyperendemic malaria by reducing the number of people capable of undergoing intense parasitism and of infecting mosquitoes. High sporozoite rates in the mosquitoes, caused by the fact that a relatively high proportion of the human population is capable of infecting mosquitoes, allow development of proportionately high equilibrium frequencies of the gene, which in turn cause marked reductions in the basic reproduction rate (Fig. 5, top, curve *A*). When the proportions of human populations capable of infecting mosquitoes are lower, this allows the development of lower equilibrium frequencies, and this in turn causes lesser reductions in the basic reproduction rate of malaria (Fig. 5, top, curves *B* and *C*). Notice also that it takes more time for lower frequencies to reach equilibrium because of the lower pressures of malaria on the population as a whole.

Figure 5 also shows the effect of varying the mosquito man-biting habit—its effect on the frequencies of the gene developed,

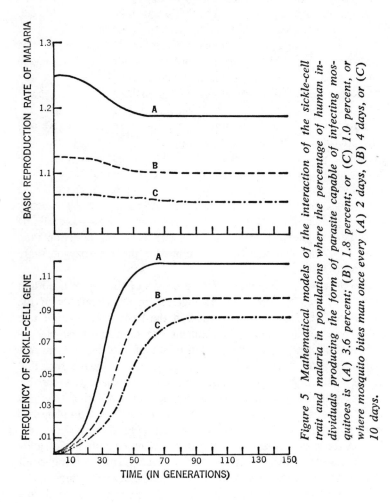

Figure 5 *Mathematical models of the interaction of the sickle-cell trait and malaria in populations where the percentage of human individuals producing the form of parasite capable of infecting mosquitoes is (A) 3.6 percent; (B) 1.8 percent; or (C) 1.0 percent, or where mosquito bites man once every (A) 2 days, (B) 4 days, or (C) 10 days.*

and its subsequent effect on the reduction of malaria in a population. The frequencies with which mosquitoes bite man vary a great deal with various species and have profound effects on the nature of malaria in a region. Stable, hyperendemic malaria is associated with high frequencies of biting. Where mosquitoes bite man regularly, the number of infected mosquitoes (the sporozoite rate) is high, the selective advantage of the heterozygote is high, and the frequency of the gene rises rapidly to a high equilibrium value (Fig. 5, bottom, curve *A*). This increase in the gene frequency causes a marked reduction in the basic reproduction rate of malaria. Lower values for the man-biting habit of mosquitoes allow lower frequencies of the gene to develop, with proportionately milder reductions in the basic reproduction rate (Fig. 5, bottom, curves *B* and *C*).

Increases in the man-biting habit of the mosquito have significant effects on the intensity of malaria and hence on the frequency of the sickle-cell trait. In many parts of the world an increase in the mosquitoes' man-biting habit is caused by the displacement or reduction in numbers of cattle or other animals that previously served as hosts for the mosquito. This displacement is caused by growth in human population, so the mosquito must turn increasingly to man as the major host. Epidemics caused by such a situation have been reported in India (Christophers 1911), and it has been speculated that man has caused the displacement of original hosts for many parasites in densely populated parts of the world, especially in the tropics.

Figure 6 shows the effect on the interaction of the sickle-cell trait and malaria of varying the longevity of the mosquito. The daily mortality of mosquitoes depends mainly on humidity and on seasonal climatic variations. Throughout tropical Africa there is relatively little seasonal climatic variation and the relative humidity is constantly high, so the daily mortality of mosquitoes is low. Figure 6, top and bottom, curve *A*, shows a simulation in which a low value was used for mosquito daily mortality, one typical for hyperendemic malaria in Africa, which was determined from actual field studies (Davidson 1955; Davidson and Draper 1953). The model stabilized after about 40 generations or 1000 years, and the equilibrium values approximate very closely the values determined for malaria and the sickle-cell trait in

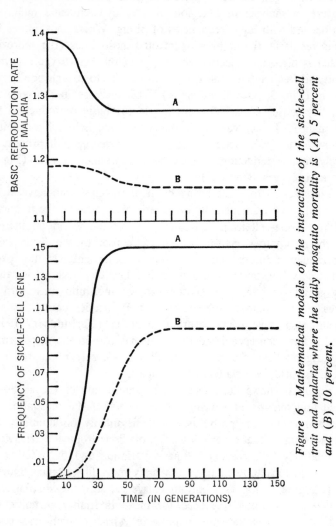

Figure 6 Mathematical models of the interaction of the sickle-cell trait and malaria where the daily mosquito mortality is (A) 5 percent and (B) 10 percent.

Uganda, where values for all the parameters in the model were obtained. MacDonald determined the basic reproduction rate to be around 1.25, and various field studies on frequencies of the sickle-cell trait show values ranging from 27 to 39.1 percent (Allison 1954b; Lehmann and Raper 1949; MacDonald 1955).[4] For the sickle cell, the gene frequency is half the trait frequency.

On the fringe of the tropical rain forest large areas of savanna are found, where the humidity is lower and where there is more seasonal climatic variation. These conditions cause a reduction in the longevity of the mosquito, the results of which are represented in Fig. 6, top and bottom, curve *B*. The model reaches equilibrium in about 60 generations or 1500 years, and the equilibrium values reached are similar to the values reported for northwestern Nigeria, where the values for the parameters of the model were obtained (Allison 1956; Archibald 1956a; Livingstone 1958). The time necessary for the development of equilibrium in all models is well within 2000 years—the interval since the Malaysian agricultural system was introduced into Africa.[5]

---

[4] Gene frequencies represent, almost exclusively, heterozygotes.

[5] Since the original publication of this paper, D. Coursey and J. Alexander (1968) have presented strong botanical and archeological evidence against the early presence of Murdock's "Malaysian agricultural complex" in west Africa. The hypotheses developed in my article were based primarily on the differences between root and tree crops and other crop complexes. Since the indigenous "Guinea yams" of west Africa and the Asian crops involve similar slash-and-burn agricultural patterns that contrast markedly with other forms of agriculture, I believe the general concepts developed are still valid.

To obtain sickle-cell trait percentages as high as thirty percent in many west African populations required a period of *at least* 1500 years. The only agricultural system that could have allowed both malaria and the abnormal hemoglobins to prosper so early in west Africa must have been based on cultivation of indigenous crops.

North and west Africa, while always considered separately, appear to have much in common in regard to hemoglobinopathies (Livingstone 1967). Hemoglobins S, C, and K, thalassemia, and glucose-6-phosphate dehydrogenase deficiency are present in both areas and across the Sahara in high frequencies. Archeological evidence and data pertaining to taro as a root crop and to abnormal hemoglobins suggest that the cultural, economic, and biological development of west Africa may owe more to the eastern Mediterranean than to east Africa or southeast Asia.

CONCLUSION

The particular agricultural adaptation we have been considering is the ultimate determinant of the presence of malaria parasites in the intracellular environment of the human red blood cell. This change in the cellular environment is deleterious for normal individuals, but individuals with the sickle-cell gene are capable of changing their red-cell environment so that intense parasitism never develops. Normal individuals suffer higher mortality rates and lower fertility rates in a malarious environment than individuals with the sickle-cell trait do, so the latter contribute proportionately more people to succeeding generations.

In the case of an intensely malarious environment created by a new agricultural situation, the viability of the normal individual is reduced and there is selection for the individual with the sickle-cell trait; this means that the nature of the gene-pool of the population will change through time. This biological change helps to maintain the cultural change causing the new cellular environmental change, and the biological change may allow further development of the cultural adaptation, which in turn increases the selective pressure to maintain the biological change. In this way it is possible to see human biology and culture interacting and differentiating together in a stepwise fashion. If valid, the hypothesis developed here serves to demonstrate the important role that disease may have in human evolution.

APPENDIX

The mathematical analysis. The purpose of this mathematical analysis is to allow the development of models in which various factors may be varied to determine their effects on the process being considered. The mathematics of the epidemiology of malaria has been developed by MacDonald (1957), and the basic statements about malaria in this simulation are his. Equations relating to changes in the gene frequency are derived from the Hardy-Weinberg law and the notation of Wright used by Livingstone (1964).

1) The equation for the relationship between the sporozoite rate and the selective advantage of the sickler over the normal individual shown in Fig. 4 is

$$(1) \qquad w_{12} = 1.075 + 1.289s$$

where w_{12} is the selective advantage of the heterozygote sickler and s is the sporozoite rate, or the proportion of mosquitoes capable of transmitting the parasite to man.

2) The expression for the change in gene frequency for one generation is derived from the Hardy-Weinberg law and is given as follows:

$$(2) \qquad q_{i+1} = \frac{1}{\left(\dfrac{w_{11}(1 - q_i)}{w_{12i}q_i} \right) + 2}$$

where q is the gene frequency, i is the number of the generation being considered, and w_{11} is the selective advantage of the normal population.

3) The expression for the sporozoite rate is given by Mac-Donald as

$$(3) \qquad s = \frac{p^n ax}{ax - \log_e p}$$

where p is the probability of a mosquito's surviving through the first day of life; p^n is the probability of its surviving through n days, or the time that it takes for the parasite to develop within the mosquito; a is the number of times a mosquito bites a man in one day; and x is the proportion of the human population capable of infecting mosquitoes.

4) To Eq. 3 I have added the following factors: $2q$, the proportion of the human population incapable of being infected due to genetic immunity, and $\alpha = (1 - 2q)$, or the proportion of the population capable of being infected due to lack of genetic immunity. Rewritten, the sporozoite rate is

$$(4) \qquad s = \frac{p^n ax\alpha}{ax\alpha - \log_e p}$$

5) MacDonald defines z_0, or the basic reproduction rate, as

(5) $$z_0 = \frac{p^n}{p^n - s}$$

Substituting the value of s from Eq. 4 into Eq. 5, we get

(6) $$z_0 = 1 - \frac{ax(1 - 2q)}{\log_e p}$$

6) The selective advantage of the heterozygote may be expressed in terms of the basic reproduction rate through substitution of the expression for s in Eq. 1 into Eq. 5; the substitution yields

(7) $$w_{12i+1} = 1.289 p^n \left[1 - (1/z_0)\right] + 1.075$$

BIBLIOGRAPHY

Alland, Alexander, Jr.
  1966 "Medical Anthropology and the Study of Biological and Cultural Adaptation." *American Anthropologist,* 68: 40–51.
Allison, A. C.
  1954a "Protection Afforded by Sickle-cell Trait Against Subtertian Malarial Infection." *British Medical Journal,* 1: 290–94.
  1954b "The Distribution of the Sickle-cell Trait in East Africa and Elsewhere and Its Apparent Relationship to the Incidence of Subtertian Malaria." *Transactions of the Royal Society of Tropical Medicine and Hygiene,* 48: 312–18.
  1956 "The Sickle-cell and Haemoglobin C Genes in Some African Populations." *Annals of Human Genetics,* 21: 67–89.
  1961 "Genetic Factors in Resistance to Malaria." *Annals of the New York Academy of Sciences,* 91: 710–29.
Angel, J. Lawrence
  1966 "Porotic Hyperostosis, Anemias, Malarias, and Marshes in the Prehistoric Eastern Mediterranean." *Science,* 153: 760–63.
Archibald, H. M.
  1956a "Malaria in South-Western and North-Western Nigerian Communities." *Bulletin of the World Health Organization,* 15: 695–709.
  1956b "The Influence of Malarial Infection of the Placenta on Incidence of Prematurity." *Bulletin of the World Health Organization,* 15: 842.
Audy, J. R.
  1954 "A Biological Approach to Medical Geography." *British Medical Journal,* 1: 960–62.
Baker, W. E., T. E. Dempster, and H. Yule
  1847 Report of a committee assembled to report on the causes of unhealthiness which has existed at Kurnaul, reprinted 1929, *Records of the Malariological Survey of India,* 1: 1–68.
Burkill, I. H.
  1953 "Habits of Man and the Origins of the Cultivated Plants of the Old World." *Proceedings of the Linnean Society of London.* 164: 12–42.

Chevalier, A.

1946 "Nouvelles recherches sur les ignames cultivées." *Revue de Botanique Appliqué et Agriculture Tropicale,* 26: 26–31.

1952 "De quelques *Dioscorea* d'Afrique Equatoriale Toxiques dont Plusieurs Variétés sont Alimentaires." *Revue de Botanique Appliqué et Agriculture Tropicale,* 32: 14–19.

Christophers, S. R.

1911 *Malaria in the Punjab.* Scientific Memoirs by Officers of the Medical and Sanitary Department of the Government of India, New Series, No. 46.

Coursey, D., and J. Alexander

1968 "African Agricultural Patterns and the Sickle Cell." *Science,* 160: 1474–75.

Dahl, D. C.

1951 "Malgache et Maanjan." *Avhandlinger utgitt av Egede-Instituttet,* 3: 1–408.

Davidson, G.

1955 "Further Studies on the Basic Factors Concerned in the Transmission of Malaria." *Transactions of the Royal Society of Tropical Medicine and Hygiene,* 49: 339–50.

1964 "The Five Mating-types in the Anopheles gambiae Complex." *Rivista di Malariologia,* 43: 167–83.

Davidson, G., and C. C. Draper

1953 "Field Studies of Some of the Basic Factors Concerned in the Transmission of Malaria." *Transactions of the Royal Society of Tropical Medicine and Hygiene,* 47: 522–35.

Dyen, I.

1953 Book Review (of Dahl 1951). *Language,* 29: 577–90.

Geertz, Clifford

1963 *Agricultural Involution.* Berkeley: University of California Press.

Lehmann, H., and A. B. Raper

1949 "Distribution of the Sickle Cell Trait in Uganda and Its Ethnological Significance." *Nature,* 164: 494.

Linton, Ralph

1958 *The Tree of Culture.* New York: Knopf.

Livingstone, F. B.

1958 "Anthropological Implications of Sickle Cell Gene Distribution in West Africa." *American Anthropologist,* 60: 533–62.

1964 "Aspects of the Population Dynamics of the Abnormal Hemoglobin and Glucose-6-Phosphate Dehydrogenase Deficiency Genes." *American Journal of Human Genetics,* 16: 435–50.

1967 *Abnormal Hemoglobins in Human Populations.* Chicago: Aldine.

MacDonald, George

1955 "The Measurement of Malaria Transmission." *Proceedings of the Royal Society of Medicine,* 48: 295–301.

1957 *The Epidemiology and Control of Malaria.* London: Oxford University Press.

Motulsky, A. G.
  1964 "Hereditary Red Cell Traits and Malaria." *American Journal of Tropical Medicine and Hygiene,* 13: 147.
Murdock, George Peter
  1959 *Africa: Its Peoples and Their Culture History.* New York: McGraw-Hill.
Paulme, Denise
  1954 *Les Gens du Riz.* Paris: Librairie Plon.
Rucknagel, Donald L., and James V. Neel
  1961 "The Hemoglobinopathies," in A. G. Steinberg (ed.), *Progress in Medical Genetics.* New York: Grune and Stratton.
Russell, P., L. West, R. Manwell, and G. MacDonald
  1963 *Practical Malariology.* London: University of Oxford Press.
Schoff, E. H. (translator and annotator)
  1912 *The Periplus of the Erythraean Sea: Travel and Trade in the Indian Ocean by a Merchant of the First Century.* London: Longmans Green.
Seligman, C. G., and B. Z. Seligman
  1932 *Pagan Tribes of the Nilotic Sudan.* London: Routledge.
Vavilov, N. I.
  1949 "The Origin, Variation, Immunity and Breeding of Cultivated Plants," translated by K. S. Chester. *Chronica Botanica,* 13: 1–364. New York: Ronald Press.
Wilson, D. B.
  1949 "Malaria Incidence in Central and South Africa," in M. F. Boyd (ed.), *Malariology.* Philadelphia and London: Saunders.

17 SWIDDEN AGRICULTURE AND THE RISE OF MAYA CIVILIZATION[1]

D. E. Dumond

I T IS A COMMONPLACE to assert that one precondition for the rise of civilization is a degree of efficiency in the production of foodstuffs, whether stated in terms of economic surplus or of the harnessing of energy. This precondition customarily has been met through some system of agriculture, and it seems frequently to be assumed that the more intensive the agriculture, the more likely it is to produce the requisite surplus. Conversely it has also been argued that civilization has not developed where intensive agriculture did not exist—specifically in cases in which the only support was some form of shifting cultivation.[2] It is this thesis which will be briefly examined here, with special reference to the lowland Maya.

One approach is that of Meggers (1954:815), who postulated a law to the effect that "the level to which a culture can develop

Reprinted from *Southwestern Journal of Anthropology*, Vol. 17 (1961), pp. 301–16, by permission of the author and publisher.

[1] Thanks are due R. D. Gastil, T. Stern, V. R. Dorjahn, and L. S. Cressman, who kindly read and commented upon a version of this paper, the L. S. and D. C. Cressman Prize Essay in Anthropology for 1960–61. None, of course, is responsible for its shortcomings.

[2] Civilization as here used refers to societies characterized by the most recognizable of the criteria presented by Childe (1950): the possession of "truly monumental public buildings," to which the concentration of "social surplus," some labor specialization, etc., are assumed to be corollary. Swidden agriculture, slash-and-burn or shifting cultivation, is defined after Pelzer (1945:17), as involving rotation of fields rather than crops; clearing by means of fire; use of human labor only; lack of manuring; use of dibble or hoe; use of short periods of cultivation alternating with long periods of fallow.

is dependent upon the agricultural potentiality of the environment it occupies." The tropical forest, doomed by natural conditions to be tilled by some method of shifting cultivation, is said thereby to possess a low absolute ceiling for cultural development. She includes the lowland Maya area within this land of little opportunity, and concludes that the lowland Maya developed civilized knowledge and skills before their arrival in the Petén, and subsequently spent their most spectacular era in a recessionary decline to which the system of agriculture was causal. Swidden agriculture as a basis for civilized developments is held in similar low esteem by others. Barrau (1959:55), for instance, indicates it can provide only for subsistence. The FAO staff (1957:9) assert that under such a backward system no concentration of population, and hence no urbanization, is possible. Palerm and Wolf (1957:26) state flatly that "slash and burn agriculture . . . could not provide a stable economic basis for the growth and existence of Maya civilization" (cf. Palerm 1955:31; Wolf 1959:77).

But the objection made is not necessarily based upon a lack of productivity, in terms of the return for an hour's labor. On the contrary, efficient swidden farming is seen by many students to be capable of producing a definite surplus. Although this potentiality seems fairly well established, a short review may be in order. It must be emphasized, however, that data are generally scanty, often unreliable, and that efficiency of shifting cultivation practices varies tremendously.

In Mexico, Lewis (1955:155f.) indicates that yields per acre from maize swiddens of Tepoztlán farmers average twice as high as those from continuously cropped lands.[3] Kelly and Palerm (1952:118) report that Tajín Totonac swidden farmers as a whole tend to produce a small amount more than they consume. La-Farge and Byers (1931:71) state that the swidden farmers of Jacaltenango, in western Guatemala, raise enough maize to carry on a considerable export business. Figures provided by Villa Rojas (1945:60, 65) suggest that in 1935–36—a better-than-average year—the X-Cacal Maya harvested almost three times

---

[3] Productivity per hour of labor *with oxen* in the continuously cropped fields is about fifty percent higher than that without oxen in swiddens. Such a comparison is of course not valid when applied to pre-Columbian Mexico.

their annual requirement of maize, and that without farming to capacity they are able to develop and maintain a surplus sufficient to tide them over two or three lean years. Various other studies indicate that swidden farms in the Mexican tropics are capable of producing a maize surplus from 20 to 100 percent of subsistence needs (Morley 1947:154; Emerson and Kempton 1935:140; Drucker and Heizer 1960).

In temperate Europe the Finno-Ougrian peoples in the nineteenth century are reputed to have obtained from shifting cultivation a yield of rye three to four times as high as that possible from continuously cropped fields (Clark 1952:92).

The situation reported from southeast Asia is similar. Conklin (1957:152) suggests that production per man-hour in Hanunóo rice swiddens in the Philippines "compares favorably with labor cost figures for rice production under the best conditions elsewhere in the tropics." Figures presented by Gourou (1956:342) suggest that irrigated rice agriculture in the heavily populated Tonkinese Delta is less than half as productive as the Hanunóo swiddens, in terms of expended man-hours. Among the Land Dayak of Sarawak, Geddes (1954:65f.) reports that irrigated (swamp) swiddens—presumably of higher fertility than would be unfertilized, continuously cropped wet fields in the same area —may not yield more than good upland swiddens. Halpern (1958:33) cites figures from Laos and other portions of Indo-China which "indicate the possibility that hectare for hectare in any given season swidden cultivation can be more productive" than irrigated rice farming. Gourou also points out that a shift from swiddens to "intensively cultivated, permanent fields does not necessarily carry with it an increase of productivity—not if the available arable area is so spacious as to permit suitable fallows and thus evade the risk of soil exhaustion. Tropical cultivators are aware of this." Consequently, he says, swidden agriculturalists may oppose changes in their agricultural systems on purely material grounds:

> The peoples of some mountains of West Africa (Atacora Mountains, Bauchi Plateau, Mandara Mountains, Adamawa, etc.) learned relatively intensive agricultural techniques, such as artificial terracing and manuring, in response to a crisis: they had retreated into the mountains primarily for defense against external dangers,

particularly against the raids of slavers. The establishment of peace and the suppression of slavery allowed these peoples to abandon their mountains and to clear the surrounding plains where arable areas were plentiful. In the new environment they are forgetting these techniques and returning to *ladang* [i.e., swidden farming], in which they find greater productivity. In the same way, all the efforts made between 1920 and 1940 to lead the Moi Rhade (Annamite Cordillera of Indochina) to utilize the plow and to till inundated rice fields have been wasted. . . . They have observed that permanent rice fields, without manure, gave a lesser output per day of work than *ladang*. . . . Still worse, the Vietnamese colonists of Ban Methuot, Darlac, have turned for the first time to *ladang* and have abandoned the ancestral plow (Gourou 1956: 345).

Leach (1959:64f.) has thrown further light on the change from extensive to intensive cultivation, with evidence from North Burma:

It is noticeable that in the areas of very low population density where the land was plentiful, shifting cultivation was always the preferred technique; effort by the government to persuade the population to adopt fixed agriculture was almost completely futile. On the other hand wherever the local population density was high so that land was scarce, terraced agriculture is the standard, traditionally established, preferred technique. There is no cultural difference between the shifting agriculturalists and the terraced field agriculturalists. Precisely the same tribal peoples practice both forms of cultivation. They recognize the two techniques as alternatives and are prepared to discuss the relative merits of both. Terraced agriculture represents much harder work but can be relied upon to produce a moderately good yield. Shifting agriculture on the other hand will produce a very high yield in areas where the forest cover has been thick but a very poor yield in areas of deforestation. There is therefore a perfectly definite economic point at which, from the villager's point of view it becomes advantageous to change from shifting agriculture to terraced agriculture.

Clark (1952:98f.) indicates that the Danubians of Neolithic Europe probably abandoned their swidden agriculture in favor of more intensive methods of tillage only when the population density was too great to permit the shifting system to operate. This may be of general occurrence. It seems not unlikely, for instance, that in ancient Mesopotamia a similar cause existed for the movement of peoples from the hills where agriculture had

begun, down toward the dry Mesopotamian plain itself, about
5000 BC (Braidwood 1960:148), a movement which seems to
have necessitated the first use of irrigation (Adams 1955:9), and
perhaps of intensive farming techniques.

Bartlett (1956:709) suggests that "wherever a few colonists
of a higher culture have gone into countries of primitive culture,
they have largely dropped to the primitive [generally swidden-
using] level of agriculture. This is well demonstrated by the history
of the colonization of the eastern United States. . . ."

Rather than find swidden farming of doubtful productivity,
therefore, it seems reasonable to suggest that for reasons of productivity there is everywhere a tendency to employ patterns of
cultivation which rely upon movement of the field when fertility
drops from over-cropping, rather than systems of intensive cropping. One might go farther and suggest that such practices of extensive agriculture are normally adhered to until population pressure becomes such that the system ceases to be viable through
lack of sufficient land for rotation. Such a tendency toward extensive use would not operate, of course, where soil fertility does
not diminish—for whatever reason—after continued cultivation,
and might be modified in cases where use of draft animals makes
intensive but less productive cultivation easier in terms of human
effort (cf. note 3 above).

But as indicated previously, a lack of productivity per man-
hour does not constitute the grounds for the final censure of swidden agriculture. Most critics condemn swidden systems as "a
wasteful method" (Childe 1951:64; also, e.g., LaFarge and Byers
1931:69; FAO Staff 1957:9). Leach (1959:64) suggests that
most criticisms base themselves on the destruction of timber and
the dangers of deforestation and erosion. That it is wasteful
of forest cover is to an extent clear. In its better examples, however, it seems generally to be conservative of soil fertility: Popenoe
(1959:76), for example, suggests that swidden agriculture in the
valley of the Polochic River in northern Guatemala represents
a very conservative practice, with the soil exhibiting comparatively
high levels of fertility. Many other students agree with him (as
Barrau 1959:55; Lafont 1959:56; Meggers 1957:81). The
significance of this for the support of civilization is clear. A well-
balanced system of shifting cultivation should be capable of indefinite duration.

But criticisms of systems of shifting cultivation as foundations for civilizations go beyond productivity and the waste of resources. Meggers (1957:82) states that the shortcomings (for present purposes) of swidden agriculture are notably two: a relatively large amount of land per capita must be available for agricultural use; and settlements cannot remain permanently in one place. Wolf (1959:77) states that "slash-and-burn cultivation usually implies a scattered population, a population unwilling to pay homage to a center of control." Other critics agree (e.g., FAO Staff 1957).

That settlements are in some instances forced to move to keep up with swiddens is undeniable. It is apparently documented in the case of the temperate zone Finno-Ougrians cited above, even though in preference to moving, lands might be cultivated as much as forty miles away (Clark 1952:96, with references); it is also strongly suggested for the Danubians (idem:95). It is the case with modern peoples, as for instance with the Djarais of central Vietnam, who reportedly succeed in wrecking each piece of land they utilize by continued burning of undergrowth, and consequently are forced into periodic moves (Lafont 1959). It is also true in the case of pioneer agriculturalists like some Iban of Sarawak who exhibit a habitual preference for virgin timber, and move in order to find it (Freeman 1955).

But this pattern is by no means universal. A great proportion of swidden farmers are in sufficient balance with their environment that they remain sedentary (Barrau 1959:55; Pelzer 1958:127). Both Conklin (1959) and Carneiro (1960) present formulas by means of which the balance between population and land may be calculated, in terms of the number of people which may be supported permanently in a given area. With his, Carneiro calculates that a swidden farming group of low-average efficiency in tropical South America should be able to support nearly five hundred people in a single sedentary settlement, and that the Kuikuru of the Upper Xingú region of Brazil could support a farming population of two thousand people in a single sedentary village, in place of their present 145. These figures are in terms of manioc cultivation with 0.7 acre to a full acre per person per year in cultivation. This compares with the figure furnished by Drucker and Heizer (1960) for the amount of maize land per year per capita needed in the La Venta region; but the fallow time is shorter in La Venta, so that it seems likely that even larger sedentary farming towns could be supported there.

If the compulsion to frequent movement of villages is not found a necessary part of much tropical swidden farming, the need for large amounts of land per capita cannot be avoided. It is this need which provides the limiting factor in swidden agriculture— a limit to productivity per area, rather than productivity per man-hour. The total number of people supportable in a given area is smaller; population density is of necessity more sharply limited.

In the case of some extremely low-density populations, areas of population concentration are possible and usual—as, for instance, in the case of nomadic peoples who come together in a periodic throng, and remain together in certain seasons with the throng moving as a unit. Such mobility is lacking in the case of swidden agriculturalists, for the most part; it seems likely that in addition to supporting a population of limited overall density the tendency will be for the population to be dispersed in small towns or villages—at least that portion of the population directly engaged in agricultural pursuits, and during the period in which agricultural labor is necessary.

This is the situation envisioned by Wolf (1959:60), when he terms such a system "centrifugal." And it is perhaps at this point that the crucial question has been raised. It seems clear that the better swidden systems in reasonably adequate areas are capable—in terms of return on labor invested—of producing an amount adequate to support not only ceremonial centers but population centers, and a number of specialists. Emerson and Kempton (1935:140) suggest, for example, that where present agricultural practices in Yucatán and Campeche produce a surplus of about twenty percent over the subsistence needs of the cultivators, the same farming population should be capable of doubling its grain output, "thus making possible the food requirements of a non-productive population four or five times that of the present one" of Mérida and Progreso. To be sure, Palerm (1955:31) argues that such support would be impossible for dispersed farmers to provide under aboriginal conditions, from sheer awkwardness of distribution when transportation depended only upon human carriers. But in spite of this assertion the pre-Columbian city of Mayapán in Yucatán remains an example of a center of concentrated population, traditionally supported for two hundred fifty years in an area for which nobody, so far as I am aware, has suggested the practice of anything but swidden agriculture, with a transportation system depending upon nothing but manpower. Palerm and Wolf (1957:27f.) state that this particular argument "is deceptive in its superficiality," insofar as it supports the case for development of civilization in swidden farming regions, for "the Northern Maya territory was conquered by war-like groups who settled in nucleated and fortified sites from which they dominated and subjected the rural population. The basic patterns of social, political and military organization, however, were introduced from the Mexican highland." Superficial or not, the example supports the supposition that swidden agriculture and transport by human porters is sufficient to provide for an urban settlement, once it has developed.

The problem remaining, then, concerns the assertion that shifting cultivation is by its nature socially "centrifugal," and hence is inimical to the centralization implicit in any civilization, including the Maya—whether the latter in its Classic manifestations in the Petén involved "urban" concentrations of city dwellers or whether it existed in terms of ceremonial centers supported by a dispersed population. At this point little argument should remain in terms of subsistence economics. The problem is one of social organization.

Kroeber (1948:272ff.), when discussing the effect of the size of a society on its organization, suggests that urbanism—civilization in the present sense—is more likely in larger societies. Steward (1955:73ff.) argues that high population density without centralization does not produce cities. That is to say, the size of the society, in Kroeber's terms, is a matter of organization; a large society is possible—theoretically, at least—in an area of dispersed population as well as in an area of population concentration. The question to be raised here is whether a measure of social centralization may be achieved by people who live as dispersed as do swidden farmers.

What population densities are possible under swidden agriculture? Pelzer (1945:23, 29) suggests that up to one hundred thirty per square mile may be supported in the Asiatic tropics without soil damage. Ooi Jin-Bee (1958:113) provides a list of carrying capacities of lands under shifting cultivation in tropical areas, varying from eighteen to one hundred sixty persons per square mile, with more than half the eleven figures above eighty. Some of these involve root crops, but more involve the cultivation of upland rice. One citation refers to a maize producing area, British Honduras, with a figure of sixty per square mile. Drucker and Heizer (1960:43) provide figures for La Venta which indicate that one person could be fed indefinitely by a maize production of 3.75 acres. If somewhat less than sixty percent of the total land area is arable—about the proportion found usable in a study at Uaxactún (Morley 1947:313f.)—such a region would support one hundred per square mile. Emerson and Kempton (1935) suggest that with farming methods in practice at the time of their study, Campeche and Yucatán could support sixty per square mile, and that the carrying capacity could be increased without drastic or harmful change in methods.[4] Densities such as those mentioned here, one might point out, are not extremely low.

That populations no more dense than these are capable of centralized organization seems evident from the most superficial consideration of evidence from Africa, a continent of relatively light population, but

> from the point of view of organization and administration, the political acumen . . . in tribe after tribe equals, where it does not surpass, anything in the nonliterate world. Not even the kingdoms of Peru and Mexico could mobilize resources and concentrate power more effectively than could some of these African monarchies, which are more to be compared to Europe of the middle ages than referred to the common conception of the "primitive" state (Herskovits 1948:332).

Although population figures for portions of Africa are notorious for their inaccuracy, at least a rough idea may be gained of certain aboriginal densities. According to figures presented by

---

[4] By way of comparison, Thompson (1954:29) suggests population figures such that ancient inhabitants of the Petén and Yucatán would not have exceeded one million at their most populous; using Morley's (1947:316) estimate of 50,000 square miles for the habitable (not total) area of the Yucatán peninsula, one arrives at a figure of twenty inhabitants per habitable square mile, or ten per square mile of total area. This seems modest indeed. Morley's more ambitious figure of 13,300,000 inhabitants provides a density of 133 per square mile—probably too high, but no higher than figures from present-day swidden-farming areas of Java, Malaya, and northern Nigeria (Ooi 1958:113).

Forde (1951:3), estimated census figures for the Yoruba in 1921 were slightly over two million, with those of 1931 running slightly more than three million, an unlikely increase of fifty percent in ten years. Hardly more believable is the increase necessary to achieve the 1952 census figure of more than five million. There are, however, a number of estimates of the size of individual Yoruba settlements, and it seems reasonable that these figures are more apt to be accurate than those for the Yoruba as a whole. Bascom (1959:31–33)[5] presents figures for a number of large Yoruba settlements which may be compared; summing these for 1911 and for 1952—and excluding figures for the modern city of Lagos—one obtains a suggestion of an increase in these populations of some one hundred percent in the indicated forty years. Bascom's citation of Moloney's estimates of ten city populations of 1890 are higher in total than are the same cities in the 1911 census, perhaps as the result of inaccuracy of estimates in either count, or it may be that in 1890, at the end of a long period of slave wars, the population was more concentrated than it was twenty years later. Allowing for a considerable population decline in the nineteenth century as a result of the wars, or for a modern increase in urbanization, one might rather tentatively suggest an increase of fifty percent in general population between 1850 and 1952. Applying this proportion to figures for population density cited by Bascom from the 1952 census, one obtains an approximate range of 1850 population densities between fifty-five and two hundred forty per square mile.[6] Of these, only the density of Ibadan province (at two hundred forty) exceeds one hundred per square mile, and the city of Ibadan itself, with a population in 1952 of nearly 460,000, is known to have developed principally as a nineteenth century military center (Bascom 1959:35). These people are swidden agriculturalists, today raising chiefly yams, maize, bananas, and manioc as subsistence foods (Forde 1951:6). Their penchant for dwelling in big settlements, however,

---

[5] All subsequent Yoruba census figures are from Bascom 1959:31–33.
[6] In a personal communication, William Bascom generously provided suggestions of means for tentatively estimating 1850 Yoruba population density, emphasizing that all such estimates must remain somewhat questionable for lack of sufficient and reliable data. His assistance is greatly appreciated, but it should go without saying that he can in no way be held responsible for any untoward results.

was well developed at the time of the first European contact. Such centers are reported from early in the sixteenth century. In the 1850's they were estimated to have at least nine settlements with populations between twenty and seventy thousand, with craft specialization and social stratification (Bascom 1959:31, 38ff.).[7]

Less spectacularly, the Azande of Sudan are estimated at 231,000, in figures cited by Baxter and Butt (1953:13). The Zande district of Sudan, as mapped by De Schlippe (1956:5), cannot include more than twenty thousand square miles. The density, therefore, should not exceed twelve per square mile. The Azande maintain dispersed settlements, and their traditions and swidden agricultural operation—the latter utilizing millet, maize, sorghum, rice, pulses, and some oil seeds (De Schlippe 1956:48ff.)—are such that moves of homesteads are fairly frequent, some of them motivated by soil depletion, but others brought about by other causes (De Schlippe 1956:191ff.). This is an indigenous pattern, yet the indigenous organization was markedly centralized, with a pyramidal organization headed by a king from a hereditary ruling clan, to whom were owed services and tribute. In some areas at least, the number of people under a semi-independent chief, subordinate to a king, might reach or exceed ten thousand (Baxter and Butt 1953:48ff.).

In sum, although it seems reasonable that shifting cultivation

---

[7] The Yoruba base much of their subsistence upon root crops, and it seems possible that such crops may produce more heavily than will cereals or maize. Barrau (1959:54), for instance, indicates that in Melanesia generally about one quarter acre of garden suffices to feed one person for one year, and that a total of about two and one half to five acres suffices to feed one person indefinitely. Figured as above, with about sixty percent of the area cultivable, one finds that in Melanesia between about seventy-five and one hundred fifty people could be supported per square mile. It may be noted, however, that anthropologists have not always agreed on the potentiality of root crop cultivation: Palerm and Wolf (1957:28) suggest that large sedentary populations may be supported by root crops in tropical areas more easily than by maize; Meggers (1957: 28f.) suggests the reverse—that root crop cultivation is more centrifugal than cultivation of temperate crops, because the lack of a single season of maturation means that farm work is more constant, hence dispersed fields must be tended more frequently. At any rate, with the exception of those for the Ibadan area, the Yoruba densities arrived at above seem in general accord with the carrying capacity of land in the lowland Maya area as estimated by Emerson and Kempton (1935) and others.

should tend to produce scattered populations, such scattering is apparently not always the result, and even when it does occur it may not preclude the support of a centralized social or political organization. Parenthetically, Kroeber's citation of Mooney's figure for the population density of the federally-bent five Iroquois tribes is less than one per five square miles (Kroeber 1939:140).

That some patterns of shifting cultivation do militate against social cohesion in terms of supra-village units, is not denied. This must certainly be the case with peoples who are still "pioneers"—breakers of virgin soil—as in the case of the Iban of Sarawak mentioned above. Here, on rather poor land, is possible a density of thirty-five to forty people per square mile, although present density is much less as the population continues to spread in search of virgin timber, utilizing techniques which are generally destructive of soil (Freeman 1955:134). In this area there is still new land to be gained. Here, village long-house communities are the only groups with any cohesion above the nuclear family, having functions in the sphere of religion and the settlement of land claims, but without productive economic role (Freeman 1955:8–10).

The situation is somewhat changed among the Land Dayak of Sarawak, however. Here Geddes (1954) reports a heavier population, having little virgin timber land available. When villages multiply through a process of hiving off, daughter villages may continue to pay allegiance to the mother village (Geddes 1954: 10). And this situation is important to the present argument, for in the maintenance of such ties may be found the seeds of a later centralized development.

Lacking such affective ties, village units might be united by warfare. Herskovits (1938, II:3) suggests that,

> In all West Africa, the early organization seems to have been that of village autonomy or, at most, the rule of several neighboring settlements by the head of the largest village, so that the number of petty kingdoms which existed before the time of their consolidation into great kingdoms such as Dahomey, Benin, Ashanti, and others, was extensive.

The extent to which warfare was causal, however, is not certain. Bascom (1959:38), for instance, indicates that "we cannot say either that the early Yoruba cities did or did not develop as defensive or predatory centres, as Ilorin, Abeokuta and Ibadan did in the 19th century. But urbanism clearly antedated the slave trade to the Americas. . . ."

It has been suggested by Willey (1957:1), based in part on work by the Coes at Nohoch Ek (Coe and Coe 1956), that even the smallest Pre-classic villages in Mesoamerica may be found eventually to have been constructed around modest ceremonial centers. If the situation is such that new villages retain some allegiance to the ceremonial centers of parent villages, the seeds of centralization have been sown.

Pre-classic remains are not plentiful in the lowland Maya area, to judge by excavations to date. It seems possible that during Pre-classic times small, more or less autonomous villages spread through the lowland Maya area, perhaps in search of virgin land. As the land was filled, migrations became less frequent, and ties between related villages became stronger, with ceremonial relationships elaborated. From this developed the centralization of Classic times, aided, perhaps, by a little warfare here and there. The result of such a process should be very close to the organization of the Maya as formulated by Willey (1956).

The foregoing should not be construed as an argument that Classic Maya civilization in the lowlands was never supported by anything but swidden agriculture. The question as to what was in fact the basis of subsistence can be answered only from work in the field. Rather, this paper is intended to suggest that the development of a centralized, stratified system such as seems indicated for the Classic Maya is by no means impossible under conditions of shifting cultivation. Indeed, present indications of intensive agriculture in ancient Mesoamerica are not demonstrably as early as the rise of notable ceremonial centers at the beginning of the Classic and earlier. Consequently, on the basis of present evidence and in spite of the argument of Palerm (1955:31) that concentration of resources and major ceremonial centers are impossible under conditions of rainfall agriculture in Mesoamerica, it seems only reasonable to conclude that the development of such concentrations and such centers began under conditions of extensive—as opposed to intensive—agricultural practices, probably largely swidden agriculture. It is further suggested—although a consideration of the question has not been attempted here—that a similar development may have occurred in other areas generally conceded to have supported civilizations, at least in those areas in which rainfall agriculture is possible at all.[8] In areas where feasible, however, the growth of population would shortly have made the practice of some form of intensive agriculture necessary.

That is to say, it seems likely that centralization and urbanization tend to pre-date the appearance of intensive cultivation and of heavy population growth. Although a discussion of the mechanisms involved is again outside the scope of this paper, it seems likely that by increasing the chances of human survival such centralized organization may stand in a causal relation to population growth, rather than vice versa.

---

[8] Pelzer (1945:20), for example, cites suggestions to the effect that swidden agriculture was basic, or at least extremely important, to other tropical civilizations, specifically that of Angkor, in Cambodia, and that of Anuradapura, in Ceylon.

BIBLIOGRAPHY

Adams, R. M.
  1955 "Developmental Stages in Ancient Mesopotamia," in *Agricultural Civilizations: A Comparative Study*. Pan American Union, Social Science Monographs, No. 1. Washington.
Barrau, J.
  1959 "The 'Bush Fallowing' System of Cultivation in the Continental Islands of Melanesia," in *Proceedings of the Ninth Pacific Science Congress (1957)*, Vol. 7. Bangkok.
Bartlett, H. H.
  1956 "Fire, Primitive Agriculture, and Grazing in the Tropics," in W. L. Thomas (ed.), *Man's Role in Changing the Face of the Earth*. Chicago: University of Chicago Press.
Bascom, W.
  1959 "Urbanism as a Traditional African Pattern." *The Sociological Review*, n.s., 7: 29–43.
Baxter, P. T. W., and A. Butt
  1953 *The Azande and Related Peoples of the Anglo-Egyptian Sudan and Belgian Congo*. Ethnographic Survey of Africa, East Central Africa, pt. 9. London: International African Institute.
Braidwood, R. J.
  1960 "The Agricultural Revolution." *Scientific American*, 203 (3): 130–48.
Carneiro, R. L.
  1960 "Slash-and-burn Agriculture: A Closer Look at Its Implications for Settlement Patterns," in A. F. C. Wallace (ed.), *Men and Cultures*. Philadelphia: University of Pennsylvania Press.
Childe, V. G.
  1950 "The Urban Revolution." *Town Planning Review*, 21: 3–17.
  1951 *Man Makes Himself*. New York: Mentor Books.
Clark, J. G. D.
  1952 *Prehistoric Europe: The Economic Basis*. New York: Philosophical Library.
Coe, W. R., and M. D. Coe
  1956 "Excavations at Nohoch Ek, British Honduras." *American Antiquity*, 21: 370–82.

Conklin, H. C.
  1957 *Hanunóo Agriculture.* FAO Forestry Development Paper No. 12.
    Rome: Food and Agriculture Organization of the United Nations.
  1959 "Population-Land Balance under Systems of Tropical Forest Agri-
    culture." *Proceedings of the Ninth Pacific Science Congress (1957),*
    Vol. 7. Bangkok.
Drucker, P., and R. B. Heizer
  1960 "A Study of the Milpa System of La Venta Island and Its
    Archaeological Implications." *Southwestern Journal of Anthropology,*
    16: 36–45.
Emerson, R. A., and J. H. Kempton
  1935 "Agronomic Investigations in Yucatán." *Carnegie Institution of
    Washington Yearbook,* 34: 138–42. Washington.
FAO Staff [Food and Agriculture Organization of the United Nations]
  1957 "Shifting Cultivation." *Unasylva,* 11: 9–11 (Rome: FAO).
Forde, D.
  1951 *The Yoruba-Speaking Peoples of South-Western Nigeria.* Ethno-
    graphic Survey of Africa, Western Africa, pt. 4. London: International
    African Institute.
Freeman, J. D.
  1955 *Iban Agriculture.* Colonial Research Studies, No. 18. London:
    Colonial Office.
Geddes, W. R.
  1954 *The Land Dayaks of Sarawak.* Colonial Research Studies, No. 14.
    London: Colonial Office.
Gourou, P.
  1956 "The Quality of Land Use of Tropical Cultivators," in W. L.
    Thomas (ed.), *Man's Role in Changing the Face of the Earth.*
    Chicago: University of Chicago Press.
Halpern, J. M.
  1958 *Aspects of Village Life and Culture Change in Laos.* Special
    Report for the Council on Economic and Cultural Affairs, Inc.
    New York: Council on Economic and Cultural Affairs, Inc.
Herskovits, J. J.
  1938 *Dahomey: An Ancient West African Kingdom.* 2 vols. New York:
    J. J. Augustin.
  1948 *Man and His Works.* New York: Knopf.
Kelly, I., and A. Palerm
  1952 *The Tajin Totonac: Part 1, History, Subsistence, Shelter, and
    Technology.* Smithsonian Institution, Institute of Social Anthropology,
    Pub. 13. Washington.
Kroeber, A. L.
  1939 *Cultural and Natural Areas of Native North America.* University
    of California Publications in American Archaeology and Ethnology,
    38. Berkeley: University of California Press.
  1948 *Anthropology.* New York: Harcourt, Brace.

LaFarge, O., II, and D. Byers
  1931 *The Year Bearer's People.* Tulane University Department of
    Middle American Research, Middle American Research Series, Pub.
    3. New Orleans.
Lafont, P. B.
  1959 "The 'Slash and Burn' (Ray) Agricultural System of the Mountain
    Populations of Central Vietnam." *Proceedings of the Ninth Pacific
    Science Congress (1957)*, Vol. 7. Bangkok.
Leach, E. R.
  1959 "Some Economic Advantages of Shifting Cultivation." *Proceedings
    of the Ninth Pacific Science Congress (1957)*, Vol. 7. Bangkok.
Lewis, O.
  1955 *Life in a Mexican Village.* Urbana, Illinois: University of Illinois.
Meggers, B. J.
  1954 "Environmental Limitation on the Development of Culture." *Ameri-
    can Anthropologist,* 56: 801–24.
  1957 "Environment and Culture in the Amazon Basin: An Appraisal
    of the Theory of Environmental Determinism," in *Studies in Human
    Ecology,* Pan American Union, Social Science Monographs, No. 3.
    Washington.
Morley, S.
  1947 *The Ancient Maya.* Stanford University: Stanford University
    Press.
Ooi Jin-Bee
  1958 "The Distribution of Present-Day Man in the Tropics: Historical
    and Ecological Perspective." *Proceedings of the Ninth Pacific Science
    Congress (1957)*, Vol. 20. Bangkok.
Palerm, A.
  1955 "The Agricultural Bases of Urban Civilization in Mesoamerica,"
    in *Irrigation Civilizations: A Comparative Study,* Pan American
    Union, Social Science Monographs, No. 1. Washington.
Palerm, A., and E. R. Wolf
  1957 "Ecological Potential and Cultural Development in Mesoamerica,"
    in *Studies in Human Ecology,* Pan American Union, Social Science
    Monographs, No. 3. Washington.
Pelzer, K. J.
  1945 *Pioneer Settlement in the Asiatic Tropics.* American Geographical
    Society, Special Publication 29. New York: Institute of Pacific Rela-
    tions.
  1958 "Land Utilization in the Humid Tropics: Agriculture." *Proceedings
    of the Ninth Pacific Science Congress (1957)*, Vol. 20. Bangkok.
Popenoe, H.
  1959 "The Influence of the Shifting Cultivation Cycle on Soil Properties
    in Central America." *Proceedings of the Ninth Pacific Science Con-
    gress (1957)*, 7: 72–77. Bangkok.
Schlippe, Pierre de
  1956 *Shifting Cultivation in Africa.* London: Routledge.

Steward, J.
  1955 "Some Implications of the Symposium," in *Irrigation Civilizations: A Comparative Study,* Pan American Union, Social Science Monographs, No. 1. Washington.
Thompson, J. E. S.
  1954 *The Rise and Fall of Maya Civilization.* Norman, Oklahoma: University of Oklahoma Press.
Villa Rojas, A.
  1945 *The Maya of East Central Quintana Roo.* Carnegie Institution of Washington, Pub. 559. Washington.
Willey, G. R.
  1956 "The Structure of Ancient Maya Society: Evidence from the Southern Lowlands." *American Anthropologist,* 58: 777–82.
  1957 "Selected Papers of the Harvard Middle American Archaeological Seminar, 1955–56: an Introduction." *Kroeber Anthropological Society Papers,* No. 17: 1–6.
Wolf, E. R.
  1959 *Sons of the Shaking Earth.* Chicago: University of Chicago Press.

18 RELATIONS OF ENVIRONMENTAL AND CULTURAL FACTORS

Alfred L. Kroeber

THE ASSUMPTION upon which the discussions in this section rest is . . . that on the one hand culture can be understood primarily only in terms of cultural factors, but that on the other hand no culture is wholly intelligible without reference to the noncultural or so-called environmental factors with which it is in relation and which condition it.

An example will illustrate. Six American states stretching in a belt from Ohio to Nebraska today produce nearly half the world's maize crop. This is a region in which the Indians also farmed maize, but with less intensity than in many other regions; and their population remained scant. The difference is not in the plant, nor fundamentally in methods of farming it. It is factors extrinsic to the cultivation itself which have changed an area of below-average maize-growing into one of most successful specialization. These factors are cultural: domesticated animals, economic demand and distribution facilities, methods of transportation, improved machinery. The natural environment remained the same.

However, maize-farming of itself, like other subsistence and economic activities, and through these all cultural activities, is obviously conditioned by "natural" factors such as climate, soil, and drainage. The frostless season must be warm and long enough, the precipitation within it sufficient, and so on. Where these

Excerpt from Chapter 13 of A. L. Kroeber, *Cultural and Natural Areas of Native North America*, University of California Publications in American Archaeology and Ethnology, Vol. 38 (1939). Reprinted by permission of the University of California Press.

conditions fail, the limits of maize-growing are reached. This inability tends to affect the whole of a culture unable to farm; but quite differently according to situation: in California and eastern Canada, for instance. The difference in effect is due to both environmental and cultural causes, which vary areally. In California, nature provided other food to make population in the nonfarming territory denser rather than lighter. The local cultures thus were able to flourish with some vigor and with considerable independence of the farming ones near them. In the East, there was no comparable natural food supply, and the hunting population remained light. This put it in a position of dependence, culturally, on the adjacent farming populations. And at the same time the cultural medium was so much thinned by the smaller subsistence possibilities that many elements of the farming culture failed to obtain a foothold to the north.

It is in this way that the interactions of culture and environment become exceedingly complex when followed out. And this complexity makes generalization unprofitable, on the whole. In each situation or area different natural factors are likely to be impinging on culture with different intensity.

It does seem worth while to review briefly the more striking cases of influence of the various environmental factors, as indicated by the degree of agreement between cultural areas and natural ones of various kinds. The intent is not so much to evaluate in general terms the strength of each environmental factor as to recognize specific cases where environment is of importance.

NATURAL VEGETATION

Plant cover is obviously almost always likely to stand in relation to culture. It largely expresses climate; it tends heavily to determine the fauna; and it enters directly into subsistence, besides at times affecting travel and transport. It is rather surprising, in fact, that culture is not therefore a function of natural vegetation to a greater degree than actually obtains. That it is not, suggests the preponderant strength of purely cultural forces. However, there are a number of neat correspondences of areas of plant cover and culture. Among the principal of these are the following:

The Northwest Coast culture tallies almost perfectly with the Northwestern Hygrophytic Forest.

Within this, the area appearing most aberrant culturally, the Willamette Valley, is also aberrant phytogeographically, being classed as forest by some authorities, as grassland by others.

In the Southwest, the historically primary line of cleavage between cultures of Pueblo and of Sonora-Gila-Yuma type is closely paralleled by a division of the area into semidesert and true desert.

The Pueblo semidesert is part of the sagebrush-juniper semidesert of the Great Basin, into which both Basket Maker and Pueblo culture proliferated.

Snake River drainage affiliates not with the Columbia but with the Great Basin in prevailing plant cover, speech and, apparently, culture.

The short-grass plains and tall-grass prairies, before the introduction of the horse, probably harbored cultures respectively of prevailing western mountain and eastern forest affiliations.

The Wind River Shoshone, basically a Basin tribe with a recent overlay of Plains culture, lived in a sagebrush habitat even though this drains into the Mississippi system.

The tropical region of southern Florida corresponds to a local variant of the general Southeastern culture.

The northern Iroquoian territory is characteristically one of Northeastern Hardwood forest.

The classic Maya culture is situated in tropical rain forest, the sub-Maya culture of the other Mayan tribes in more open plant cover.

The Pacific Nicaragua or Chorotegan culture lay in a region of relatively arid vegetation.

East of the Mississippi, correspondences are less definite than elsewhere. The varieties both of culture and of plant cover differ from one another by small intervals, so that conditions are more nearly uniform on both scores. Mexico, on the other hand, presents sharp contrasts, but knowledge of the ecology is too imperfect, and that of the cultures too little organized, to make most classifications and correlations more than tentative.

CLIMATE

Climate has been incidentally rather than systematically considered in this work. It is not an easy thing to deal with; partly because of its compositeness. Temperature, precipitation, seasonal régime, besides minor factors, are all of varying influence. Here one component and there another becomes specifically influential upon culture. Temperature may be uniform in two regions and yet the precipitation cause them to vary enormously as cultural habitats; or the reverse. A climatic classification taking cognizance of all factors is obviously the desideratum. A basis for this is provided by the Köppen system. But the execution and mapping of this has been on a world-wide scheme rather summary for comparisons within a continent, and certainly not equal in accuracy of detail to the available plant-cover classifications. Since these so largely reflect climate, besides being more directly related to subsistence, I have thought it advisable to center present attention on them.

Russell has recently applied the Köppen scheme, with modifications resulting from purely American considerations, to two parts of the continent: California, and the dry parts of the United States (Russell 1926 and 1931). Geographically broader studies as intensive as these will make possible a rather exact comparison of climate and culture.

I have gone over Russell's California climate classification with care. On the whole it seems to agree somewhat more closely with ethnic than with cultural groupings. But the California situation on all three scores is notoriously intricate, and the results of the comparison cannot fairly be presented without a mass of detail going beyond the scope of the present work. I hope to give this matter separate treatment in a subsequent paper.

From Russell's second monograph I reproduce two maps in somewhat simplified form. The first (map 1) shows the dry climates of the United States, classified into cold and hot steppe and cold and hot (and torrid) desert climates.[1] In geographic and cultural terms, the distribution and correspondence of the areas of these climates is as follows.

---

[1] For a definition of these classes, especially the primary ones of desert (W), steppe (S), and humid (H), it is necessary to consult the original work, since the formulas and diagrams on which the distribution rests are complicated. The line which separates the "hot" and "cold" types within the two major dry climates is the January isotherm of 32° F. The "very hot summer desert" climate, BWhh, is hot summer desert plus three months with mean maximum temperature above 100° F.

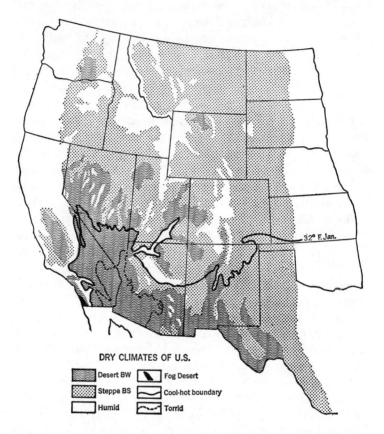

DRY CLIMATES OF U.S.

Desert BW	Fog Desert
Steppe BS	Cool-hot boundary
Humid	Torrid

Map 1 Dry climates of the United States; adapted and slightly simplified from Russell. Desert climates in heavy shading, steppe type in light shading, humid unshaded. The January isotherm of 32° F. (solid heavy line) divides cool dry from hot dry climates. Torrid desert, with three summer months above 100° F., within broken line.

The western limit of steppe and desert against humid climates is the (eastern foot of the) Cascades-Sierra Nevada wall. The San Joaquin Valley is arid; in its middle, desert. On the coast, dry climate begins between Santa Barbara and Los Angeles, to continue southward. Thus not only all the Northwest coast within the United States, but indeed most of cultural California, is humid; southern California is variegated humid and arid. The Achomawi and Washo still live mainly in humid climate.

On the east, the steppe-humid boundary follows the hundredth meridian rather closely. Most of the Plains area (as distinct from Prairie) thus lies in steppe. The climatic boundary given can be assumed as not very far from the eastern limit of range of the old, prehorse culture leaning on a Rocky Mountain habitat with seasonal incursions into the plains.

The historic and most of the prehistoric Pueblo culture lies in steppe. Pueblo occupations of hot desert were the lower Rio Grande, Chihuahua, Upper and Middle Gila, and Southern Nevada phases, all transient; an arm of cold desert also extends up the San Juan. The ancient non-Pueblo red-on-buff ware culture centering on the Gila lay wholly in desert; its focus, like the historic Lower Colorado culture, in torrid desert. The Great Basin culture area lies mostly in steppe and nearly all in cool arid climate. In Nevada, desert prevails, but broken by nearly a dozen parallel ranges rising into steppe climate.

The line separating cool from hot arid climates approximately separates the northern Plains from the southern Plains tribes. It also separates the areas occupied by Pueblos both early and late from those to the south held by them only for a time. But it seems to correspond to nothing of primary ethnic or cultural significance in Nevada and California.

Russell's second map shows the variation in seasonal precipitation in the western United States. He modifies the Köppen scheme by recognizing nine types of seasonal régime. In map 2 I have condensed these into three. The first type (western area) corresponds to his types S and Sf (dry summers, wet winters), with precipitation in the two wettest winter months as 2:1 or more compared to the two wettest summer months. The second (eastern area) corresponds to Russell's types W, Wf, fW, fw (dry winters), with precipitation in the same months as 4:7 or less; and the third (middle area) to his Sf, sf, f, with the winter-summer ratio in the same months between 2:1 and 4:7, or reasonably balanced. For precise understanding of the scheme, it is again necessary to refer to the original text.

What this map shows is that most of the true Pueblo area, ancient and modern, falls within the region of definite excess of summer rains. Such of it as does not, is not far over the boundary, being included in Russell's next régime, "f," for which there is still a summer excess, though as low as about 6:5 (western limit shown by the dotted line in map 2). Where winter rains are definitely in excess, there is no native agriculture

Map 2   Seasonal distribution of precipitation in the western United States; simplified from Russell. In the stippled area, the ratio of the precipitation in winter to that in summer (two wettest months) lies between 2:1 and 4:7. The dotted line indicates the western limit of a 6:5 ratio.

at all, except along the self-irrigating flood-plain patches of the lower Colorado.

The inference is twofold:

The definitely maize-dependent Pueblo culture remained limited to an area of sufficient precipitation during the growing season of the plant; which in an arid climate means excess of summer rains. To the south a limit to this culture was probably set by aridity, which reached a point where even heavy summer concentration no longer sufficed. To the north, the limit was

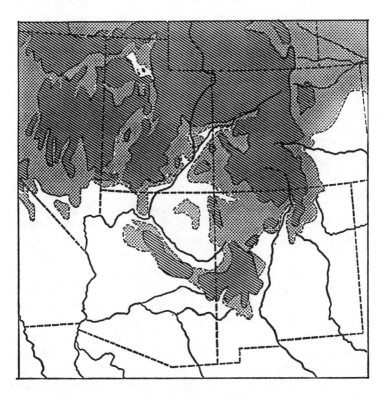

Map 3 Growing season in the Southwest in terms of average dates of last killing frost in spring and first in fall; adapted from Atlas of American Agriculture, *Pt. II, Sec. I, pp. 2, 6. Heavy shading, both dates within the period June 1 (solid line) to September 30 (broken line); that is, normal growing season definitely less than four months. Light shading, one date outside the same period; season about four months. Unshaded, both dates outside the period: hence average season longer than four months.*

evidently set by cool summers, likely to bring fatal frosts between the germination and harvesting of maize: see map 3. It is plain from this map that the area into which the Pueblos concentrated after 1500 all has a normally frostless season of more than four months. Taos alone seems to be just beyond the edge; but even the patch occupied by Laguna and Acoma is accounted

for by a west-extending arm of long-summer territory. All the
abandoned Pueblo tracts also fall partly or wholly in this climate;
in the San Juan drainage, for instance, the Kayenta district
entirely, the Chaco and Mesa Verde fractionally. Much the same
thing is shown, though the basis of computation is somewhat
different, by map 4 (p. 359, below).

Native California failed to become agricultural because of its
dry summers, for which, so far as maize was concerned, no
amount of winter precipitation could compensate. In most of the
eastern United States cold winters and winter precipitation did
not matter, because low elevation permitted the summer to be
hot and long enough, and the considerable and relatively even
precipitation contained summer rainfall enough, for maize to
thrive. Obviously, these conditions have also determined modern
maize distribution: California today is not notably a corn-raising
state. As between the summer-showered hot desert of southern
New Mexico-Arizona and the dry-summer hot steppe climate of
southern California, Pueblo culture evidently could and did cling
to its maize foundation and persist somewhat precariously in the
former, but was not able even to become established in the latter.
The country between—roughly, central and western Arizona—
in general suffered from too great absolute aridity and evaporation
to make primary maize subsistence possible except where local
natural flood conditions as on the lower Colorado, or specialized
technique as in the Gila-Salt Valley, made irrigation on a fair-
sized scale possible.

The idea that seasonal distribution of rainfall largely controlled both the successful functioning of Pueblo culture and the
nonagriculture of California, I owe to my colleague Sauer.
Russell's careful maps render possible the more precise application of the idea.

Map 4, on a smaller scale than map 3, shows the areas in
which a growing season of at least 120 and 100 days, respectively,
can be counted on in four years out of five. It is added for what
it shows concerning the northern limit of farming east of the
Pueblos. Eastern Wisconsin, the parts of Ontario and New York
occupied by Huron and Iroquois, the Hudson Valley, Connecticut, and the coasts of Massachusetts are all in territory which
could reasonably count on at least 120 days for maize to grow.
These are all districts in which culture flourished, or population

was dense, in comparison with immediately adjacent districts. By the location of settlements in specially sheltered spots, it was probably possible in this area to reduce the expectability of a loss of crop through frost from two years in ten to one or less. It is clear that, as among the Pueblos, an agriculture based on tropical plants had here been pushed to its northern limit of potentiality, at any rate as an agriculture important and not merely ancillary to existence. On the other hand, the adjustment was as stable as it was nice, indicating the firmness of the attachment of the cultures in question to their farming basis. . . .

The one successfully farming highland people, the Cherokee, were far enough south to be in good maize country. At the greatest altitudes occupied, their growing season was as long as that of their ancient northern kinsmen the Iroquois and Huron.

The 100-day line, which marks the extreme limits of native

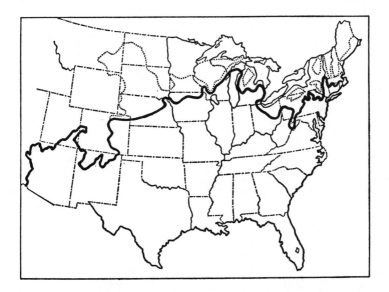

Map 4   Limits of areas within which the season without killing frosts is respectively 120 days (solid line) and 100 days (dotted line) in four years out of five; simplified from Atlas of American Agriculture, *Pt. II, Sec. I, p. 12. The lines indicate the limits, respectively, of reliable and of precarious or sporadic maize growing, and therefore of all agriculture, in native times.*

agriculture when specializing on the quickest maturing varieties of maize, is of no great importance in the Appalachian region, except locally. West of the Mississippi, however, it is significant because it adds as potential farming territory southern Minnesota and the Missouri Valley up into North Dakota, the home of most of the Dakota and of the "Plains Village" tribes. Yet the conditions are difficult enough to make it probable that only a people long and deeply addicted to agriculture would have tried to farm here. An introduction of maize-growing into this area by diffusion in the ordinary ethnological sense, by a process of imitation and learning, seems unlikely; the import was evidently by ethnic migration of farmers. This conclusion is in accord with the customary assumptions based on legendary tradition and inferences from speech relationship of the tribes concerned.

BIBLIOGRAPHY

Russell, R. J.
1926 "Climates of California." *University of California Publications in Geography*, 2: 73–84.
1931 "Dry Climates of the United States, I, Climatic Map." *University of California Publications in Geography*, 5: 1–44.

19 ECOLOGIC RELATIONSHIPS OF ETHNIC GROUPS IN SWAT, NORTH PAKISTAN

Fredrik Barth

THE IMPORTANCE OF ecologic factors for the form and distribution of cultures has usually been analyzed by means of a culture area concept. This concept has been developed with reference to the aboriginal cultures of North America (Kroeber 1939). Attempts at delimiting culture areas in Asia by similar procedures have proved extremely difficult (Bacon 1946, Kroeber 1947, Miller 1953), since the distribution of cultural types, ethnic groups, and natural areas rarely coincide. Coon (1951) speaks of Middle Eastern society as being built on a mosaic principle—many ethnic groups with radically different cultures co-reside in an area in symbiotic relations of variable intimacy. Referring to a similar structure, Furnivall (1944) describes the Netherlands Indies as a plural society. The common characteristic in these two cases is the combination of ethnic segmentation and economic interdependence. Thus the "environment" of any one ethnic group is not only defined by natural conditions, but also by the presence and activities of the other ethnic groups on which it depends. Each group exploits only a section of the total environment, and leaves large parts of it open for other groups to exploit.

This interdependence is analogous to that of the different animal species in a habitat. As Kroeber (1947:330) emphasizes, culture area classifications are essentially ecologic; thus detailed ecologic considerations, rather than geographical areas of subcontinental size, should offer the point of departure. The present

Reprinted from *American Anthropologist*, Vol. 58 (1956), pp. 1079–89, by permission of the author and publisher.

paper attempts to apply a more specific ecologic approach to a case study of distribution by utilizing some of the concepts of animal ecology, particularly the concept of a *niche*—the place of a group in the total environment, its relations to resources and competitors (cf. Allee 1949:516).

Groups. The present example is simple, relatively speaking, and is concerned with the three major ethnic groups in Swat State, North-West frontier Province, Pakistan.[1] These are: (1) *Pathans*—Pashto-speaking (Iranian language family) sedentary agriculturalists; (2) *Kohistanis*—speakers of Dardic languages, practicing agriculture and transhumant herding; and (3) *Gujars* —Gujri-speaking (a lowland Indian dialect) nomadic herders. Kohistanis are probably the ancient inhabitants of most of Swat; Pathans entered as conquerors in successive waves between A.D. 1000–1600, and Gujars probably first appeared in the area some 400 years ago. Pathans of Swat State number about 450,000, Kohistanis perhaps 30,000. The number of Gujars in the area is difficult to estimate.

The centralized state organization in Swat was first established in 1917, and the most recent accretion was annexed in 1947, so the central organization has no relevance for the distributional problems discussed here.

Area. Swat State contains sections of two main valleys, those of the Swat and the Indus Rivers. The Swat River rises in the high mountains to the North, among 18,000 foot peaks. As it descends and grows in volume, it enters a deep gorge. This upper section of the valley is thus very narrow and steep. From approximately 5,000 feet, the Swat valley becomes increasingly wider as one proceeds southward, and is flanked by ranges descending from 12,000 to 6,000 feet in altitude. The river here has a more meandering course, and the valley bottom is a flat, extensive alluvial deposit.

The east border of Swat State follows the Indus River; only its west bank and tributaries are included in the area under discussion. The Indus enters the area as a very large river; it flows in a spectacular gorge, 15,000 feet deep and from 12 to 16 miles

[1] Based on field work February–November 1954, aided by a grant from the Royal Norwegian Research Council.

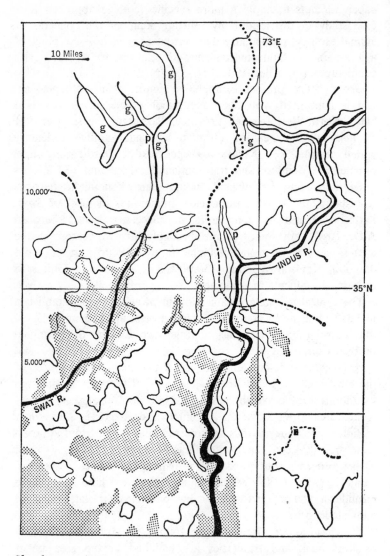

*Sketch map of area of Swat State, Pakistan. Stippled area: under culti-
vation by Pathans. Broken line: border between Pathan and Kohistani
areas. Dotted line: border of area utilized by Gujars (the two borders
coincide towards the southeast). p: outlying Pathan communities. g:
outlying communities of transhumant Gujars. Gujar nomads spend the
summer in the mountains central and north on the map, and winter
in the southernmost area of the map. Inset: location of sketch map.*

wide. Even in the north, the valley bottom is less than 3,000 feet above sea level, while the surrounding mountains reach 18,000 feet. The tributary valleys are consequently short and deeply cut, with an extremely steep profile. Further to the south, the surrounding mountain ranges recede from the river banks and lose height, the Indus deposits some sediment, and the tributary streams form wider valleys.

Climatic variations in the area are a function of altitude. Precipitation is low throughout. The southern, low-altitude areas have long, hot summers and largely steppe vegetation. The Indus gorge has been described as "a desert embedded between icy gravels" (Spate 1954:381). The high mountains are partly covered by permanent ice and snow, and at lower levels by natural mountain meadows in the brief summer season. Between these extremes is a broad belt (from 6,000 to 11,000 feet) of forest, mainly of pine and deodar.

Pathan-Kohistani distribution. Traditional history, in part relating to place-names of villages and uninhabited ruins, indicates that Kohistani inhabitants were driven progressively northward by Pathan invaders (cf. Stein 1929:33, 83). This northward spread has now been checked, and the border between Kohistani and Pathan territories has been stable for some time. The last Pathan expansion northward in the Swat valley took place under the leadership of the Saint Akhund Sadiq Baba, eight generations ago. To understand the factors responsible for the stability of the present ethnic border, it is necessary to examine the specific ecologic requirements of the present Pathan economy and organization.

Pathans of Swat live in a complex, multi-caste society. The landholding Pakhtun caste is organized in localized, segmentary, unilineal descent groups; other castes and occupational groups are tied to them as political clients and economic serfs. Subsistence is based on diversified and well-developed plow agriculture. The main crops are wheat, maize, and rice; much of the plowed land is watered by artificial irrigation. Manuring is practiced, and several systems of crop rotation and regular fallow-field rhythms are followed, according to the nature of the soil and water supply. All rice is irrigated, with nursery beds and transplantation.

Only part of the Pathan population is actively engaged in

agriculture. Various other occupational groups perform specialized services in return for payment in kind, and thus require
that the agriculturalists produce a considerable surplus. Further,
and perhaps more importantly, the political system depends
on a strong hierarchical organization of landowners and much
political activity, centering around the men's houses (*hujra*).
This activity diverts much manpower from productive pursuits.
The large and well-organized Pathan tribes are found in the
lower parts of the Swat valley and along the more southerly
tributaries of the Indus, occupying broad and fertile alluvial
plains. A simpler form of political organization is found along the
northern fringes of Pathan territory. It is based on families of
saintly descent, and is characterized by the lack of men's houses.
This simplification renders the economy of the community more
efficient (1) by eliminating the wasteful potlatch-type feasts of
the men's houses, and (2) by vesting political office in saintly
persons of inviolate status, thus eliminating the numerous retainers
that protect political leaders in other Pathan areas.

Pathan territory extends to a critical ecologic threshold: the
limits within which two crops can be raised each year. This is
largely a function of altitude. Two small outliers of Pashto-
speaking people (Jag, in Duber valley, and a section of Kalam)
are found north of this limit. They are unlike other Pathans,
and similar to their Kohistani neighbors in economy and political
organization.

The conclusion that the limits of double cropping constitute the
effective check on further Pathan expansion seems unavoidable.
Pathan economy and political organization requires that agricultural
labor produce considerable surplus. Thus in the marginal, high-
altitude areas, the political organization is modified and "econo-
mized" (as also in the neighboring Dir area), while beyond these
limits of double cropping the economic and social system can
not survive at all.

Kohistanis are not restricted by this barrier. The Kohistani
ethnic group apparently once straddled it; and, as they were
driven north by invading Pathans, they freely crossed what to
Pathans was a restricting barrier. This must be related to differences between Kohistani and Pathan political and economic
organization, and consequent differences in their ecologic requirements.

Kohistanis, like Pathans, practice a developed plow agriculture. Due to the terrain they occupy, their fields are located on narrow artificial terraces, which require considerable engineering skill for their construction. Parts of Kohistan receive no summer rains; the streams, fed from the large snow reserves in the mountains, supply water to the fields through complex and extensive systems of irrigation. Some manuring is practiced. Climatic conditions modify the types of food crops. Maize and millet are most important; wheat and rice can only be raised in a few of the low-lying areas. The summer season is short, and fields produce only one crop a year.

Agricultural methods are thus not very different from those of Pathans, but the net production of fields is much less. Kohistanis, however, have a two-fold economy, for transhumant herding is as important as agriculture. Sheep, goats, cattle, and water-buffalo are kept for wool, meat, and milk. The herds depend in summer on mountain pastures, where most of the Kohistanis spend between four and eight months each year, depending on local conditions. In some areas the whole population migrates through as many as five seasonal camps, from winter dwellings in the valley bottom to summer campsites at a 14,000 foot altitude, leaving the fields around the abandoned low-altitude dwellings to remain practically untended. In the upper Swat valley, where the valley floor is covered with snow some months of the year, winter fodder is collected and stored for the animals.

By having two strings to their bow, so to speak, the Kohistanis are able to wrest a living from inhospitable mountain areas which fall short of the minimal requirements for Pathan occupation. In these areas, Kohistanis long retained their autonomy, the main territories being conquered by Swat State in 1926, 1939, and 1947. They were, and still are, organized in politically separate village districts of from 400 to 2000 inhabitants. Each community is subdivided into a number of loosely connected patrilineal lineages. The central political institution is the village council, in which all landholding minimal lineages have their representatives. Each community also includes a family of blacksmith-cum-carpenter specialists, and a few households of tenants or farm laborers.

Neighboring communities speaking the same dialect or language[2] could apparently fuse politically when under external pressure, in which case they were directed by a common council of prominent leaders from all constituent lineages. But even these larger units were unable to withstand the large forces of skilled fighters which Pathans of the Swat area could mobilize. These forces were estimated at 15,000 by the British during the Ambeyla campaign in 1862 (cf. Roberts 1898, II:7).

"Natural" subareas. The present Swat State appears to the Kohistanis as a single natural area, since, as an ethnic group, they once occupied all of it, and since their economy can function anywhere within it. With the advent of invading Pathan tribes, the Kohistanis found themselves unable to defend the land. But the land which constitutes one natural area to Kohistanis is divided by a line which Pathans were unable to cross. From the Pathan point of view, it consists of two natural areas, one containing the ecologic requisites for Pathan occupation, the other uninhabitable.[3] Thus the Kohistanis were permitted to retain a part of their old territory in spite of their military inferiority, while in the remainder they were either assimilated as serfs in the conquering Pathan society or were expelled.

From the purely synchronic point of view, the present Pathan-Kohistani distribution presents a simple and static picture of two ethnic groups representing two discrete culture areas, and with a clear correspondence between these culture areas and natural areas: Pathans in broad valleys with a hot climate and scrub vegetation as against Kohistanis in high mountains with a severe climate and coniferous forest cover. Through the addition of time depth, the possibility arises of breaking down the concept of a "natural area" into specific ecologic components in relation to the requirements of specific economies.

---

[2] There are four main Dardic languages spoken in Swat State: Torwàli, Gawri, and Eastern and Western dialect of Kohistəi or Mayān (Barth and Morgenstierne Ms.).

[3] The Pathan attitude toward the Kohistan area might best be illustrated by the warnings I was given when I was planning to visit the area: "Full of terrible mountains covered by many-colored snow and emitting poisonous gases causing head and stomach pains when you cross the high passes; inhabited by robbers, and snakes that coil up and leap ten feet into the air; with no villages, only scattered houses on the mountain tops!"

Analysis of the distribution of Gujars in relation to the other ethnic groups requires such a procedure. Gujars are found in both Pathan and Kohistani areas, following two different economic patterns in both areas: transhumant herding, and true nomadism. But while they are distributed throughout all of the Pathan territory, they are found only in the western half of Kohistan, and neither reside nor visit in the eastern half. The division into mountain and valley seems irrelevant to the Gujars, while the mountain area—inhospitable to Pathans and usable to Kohistanis—is divided by a barrier which Gujars do not cross. The economy and other features of Gujar life must be described before this distribution and its underlying factors can be analyzed.

Gujars constitute a floating population of herders, somewhat ill-defined due to a variable degree of assimilation into the host populations. In physical type, as well as in dress and language, the majority of them are easily distinguishable. Their music, dancing, and manner of celebrating rites of passage differ from those of their hosts. Their political status is one of dependence on the host population.

The Gujar population is subdivided into a number of named patrilineal tribes or clans—units claiming descent from a common known or unknown ancestor, but without supporting genealogies. There are sometimes myths relating to the clan origin, and these frequently serve as etymologies for the clan name. The clans vary greatly in size and only the smallest are localized. The effective descent units are patrilineal lineages of limited depth, though there is greater identification between unrelated Gujars bearing the same clan name than between strangers of different clans. These clans are irrelevant to marriage regulations. There is little intermarriage between Gujars and the host group.

The economy of the Gujars depends mainly on the herding of sheep, goats, cattle, and water buffalo. In addition to animal products, Gujars require some grain (maize, wheat, or millet) which they get by their own agriculture in marginal, high-altitude fields or by trade in return for clarified butter, meat, or wool. Their essential requirements may be satisfied by two rather different patterns of life—transhumance and true nomadism. Pathans differentiate persons pursuing these two patterns by the terms Gujar and Ajer, respectively, and consider them to be ethnic subdivisions. In fact, Gujars may change their pattern of life from one to the other.

Transhumance is practiced mainly by Gujars in the Pathan area, but also occasionally in Kohistan (see map). Symbiotic relationships between Gujars and Pathans take various forms, some quite intimate. Pathans form a multi-caste society, into which Gujars are assimilated as a specialized occupational caste of herders. Thus most Pathan villages contain a small number of Gujars—these may speak Gujri as their home language and retain their separate culture, or may be assimilated to the extent of speaking only Pashto. Politically they are integrated into the community in a client or serf status. Their role is to care for the animals (mainly water buffalo and draft oxen) either as servants of a landowner or as independent buffalo owners. They contribute to the village economy with milk products (especially clarified butter), meat, and manure, which is important and carefully utilized in the fields.

In addition to their agricultural land, most Pathan villages control neighboring hills or mountainsides, which are used by Pathans only as a source of firewood. The transhumant Gujars, however, shift their flocks to these higher areas for summer pasture, for which they pay a fixed rate, in kind, per animal. This rent supplies the landholders with clarified butter for their own consumption. Gujars also serve as agricultural laborers in the seasons of peak activity, most importantly during the few hectic days of rice transplantation. They also seed fields of their own around their summer camps for harvest the following summer.

In Kohistan there is less symbiosis between Gujars and their hosts but the pattern is similar, except that the few fields are located by the winter settlements.

The transhumant cycle may be very local. Some Gujars merely move from Pathan villages in the valley bottom to hillside summer settlements 1000 or 1500 feet above, visible from the village. Others travel 20 or 30 miles to summer grazing grounds in the territory of a different Pathan tribe from that of their winter hosts.

Nomads travel much farther, perhaps 100 miles, utilizing the high mountain pastures in the summer and wintering in the low plains. While the transhumant Gujars place their main emphasis on the water buffalo, the nomads specialize in the more mobile sheep and goats. Nonetheless, the two patterns are not truly distinct, for some groups combine features of both. They spend the spring in the marginal hills of Pathan territory, where they seed a crop. In summer the men take the herds of sheep and goats to the high mountains, while the women remain behind to care for the buffalo and the fields. In autumn the men return with the herds, reap the crops, and utilize the pastures. Finally, they store the grain and farm out their buffalo with Pathan villagers, and retire to the low plains with their sheep and goats for the winter.

The true nomads never engage in agricultural pursuits; they may keep cattle, but are not encumbered with water buffalo. The degree of autonomous political organization is proportional to the length of the yearly migration. Households of locally transhumant Gujars are tied individually to Pathan leaders. Those crossing Pathan tribal borders are organized in small lineages, the better to bargain for low grazing tax. The true nomads co-ordinate the herding of flocks and migrations of people from as many as 50 households, who may also camp together for brief periods. Such groups generally consist of several small lineages, frequently of different clans, related by affinal or cognatic ties and under the direction of a single leader. Thus, though migrating through areas controlled by other political organizations, they retain a moderately well-defined organization of their own.

Gujar distribution. The co-existence of Gujars and Pathans in one area poses no problem, in view of the symbiotic relations sketched above. Pathans have the military strength to control the mountainous flanks of the valleys they occupy, but have no effective means of utilizing these areas. This leaves an unoccupied ecologic niche which the Gujar ethnic group has entered and to which it has accommodated itself in a politically dependent position through a pattern of transhumance. Symbiotic advantages make the relationship satisfactory and enduring. It is tempting to see the expansion of Gujars into the area as resulting from the Pathan expulsion of Kohistanis from the valley. The Kohistanis, through their own pattern of transhumance, formerly filled the niche and it became vacant only when the specialized agricultural Pathans conquered the valley bottom and replaced the Kohistanis.

But the co-existence of Gujars and Kohistanis poses a problem, since the two groups appear to utilize the same natural resources and therefore to occupy the same ecologic niche. One would expect competition, leading to the expulsion of one or the other ethnic group from the area. However, armed conflict between the two groups is rare, and there is no indication that one is increasing at the expense of the other. On the other hand, if a stable symbiotic or noncompetitive relationship may be established between the two groups, why should Gujars be concentrated in West Kohistan, and not inhabit the essentially similar East Kohistan area? The answer must be sought not only in the natural environment and in features of the Gujar economy, but also in the relevant social environment—in features of Kohistani economy and organization which affect the niche suited to utilization by Gujars.

East vs. West Kohistan. As indicated, Kohistanis have a twofold economy combining agriculture and transhumant herding, and live in moderately large village communities. Although most Gujars also practice some agriculture, it remains a subsidiary activity. It is almost invariably of a simple type dependent on water from the melting snow in spring and monsoon rains in summer, rather than on irrigation, and on shifting fields rather than manuring. The Kohistanis have a more equal balance between agriculture and herding. The steep slopes require complex terracing and irrigation, which preclude shifting agriculture and encourage more intensive techniques. The size of herds is limited by the size of fields, which supply most of the winter fodder, since natural fields and mountain meadows are too distant from the winter dwellings to permit haying. Ecologic factors relevant to this balance between the two dominant economic activities become of prime importance for Kohistani distribution and settlement density.

There are significant differences in this respect between East and West Kohistan, i.e. between the areas drained by the Indus and the Swat Rivers respectively. While the Indus and the lowest sections of its tributaries flow at no more than 3,000 feet, the Swat River descends from 8,000 to 5,000 feet in the section of its valley occupied by Kohistanis. The higher altitude in the west has several effects on the economic bases for settlement: (a) Agricultural production is reduced by the shorter season and lower temperatures in the higher western valley. (b) The altitude difference combined with slightly higher precipitation in the west results in a greater accumulation of snow. The Indus bank is rarely covered with snow, but in the upper Swat valley snow tends to accumulate through the winter and remains in the valley bottom until April or May. Thus the sedentary stock-owner in West Kohistan must provide stored fodder for his animals throughout the four months of winter. (c) The shorter season of West Kohistan eliminates rice (most productive per land unit) as a food crop and reduces maize (most advantageous in return per weight of seed) in favor of the hardier millet.

These features serve to restrict the agricultural production of West Kohistan, and therefore the number of animals that can be kept during the winter season. No parallel restrictions limit the possibility for summer grazing. Both East and West Kohistan are noteworthy for their large, lush mountain meadows and other good summer grazing, and are thus rich in the natural resources which animal herders are able to exploit. However, these mountain pastures are only seasonal; no population can rely on them for year-round sustenance. Consequently, patterns of transhumance or nomadism are developed to utilize the mountain area in its productive season, while relying on other areas or techniques the rest of the year. True nomads move to a similar ecologic niche in another area. People practicing transhumance generally utilize a different niche by reliance on alternative techniques, here agriculture and the utilization of stored animal fodder. There appears to be a balance in the productivity of these two niches, as exploited by local transhumance in East Kohistan. Thus, in the Indus drainage, Kohistanis are able to support a human and animal population of sufficient size through the winter by means of agriculture and stored food, so as to utilize fully the summer pastures of the surrounding mountains. In an ecologic sense, the local population fills both niches. There is no such balance in the Swat valley. Restrictions on agricultural production limit the animal and human population, and prevent full exploitation of the mountain pastures. This niche is thus left partly vacant and available to the nomadic Gujars, who winter in the low plains outside the area. Moreover, scattered communities of transhumant Gujars may be found in the western areas, mainly at the very tops of the valleys. With techniques and patterns of consumption different from those of Kohistanis, they are able to survive locally in areas which fall short of the minimal requirements for permanent Kohistani occupation. The present distribution of Gujars in Kohistan, limiting them to the western half of the area, would seem to be a result of these factors.

A simple but rather crucial final point should be made in this analysis: why do Kohistanis have first choice, so to speak, and Gujars only enter niches left vacant by them? Since they are able to exploit the area fully, one might expect Gujars eventually to replace Kohistanis. Organizational factors enter here. Kohistanis form compact, politically organized villages of considerable size. The Gujar seasonal cycle prevents a similar development among them. In winter they descend into Pathan areas, or even out of tribal territory and into the administered areas of Pakistan. They are thus seasonally subject to organizations more powerful than their own, and are forced to filter through territories controlled by such organizations on their seasonal migrations. They must accommodate themselves to this situation by travelling in small, unobtrusive groups, and wintering in dispersed settlements. Though it is conceivable that Gujars might be able to develop the degree of political organization required to replace Kohistanis in a purely Kohistani environment, their dependence on more highly organized neighboring areas still makes this impossible.

The transhumant Gujar settlements in Kohistan represent groups of former nomads who were given permission by the neighboring Kohistanis to settle, and they are kept politically subservient. The organizational superiority of the already established Kohistanis prevents them, as well as the nomads, from appropriating any rights over productive means or areas. What changes will occur under the present control by the State of Swat is a different matter.

This example may serve to illustrate certain viewpoints applicable to a discussion of the ecologic factors in the distribution of ethnic groups, cultures, or economies, and the problem of "mosaic" co-residence in parts of Asia.

(1) The distribution of ethnic groups is controlled not by objective and fixed "natural areas" but by the distribution of the specific ecologic niches which the group, with its particular economic and political organization, is able to exploit. In the present example, what appears as a single natural area to Kohistanis is

subdivided as far as Pathans are concerned, and this division is cross-cut with respect to the specific requirements of Gujars.

(2) Different ethnic groups will establish themselves in stable co-residence in an area if they exploit different ecologic niches, and especially if they can thus establish symbiotic economic relations, as those between Pathans and Gujars in Swat.

(3) If different ethnic groups are able to exploit the same niches fully, the militarily more powerful will normally replace the weaker, as Pathans have replaced Kohistanis.

(4) If different ethnic groups exploit the same ecologic niches but the weaker of them is better able to utilize marginal environments, the groups may co-reside in one area, as Gujars and Kohistanis in West Kohistan.

Where such principles are operative to the extent they are in much of West and South Asia, the concept of "culture areas," as developed for native North America, becomes inapplicable. Different ethnic groups and culture types will have overlapping distributions and disconforming borders, and will be socially related to a variable degree, from the "watchful co-residence" of Kohistanis and Gujars to the intimate economic, political, and ritual symbiosis of the Indian caste system. The type of correspondence between gross ecologic classification and ethnic distribution documented for North America by Kroeber (1939) will rarely if ever be found. Other conceptual tools are needed for the study of culture distribution in Asia. Their development would seem to depend on analysis of specific detailed distributions in an ecologic framework, rather than by speculation on a larger geographical scale.

Allee, W. C., et al.
  1949 *Principles of Animal Ecology.* Philadelphia: Saunders.
Bacon, Elizabeth
  1946 "A Preliminary Attempt to Determine the Culture Areas of Asia."
  Southwestern Journal of Anthropology, 2: 117–32.
Barth, Fredrik
  1956 *Indus and Swat Kohistan—An Ethnographic Survey.* Studies Honor-
  ing the Centennial of Universitetets Etnografiske Museum, Vol. 2.
  Oslo.
Barth, Fredrik, and Georg Morgenstierne
  Ms. "Samples of Some Southern Dardic Dialects."
Coon, Carleton S.
  1951 *Caravan.* New York: Holt.
Furnivall, J. S.
  1944 *Netherlands India—A Study of Plural Economy.* Cambridge:
  University Press.
Kroeber, A. L.
  1939 *Cultural and Natural Areas of Native North America.* University
  of California Publications in American Archaeology and Ethnology,
  38. Berkeley: University of California Press.
  1947 "Culture Groupings in Asia." *Southwestern Journal of Anthropology,* 3: 322–30.
Miller, Robert J.
  1953 "Areas and Institutions in Eastern Asia." *Southwestern Journal
  of Anthropology,* 9: 203–11.
Roberts, Field Marshal Lord
  1898 *Forty-one Years in India.* London: Bentley.
Spate, O. H. K.
  1954 *India and Pakistan.* London: Methuen.
Stein, Sir Aurel
  1929 *On Alexander's Track to the Indus.* London: Macmillan.

20 ECOLOGICAL DETERMINANTS OF CHIEFTAINSHIP AMONG THE YARURO INDIANS OF VENEZUELA

Anthony Leeds

I

FATHER JOHN COOPER is said to have remarked once that when South American Tropical Forest tribal chiefs order their people to do something, the people immediately do as they choose. Certainly, as a general pattern of chieftainship, this is true among many groups,[1] and the Yaruro Indians of the south-central Venezuelan llanos are no exception. Among them, as with others, the very word chieftainship seems inappropriate. We shall use the term here, but it should only be understood as a convenience for designating our subject matter. Whether, in general, the functions of chieftainship in South America vary in importance as ecological conditions require differing chiefly activities, or whether chieftaincies were created or reinforced through the structure of statuses engendered in acculturation situations, as seems to have occurred in parts of Venezuela, or whether the varieties of chieftainship represent different evolutionary phases of development responding to the general conditions of the culture in which they occurred, is not yet clear. Presumably some consistent set of factors may be found, perhaps along the techno-ecological lines suggested by Sahlins (1958) or Harris (1958) or the socio-economic conditions such as warfare suggested by

Reprinted by permission of the author and publisher from *Akten des 34. Internationalen Amerikanistenkongresses* (1960), pp. 597–608, Vienna: F. Berger, Horn, 1962.
[1] E. g., Akawaio, Barama River Carib and other Carib groups, Canella, Carajá, Cayapó, Kiukuru, Sherente, Taulipáng, Waika, etc. Cf. Lowie 1949, especially pages 341–50.

Carneiro (1961), which will serve as principles in the explanation of the tropical South American and other chieftainships of similar characteristics, such as some of those found in Melanesia. It is hoped that the following interpretation, largely dealing with the ecological foundations of chieftainship, will contribute towards this formulation of principles.

II

Briefly, Yaruro chieftainship is characterized by its ineffectiveness. The *capitan,* as he is called in Spanish, or *o'te-ta'ra* (elder head) in Yaruro, rarely commands. When he does, the commands most often are directed at children and young people, especially males—women, on the whole, being consulted not commanded. Most direct commands, in so far as I was able to observe, were made in Spanish![2]—essentially in acculturation contexts. In general, they concerned village care, small services, and the like. No occasion was observed of commanding older men, except for a married youth of 19, who was the youngest adult male in the village. The two or three commands he received during my stay went unnoticed, and, in one or two instances, were even directly contravened. The capitans of the Cinaruco river group and of Palmarito de Guachara both consistently complained that no one paid enough attention to them, and the Palmarito chief complained that he never was kept sufficiently informed of events by his people. The fact is that people do

---

[2] Commands and other stress situations, which generally appear to be uncongenial to the Yaruro and more overt as the people have been more subject to acculturation, seem to elicit from the Yaruro Spanish responses rather than Yaruro ones. It is as though it were not fitting to utter commands or express anger in Yaruro. Thus, the few times noisy altercation was heard among the Cinaruco Yaruro, the language used was Spanish. The chief's commands and his overt anger were always expressed in Spanish, even if he had just before been speaking in Yaruro. Though anger may often be felt, it is not shown if the participants are expressing themselves in Yaruro. Thus, the chief scolded one of the village boys for riding one of the recently acquired burros—in Spanish; he ordered a 19-year old young man to do some task—in Spanish; he complained of the actions of one of the village elders in taking on the job of guide without first consulting him (though he would certainly have permitted it)—in Spanish.

pretty much as they choose in all important decision-making situations which do not involve the community at large, or the relationship of some member of the community or the entire group to outsiders.[3] In the former situation, the chief serves as a consultative funnel through which the community discussion pours back and forth until the community achieves some clear but unstated consensus upon which community members can act, individually of course. Only in the situations dealing with outside groups does the Yaruro capitanship emerge as a more developed status which might metaphorically be described as a position similar to that of a minister of foreign relations. In behalf of his group, he talks with any representatives of outside groups, especially if they are non-Yaruro, and acts as gatherer of information and as channel of communication between the community and the outside entity. Even this is weakened, however, since it applies more by courtesy than by fact among the Yaruro themselves, and other members of the community may perform the same function even if to a somewhat smaller degree. It is also weakened in that no Yaruro is prevented from acting on his own with respect to non-Yaruro outsiders, and, in fact, many Yaruro do establish their own relationships with outsiders as a number of instances attested. Indeed, the rights of the individual members of the society to make their own decisions, at least internally if not also externally, is insisted on. In one instance, a chief who took it upon himself to represent his people to the outside world without consultation and to make arbitrary decisions for them inside the community—mainly in his own interest—was, with the consent of the community, assassinated by one of the members, now in excellent standing in that community as a respected shaman. The chief in question had stepped beyond the bounds designated for his status. In sum, the position of chief, even

---

[3] Cf. Leeds 1960a, with respect to the place of individual action in Yaruro society. Though there is individual action, choice, and responsibility, these are all carried out as an aspect of community organization and essentially with community affirmation. A person is not an individual set in counterpoint to his society—there is no polarity of individual-society, as we, in our culture, generally seem to conceive. Individualism in the latter sense does not exist among the Yaruro. The Yaruro should not be mistaken for an individualistic culture, as, I suspect, several of the cultures described as individualistic in Mead 1937 should not have been.

though formally recognized by Yaruro society and reinforced by formal recognition and appointment by Venezuelan authorities, is feeble as an institution and as a status.[4] It is our hypothesis that ecological conditions of Yaruro life determine the form of the chieftainship in such a way that its stronger institutionalization would be impossible, and we turn to this question now.

III

Yaruro subsistence activities[5] comprise swiddening, gathering, pig herding, hunting and fishing, mentioned in the order of their importance as contributors to the total food supply as measured in calories.[6] Horticulture probably provides 60–70% of the total annual food supply. The horticulture practiced is characteristic of tropical forest slash-and-burn gardens, with a slow rotation of plots in order to permit soil renewal and weed control. Trees are cut, at present with steel axes and formerly, apparently, with axes of bone or shell, and then burnt. Occasional fences are roughly made of the logs to keep out pigs. Bitter manioc (*Manihot utilissima*),[7] in several varieties, is the main crop, though sweet manioc (*Manihot aipi*), also in several varieties, is planted too, as are corn, bananas, sugar cane—each in several varieties— and a number of lesser crops such as melons, squashes, pumpkins, pineapples, sweet potatoes, and yautia or ocumo (*Xanthosoma sagittifolium*). Crops are planted with a digging stick which may also be used in harvesting. Gardens are weeded, once only, early in the growth of the crops. Other than clearing, the only soil preparation is the construction of hills for planting bananas. This

---

[4] Professor Benjamin N. Nelson informs me that in medieval Spain, village communities had an official, also called *capitan,* whose function was to treat with state functionaries representing the world beyond the village community's frontier. It is possible that the Yaruro capitan, and many others in Venezuela, are an acculturative transfer of this office to tribal groups. In the case of the Yaruro, this would have happened some 250–300 years ago.

[5] The use, here, of the terms 'activity', 'tasks', 'techniques', 'tools', 'resources', and 'habitat' corresponds to the definitions given in Leeds 1960b.

[6] Cf. Leeds 1961, which gives these data in detail and describes the habitat and horticulture *in extenso*.

[7] Native terms for these crops are given, ibid.

is done by burning hills made by a certain species of ants (*huachaquero*). The hills, which are quite wide and low, are filled with organic matter enriching the soil.[8] Harvesting is aided with baskets for carrying the crops. Baskets contain about half a bushel or less. No fertilization, no terracing, no drainage, no irrigation, no extensive turning of the soil is done.

The gathered resources include a number of roots, particularly changuango, changuanito, and guapo (*Marante arundinacea*);[9] varied fruits, especially that of the moriche palm (*Mauritia flexuosa*); several seeds, notably chiga (= chigo?; — *Campiandra comosa*); calabashes (*Crescentia Cujete*), and bees' wax and honey. None of the items gathered are large in size or difficult of access except the bees' wax, one or two of the fruits, and calabashes which grow on higher trees, or may be very far. Gathered foods may be picked up by hand or with the aid of a digging stick or machete, and may be brought back in the harvesting baskets. Other items which may be gathered include the raw materials for baskets and mat-making or for food-processing tools such as the tipití, pots, or mortars and pestles. These items include the fronds of the moriche palm, used for making cord, baskets, tipitís, mats, and sacks; in some villages, clay for pots; reeds for arrows, wood for house beams, mortars and pestles, bows, and for cooking utensils. Wood, palm fronds, and many other items are gathered with the help of the all-purpose machete.

Pig herding is unsystematically done. The pigs, a recent acquisition, spend most of their time at will in the foraging grounds. The significant herding activity occurs only at times when one or another of the groups of pigs breaks into the gardens, an almost daily occurrence. They are then driven to the foraging grounds again or, if late in the day, into a close till morning when they are either driven forth again or allowed to scavenge in the village. There are several herds of pigs of sizes varying from perhaps a maximum of 20 including piglets to the more usual six or eight animals. The only tools used in pig care include a slaughtering stick with which the pig is clubbed to death and knives to cut up the meat. The close is built of logs cut with a machete and carried

---

[8] Ibid., note 9, contains data on soil values.

[9] Identifications are from Pittier 1926.

in by one or two men. Pig meat, though eaten with regularity, is definitely a secondary element of diet.

Hunting is done almost exclusively with the bow and arrow. There are several types of arrows. One for fish has a metal point approximately 4 inches long with a side hook about five inches from the tip, where the tip is set into the shaft. This may also be used for smaller animals. One for birds has a blunt wooden head, and does not appear to be used very often. A third type is used for larger animals such as deer and capybara. It has a blade about 6 inches long shaped like a laurel leaf and, at present, made of steel. At the base of the blade, a small cross-piece is affixed in order to prevent the precious blade from piercing so deeply into the animal that, if it escapes, it would carry the arrow away with it. The fourth type of arrow is used for turtles, tortoises, and alligators or other animals which submerge. The head is short and strong with a sharp recurved hook. The entire metal head is attached to a cord, and this in turn is attached to the arrow shaft, from which the head is detachable. On detaching, the shaft floats and the game can be followed in its underwater course. The bow is generally about 6 feet long or a little more. It is made rather crudely of the wood of the macanilla palm (*Bactris Gaspiaes*). Some animals, especially land tortoises and armadillos, may be caught by hand. Alligators may also be hunted with exceedingly heavy steel hooks and a strong line. In hunting, no traps, nets, surrounds, or drives are used.

Fishing is done chiefly with bows and arrows, though an arrow may sometimes be used as a spear, repeatedly jabbed into grassy waters near the river banks. Fishing may also be done with hooks and lines of different sizes. Bait is also used. A man may fish from a platform built by lashing logs horizontally to two trees and then shooting into the still side pools of a stream into which he has driven a post with bait attached. He may also stand in a canoe to shoot. It is reported, though I have not myself seen it, that barbasco (*Jacquinia revoluta* or *mucronulata*) poison is used by some Yaruro.[10] No nets, weirs, traps, sweeps, or artificial fish pools are used.

---

[10] Personal communication from Mr. Thomas Rootes who has studied Yaruro linguistics for a number of months, having visited several groups.

Given the techniques and tools of the Yaruro, all the subsistence activities described can conveniently be done by one person. Some *must* be done by one person only, since the tools and techniques themselves do not permit two or more persons to operate jointly. As it were, the logic of the tools and techniques concerned demands utilization by single persons.[11] Some of the tools and techniques might conveniently involve two or more persons, e.g. lashing tree trunks together to make a fence or cornering a capybara, but do not definitively *require* more than one person. Activities of all sorts may be done by aggregates of persons, each utilizing his own tools and techniques individually but neither the activity, the tools nor the techniques entail the aggregation of individuals. Thus, from the point of view of human organization, the technology, by itself, entails no managerial functions, no coordination of tasks which must be overseen by someone occupying an appropriately defined status.[12] That is, there are no technologically determined positions of leadership in Yaruro society. Further, the technology as such entails no significant cooperation in work organization, even when this is convenient, and correspondingly, no standard work groups or management functions, as represented in some defined status, for facilitating cooperation are to be expected or to be found. In fact, Yaruro technology and resource distribution are such as to elicit considerable dispersion of activities and actors at any given time of work, and to inhibit the development of rank and the personal acquisition of superordinating prestige.

IV

We may now examine the habitat aspect of the ecological relationship. A clearly marked annual cycle occurs in the Yaruro

---

[11] Different kinds of tools require different kinds of organization. A simple hand saw can be used by only one person at a time. A logging saw, though it can awkwardly be used by one person, is surely best used by two persons. Certain other saws, e.g. jig saws, make up one of a series of machine processes on a single part of a product, the entire series being the unit of operation which requires a still more complex level of organization. Cf. Leeds 1960b.

[12] For the structure of argument which is involved here, see Leeds 1960b.

habitat.[13] However, despite a sharp seasonal change from heavy rains up to 60 inches in one half of the year to almost desert-like conditions in the other, temperature, sun, soil, and water-table conditions are such that plants will grow all year round, supplying a steady flow of vegetable foods to the people. The change of the water level in the rivers and in the water-table and the sharp increases and decreases of rain strongly affect the patterns of animal and plant life in the Yaruro environment. Annual cyclical variations in wind, humidity, and temperature are also quite marked. Plants and most especially animals, experience a kind of seasonal pulsation. As the rivers fill during the rainy season, the larger animals, such as the cayman, alligator, manatí, and dugong, move upstream to somewhat shallower waters, where their food supply is easier of access. Fish also move upstream and even up small brooks, where this is possible. If the savannas flood, many fish swim out into the savannas where numerous insects and other foods are now to be found. The insects themselves multiply and are distributed farther and farther back from the rivers as the rains progress and the savanna floods widen. Meanwhile, foraging animals move farther from the rivers and ponds, and range over greater distances as the rains and the elevated water-tables foster greater plant food resources. Insects in part follow the animals, in part the vegetation as it wakens to winter life in the interfluves. As the dry season begins to return, the reverse process takes place, and all life concentrates nearer and nearer the permanent waters such as the big rivers and some lakes, or at points where the land surface is near enough the permanent water-table to maintain some vegetation, notably the gallery forests and the woodlots, called *montes* in Spanish. Thus one may ideally describe a summer and a winter organization of the habitat. The incidence of resources varies accordingly,

---

[13] 'Habitat' here refers to all physical objects and conditions of the environment which are relevant to the existence or production of resources as defined by the culture. For the most part, then, 'habitat' refers to those environmental conditions such as humidity, temperature, insolation, rainfall, etc., which affect the food supply, as well as the food and water available for animals and plants and other culturally relevant physical objects. By extension, it refers to daily, seasonal, annual, and long-term variations and cycles in the various relevant factors of the environment, whether climatic, geologic, or biotic, which affect any of these supplies.

and consequently so do the technological activities and tasks to be done. In the dry season, there is a marked increase of gathering, particularly of roots and seeds which appear to store starches for dry season use in the wet season, whereas fruits appear mainly in the rainy season. Hunting increases in the dry season when animals are more highly concentrated in and near the rivers and tributary brooks and streams. Fishing also increases in the dry season as the waters become shallower, less grass-choked, and no longer laden with muds from upstream erosion which makes it impossible to see the fish. Garden production appears to decrease in summer as the dry season precludes growing some crops, such as pineapples, altogether, and reduces the possibility of growing sugar cane and corn.

Despite this marked seasonality, the habitat conditions of both seasons resemble each other in certain formal respects vital to our argument (see Leeds 1961 for further details and maps of the seasonal resource locations). First, at any given moment of either season, from the point of view of work organization, the resources are what we may call dispersive. Thus, in mid-rainy season, swiddens are to be found dispersed along the streams and brooks flowing into the rivers and these adits are distributed irregularly over the land within a distance of 4–5 miles of the river. Even low slip-off slopes of the river may be used for growing sugar cane in the wet season, though they are too dry in the dry season. Game, such as tortoise, armadillo, deer, birds, and occasional other animals, are to be found throughout the savannas and about the river banks. Fish are found in most streams and in the rivers including those which have no useful banks for horticulture. Gathered resources are found near the streams in marshy places where the moriche palm grows, and to a lesser extent in the savannas (Leeds 1961:Map I). The dry season resources are also distributively located though the pattern is somewhat different (Leeds 1961:Map II). Quanta of production from these resources at any one time are rarely great. The larder, as it were, must be filled from a number of sources at once, even though one crop, particularly bitter manioc, and occasionally sweet manioc and corn, may rise briefly to as much as 50 or 60% of the food supply. Thus the available quanta of resources and their distribution at given moments in time are such as to demand a distributive form of labor organization: workers, as individuals or in very small groups, must go off in different directions at the same time. The obverse of this, of course, is that no sizable or permanent working groups are to be expected and none in fact occur. Further, because a dispersion of the labor force and a constant flux in the constitution of work groups is entailed by the relationships between the technology and the habitat, organized and permanent managerial functions can scarcely occur, and no fixed status with significant managerial powers would be expected. The observed data of leadership among the Yaruro and many other tribes in South America and other parts of the world, such as Melanesia, having fundamentally similar ecologies, corresponds precisely with what one is led to expect logically from the form of the ecology.

The absolute size of work groups achievable in the Yaruro habitat is limited not only by the dispersed locations and temporal harvest patterns of resources, but also by the absolute productivity of the ecology. If one calculates the distribution per land area of those calories potentially convertible to human energy, the rate of calories per unit of land surface is so low that even at maximum utilization only a very low population density of about 2 persons per square mile would be possible. If concentrated in the center of an effective walking distance for exploiting resources of, say, six miles radius from a village, with a resultant total area of about 110 square miles, there would be about 220 souls. Of these, perhaps 70% (all persons over age 10), at maximum, might constitute the labor force, i.e. 154 adults and older children. The actual conditions are, of course, much more limiting, since the efficiency of the technology is such that it cannot exploit the totality of calories potentially available for conversion to human energy at any one time.[14] The actually harvested calories are

---

[14] For example, all the fish available in the streams at a given time cannot be caught. More could be caught with an improved technology, such as the use of fish traps, weirs, or fish poisons, which, as we have said, are absent from the technology of the Cinaruco Yaruro. Density of fish, or any other biotic population, can be estimated (cf. Dice 1952: Ch. IV), and then compared with rates of harvesting. Furthermore, it should be noted that often the totality of an actually harvested resource may not be available. For example, in the Trobriand Islands, in a good

considerably less, though I have no estimates as to how much less. Let us estimate half, or enough to support one person per square mile, that is, 110 persons. With a somewhat smaller per cent of the population available for the labor force, say 60% of the 110, the force would have only about 67 persons at most. This appears to be a reasonable number for the Cinaruco Yaruro groups, although due to depopulation from disease and massacre, the labor force actually observed in "my" group was a little more than 25% of that number, or 18, and neighboring groups were generally still smaller. These 154, 67, and especially the actual 18 workers, even if, at any given moment, *all* were working at subsistence activities, would be distributed over various parts of the 110 square miles of territory under the kind of dispersive habitat and technological conditions described. They are in fact so thinly scattered as to preclude any sort of continuing managerial functions.

V

A consideration of the forms of the harvest surplus[15] is relevant to our discussion. Harvest surpluses must be considered with respect both to individual subsistence resources and to all subsistence resources taken together. In the annual cycle, there is considerable variation in the amount produced of any given crop, except for sweet and bitter manioc which together constitute perhaps 40% of the annual food supply of the Yaruro. Manioc produces throughout the year. Given that the manioc-growing

---

year, all the yams harvested cannot be eaten at once, nor can they be stored. Some portion of the crop is then lost by spoilage. We may construct, in terms of calories or other significant food values, two ratios:

$$\frac{C_h}{C_p} \qquad \frac{C_e}{C_h}$$

C — Calories
c — consumed
p — potential
h — harvested (= available for use)

The first may be used as a measure of the efficiency of the productive capacity of the technology; the second as a measure of the efficiency of the distributive capacity of the technology.

[15] The technological, producers, and harvest surpluses are defined in Harris 1958, and implied in Harris 1959. They are dealt with in detail with respect to the Yaruro in Leeds 1961. Other relevant discussions of surplus are found in Sahlins 1958; Jacobs and Stern 1952: Ch VI.

areas are widely dispersed and that considerable labor is drawn
from manioc areas by still more dispersed resources, it follows
that most work units for manioc gardens will consist of only one or
two men, each having their own swidden or sharing it with one or
two others to supply themselves and their immediate families
throughout the year. As might be expected, land tenure and land
usage patterns are in accord with this inference. Occasionally
small oscillations in the manioc crops may produce small harvest
surpluses. These, at least nominally, belong to the man in whose
swidden they grow and are his for disposal. The quantities, however, are exceedingly small, and present no problems of storage or
disposal necessitating more centralized supervision and allocation.
Most other resources display a similar pattern though to an even
smaller degree. Fish are obtainable, for the Cinaruco Yaruro, all
year round with almost equal ease, though the Palmariteños
have a more difficult time because of the grassy and muddy
waters in the rainy season. Hunting windfalls and large pigs are
the only animal sources which present harvest surpluses of any
size. However, these are small enough so that they last at most
two or three days, and they are so irregular both as to occurrence
and as to personnel involved that no regular centralized in-
stitutional mode of handling them is entailed. The virtual absence
of meat storage also inhibits any such development because it
forces the immediate distribution of most of the meat of the
slaughtered pig or captured game. There is no constantly or
repeatedly stored supply to be supervised or allocated. In fact
swine and windfall game, properly considered, correspond to the
small oscillations of the manioc supply and are totally different
from the regularly occurring massive incidence of food sources
like buffalo herds, salmon runs, and wheat harvests of temperate
climates or crab runs in the tropical Orinoco delta of Venezuela.[16] Of all the food resources, the only one with a marked
harvest surplus is corn. The significance of even this harvest
surplus is reduced by a) the smallness of the quanta involved
relative to the total food supply, and b) the fact that there are
two corn seasons, one beginning in June, one about the beginning
of February. Temporary harvest surpluses of corn may, how-

---

[16] Personal communication from Johannes Wilbert who has done extensive
fieldwork with the Warrau in the Amacuro Delta of the Orinoco River.

ever, contribute slightly to the enhanced prestige of those individuals who by their own will and work have been most productive.[17] They say with appreciation, "He is a hard worker," but the prestige is relevant only to the sphere in which it is gained. It does not necessarily give him prestige in some other spheres of cultural life, such as, for example, the ceremonial or decision-making activities.

In taking an overall view of the food resources, it will be noted that there are no clear harvest surpluses, and that the oscillations in supply, which are in truth minute and momentary harvest surpluses, are so small and irregular and varied in location as to be insignificant determiners of managerial functions. At most one might expect the harvest surplus of corn to elicit some small allocative function, generally none. Storage, too, in this case, is not a technique requiring administration as with wheat in grain elevators. It would in fact be better to consider this kind of storage as a steady presence of food rather than as storage at all, even though it functions as such.

The extra labor requirements of these small upward oscillations of the harvest surplus are likewise, in general, indistinguishable from regular labor requirements and are easily absorbed by individual workers. Or a worker may take along a child, who goes as much for the fun of being with his father or grandfather, but nevertheless carries back some produce. This type of situation is in sharp contrast with, say, the labor requirements of a large harvest surplus like the wheat crop in the United States which demands a large amount of labor quickly and temporarily. Such a harvest surplus entails a number of organizational problems foreign to the harvest oscillations.

Finally, the Yaruro deny any considerable long-term oscillations

---

[17] Yaruro individuals differ in productivity not only because of inborn qualities such as strength and native abilities, but also by choice based on tastes. Some do not like to grow corn, others do not like to grow pigs, others still prefer to hunt or trade. The food quanta produced by these several activities vary greatly. The individual may exercise these choices in a cultural setting where any such choice benefits the community. All produce eventually finds its way into the community at large through the distribution mechanism. The person is not acting as an individualist regardless of the interest of others, but at his own optimum, given his unique person, in the community as a whole. Cf. fn. 3 *supra*.

in the environment and consequently in the resources. The extremes, particularly the minima, of habitat factors which regulate food and population balances, according to Liebig's Law, fall within narrow limits and again elicit no special institutions of management or of equilibrium maintenance to compensate for them, as in the case of the potlatches of the Northwest Coast of America, the buffalo hunts in the Great Plains of the United States, or the use of pigs in Melanesia (cf. Suttles 1960, 1962; Llewellyn and Hoebel 1941; Vayda 1961; Vayda, Leeds, and Smith 1961).

V I

One more point may be made regarding the ecology as limiter of chieftainship among the Yaruro. The tools, techniques, and resources require no very extensive, highly specialized or esoteric knowledge. In fact any man or woman, and any child as well, has access to such knowledge, and it is easily acquired by all members of the society who thus have, at least potentially, equal access to control over the means of life. There is no specialized knowledge, at least with respect to technology and habitat, which requires a specialized respository in the form of a chief or learned person. Yaruro knowledge, itself dependent upon the inventory of tools, techniques, and resources, inhibits any tendency towards the development of any sort of specialist in technical or managerial knowledge. As one might expect, there are no true specialists in Yaruro society. Here and there women make pots and certain women seem to have a special bent for making woven sacks but these are not properly specialties. Nor, from a technological or ecological point of view, is male or female shamanism in any way a speciality. There do not appear to be specialists even in esoteric knowledge. Knowledge of the general type described here might be called 'dispersive' or 'egalitarian' since it tends to become more or less uniformly distributed among the members of the society. A consequence of the existence of this type of knowledge, associated with the kind of technology described, is that there will be no specialised training of any specialists and, of course, no specialised personnel to do such training. This is the situation which obtains among the Yaruro both with respect to technical and managerial activities. Thus, in Yaruro knowledge, there is no source for the support of an institutionalized and strong chieftainship.

VII

In one respect, the ecology encourages chiefly functions. A balance is struck between the cultural resources, the possibilities that the habitat affords for their production, and the length of time that areas of land can be exploited. This is particularly true of the horticultural lands since they can no longer be used after three years of cropping, and it becomes necessary to move on. The result is that there is a slow migration of resources areas, chiefly of horticultural areas across the tribal territory. The lands in cultivation move further and further from any given village until a point of suspension is reached at which the walking and working distance of the gardens is too far from the village for effective or efficient exploitation. At this point a village or part of a village must move. Moving the villages involves decision-making with respect to time, new location, and so on. Plainly, moving a village involves a community decision. A community institution for handling the decision-making is necessary. Technologically speaking, the moving itself is not a community task and does not involve supervision and direction. Therefore, one would not expect the institution of decision-making to be a directive one, but a consultative one. Again this corresponds to the observed modes of action of the Yaruro chiefs. The chiefs' function is to facilitate the formation of the decisions of the community by funnelling and interpreting individuals' feelings and expressions to the rest of the members of the community.

In sum, I have presented a model of a form of ecology which, hypothetically, determines the limits within which any sort of chiefly functions may operate. This model, again hypothetically, is applicable to all cultures having the kind of technological and habitat characteristics and forms of surplus here described. I think the model applies particularly to cultures which grow root-crops such as manioc, which utilize no labor-concentrative techniques, such as irrigation, and for whose food resources notable seasonality is absent. Such cultures have been noted widely in tropical South America and also in Melanesia. In both areas, chiefly functions are notably limited as contrasted, say, with Circum-Caribbean corn-raising cultures with some irrigation and other intensive techniques (Sturtevant 1961; Reichel-Dolmatoff 1961) and with Polynesian high cultures with elaborate irrigation and other public works (Sahlins 1958). It should be noted, first, that the Yaruro were not far from these Circum-Caribbean chiefdoms and even show a number of trait similarities, and, second, that the Yaruro have been under Spanish acculturation, which has involved encouragement of chiefly functions, for probably 250 years. Yet, despite the pressures of both diffusion and acculturation to produce a more developed chieftaincy, the attenuated form described persists. The explanation of this persistence seems to me to be ecological. I suggest that the model of explanation presented here is based on a set of analytic dimensions —the characteristics of the technology, those of the habitat, those of the harvest surplus, and the interrelationships of these—which may be used for all cultures, but whose formal, systemic relations vary from culture to culture, or class of cultures to class of cultures, thus giving different models for different cultures or classes of cultures. By using such dimensions, one can account for cultural differences by means of a standard set of principles, thus facilitating genuine comparisons and generalizations.

BIBLIOGRAPHY

Carneiro, Robert
  1961 "Slash and Burn Cultivation Among the Kuikuru and Its Implications for Cultural Development in the Amazon Basin," in Johannes Wilbert (ed.), *The Evolution of Horticultural Systems in Native South America: Causes and Consequences. A Symposium. Antropologica,* Supplement Publication No. 2. Caracas.
Dice, Lee R.
  1952 *Natural Communities.* Ann Arbor: University of Michigan Press.
Harris, M.
  1958 "A Taxonomy of Significant Food Surpluses." Paper read at the annual meeting of the American Anthropological Association, Washington, D.C.
  1959 "The Economy Has No Surplus?" *American Anthropologist,* 61: 185–99.
Jacobs, M., and B. Stern
  1952 *General Anthropology.* College Outline Series, No. 20. New York: Barnes & Noble.
Leeds, A.
  1960a "The Ideology of the Yaruro Indians in Relation to Socio-Economic Organization." *Antropologica,* 9: 1–10.
  1960b "Some Preliminary Considerations Regarding the Analysis of Technology." Paper presented at the 6th International Congress of Anthropological and Ethnological Sciences, Paris.
  1961 "Yaruro Incipient Tropical Forest Horticulture—Possibilities and Limits," in Johannes Wilbert (ed.), *The Evolution of Horticultural Systems in Native South America: Causes and Consequences. A Symposium. Antropologica,* Supplement Publication No. 2, Caracas.
Llewellyn, K. N., and E. A. Hoebel
  1941 *The Cheyenne Way: Conflict and Case Law in Primitive Jurisprudence.* Norman: University of Oklahoma Press.
Lowie, R. H.
  1949 "Social and Political Organization of Tropical Forest and Marginal Tribes," in Julian Steward (ed.), *The Handbook of South American Indians,* 5: 313–50. Bureau of American Ethnology Bulletin No. 143.

Mead, Margaret (ed.)
1937 *Cooperation and Competition Among Primitive Peoples.* New York: McGraw-Hill.

Pittier, H.
1926 *Manual de las Plantas Usuales de Venezuela.* Caracas, Venezuela: Litografia del Comerico.

Reichel-Dolmatoff, G.
1961 "The Agricultural Basis of the Sub-Andean Chiefdoms of Colombia," in Johannes Wilbert (ed.), *The Evolution of Horticultural Systems in Native South America: Causes and Consequences. A Symposium. Antropologica,* Supplement Publication No. 2, Caracas.

Sahlins, M. D.
1958 *Social Stratification in Polynesia.* Seattle: University of Washington Press (for the American Ethnological Society).

Sturtevant, W. C.
1961 "Taino Agriculture," in Johannes Wilbert (ed.), *The Evolution of Horticultural Systems in Native South America: Causes and Consequences. A Symposium. Antropologica,* Supplement Publication No. 2, Caracas.

Suttles, W.
1960 "Affinal Ties, Subsistence, and Prestige among the Coast Salish." *American Anthropologist,* 62: 296–305.
1962 "Variation in Culture and Habitat on the Northwest Coast," in *Akten des 34. Internationalen Amerikanistenkongresses (1960)* Vienna: F. Berger, Horn.

Vayda, A. P.
1961 "A Re-examination of Northwest Coast Economic Systems." *Transactions of the New York Academy of Sciences,* Ser. II, 23: 618–24.

Vayda, A. P., A. Leeds, and D. Smith
1961 "The Subsistence Use of Pigs in Melanesia," in Viola E. Garfield (ed.), *Proceedings of Spring Meeting of the American Ethnological Society Annual Meeting.* Seattle: University of Washington Press.

21 LAND USE AND THE EXTENDED
FAMILY IN MOALA, FIJI[1]

Marshall D. Sahlins

THE HYPOTHESIS of this paper is that the traditional extended family organization of Moala Island, Fiji, depends for its continued existence on particular customs of land tenure and land use; that when these customs change, the familial form tends to change. An analysis of the family in two contemporary villages will show that in one, Keteira, the traditional family structure has been largely maintained, while in the second, Naroi, it barely survives. It is submitted that exploitation of scattered land resources in Keteira is responsible for the continuance of the extended family there, while dependence on land only in the environs of the village has contributed to the emergence of the independent nuclear family in Naroi. It is concluded that the patterns of land use are necessary determining conditions of familial structure in Moala.

To demonstrate the proposition, I will first describe the composition and operation of the traditional Moalan extended family. The familial forms present in Keteira and Naroi will then be analyzed. Finally, the relationship between family types and land usage will be described, and conclusions drawn.

Moala is an island of volcanic origin, some 24 square miles in

Reprinted from *American Anthropologist,* Vol. 59 (1957), pp. 449–62, by permission of the author and publisher.
[1] The ethnographic materials presented here were collected by the author from October, 1954, to August, 1955. The field trip was made possible by a fellowship granted by the Social Science Research Council of Washington, D.C. Preparation of the field data for publication is being aided by a grant from the Columbia University Council for Research in the Social Sciences.

area. It is quite hilly; the highest peak is 1535 feet. The hills
descend sharply to rocky or mangrove-bordered coasts, leaving
relatively little flat land on the island. The population, numbering
approximately 1200 (all Fijian with the exception of three Chinese
shop-keepers), is settled in eight coastal villages. Basic subsistence activities are the growing of root crops, taro, yams, sweet
potato, and sweet manioc, by slash and burn techniques. Some
wet taro is also grown. Copra and money have become increasingly important in the local economy, especially since the
beginning of World War II. The two villages considered here,
Naroi and Keteira, are located at the extreme northeastern end
and on the eastern side of the island, respectively (see map).
Naroi is the largest Moalan village and the home of the paramount
chief of the island, Roko Tui Moala. Keteira is about one-third
as large and boasts no important chief. However, neither differences in population nor the relative political standing of the two
villages has any particular bearing on the present analysis.

THE TRADITIONAL MOALAN FAMILY

This description of the traditional Moalan family is built from
observation and from informants' opinions, ideas, and ideals. The
term "traditional" does not necessarily denote "aboriginal." Moala
has been subject to European influences for over a century, and
to Tongan influences for an even longer period. In its essentials,
the family pattern described here is almost certainly of great
antiquity, but there have been minor changes in house and hearth
arrangements over the past two or three centuries.

In the local dialect the traditional family may be designated
vuvale[2] or *vale* ("house"). It is of the patrilocal extended variety,
usually composed of a man, his wife, his unmarried daughters
and sons, and married sons with their wives and children.
Occasionally a man will reside with his wife's family after marriage. This arrangement, which can continue for life, most often
occurs when the wife has no brother to carry on her family. If a
man comes from another island or is orphaned, he might also
live with his wife's family.

---

[2] The Standard Fijian orthography now in general use in the Colony is
adopted here. For English speakers the most unusual aspects of this
orthography are: c, English *the;* g, si*ng*er; and q, fi*ng*er.

The extended family occupies a compound of closely grouped living houses sharing a single cook house. Each living house holds one of the nuclear family constituents of the extended family. Informants state that in the "old times" more than one married pair often lived in a house, but this practice was made illegal by an early (1877) British regulation. While there is no evidence that the regulation was ever rigorously enforced—and it was later rescinded (Roth 1953:22)—nowadays each married pair and their offspring almost invariably occupy a separate living house. A single, common hearth has always been a feature of the extended family, although in pre-British times it may have been located in one of the living houses rather than in a distinct cook house. The Government also legislated that each living house should have a separate cook house, but despite prosecutions under the regulation, this has never become a customary practice in Moala. Not only does an entire extended family share a common

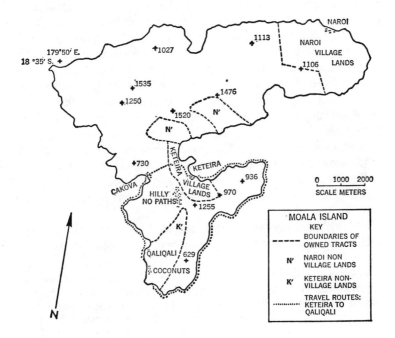

Moala Island

cook house, but the group takes it meals in common, either in the cook house or in one of the living houses.

The extended family is firmly organized by a system of internal ranking based on generation and birth order. The father is leader of the family, followed by his children in order of birth. In pre-Christian times, polygyny was practiced (especially by chiefs), in which case children took precedence first by the order of marriage of their mothers and then, between full siblings, by birth order. The principles of ranking regulate succession to family headship. Here we can focus our attention on the males of the family, since females rarely become family heads and moreover, daughters can be expected to leave the group upon marriage. The oldest son will accede to family leadership at his father's death, and indeed gradually usurps the prerogatives of headship during his father's old age. Should the oldest son die or be disqualified from succession by personality defects, his younger brothers become eligible in the order of their birth. This ranking system and succession pattern is reflected in the kin terminology appropriate between males of an extended family as described in Table 1.

As the table indicates, distinctions of seniority (based on birth order) are consistently made in the kin terminologies of reference and address among males of the extended family. This is true everywhere in Moala, despite the fact that the words used for kin designations may vary from village to village. Status titles such as *Roko* or *Ratu,* qualifying terms such as *levu* and *lailai* ("big" and "little"), and the use of teknonomy as a sign of respect all help to express the relative rank of any pair of males in the family. I should stress that the older-younger terminological distinctions which indicate relative rank do not as consistently apply to more distant classificatory brothers and fathers than are listed in the table.

The wives of brothers of the extended family should address each other as sisters,[3] but they usually make no rank distinctions

---

[3] Ideally they would be classificatory "sisters" to each other. Since the preferred marriage is between classificatory cross-cousins and since parallel cousins are terminologically merged with siblings and distinguished from cross-cousins, wives of brothers would be sisters. Very rarely, however, would they be "true" sisters, i.e., offspring of the same married pair. Even if cross-cousin marriage is not practiced, wives of brothers should use "sister" terminology with each other.

Table 1. Kin Terms for Males in the Extended Family;
Man Speaking

Relation to Ego	Terms of Address		Terms of Reference	
	Naroi	Keteira	Naroi	Keteira
Father	Ratu[1]	Tata	Tamaqu	Tamaqu
Father's older brother	Ratu levu ("Big father") or Roko[2] *name*	Ratu	Tamaqu levu ("Big father")	Tamaqu levu ("Big father")
Father's younger brother	as father	as father	Tamaqu lailai ("Little father")	Tamaqu lailai ("Little father")
Older brother and father's older brother's sons	Roko *name*	tekno-nomy,[3] "Father of So—and—So"	Tuakaqu	Tuakaqu or teknonomy, "Father of So—and—So"
Younger brother and father's younger brothers' sons	by name	by name	Taciqu	Taciqu

[1]"Ratu" is also a title used in addressing people of high rank, especially in the Bauan dialect of Fijian.

[2]"Roko" is another status term, reputedly ancient in the Moalan dialect.

[3]It is improper to address a superior by name only, hence teknonomy is used here as an indication of respect. Note the distinction thereby made between older and younger brothers and between father's older brothers' sons and father's younger brothers' sons.

in terminology since they are almost invariably of different natal groups. The relations among women married into a family reflect their husbands' rank, but aside from the wife of the family head, who leads the women's affairs, this ranking is not of great significance. A father treats his daughters-in-law as of approximately equal status. A man considers both older and younger brothers' wives as "secondary" wives, able to perform all the household duties of his own wife in her absence. However, sexual intercourse with brothers' wives is expressly forbidden, nor is there any leviritic marriage. If a man dies, his widow and children may simply remain with his extended family, but she may also return to her natal group or remarry. If she leaves, she takes her immature children with her, the father's family keeping older children and later reclaiming the children taken by their mother.[4]

Ranking within the extended family is not simply a matter of kin terminology. Also involved is a complex system of etiquette which governs behavior of people of different status in the system. The behavior of senior and junior members of the family toward each other parallels in specific detail that appropriate between chiefs and people of inferior status. Chiefly etiquette is in many respects an elaborate version of familial etiquette. In fact, the genealogical position of the chief, as scion of the main line of a common descent which embraces his people, is identical in principle to the genealogical position of the head of the family relative to the junior members. The similarity goes further: a younger brother may be described as the *kaisi* of an older brother, and the older is *turaga* to him—the more common referents of the terms "kaisi" and "turaga" being "people of low status" and "chiefs" respectively. Relative status in the family is symbolized by many customary rules of every-day behavior. For example, in their common meals, father and sons are seated at the "upper" end of the eating mat according to rank; the higher the rank, the closer to the position of high status toward the rear of the house. They are served in rank order by the women, who, with the immature

---

[4] If a woman separates from or divorces her husband, she returns to her natal group, taking immature children with her. The father will later reclaim these children. (A man will similarly "reclaim" illegitimate children.) Occasionally, a woman separating from or divorcing her husband will leave behind even immature children; they would be raised by the father's brothers' wives.

children, eat afterwards. So also in any gathering of men of a family under one roof, the higher one's status, the nearer he may sit toward the rear of the house. Like the relationships between Fijian chiefs and commoners, there is a distinct atmosphere of reserve between a man and his younger brothers (although less so between fathers and sons). In a family gathering, especially one involving a serious discussion, a younger brother or young son will not venture an opinion until he is asked; he generally speaks only when spoken to. This is not to say that family gatherings are drab affairs, but they are not often very gay. It is common for the reserve between brothers to amount to what is practically an avoidance relationship. The Moalans say, and I have observed it to be true, that it is "easier" to be with cross-cousins (terminologically and behaviorally distinct from brothers) or distant brothers than with full siblings.

Nevertheless, the traditional extended family is a unit of considerable solidarity. In village affairs it frequently acts as a collectivity. Before the firm establishment of British law, the family as a whole bore the responsibility of making amends if one of its members committed a wrong against another person of the community. By the same token, a man's extended family was his first line of retaliation if a wrong were committed against him. Until quite recently, it was difficult to limit a fist fight to just two opponents.

The fundamental activities of the extended family are economic: the members form a labor pool; property and produce are pooled in providing for the common hearth; and the internal ranking scheme is primarily a means of organizing production and distribution. The women contribute a great deal to extended family living. They care for the children, keep the houses in order, prepare meals (which sometimes involves gathering firewood and vegetable greens), make mats, do most of the fishing, and collect shellfish, sea slugs, and the like. The women are organized as a co-operating labor unit, each contributing her part to the day's work. It is the role of the wife of the senior male to decide the daily work, and to delegate and apportion the labor accordingly. The most strenuous jobs, such as net fishing, generally go to the younger women, but the particular activities of any woman may vary from day to day.

The men also form a labor pool. The men's primary tasks are

gardening, housebuilding, and some fishing. In earlier times, the men of an extended family often formed a work unit for housebuilding, clearing land and firing it, digging irrigated taro patches, and planting and weeding gardens of yams, sweet potato, taro, and other crops. Nowadays, some of these tasks are done by suprafamilial organizations such as the village, although it is still common for members of an extended family to work together as a single labor group. When working as a unit the men are directed by the family head—father or eldest brother. But even when not working together, they act as members of a single production group since all their economic activities are directed toward providing for the entire family. On a given day any number of tasks might be apportioned among the men, such as planting, weeding, or harvesting certain gardens, bringing in food for the next day's meals or for a feast contribution, attending to business in the village or in another village, and so forth. The regulation and co-ordination of the men's daily activities is the most important function of the family head. At the morning meal, or perhaps the night before, he divides the day's work. Again, the heaviest burdens usually fall to the youngest. The younger sons and brothers are conceived of as the strong arms of the family; their primary duties are to serve and provide for their elders. The working sphere of the elders is generally confined to the village and its environs. Ideally, the head of a large extended family should do little other than supervise the division of labor, drink kava, and sleep. Actually he will often work in the gardens, since a knowledge of familial resources is required of him in order to co-ordinate the men's work properly and efficiently. When the family head is too enfeebled by age to work in the "bush," he must abdicate his position of leadership in favor of his oldest son.

The traditional extended family pools its property resources as well as its labor resources. Each mature man has a yam garden, taro patches, and plots of other plants which he calls his own, but the products are not his to dispose of. All gardens of family members are subject to the control (*lewa*) of the family head. He determines where and (formerly) when gardens are to be planted, when they are to be weeded, and when crops are to be harvested. Since the food produced is for a common hearth, and since control of the plots is centralized, the various gardens are in effect joint property. As one informant puts it, "We are planting for one pot. The gardens are separate, but they are as one garden. Any one of us can and does take without permission from any of these gardens." Very often the gardens of the extended family are quite close to each other. Extended families tend to plant gardens of each of the major crops in distinct areas, with no other family's gardens intervening in these areas.

The houses that make up the family compound are similarly owned. The husband of the married pair occupying each house is considered the house owner, but all houses in the compound are subject to the decisions of the family head as to who is to live in them, the rearrangement of occupants, and the like. Household animals, pigs and chickens, are today owned in the same way; they are considered the property of a man and his wife, but control over them can be exercised by the leader of the extended family. Nowadays, the extended family head and his wife occasionally have full possession and control of all domestic animals, and other married pairs in the group have none. I cannot say with certainty which of these usages is older. Productive property such as canoes or fishing nets may be considered personal goods, but use is shared throughout the family.

While simple pooling of goods is the major form of distribution within the family, there is also a type of distribution which operates specifically between individuals. Here rank considerations are important. Any goods or services needed by seniors may be demanded from juniors or, in the case of goods, taken from juniors without permission. By the same token, the great responsibility of seniority is to give aid to younger relatives when they are in need. However, such aid cannot be taken by a junior without permission, but must be humbly requested (*kerekere*). Goods and services thus flow both up and down the hierarchy. But the milieu in which goods are given by an elder to a junior is one which emphasizes the "weakness" and inferiority of the younger, whereas the transfer of goods from younger to elder emphasizes the latter's inherent rights of control. In neither case, however, is any return of goods expected.

As a solid social and economic unit, the extended family does not go on forever. When a man's sons start to raise families of their own, the extended family gradually begins to segment. When the family head becomes too old to visit the gardens, control over them passes to his eldest son, or in the immaturity of the son, to the head's younger brother. The old man and his wife will usually move out of their large house into a smaller one, and his successor takes over his house. By slow process, the family head is thus divested of former status and power. "His time is up," Moalans say, and he is literally waiting to die. By modern, missionary-influenced ethics, an old father or family head should be properly fed and cared for by his brothers and sons. Actually he sinks into a pitiable position; aboriginally, his family might have killed him (Williams and Calvert 1859:144). Today he is barely kept alive; his counsel is never sought, and he is more often considered silly (even when not senile) than wise. He has no place or contribution to make in the family or in the community. When the head of a large family dies, the segmentation of the group is imminent. If the family is small, the division will be delayed until some of the men have grown children, preferably married sons, so that the new families will have the necessary labor forces. The break-up of an extended family is signalled by the division of control over houses, division of coconuts (only a recent practice), and division of control over productive property. When the family splits, each married male comes into full possession of the house which he and his family have been occupying. The successor of the former leader, usually the eldest surviving son, will divide among the mature males the coconuts formerly used by the family as a whole. The principle governing the allotment of coconuts is that an equitable division be made according to need. The older brother is here still guided by the ethic that senior members of the group are responsible for the well-being of juniors. Occasionally, however, the prerogative of coconut allotment is abused by an older brother in his own favor, and hostility breaks out among the segmenting groups. Land as such is not divided, for the traditional extended family does not hold land privately. (Rather, land is held communally by larger social units of which families are constituent elements. Families and individuals hold usufructory rights in any land which they have cleared. Such rights cease when cultivation ceases, and the land is left to regain its fertility.) But while lands are not divided, the leader's unified control of family gardens is divided. Each of the heads of the segmenting components of the family takes over full control of the gardens which any member of his household cultivates. This decentralization of control produces the ultimate sign of segmentation, the building of new cook houses for each house group—the division of the common hearth. Each house group is now an independent unit. In each, the formation of an extended family begins anew. The various extended families so formed become bound in a larger social unit, *tokatoka,* united by common descent and led by the genealogically senior male. Eventually a tokatoka grows large, segments, and thus gives rise to a still larger descent group, *mataqali.* Tokatoka and mataqali are land-owning groups, and are of great social and political significance in the local community. However, a precise description of the nature and functioning of these groups would be outside the scope of this paper.

It should be kept in mind that this description of the traditional extended family is a generalized one. Exigencies of death, different ratios of daughters and sons, residence of a man in his wife's father's family, and other circumstances, may produce differences in the composition of family groups. But wherever the extended family occurs, it operates in the manner I have described.

FAMILY ORGANIZATION IN KETEIRA AND NAROI

Family organization has undergone considerable modification during the past century in Moala. However, the traditional extended family still predominates in one village in particular, Keteira. In other villages, such as Naroi, it is in the minority, having been largely replaced by independent nuclear forms of family. In this section, family composition in these two villages, Keteira and Naroi, is described in detail.

In analyzing Moalan family types, I shall use the term *nuclear family* to denote a group consisting of a married pair, with or without offspring, living in one house and exclusively using a nearby cook house. The exclusive use of a cook house is indicative of the economic and social independence of the nuclear family. *Nuclear core family* will be used for groups composed of a married pair, with or without offspring, and additional single relatives (of any kin category) of either spouse, exclusively occupying one living house and one cook house. *Extended family* will stand for the traditional extended family described in the last section. Extended families have nuclear constituents, but these share a common cook house and hence are not economically and socially independent. Table 2 summarizes the pertinent data on family composition in Naroi and Keteira.

Table 2. A comparison of family forms in Naroi and Keteira
(1954–1955)

	Naroi	Keteira
1. Number of People	340	115
2. Number of Independent Nuclear Families	11	1
3. Number of Independent Nuclear Core Families	18	2
4. Number of Extended Families	6	6
5. Total Number of Families	35	9
6. Average Number of People per Family	9.7	12.8
7. Percentage of People in Independent Nuclear and Nuclear Core Families	71.2	19.1
8. Percentage of People in Extended Families	28.8	80.9

The data indicate clearly that the traditional extended family remains dominant in Keteira, while in Naroi it has been superseded by nuclear and nuclear core families. The distribution of each type of family and the percentages of people living in extended families in the two villages offer the most striking evidence of this fact. Six of the nine Keteira families are extended, compared to six extended families of the 35 in Naroi. Over 80 percent of the Keteira population lives in extended families, compared to less than 30 percent so residing in Naroi. The extended family is the major form in Keteira and the minor form in Naroi.

Moreover, some of the extended families in Naroi are markedly unstable, which is not true of any in Keteira. For example, the large family of the paramount chief of Moala, composed of six nuclear families, has several times broken into small house groups for eating purposes. There has been considerable reshuffling of the nuclear components of these eating groups. Although food is still cooked in the cook house which serves the entire extended family, fish and other additions (*i coi*) to the basic vegetable diet are usually cooked separately by the women of each eating house group. Segmentation of this family into independent nuclear families has been discussed several times and seems imminent. In general, extended family life in Naroi is less serene than in Keteira. In Naroi, quarrels between women over proprietorship of cooking utensils and over the burdens of food preparation are common. These quarrels are quickly communicated to the men, who are often hard pressed to smooth things over.

The differential survival of the traditional extended family in these two villages gives an excellent opportunity to study not only the causes of its decay but also the factors which are necessary to its continued existence. I will undertake to do this in the following section.

LAND USE AND THE FAMILY
IN KETEIRA AND NAROI

It is frequently noted that primitive forms of extended family do not survive the process of acculturation to civilization. In many cases the emergence of independent nuclear families is a result of contact with European culture. Entrance into a money economy in particular has the effect of breaking down extended family customs of pooling goods and services. But this is not a sufficient explanation of what has occurred in Moala.

Naroi and Keteira are both subject to heavy influences from European culture, and are both becoming involved in the money economy of the Colony to a substantial extent. Naroi has two Chinese storekeepers and it is the main port of Moala, connecting by boat to European centers in Suva, Viti Levu, and Levuka, Ovalau. Keteira uses a Chinese-operated store in the village of Cakova, twenty minutes walk from Keteira. In some ways, Keteira has felt more European influence than Naroi. At any given time a greater proportion of Keteira people are visiting or working in Suva or Levuka than are Naroians. (The figures run roughly 20 to 30 percent of the married males of Keteira absent from the village as compared to five to 15 percent married Naroi men absent.) The Keteira school is better staffed than that of Naroi; more people of Keteira learn at least a smattering of English, as well as more of other tidbits of European culture. As copra is the main source of money for Moalans, an indication of the degree to which participation in a money economy has influenced production can be had by comparing the average number of coconuts planted per man per year in each village. In Naroi the average number of coconuts planted among 29 of the approximately 75 able-bodied men in 1954 was 114; in Keteira, the average among 17 of the approximately 25 able-bodied men was 181 coconuts. To the degree that these figures represent involvement with things monetary, Keteira cannot be said to be backward. Keteira is no less acculturated than Naroi and perhaps is more so, yet the traditional extended family has survived in Keteira. It can be concluded at this point that culture contact with Europeans per se does not cause the breakdown of the old family form.

Why has Keteira maintained the traditional extended family? The answer appears to be that Keteira continues to follow an old practice of exploiting land resources both near and at some distance from the village, and that the extended family is adapted to such a pattern of land use. In recent years, Naroi and most other Moalan villages have abandoned the practice of using distant lands and have confined agricultural activities to the village environs. It is in these villages that independent nuclear families have developed at the expense of extended families. (Quantitative evaluation of this trend can only be given for Naroi, but I have noted the same phenomenon in other villages which use only nearby land.)

To support this hypothesis, it is necessary to examine the traditional patterns of land use. Since prehistoric times the lands held by Moalan villages have not merely been concentrated around the settlement sites. Until quite recently, every village laid claim to and worked land so far away that farming necessitated the periodic and sometimes prolonged absence of the cultivators. Yam gardens, wet and dry taro gardens, and plots of other food plants were made in these distant lands. Huts were erected near the fields for shelter during the periods of clearing, planting, weeding, and harvest. Meanwhile, similar occupations were taking place in gardens near the village.

Villages obtained lands far from the settlement site by various means. The most common method was the retention of claims to land near former habitation sites. Moalan villages did not move frequently, but within a few centuries a village might occupy several sites. In time, it would come to be situated far from its old location, perhaps on another coast or side of the island. If, as was usually the custom, claims to land used in ancient times were maintained by periodic cultivation, a village came to hold widely dispersed areas of land. Traditions sometime assign defeats in war as the cause of village shifts, but even in this case a defeated village maintained land rights around the old settlement. Very rarely, victorious villages appropriated some land of conquered villages, giving them lands in distant areas.

Although Moala is small, land more than a mile or two from any village is apt to be relatively inaccessible. The interior of the island is hilly, the gradients are often quite steep, and the "bush" cover is thick; hence, a journey of even two miles inland is quite arduous and time consuming. Travel along the coast is also limited, for the rocky shore permits walking only at low tide, and only at high tide can a boat be poled along the fringing reef. Nor are the winds favorable for daily round trips from a village to distant points by sailing canoe. Due to these difficulties, land more than one or two miles from a village can be most effectively exploited if the producers remain near it overnight.

There are a number of reasons why Moalans frequently found it worthwhile to continue to exercise claims to land far from their villages. In some cases where villages have remained in situ for long periods, slash and burn agriculture resulted in deforestation of surrounding lands and replacement by a thick cover of reed (*gasau*), which lowers the soil fertility. The forest has a better chance of regaining its former density—and the soil has a better chance of being replenished with organic materials— around abandoned habitation sites. Claims to old village lands, therefore, are valuable.

A second reason for retaining distant lands is that they may be suitable for growing types of crops that cannot be as successfully cultivated in the vicinity of the village. As a result of differences in soils, topography, and rainfall, given parts of the island have variable potentials for the growth of different plants. For example, some villages today produce more than twice the poundage per capita of taro than do others because of superior facilities (water and topography) for irrigation. Yam yields vary in different villages because of differences of rainfall. Food gathering possibilities are different in various parts of the island. The lowly mussel, *Arca culcullaea concomerata* (*kai koso,* Fijian) is so abundant in the bay off Keteira that it is daily food in almost all seasons, whereas it is extremely rare in other villages.

Fish, edible sea slugs, crabs, and prawns are abundant only in particular locales. It is to the advantage of a village to hold lands in different areas of the island, thereby gaining access to soils of high potential for a number of crops and to a number of natural food resources.

The traditional Moalan extended family is well constituted for the tasks of production in different areas and for the uniform distribution of the diverse produce. The size of the family made it possible to release some members for work on distant fields without hardship for those left in the village. A man might take his wife with him to a distant garden, leaving his children to be cared for by others in the group. A common cook house and common meals, and centralized supervision of gardens ensure that the different foods will be shared among all members, regardless of their particular contribution to production. The family authority system permits the division and co-ordination of labor which is necessary for its multifarious and spatially separated activities. Even the usual provision that the hardest work goes to the younger members of the family is adaptive. Cultivation of distant gardens is thus undertaken by the youngest and strongest, while those older and weaker may carry out lighter tasks near the settlement—the elder men perhaps do no more than pull up crops for the daily meals. This type of family group is an ideal unit for working scattered resources without sacrificing any of the usual familial functions of child care, socialization, and the production of capable, mature members of the society. Proof of this contention is the fact that the traditional extended family has been maintained in Keteira, where the pattern of using distant lands still obtains, whereas it has broken down in Naroi, where only land around the village is used.

Naroi also continues to hold tenure to land far from its present site, not because cultivation is maintained there, but because the Government-sponsored Lands Commission in the 1930's confirmed Naroian ownership in conformity with traditional custom. But only Keteira, in contrast to Naroi and most other Moalan villages, still uses its distant lands. A large tract in the southeast of the island, called Qaliqali (area K', map), is extensively worked by all Keteira families. The area is claimed because of its proximity to an ancient village site of the major patrilineal descent group (*mataqali*) of Keteira. However, the use to which the land is presently put and the reasons for its continued exploitation are not traditional. Keteira retains an interest in Qaliqali because of the abundance of coconuts there, in contrast to the scarcity of these "money trees" around the village proper. The area in which Keteira is located has been a center of population concentration since prehistoric times, and as a result the environs of the village have been largely deforested by slash and burn agriculture. Although food plants can be grown with moderate success in this reed-covered area, coconuts do not thrive. For the all-important copra trade, Keteira continues to use Qaliqali. Due to excessive rainfall in Keteira Bay, many men (about one-third) also make their yam gardens in Qaliqali, and several have manioc plots there as well. The men of Keteira frequently go to Qaliqali for days or even weeks on end (especially during the customary May-June period of intensive copra preparation) to plant coconuts, make copra, or cultivate their gardens.

Naroi is situated in an area which has not been extensively occupied for a long period of time and which has not been so heavily deforested. The Naroi region, both near the coast and extending far upland, is planted with sufficient coconuts to take care of the villagers' needs. Because of this local supply, the Naroi people only infrequently visit their old village sites (areas N' on map). In fact, Naroians have not extensively cultivated the old sites for at least 30 to 40 years, despite coconuts growing there. Time which would otherwise be available for work in the vicinity of the ancient villages is nowadays largely consumed by copra production in Naroi. And food purchased from stores with copra money substitutes for any advantage that could be gained by growing certain crops, such as taro, in the old sites. Rarely do Naroians exercise their ancient land claims, and then only to augment the supply of copra in an emergency. Conditions in most other Moalan villages (besides Keteira) approximate those in Naroi, and hence there has been a general abandonment of the traditional land use pattern.

A calendar of the activities of the Keteira population during several weeks in May and June, 1955, will give some indication of their dependence on Qaliqali. These were weeks of intensive copra production. A tabu placed on the nuts had been lifted so that the men could earn money to pay the head tax required of all Fijians. The calendar may also indicate some of the advantages of extended family life in light of this pattern of land use.

1. Week beginning Monday, May 16, 1955.

Monday was the first exodus to Qaliqali for copra preparation. Most of those leaving traveled overland to Cakova and along the western shore (see map). Others poled around the southern part of the island. By Monday night, about one-half of the married men and their mature sons were at Qaliqali. A few women accompanied their husbands, but most remained in the village to care for their children and to make mats in preparation for an interisland trade scheduled for August. By Wednesday the village was even more deserted, as more of the men, after bringing in several days' food supply for the women, joined their fellows in Qaliqali. On Thursday night, only seven men remained in the village, one a school teacher and two who were too old for extensive travel. On Saturday most of the men returned from Qaliqali to provide food for the weekend and to attend Sunday church.

2. Week of Monday, May 23.

The pattern of movements this week was the same. Most of the able-bodied men left for Qaliqali Monday morning. Some were accompanied by their wives, but most of the women and children remained behind. A few married couples stayed at Qaliqali into the next week, but the rest of the people returned to Keteira on Saturday.

3. Week of Monday, May 30.

The same pattern as the previous two weeks.

4. Week of Monday, June 6.

This week most of the men delayed their departure in order to clean up the village in preparation for inspection by the Government chief (*Buli*) of the island. (These inspections are supposed to take place monthly, but they are frequently neglected.) Only a few men and boys could be spared for copra making during the early part of the week. The inspection was completed Thursday morning and most of the workers left immediately for the coconut area, returning on Saturday.

5. Week of Monday, June 13.

The same as weeks 1 and 2. By the end of this week the period of intensive copra preparation was over.

No movement of this type occurs in Naroi during these weeks. A few families (nuclear and nuclear core), whose coconuts are a mile or so from the village, do stay on their lands during this period. However, most remain in the village.

CONCLUSIONS

Comparison of family organization and patterns of land utilization in Keteira and Naroi reveals that the maintenance of the traditional extended family is dependent on strategic exploitation of productive lands distant from the village site. The Keteira extended family is adjusted to working spatially separated resources. The large size of the group, the internal ranking system and authority hierarchy, the centralized control of resources, the provisions for distribution of work on the basis of capability, and the sharing of property and food, all make it possible for the group to extend its productive operations over a large area and to distribute equitably the fruits of such production. Considered in this light, the fragmentation of the extended family after three or four generations is also understandable. Given sufficient time and patrilocal residence, each nuclear constituent of an extended family would normally expand to the point where the full complement of members necessary for carrying out extended family activities is present. By this time also, the burdens of food preparation and administration of the resources of an extended family composed of such large segments have become unwieldy. Thus there is no reason for an extended family to continue beyond three or four generations of common descent, and there is good reason for segmentation into a number of discrete families.

In Naroi, where only land in the environs of the village is productively utilized, the traditional extended family has no longer any raison d'être. Nuclear families can effectively undertake all necessary exploitative and distributive activities. With a land use pattern of this type, the influences of acculturation, especially involvement in a money economy, can be expected to hasten the disappearance of the extended family. Such indeed is the most plausible explanation of the demise of the traditional family system in Naroi. In Keteira the extended family maintains itself in the face of the encroaching money economy because the traditional land use customs have not been changed. On the contrary, the greater dependence upon money in the economy has confirmed adherence to the old practices of land tenure, since land near the village cannot support sufficient coconut growth.

That the Moalan extended family is adapted to the exploitation of scattered resources is a conclusion of great interest and possibly of more widespread application. The extended family does not characterize primitive society in every ecological situation or at every level of development. Differences in family forms are not only of themselves significant, but in view of their importance as determinants of kinship structure (Murdock 1949:153–54) the study of differences in family type assumes critical proportions in the field of social organization. It is hoped that this examination of the Moalan data provides an hypothesis that can be more generally applied in explanation of crucial variations in the family systems of the primitive world.

BIBLIOGRAPHY

Murdock, George P.
   1949 *Social structure.* New York: Macmillan.
Roth, G. K.
   1953 *Fijian way of life.* London: Oxford University Press.
Williams, Thomas, and James Calvert
   1859 *Fiji and the Fijians.* New York: Appleton.

22 EFFECTS OF CLIMATE ON
CERTAIN CULTURAL PRACTICES

John W. M. Whiting

IN THE COURSE of research at the Laboratory of Human Development during the last few years, it was discovered quite
unexpectedly that there is a biased geographical distribution of
societies in which boys are circumcised. They occur more commonly in tropical than temperate regions and more commonly
in the Old World than in the New World. This distribution is
shown in Table 1.

It can be seen from this table that genital mutilations are almost
entirely restricted to Africa and the Insular Pacific, which regions
are largely situated in the tropics. It should also be noted that
they do not occur in tropical South America. It is the purpose
of this paper to explore the possibility that certain ecological
factors may account in part for this biased distribution.

Two recent studies (Whiting, Kluckhohn, and Anthony 1958;
Burton and Whiting 1961) concerned with the function of male
initiation rites have shown that the circumcision of boys, particularly when it forms a part of such rites, is associated with
exclusive mother-infant sleeping arrangements, a prolonged postpartum sex taboo, and patrilocal residence. It is not appropriate
in this paper to discuss the various interpretations of these
associations (Burton and Whiting 1961; Young 1962) but simply
to report that they are strong enough to make the presence of one
or more of these customs in a society a good predictor of the
presence of circumcision in that society. An investigation of the

Reprinted by permission of the author and publisher from *Explorations in
Cultural Anthropology*, W. H. Goodenough, ed., pp. 511–44, New York:
McGraw-Hill, 1964.

Table 1. *Regional distribution of male genital mutilation**

Region	Absent	0–2 yrs	3–5 yrs	6–10 yrs	11–15 yrs	16–25 yrs	% present
Africa †	18	2	4	12	10	3	65
Eurasia	29	0	1	0	0	0	3
Insular Pacific	14	0	1	4	3	1	39
North America	39	0	0	0	0	0	0
South America	31	0	0	0	0	0	0

* The judgments used for determining the presence or absence of circumcision rites represent the pooling of scores from two sources—column 36 of the Ethnographic Atlas (Murdock et al. 1962:270) and judgments made at the Laboratory of Human Development. There was 83 per cent agreement on 53 overlapping cases. Where there was disagreement the sources were consulted, and if they were ambiguous the society was omitted from the sample. If one of the judgments was clearly correct, it was chosen. Cases in which Laboratory of Human Development scores have been chosen over those in the Ethnographic Atlas are presented in Table 9 with supporting evidence. The sample and method of choosing it are also presented in the introduction to Table 9.

† Societies classified by Murdock (1957) as belonging to the Circum-Mediterranean region have been placed in Africa if they are situated in the continent. Otherwise they have been placed in the Eurasian region.

possible functions of these three customs therefore provides a good starting point for this inquiry into the possible effect of ecology on certain cultural practices. If any of these customs can be interpreted as a solution to environmental problems peculiar to the regions of the world in which circumcision occurs, then their distribution among the regions of the world will be less mysterious.

The inquiry can be begun by considering the various arrangements for sleeping found over the world. The way a mother, father, and infant arrange themselves when they go to bed at night can be divided into four types, which may be defined as follows. The first one is familiar to the American middle class. In this type the father and mother sleep together in a double bed and the infant sleeps apart from them in a crib or cradle. Using M for mother, F for father, B for baby, and a hyphen to indicate separate beds, this type can be designated as MF-B. In most societies where this type is customary the infant's cradle is placed near the parental bed, but in rare instances, as often in our own society, the infant may be given a room of his own. The second type, the exclusive mother-infant arrangement (MB-F), is the one that was found to be so strongly associated with male initiation rites at puberty. In this arrangement the mother and infant sleep together in the same bed and under the same blanket while the father sleeps in a different bed—either at the other side of the room, or in a separate bedroom, or even in a separate hut. The third type (MBF) consists of a mother, a father, and an infant all sleeping together in one bed. In the fourth type (M-B-F) each member of the triad has a separate bed of his or her own.

It should be noted here that in certain societies in which polygynous marriages are the rule two arrangements may commonly occur. When a man first marries, he and his wife constitute a monogamous family. This couple may often sleep together until he acquires his second wife. Cowives apparently do not make good bedfellows, so some change in sleeping arrangements is necessitated. Under such circumstances the husband will either sleep apart from each of his wives or rotate between them, sharing a bed first with one wife and then with another. In the latter case, since we are concerned with the relation of parents to an infant, it should be pointed out that more often than not, a man will not sleep with any of his wives while she has a nursing infant, but will spend his nights with his other wife or wives. Thus, in polygynous societies we may have two common forms of sleeping arrangements, the monogamous which may be either MF-B or MBF, and the polygynous which is MB-F. More often than not in polygynous societies, however, husbands and wives sleep apart even when monogamously married.

The relative frequency of these four types of sleeping arrangements[1] is presented in Table 2. It can be seen from this table that an infant sleeps in bed with his mother in approximately two-thirds of the societies of the sample and does so exclusively in nearly half the societies.

It is reported in various ethnographies that the sleeping arrangements customary in a given society may be in response to tem-

---

[1] The judgments on sleeping arrangements were made at the Laboratory of Human Development. The agreement between independent judges was 80 per cent. The scores available for the present sample are presented in Table 9.

Table 2. *Relative frequencies of the four types of sleeping arrangements*

	Number of societies	% of total
Mother, father together; baby separate (MF-B)	28	20
Mother separate; father separate; baby separate (M-B-F)	19	14
Mother, father, baby together (MBF)	21	16
Mother, baby together; father separate (MB-F)	68	50
Total no. of societies	136	

perature. Thus Gusinde (1937:25) says of the Yaghan, "During sleep they move as close as possible to one another to give each other the benefit of their body warmth." Although we have found no such statement in an ethnography, perhaps members of a family sleep apart from each other in the tropics to keep cool. If sleeping arrangements are in fact differentially distributed by temperature, it might help solve the problem posed in this paper.

An estimate of the average winter and summer temperatures was therefore made for each society[2] and these scores were related to sleeping arrangements. Variations in summer temperature showed little relationship to sleeping arrangements, but winter temperature showed a striking association that is presented in Tables 3, 3a, and 3b.

Table 3. *The relation between winter temperature and the arrangements for sleeping among mother (M), father (F), and a nursing infant (B)* *

Winter temperature		Sleeping arrangements			
		MF-B	M-B-F	MBF	MB-F
Hot	(>68° F)	4	9	10	46
Mild	(>50° F)	0	1	5	16
Cool	(>32° F)	8	2	5	3
Cold	(<32° F)	16	6	1	4

* A hyphen separating any two persons indicates that they do not sleep under the same blanket.

---

[2] These scores were taken from a map of world surface temperatures (Finch et al. 1957: map 9), together with the latitude and longitude for each society as given in the World Ethnographic Sample (Murdock 1957) and the Ethnographic Atlas (Murdock et al. 1962). These scores have not been checked from ethnographic sources.

As can be seen from the tables, the simple hypothesis of sleeping arrangements as a method of temperature control is strongly
confirmed as far as the mother and father are concerned. They

Table 3a. Data from Table 3 rearranged to show the relation between
winter temperature and mother and father sleeping together (MF-B,
MBF).*

Winter temperature	% and 95% confidence limits for MF sleeping arrangements (MF-B or MBF)
Hot and mild	21% ⊢─┴─┤
Cool and cold	67% ⊢──┴──┤
$x^2 = 27.4$ $p < .001$	⊢────┴────┴────┤ 0% 50% 100%

* Winter temperatures have been combined into two classes and the
percentage of societies in which the mother and father ordinarily sleep
together has been indicated. Ninety-five per cent confidence limits have
also been indicated by a line under each percentage.

Note: In all the tables to be presented in this paper that show a
relation between two variables or customs, the significance of the
association is evaluated by the chisquare test. In addition, the percentage of cases in which a custom is observed is reported and the 95 per
cent confidence limits for that percentage have been indicated by a
line under the observed per cent. These confidence limits indicate that
we are 95 per cent confident that the "true" percentage lies somewhere
on this line. Thus, in the above case we are 95 per cent sure that in
societies where the winter temperature is hot or mild, a mother and
father will sleep together in not more than 31 per cent or less than 14
per cent of the time.

generally sleep together if the temperature falls below 50° F in the
winter and apart in climates where the temperature is continuously mild or warm. Rather unexpectedly, however, the
exact opposite is true for predicting whether an infant will sleep
in the same bed with his mother. In this case he does so in
climates with mild winters but does not when the winter temperature drops below 50° F. A closer look at the ethnographic data
suggests a reason for this. In every instance where an infant
sleeps apart from his mother he has his own cradle, crib, or
sleeping bag. Apparently this is a more effective means of ensuring
an appropriate body temperature for the infant than taking him

Table 3b. Data from Table 3 rearranged to show the relation between the mother and baby sleeping together (MB-F, MBF) and winter temperature.

Winter temperature	% and 95% confidence limits for MB sleeping arrangements (MBF, MB-F)
Hot and mild	85%
Cool and cold	29%
$x^2 = 41.89$ $p < .001$	0%　　　　　50%　　　　　100%

into the parental bed. Perhaps this is partly because an infant's sleeping hours do not correspond to those of an adult.

Thus, since exclusive mother-infant sleeping arrangements occur in warm climates, and since, as reported above, they have been shown in previous studies to be strongly associated with male rites involving circumcision, this helps solve the problem of the frequent occurrence of such rites in tropical regions. It accounts for their frequent presence in Africa and the Insular Pacific, where the winters are generally warm, and it accounts for the infrequent occurrence of such rites in Eurasia and North America, where the winters are cold, but it does *not* account for their absence in tropical South America. In other words, the results so far only partially explain the distribution of circumcision rites over the world. Perhaps a look at the other two customs found to be associated with circumcision, e.g., patrilocal residence and a long postpartum sex taboo, will help the dilemma of tropical South America.

Since no obvious hypothesis comes to mind that might account for a direct influence of the environment upon patrilocal residence, an indirect approach is indicated. Perhaps patrilocal residence is associated with other cultural variables which in turn are determined by ecology. Polygyny is one such factor. The reason for the association between polygyny and patrilocal residence has been suggested by Murdock (1949:206).

Polygyny is relatively inconsistent with the individualism under neolocal residence and with the high and independent position of women under bilocal residence, and it is practically impossible, except in the sororal form, under matrilocal residence. It is, however, particularly congenial to patrilocal residence, where women are isolated from their kinsmen and tend to be economically and socially inferior to men. Hence anything which favors polygyny likewise favors the development of patrilocal residence.

Table 4. *The relationship between polygyny and residence*

	Residence			
% polygyny*	Matrilocal and uxorilocal	Neolocal and bilocal	Avunculocal and virilocal	Patrilocal
High (over 30%)	1	4	12	30
Medium (16%–30%)	7	1	10	7
Low (1%–15%)	7	7	4	16
Monogamous	7	6	4	13

* The frequency of polygyny score was made at the Laboratory of Human Development, and based upon an estimate of the proportion of adult women of childbearing age who were polygynously married. Since this method gives a higher figure for polygyny than that used by Murdock (1949, 1957) 30 per cent rather than 20 per cent is used as a dividing point between high and limited polygyny.

Table 4a. Data from Table 4 rearranged to show the per cent and 95 per cent confidence limits of societies with patrilocal residence that also have high polygyny (over 30 per cent) compared with the per cent and 95 per cent confidence limits for patrilocal residence among societies where polygynously married women are less common.

Polygyny	% and 95% confidence limits for patrilocal residence
High	64%
Not high	40%
$x^2 = 6.75$ $p < .01$	0% 50% 100%

Murdock's insight is clearly supported by the sample used in this study as is shown in Table 4. If a society has a high frequency of polygyny (i.e., over 30 per cent of the women of childbearing age are polygynously married) then it is more likely (64 to 40 per cent) to have patrilocal residence than a society with a lower frequency of polygyny.

This association is interesting, but does not help solve the problem posed in this paper. There is no evident reason why polygyny should be better adapted to one type of environment than another. A further step is needed. Is there some indirect association between polygyny and the environment? What are the functions of polygyny?

Native theory suggests that polygyny may be an adjustment to a prolonged postpartum sex taboo. A Yoruba informant interviewed on the reasons of polygyny put it this way. "When we abstain from having sexual intercourse with our husband for the

Table 5. *The relation between the duration of the postpartum sex taboo and the proportion of polygynously married women of childbearing age in any society*

Postpartum sex taboo	Monogamy	Polygyny		
		Low (1–15%)	Medium (16–30%)	High (>30%)
Long (>1 year)	6	3	12	28
Short (<1 year)	23	29	12	19

Table 5a. Data from Table 5 rearranged to show the per cent and 95 per cent confidence limits of societies with a long postpartum sex taboo that have high (73 per cent) polygyny as compared with the per cent for societies with a short postpartum sex taboo.

Postpartum sex taboo	% and 95% confidence limits for high polygyny
Long	57%
Short	23%
$x^2 = 15.91$ $p < .001$	0% 50% 100%

two years that we nurse our babies, we know that he will seek some other woman. We would rather have her under our control as a cowife so that he is not spending money outside the family."

Sexual abstinence for two years following parturition seems unusually long. Perhaps the Yoruba informant was talking about an extreme instance. A look at the data on the duration of the taboo shows that this is not the case. Over one-third of the societies of our sample have a postpartum sex taboo of twelve months or more. Some evidence suggesting the generality of the Yoruba explanation of polygyny is shown in Table 5. It can be seen from this table that societies characterized by a prolonged postpartum sex taboo also tend to have a high frequency of polygynous marriage.

From Tables 4 and 5 it can be seen that there is a strongly patterned relationship between the three variables under consideration—a relation that can be interpreted as being a consequence of the following causal chain:

Long postpartum sex taboo → high polygyny → patrilocal residence

If this causal sequence is correct, a prolonged postpartum sex taboo becomes the best candidate for the solution to the problem of the distribution of circumcision rites.

Societies may be divided into two large categories with respect to the reasons given for the postpartum sex taboo. In many of the societies of the world there is a brief period following the birth of a child during which sexual intercourse is taboo, the reason given being that the mother's wounds occasioned by childbirth should be given time to heal before sexual intercourse is resumed. The remainder of the societies of the world are of greater interest to the problem at hand. In these societies abstinence following parturition is said to be practiced for the health of the infant rather than that of the mother and may last from one to four years, generally ending when the infant is weaned. The following quotation from a Hausa informant (Smith 1954:148) clearly expresses common ethnotheory for a long taboo.

A mother should not go to her husband while she has a child she is suckling. If she does, the child gets thin, he dries up, he won't be strong, he won't be healthy. If she goes after two years it is nothing, he is already strong before that, it does not matter if she conceives again after two years. If she only sleeps with her husband and does not become pregnant, it will not hurt her child, it will not spoil her milk. But if another child enters in, her milk will make the first one ill.

Statements such as this are frequently reported in ethnographies as native explanations for extended postpartum sex taboos. This strongly suggests that under certain conditions the demands of a fetus adversely affect either the quantity or quality of a nursing mother's milk. An inadequate protein diet is suggested as the necessary condition for pregnancy to have such an effect.

Although the evidence from medical research indicates that the quality of a mother's milk is probably not affected by inadequate amounts of protein in her diet, it is improbable that any of the subjects studied were pregnant (Ashdhir 1962). Conversely, studies of the effect of pregnancy upon lactation seem to be limited to animals. Therefore there seems to be no evidence to refute the hypothesis that if a mother with a diet inadequate in protein should become pregnant, her milk would be "spoiled" in some way, as the Hausa informant put it, and thus would endanger the health of her nursing child. It seems likely that a motive as powerful as this would be needed to induce a woman to forego sexual intercourse for two to three years.[3]

Further evidence in support of this hypothesis is provided by the geographic incidence of kwashiorkor in recent years. This

---

[3] Nomadism provides another and quite different reason for a postpartum sex taboo. In nomadic societies which have no means of carrying children such as a wagon, sled, packsaddle, or canoe, and in which the women have to carry infants unable to walk by themselves, some means of spacing children is required. Nine of the ten societies in our sample who were judged (Ethnographic Atlas, *Ethnology,* 1962, Vol. 1, No. 2, Col. 30) to have a nomadic band organization, but to lack a means of transport other than the mother's back, are reported to practice some method of spacing children. These methods consist of one or more of the following customs: a prolonged postpartum sex taboo, abortion, and infanticide. Infanticide alone or in combination with abortion is the most common method, accounting for four of the nine cases, whereas the postpartum sex taboo and abortion alone or in combination account for but three of them. The remaining two societies are reported to use all three methods. Infanticide is as efficient as a postpartum sex taboo for solving the problem posed by nomadism, but only the latter solves the problem of protein deficiency.

protein deficiency disease, which affects young children at or about the time of weaning, has received considerable attention, especially by the World Health Organization and the Food and Agriculture Organization of the United Nations. This has resulted in an active research program (see, for example, Brock and Autret 1952; Autret and Béhar 1954; Waterlow and Vergara 1956) the results of which are summarized in a recent issue of *Science* (Scrimshaw and Béhar 1961). Although the evidence strongly indicates protein deficiency as a primary cause of the disease, other factors such as caloric intake and possibly the absence of other nutrients may also be important. Furthermore, the geographic location of the societies listed in Table 6 suggests that the disease seldom occurs in parts of the world that are not both hot and humid.

Table 6. *Specific mortality rates, per 1,000 population, of children one to four years of age in selected countries (1955–1956).* (Scrimshaw and Béhar 1961)

Kwashiorkor rare or unknown	Mortality rate	Kwashiorkor common	Mortality rate
Argentina	3.8	Colombia	20.3
Australia	1.3	Ecuador	28.8
Belgium	1.6	Egypt	60.7
Canada	1.5	El Salvador	22.7
France	1.6	Guatemala	42.7
Japan	3.8	Guinea	55.4
Netherlands	1.2	Mexico	24.0
Sweden	1.0	Thailand	14.5
United States	1.1	Venezuela	12.5

The high incidence of kwashiorkor in tropical areas of high rainfall and low availability of protein is of importance to the present inquiry. If a prolonged postpartum sex taboo is a cultural means of reducing the frequency of this disease by both prolonging the nursing period and ensuring that the protein content of the lactating mother's milk is not reduced below the danger point, then this taboo should also occur in societies situated in the humid tropics with a food supply low in protein.

To test the above hypothesis, judgments as to the nature of the staple food were used as a rough estimate of the amount of protein available to a lactating mother.[4] Such judgments are available in column 7 of the Ethnographic Atlas (Murdock et al. 1962:115) and in columns 1–5 of the World Ethnographic Sample (Murdock 1957).

From these codes the societies of our sample have been divided into three major classes according to the protein value of their staple food. The rationale for this division is found in a food composition table in a bulletin put out by the Food and Agriculture Organization (Chatfield 1954:10–49). In this table animal proteins including fish and eggs, which vary from 22 per cent (seal and walrus meat) down to 8.4 per cent (pork), dairy products, which vary from 46 per cent (cheese) to 3.3 per cent (milk), and seeds, 27 per cent (squash) to 18 per cent (sesame) have been classed as high in protein. The cereals, which range from 13.8 per cent (whole-wheat flour) to 6.7 per cent (milled white rice) have been classified as providing a medium protein diet; while roots, varying from 2.4 per cent (yam) to 1.2 per cent (cassava), and fruit, 1.2 per cent (banana) to 1.1 per cent (breadfruit) are classified in the low-protein category.

From the above protein values and the judgments available in the Ethnographic Atlas, the societies of our sample were classified as follows:

1. *High-protein.* Societies in which hunting, fishing, gathering,[5] herding, or any combination of these subsistence activities were judged to be more important than agriculture.

2. *Medium-protein.* Societies in which agriculture was judged to be equal to or greater than hunting, fishing, gathering, and/or herding in importance, and cereal grain was judged to be the staple crop.

3. *Low-protein.* Societies in which agriculture was judged to be equal to or greater than hunting, fishing, gathering, and/or herding in importance, and roots or fruit were judged to be the staple crop.

---

[4] Although a more direct estimate of the amount of protein available in the daily diet was available for approximately half the societies of our sample (M. Whiting 1958), the Atlas scores were chosen since they enabled the use of a much larger sample.

[5] It was assumed that high-protein seeds, insects, eggs, and small animals formed a large part of the diet of most gatherers. Those societies who are primarily root gatherers will have been improperly classified.

A test of the assumption that low protein leads to kwashiorkor and kwashiorkor to a prolonged postpartum sex taboo to protect

Table 7. Per cent and 95 per cent confidence limits of societies with a long postpartum sex taboo for three degrees of availability of protein based upon an estimate of the protein value of their staple crop.

| Availability of protein | Duration of postpartum sex taboo | | % and 95% confidence limits for long postpartum sex taboo |
	Short (0–1 yr)	Long (>1 yr)	
High	47	15	24%
Medium	38	25	40%
Low	20	27	57%
$x^2 = 12.53$ $p < .01$			0% 50% 100%

the nursing infant from this disease is presented in Table 7. It can be seen from this table that there is some support for this hypothesis.[6] The proportion of societies with a long taboo increases as their protein availability decreases. Furthermore, the difference between the high-protein and the low-protein groups reaches statistical significance.

But the above association still does not tell us why this associated custom should have a biased geographic distribution. If the above findings are meaningful for the problem of this paper, then low-protein crops must be the staples in regions where circumcision is common, and high-protein crops the staples where it is rare. Since roots and fruits have long been assumed to be more common in the tropics than elsewhere, it was decided to discover if protein availability from the staple crop was related to climate.

---

[6] The relation of the incidence of kwashiorkor to postpartum sex taboo would, of course, provide a more direct test of the hypothesis under consideration. Ratings on the incidence of this disease could not be made from the ethnographic literature, however, on enough cases to make such a test possible.

To do this each society was coded for climate[7] from a map after Glenn T. Trewartha appearing in *Goode's World Atlas,* 10th ed., p. 8. In this map the climates of the earth have been divided into six categories and a number of subcategories based upon a combination of rainfall and temperature as indicated in Table 8.

From this table it appears that societies whose staple crop has been judged to be low in protein are most likely to be found in the rainy tropics (94 per cent). In contrast, only one-fourth of the high-protein societies are found in such a climate. Societies judged to be medium in protein availability are split 60–40 between humid tropical and other climates.[8]

It seems, then, that there is some evidence for a long causal chain leading from the rainy tropics to circumcision. Such a climate is conducive to the growing of low-protein root and fruit crops. A diet based largely upon such crops is assumed to lead to a high incidence of a protein deficiency disease called kwashiorkor. This, in turn, leads a mother to avoid getting pregnant while she is lactating, since this might reduce the already low protein value of her milk below the danger point and result in the illness of the nursing child. The avoidance of pregnancy in these societies without an alternative effective means of contraception is generally accomplished by abstinence, which leads the husband to seek another wife, and thus to the acceptance of polygyny as a form of marriage. Finally, there is some indication that polygyny is more compatible with patrilocal than other forms of residence. Since both a long postpartum taboo and patrilocal residence have

---

[7] Two independent coders agreed on 91 per cent of the judgments.
[8] The fact that the medium-protein group does not predict postpartum sex taboo needs some comment. A further analysis of this group of societies indicates that interaction of climate and protein should be taken into account. Tropical rainy climates in which cereal crops are the staple have greater likelihood of having a long postpartum sex taboo (55 per cent) than societies with a similar economy in other climates (18 per cent). The reason for this interaction is unclear, but the effect of heavily leached tropical soils upon the quality of food is a possibility. Another is suggested by the fact that for many of the tropical cereal-growing societies, maize is the staple crop. This cereal is reported to be lacking in certain amino acids which are necessary to health (Food and Agriculture Organization Report No. 9, 1953). Much more research must be done before these or other possible reasons can be pinned down.

been shown to be associated with circumcision rites, a second reason for the tropical distribution of such rites is suggested.

The absence of circumcision in tropical South America, how-

Table 8. *Distribution of availability of protein based on an estimate of protein value of the staple crop for societies situated in various climates*

Climate	Availability of protein		
	High	Medium	Low
Tropical rainy:			
Rain forest	5	8	29
Savannah	11	32	16
Dry climates:			
Steppe	9	3	
Desert	9	7	
Humid mesothermal	11	9	1
Humid microthermal	9	5	
Polar	4		
Undifferentiated highlands	4	3	2

Table 8a. Data from Table 8 rearranged to show the per cent and 95 per cent confidence limits of tropical rainy climates (combining rain forest and savannah) for each of three classes of protein availability based on the protein value of the staple crop.*

Availability of protein	% and 95% confidence limits for tropical rainy climates
Low	94%
Medium	60%
High	26%
$x^2 = 51.32$ $p < .001$	0% 50% 100%

* The direction of the table has been reversed in order to retain the three protein classes.

ever, still remains unexplained. By all odds this custom should be common in this area, and yet it is not. One of the South American societies of our sample, the Tucuna, were reported to have previously circumcised their boys. None do so now. Is there any reason for this strong exception to the findings of this paper?

In searching for the answer to this question, a look at the incidence in the rainy tropics of South America of the variables which predict circumcision might be useful. This search yields the following results. Although the frequency of exclusive mother-infant sleeping arrangements (65 per cent) is slightly low (see Table 3) it is not as far out of line with tropical societies in other parts of the world as are the other two predictors, patrilocal residence (21 per cent) and a long postpartum sex taboo (38 per cent) which are 57 and 59 per cent respectively among tropical societies in the rest of the world. The low frequencies of these latter two customs might be accounted for if tropical South America were high in the availability of protein. Such, however, is not the case. With the exception of a few hunters, gatherers, and fishers, most societies in this region live on low-protein roots and fruit. Furthermore, the incidence of kwashiorkor is reported to be high throughout the area.

Perhaps in the rainy tropics of South America some other cultural solution to the problem of protein deficiency has been discovered. That only 50 per cent of the societies in this region with a low-protein diet have a long taboo as compared to 70 per cent of low-protein societies in other tropical regions, although not striking, is at least suggestive.

The frequent occurrence of abortion in tropical South America is a possible explanation. This custom is an alternative to sexual abstinence (or effective contraception) as a cultural means of avoiding pregnancy during lactation. Fourteen of sixteen societies in this area on which we have data openly practice abortion, and in three of them married women do so if they have a nursing child. Furthermore, in many societies of this area there are professional abortionists. The data on abortion by married women for the purpose of spacing children is not well reported, but for the seventeen societies of our total sample which were judged to have such a practice, eleven were situated in the rainy tropics. Data are not available, however, for enough South American cases to be at all conclusive.

In summary, some ecological reasons for the biased geographical distribution of circumcision rites have been presented. Starting with the findings of former research that exclusive mother-infant sleeping arrangements, a long postpartum sex taboo, and patrilocal residence are associated with circumcision rites, it has been shown: (1) that exclusive sleeping arrangements are influenced by the winter temperature (see Table 3); (2) that a long postpartum sex taboo is influenced by protein deficiency which, in turn, is related to rainy tropical climates (see Tables 7 and 8); and (3) that patrilocal residence is associated with polygyny which is, in turn, associated with a long postpartum sex taboo (see Tables 4 and 5). The notable exceptions to these findings occur in South America. Analysis of the distribution of the customs predicting circumcision in this area suggests that abortion might possibly be an alternative to the long postpartum sex taboo as an adjustment to protein deficiency.

Although the above associations are for the most part statistically significant, a close look at any of the tables shows that there are many exceptional cases. Some of these are no doubt due to the operation of other factors which have not been taken into account in the study. Still others are due to coding errors. Some of these errors could have been corrected on the basis of a more thorough and careful assessment of ethnographic evidence. Other errors are due to inadequate reporting in the ethnographic sources. As is the case with all cross-cultural studies, the interpretations suggested in this paper should be followed up by intensive field studies in critical societies. Tropical South America is an obvious place for such a study.

It will be noted that the hypotheses are dependent on accurate assessments of climate, nutrition, and health. For the purpose of this paper crude estimates were used. For further research regarding this problem the assistance of specialists in these matters is indicated.

This study further suggests a method of attacking the knotty problem of causality. The correlational method used in cross-cultural research cannot, of course, show the direction of causation. It must rest upon other evidence suggesting the relative plausibility of one or the other assumption as to causal direction. In this study temperature and climate cannot be reasonably assumed to be the *effect* of a custom. Any association between a climatic variable and a custom can plausibly be interpreted either as an effect of climate upon the custom or as an effect of climate upon some other factor associated with such a custom. For example, in this paper it is not plausible to assume that exclusive mother-infant sleeping arrangements cause a warm winter, or that a long postpartum sex taboo causes a rainy tropical climate. Thus, it is the assumption of this paper that ecological variables determine the customs associated with them.

Frank Young (1962), in discussing the function of male initiation rites, has argued that they are caused by an exclusive male organization which is in turn caused by a "middle level" of economic production which he suggests may be in part determined by the physical environment. He interprets a long postpartum sex taboo and exclusive mother-infant sleeping arrangements as only very indirectly related to the environment since they are presumed to be a consequence of the interaction between the presence of exclusive male organization and polygyny. The close association between climate and both a long postpartum sex taboo and exclusive sleeping arrangements provides greater plausibility to the position taken by Whiting, Kluckhohn and Anthony (1958) and by Burton and Whiting (1961) that these customs are a cause rather than effect of male initiation rites involving circumcision, polygyny, and presumably also Young's exclusive male organization.

APPENDIX: SUMMARY OF DATA

The data used in this paper are presented in Table 9. Columns 1–5, 12 and 13 have been taken from the Ethnographic Atlas (Murdock et al. 1962) or the World Ethnographic Sample (Murdock 1957) in cases where the appropriate scores were not available in the former source. Since scores for the age of circumcision (column 5) and the duration of the postpartum sex taboo (column 13) were also available at the Laboratory of Human Development, these have been used to supplement the Ethnographic Atlas. Furthermore, in cases of disagreement between our scores and those presented in the Atlas, we have rechecked the sources and used whichever score seemed to be more strongly supported by the evidence. When no decision could be made, the case was omitted. If our scores were chosen over

the Atlas scores, documentary support has been supplied at the
end of the table. This has been done only if (1) the disagree-
ments were of more than one scale point, (2) between "present"
and "absent," or (3) between "present" and "not ascertainable."
All such cases are marked with an asterisk (*) in Table 9.

Two changes were systematically made in column 13. First,
coitus interruptus was scored as a sex taboo. Second, interval
3 was defined as ending at eleven rather than twelve months as
was the case in the Ethnographic Atlas. As a consequence the
scores for a few tribes judged to have a taboo of one year's
duration were changed from a 3 to a 4 rating. This has been
indicated by a double asterisk (**). There was a high agreement
(85 per cent) between the two sets of judgments when both
were made. A fairly large number of societies (27) however,
judged as nonascertainable in the Ethnographic Atlas, were given
a score by our judges.

The scores for infanticide and abortion (columns 14 and 15)
were largely made from abstracts published by George Devereux (1955) supplemented by ratings made at the Laboratory
of Human Development on a few additional societies. A systematic
search for information on these variables has not been made for
many of the societies of this sample.

The remaining scores were all made at the Laboratory of
Human Development. Reliability checks were made on all of
them, and the percentage of agreement varied between 75 and
95 per cent. In cases where two or more judges rated a society
and disagreed, discussed ratings were used.

The sample was determined by the availability of coded data.
It consists of all societies appearing either in Murdock's World
Ethnographic Sample (1957) or vol. 1 of his Ethnographic Atlas
(1962) on which coded data on either the age at circumcision
or duration of the postpartum sex taboo, or both these variables,
were available. This resulted in fifty-six of Murdock's (1957)
sixty culture areas being represented, which indicates a reasonable spread. On the other hand, North America and Africa
are probably overrepresented and the Circum-Mediterranean
underrepresented. The universe represented by this sample can
clearly be called into question. Although we do not believe the
findings would be substantially different if a random sample of

societies had been drawn, this is an empirical question which can be solved only when the customs under consideration are adequately described on a larger number of societies than is now the case.

The code for Table 9 is as follows:

Column 1.	Area: A, Africa; C, Circum-Mediterranean; E, East Eurasia; I, Insular Pacific; N, North America; S, South America.
Column 2.	Tribe.
Columns 3 and 4.	Latitude and longitude.
Column 5.	Age of circumcision: 1, birth to two weeks; 2, two weeks to two years; 3, two years to six years; 4, six years to ten years; 5, eleven years to fifteen years; 6, sixteen years to twenty-five years; 9, present but age not ascertainable; 0, absent.
Column 6.	Most common type of sleeping arrangement: M refers to mother, F to father, and B to a nursing infant. Persons represented by letters that are separated by a hyphen do not sleep in the same bed (e.g., in body contact or under the same blanket). In those societies in which there is a different arrangement for monogamous and polygynous households the latter has been indicated if the percentage of polygyny is high (i.e., over 30 per cent of the women of childbearing age are members of a polygynous household).
Column 7.	Winter temperature: hot, over 68°; mild, 50 to 67°; cool, 32 to 49°; cold, below 32°.
Column 8.	Type of climate: Af or Am – tropical rain forest, Aw – tropical savannah, B – dry climates, C – humid mesothermal climates, D – humid microthermal climates, E – polar climates, H – undifferentiated highlands.

Column 9.	Sleeping distance, mother-father, monogamous position: Distances are indicated according to the following code: 1, mother and father sleep in body contact; 2, mother and father sleep in the same room but not in body contact; 3, mother and father sleep in separate rooms; 4, mother and father sleep in separate huts in the same compound; 5, mother and father sleep in different huts in the same village; 6, mother and father reside in different villages. All ratings refer to the sleeping arrangement used while the mother has a nursing infant.
Column 10.	Sleeping distance, mother-father, polygynous position. (See col. 9 for code.)
Column 11.	Per cent polygynously married women: The actual percentage is given if it could be ascertained from census material. Otherwise, the percentage was estimated and coded L, low or 1–15 per cent; M, moderate, 16–30 per cent; H, high, over 30 per cent. O represents monogamy and P polyandry.
Column 12.	Amount of available protein: L, low; M, medium; H, high.
Column 13.	Duration of the postpartum sex taboo: 1, less than one month; 2, one month to six months; 3, over six months but less than one year; 4, one year to two years; 5, over two years. Coitus interruptus is coded as a postpartum sex taboo.
Column 14.	Infanticide: 1, infanticide is present, but whether it is used as a method of spacing children is not ascertainable; 2, infanticide is present, but not as a means of spacing children; and 3, infanticide is used by married women as a means of spacing children. The 0 rating indicates that infanticide is stated absent.
Column 15.	Abortion: See col. 14.

Table 9

(1)	(2)	(3)	(4)	(5)	(6)	(7)	(8)	(9)	(10)	(11)	(12)	(13)	(14)	(15)
Aa	Kung	20S	21E	0	..	Mild	B	..	..	..	H	2	3	·
	Nama	26S	18E	0	MB-F	Mild	B	2	4	L	H	2	·	1
Ab	Lovedu	24S	31E	5	MB-F	Mild	Aw	·	4	42	M	4	2	1
	Pondo	31S	30E	0(5)	MB-F	Mild	C	4	4	21	M	4	..	..
	Thonga	24S	32E	5	MB-F	Mild	Aw	2	4	66	M	4*	2	0
	Venda	23S	30E	6	MB-F	Mild	Aw	4	4	H	M	5*	·	2
Ac	Bemba	11S	31E	0(5)	MB-F	Mild	Aw	1	4	H	M	5*	2	1
	Ila	16S	27E	5°	MFB	Mild	Aw	·	4	H	M	5	·	·
	Lamba	13S	28E	0	MB-F	Mild	Aw	1	4	9	M	1	2	1
	Yao	13S	36E	4	MB-F	Mild	Aw	6	4	30	M	4	2	·
Ad	Chagga	3S	37E	5	MB-F	Mild	Aw	·	4	H	L	5*	·	3
	Ganda	1N	32E	0	M-B-F	Hot	Aw	2	4	62	M	4	2	·
	Gusii	1S	35E	4	MB-F	Hot	Aw	1	4	63	M	1	0	2
	Kikuyu	1S	37E	5	MB-F	Mild	Aw	4	4	32	M	2	2	·
	Nyakyusa	9S	34E	0	MB-F	Mild	Aw	4	4	61	L	4*	·	1
Ae	Bamileke	5N	10E	5	..	Hot	Af	·	·	..	M	4	·	·
	Fang	2N	12E	4	MB-F	Hot	Af	2	4	H	L	4	·	3
	Kpe	4N	9E	4(6)	..	Hot	Af	·	·	..	L	4	·	·
	Mongo	0	20E	4	MB-F	Hot	Af	·	4	H	L	4	·	3
	Rundi	3S	30E	0	MB-F	Mild	H	1	5	H	L	1	3	3
Af	Ashanti	7N	2W	0	MB-F	Hot	Aw	5	4	72	L	2	2	2
	Dahomeans	7N	2E	6(5)	MB-F	Hot	Aw	·	4	H	L	1	·	3
	Mende	8N	11W	4	MB-F	Hot	Aw	4	4	79	M	5*	·	2
	Nupe	9N	6E	4	MB-F	Hot	Aw	4	4	82	M	5	·	1
	Yako	6N	8E	0	..	Hot	Af	·	·	..	L	4	·	·

Table 9 (Continued)

(1)	(2)	(3)	(4)	(5)	(6)	(7)	(8)	(9)	(10)	(11)	(12)	(13)	(14)	(15)
Ag	Yoruba	8N	4E	1(6)	MB-F	Hot	Aw	3	3	29	L	5*	2	0
	Bambara	13N	7W	5	MB-F	Hot	Aw	2	4	H	M	5*	2	2
	Birifor	10N	3W	0	:	Hot	Aw	..	..	..	M	5	..	2
	Mossi	13N	2W	5	MB-F	Hot	Aw	4	4	60	M	5*	2	2
	Tallensi	11N	1W	0	MB-F	Hot	Aw	4	4	62	M	5	2	3
	Tenda	13N	13W	4	:	Hot	Aw	..	..	..	M	4	..	..
Ah	Katab	10N	8E	0	MB-F	Hot	Aw	4	4	41	M	5	2	2
	Tiv	7N	9E	4	MB-F	Hot	Af	2	4	49	L	4	2	2
Ai	Azande	5N	27E	4	MB-F	Hot	Aw	4	4	57	M	4	..	2
	Shilluk	10N	32E	0	MB-F	Hot	Aw	6	4	23	M	4	2	2
Aj	Dorobo	0	36E	6	MB-F	Mild	Aw	5	5	L	H	2*	..	..
	Lango	2N	33E	0	:	Hot	Aw	..	..	..	M	5*	..	2
	Luo	1S	34E	0	MB-F	Hot	Aw	4	4	H	M	2	..	2
	Masai	2S	36E	5	:	Mild	Aw	..	..	..	H	3	..	2
	Nandi	0	35E	5	:	Mild	Aw	..	..	..	M	2	..	..
	Nuer	8N	32E	0	MB-F	Hot	Aw	2	3	M	H	4	2	2
	Turkana	4N	35E	0	:	Hot	Aw	..	..	..	M	..	..	..
Ca	Amhara	12N	38E	1	MFB	Mild	H	1	4	L	M	2	2	1
	Somali	9N	49E	3	MB-F	Hot	Aw	2	4	L	H	2	1	2
Cb	Hausa	12N	9E	4	MB-F	Hot	Aw	2	4	59	M	4	2	2
	Songhai	17N	1W	3	MFB	Hot	B	1	1	L	M	2*	..	..
	Wolof	15N	17W	4(6)	MB-F	Hot	B	4	4	61	M	4	..	1
Cc	Tuareg	17N	5W	3	MB-F	Hot	B	2	·	0	M	2	2	1
Cd	Silwa	25N	33E	3	MFB	Mild	B	1	·	7	M	2	0	0
Ce	French	44N	4E	0	MF-B	Cool	C	1		0	M	1	..	..
Cf	Yankee	42N	72W	0	MF-B	Cold	D	1		0	M	1	0	2

Code	Society	Lat.	Long.		M-F-B	Temp.								
Cg	Lapps	68N	21W	0	M-F-B	Cold	E	2		0	H	2	0	0
Ch	Bulgarians	43N	23E	0	MF-B	Cold	D	1		0	M	2		
	Serbs	44N	20E	0	MF-B	Cold	D	1	3	0	M	1*		1
Cj	Rwala	33N	37E	3	M-F-B	Mild	B	3	4	M	H	2*	2	2
Ec	Ainu	44N	144E	0	MB-F	Cold	D	1	3	H	H	2	2	2
	Chukchee	66N	177E	0	MB-F	Cold	E	1	2	H	H	1	1	1
	Koryak	62N	164E	0	MF-B	Cold	D	1		19	H	2	2	2
	Samoyed	68N	75E	·	MF-B	Cold	D	1		L	H	1*	0	
	Yukaghir	72N	145E	0	··	Cold	E		5	··	H	1*		
Ed	Japanese	35N	136E	0	MB-F	Mild	C	2		L	M	1		2
	Lolo	27N	102E	0	·	Cool	C			L	M	1		
	Miao	28N	106E	0	MFB	Cool	C	1		0	M	5*	2	2
	Min Chinese	24N	115E	0	··	Mild	C			··	L	1		
	Okinawa	26N	128E	0	MFB	Cool	C	1		0	M	2	2	2
Ee	Burusho	37N	75E	·	M-F-B	Cold	B	2	2	L	M	1		
	Lepcha	29N	89E	0	M-F-B	Cold	H	1	4	35	M	2		
Ef	Bhil	22N	74E	0	MB-F	Mild	Aw	2	2	H	L	1		
Eg	Baiga	22N	81E	0	MB-F	Hot	Aw	2	2	33	H	*		
	Bhuiya	22N	85E	0	··	Hot	Aw			··	M	1		
	Chenchu	16N	79E	0	··	Hot	Aw	2		4	M	2	2	2
	Coorg	12N	76E	0	M-F-B	Hot	Am	3	6	L	H	1	0	0
	Gond (Maria)	21N	80E	0	M-F-B	Hot	Aw	1	3	8	H	2*	2	2
	Toda	12N	77E	0	MFB	Mild	B	1		P	M	1*	0	0
Eh	Andamanese	12N	93E	0(3)	MFB	Hot	Af	1		0	H	1		
	Tanala	22S	47E	0	MB-F	Mild	Af	1	4	33	M	2°		
	Vedda	8N	81E	0	;	Hot	Aw			··	H	1		
Ei	Burmese	20N	95E	0	MF-B	Hot	Aw	1	6	L	M	2		

Table 9 (Continued)

(1)	(2)	(3)	(4)	(5)	(6)	(7)	(8)	(9)	(10)	(11)	(12)	(13)	(14)	(15)
	Lakher	22N	93E	0	MFB	Hot	Am	1	·	·	M	M	1*	·	·
	Purum	25N	94E	0	··	Cool	C	··	··	··	··	M	2	··	··
Ej	Semang	5N	102E	0	MFB	Hot	Af	1	·	·	3	H	1*	·	3
Ib	Balinese	8S	115E	0	MB-F	Hot	Aw	2	5	·	L	M	2	·	2
	Javanese	7S	110E	5	··	Hot	Af	··	··	··	··	M	2	·	2
Ic	Alorese	8S	125E	·	MB-F	Hot	Aw	2	5	5	22	M	3	2	2
Id	Aranda	24S	134E	5	MB-F	Hot	B	2	2	2	H	H	1	3	3
	Murngin	12S	136E	4	MB-F	Hot	Aw	1	1	2	82	H	1	3	3
Ie	Arapesh	4S	144E	·	MB-F	Hot	Af	1	4	4	H	L	4**	·	··
	Kapauku	4S	136E	0	M-F-B	Hot	Af	3	3	3	32	L	1	·	2
	Keraki	9S	142E	0	··	Hot	Aw	··	··	··	··	L	3	·	··
	Kwoma	4S	142E	5	MB-F	Hot	Af	2	2	2	55	L	5	·	··
	Wogeo	3S	144E	6*	MB-F	Hot	Af	·	2	2	53	L	5	1	2
If	Chamorro	7N	145E	0	··	Hot	Af	·	·	·	0	M	1	·	··
	Marshallese	12N	165E	0	MB-F	Hot	Af	2	·	·	0	L	1	2	1
	Ponapeans	7N	158E	0	··	Hot	Af	·	··	··	··	L	2	·	2
	Trukese	7N	152E	0	MBF	Hot	Af	1	·	·	0	L	4*	·	3
	Ifaluk	7N	147E	0	MBF	Hot	Af	1	·	·	0	L	4**	0	··
	Yapese	9N	138E	0	··	Hot	Af	··	··	··	··	L	5*	0	·2
Ig	Kurtatchi	5S	154E	0*	MB-F	Hot	Af	2	4	4	50	L	4	··	··
	Lesu	3S	153E	4*	MB-F	Hot	Af	5	5	5	M	L	5*	·	1
	Malaita	9S	161E	0	MB-F	Hot	Af	4	4	4	L	L	2	·	··
	Siuai	6S	155E	0	·	Hot	Af	·	4	4	28	L	5	·	··
	Trobriands	8S	151E	0	MB-F	Hot	Af	2	·	·	38	L	4	2	1
Ih	Bunlap	16S	168E	3	··	Hot	Af	··	··	··	··	L	4	·	··
	Lau	18S	179E	4	M-F-B	Hot	Af	5	5	5	0(H)	L	4	2	2

	Tribe	Lat	Long		Type	Temp	Climate	3	4	O(H)		2*		
Ii	Ontong-Java	5S	160E	·	M-F-B	Hot	Af	·	·	··	L	2*	··	··
	Samoa	14S	170W	5	MBF	Hot	Af	1	2	··	L	4	0	2
	Tokelau	9S	172W	9	:	Hot	Af	1	·	P	H	5	··	··
Ij	Maori	24S	175E	0°	MF-B	Hot	Af	1	·	M	L	1	1	1
	Marquesans	9S	140W	4°	MFB	Hot	Aw	1	·	L	L	1	0	2
Na	Aleut	54N	167W	0	MF-B	Cold	D	1	·	O	H	2	2	·
	Copper Eskimo	69N	110W	0	MB-F	Cold	E	2	2	L	H	1	3	0
	Kaska	59N	128W	0	M-F-B	Cold	D	2	·	··	H	2	2	·
	Kutchin	67N	140W	0	M-F-B	Cold	D	2	·	··	H	1	··	·
Nb	Bella Coola	52N	127W	0	··	Cool	C	·	·	··	H	1	··	··
	Haida	54N	132W	0	··	Cool	C	·	·	··	H	5*	2	1
	Kwakiutl	51N	128W	0	MF-B	Cool	C	1	·	··	H	4*	·	1
	Tolowa	42N	124W	0	··	Cool	C	·	·	··	H	2	··	1
	Twana	48N	123W	0	··	Cool	C	·	·	··	H	2	··	··
	Yurok	41N	124W	0	M-F-B	Cool	C	5	5	M	H	3°	··	2
Nc	Atsugewi	41N	121W	0	··	Cold	H	·	·	··	H	1	··	··
	Diegueno	32N	116W	0	··	Mild	B	·	·	··	H	4**	··	··
	Miwok	38N	120W	0	··	Cool	C	·	·	··	H	2	··	1
	Tubatulabal	36N	118W	0	MF-B	Cool	H	1	·	O	H	2	··	1
	Yokuts	36N	120W	0	MF-B	Cool	B	1	·	L	H	2*	2	2
Nd	Klamath	43N	122W	0	MF-B	Cold	H	1	2	M	H	5	·	1
	Paiute	42N	120W	0	MFB	Cold	B	1	2	18	H	2	2	2
	Sanpoil	48N	119W	0	M-F-B	Cold	B	1	5	H	H	1	1	3
	Ute	40N	110W	0	MF-B	Cold	H	1	·	L	H	4	··	1
Ne	Walapai	35N	113W	0	MF-B	Cool	B	1	2	L	H	1*	2	3
	Cheyenne	39N	104W	0	MF-B	Cold	B	1	4	M	H	5*	·	3
	Crow	45N	108W	0	MF-B	Cold	B	1	2	M	H	1	2	2

Table 9 *(Continued)*

(1)	(2)	(3)	(4)	(5)	(6)	(7)	(8)	(9)	(10)	(11)	(12)	(13)	(14)	(15)
	Gros Ventre	49N	109W	0	..	Cold	B	..	..	..	H	2	1	..
	Teton	43N	103W	0	M-F-B	Cold	B	..	..	..	H	5*	..	2
Nf	Ojibwa	49N	91W	0	MF-B	Cold	D	1	2	M	H	4*	2	2
	Omaha	41N	96W	0	MF-B	Cold	D	1	.	0(L)	H	1*	2	2
	Pawnee	42N	100W	0	MF-B	Cold	D	1	2	M	M	1*	0	..
	Wichita	34N	98W	0	..	Cool	C	..	..	..	M	5	..	..
Ng	Creek	33N	84W	0	..	Cool	C	..	..	L	M	2*	2	2
	Delaware	40N	75W	0	MF-B	Cool	D	1	.	M	M	1*	0	2
	Micmac	46N	65W	0	MF-B	Cold	D	1	.	0(M)	H	2	..	3
Nh	Chiricahua	31N	108W	0	MB-F	Cool	B	2	2	M	M	5	..	..
	Cochiti	32N	115W	0	..	Mild	B	..	..	..	M	1	..	2
	Hopi	36N	111W	0	MF-B	Cold	B	1	.	0	M	2	2	2
	Navaho	37N	110W	0	MF-B	Cold	B	1	4	13	M	2	2	0
Ni	Papago	31N	112W	0	MFB	Cool	B	1	.	0(M)	M	1*	1	2
	Tarahumara	28N	107W	0	MFB	Cool	B	1	4	L	M	1	2	2
Nj	Mixtecans	17N	95W	0	MFB	Hot	Aw	1	.	0	M	1	..	2
	Tarascans	19N	101W	0	MB-F	Mild	H	2	.	0	M	2	..	2
Sa	Cuna	9N	78W	0	M-F-B	Hot	Af	2	2	L	M	1*	2	2
	Mosquito	13N	85W	0	MF-B	Hot	Af	1	2	L	L	1	2	1
	Talamanca	9N	83W	0	..	Hot	Af	..	..	..	M	2*	.	(0)
Sb	Cagaba	11N	74W	0	M-F-B	Hot	Aw	4	4	L	L	2*	.	1
	Callinago	15N	61W	0	MB-F	Hot	Am	2	5	M	H	2*	.	2
	Goajiro	12N	72W	0	MB-F	Hot	B	2	4	H	H	1	.	1
Sc	Bush Negro	4N	56W	0	MB-F	Hot	Am	4	4	H	L	4	.	1
	Carib	5N	59W	0	M-F-B	Hot	Aw	2	2	37	L	1	.	1
	Warrau	9N	68W.	0	..	Mild	Aw	..	..	.	H	2	.2	'

		Lat	Long												
Sd	Yaruro	7N	68W	0	MB-F	Hot	Aw	2	2	•	L	L	1*	•	•
	Tapirape	11S	52W	0	MB-F	Hot	Aw	2	2		0	L	4	2	•
Se	Siriono	16S	64W	0(1)	••	Hot	Aw	2	2	2	H	H	1	0	2
	Tucuna	3S	70W	0	••	Hot	Af	••	••	••	••	L	4*	•	1
	Witoto	1S	73W	0	MB-F	Hot	Af	2	2		0	L	5	•	•
	Yagua	3S	72W	0	MB-F	Hot	Af	2	2		0	H	3	•	1
Sf	Aymara	16S	69W	0	MFB	Cool	H	1	1		L	L	1*	•	1
Sg	Araucanians	39S	68W	0	M-F-B	Cool	B	1	1	2	58	M	4	2	0
	Ona	54S	69W	0	MF-B	Cool	C	1	1		M	H	1*	2	•
	Tehuelche	46S	70W	0	MF-B	Cool	B	1	1	•	L	H	4**	2	2
	Yaghan	55S	69W	0	MB-F	Cool	C	2	2	2	••	H	2	1	3
Sh	Abipon	29S	61W	0	••	Mild	Aw	••	••	••	••	H	5	3	3
	Caduveo	22S	57W	0	••	Mild	C	••	••	••	••	H	4*	3	3
	Mataco	24S	63W	0	MFB	Mild	C	1	1	6	L	H	2*	2	3
Si	Camayura	12S	54W	0	MB-F	Hot	Aw	2	2	2	18	L	•	3	3
	Nambicuara	12S	59W	0	MB-F	Hot	Aw	1	1	•	55	H	4*	•	1
	Trumai	12S	53W	0	MB-F	Hot	Aw	2	2	2	22	L	4*	3	2
Sj	Apinaye	6S	49W	0	MF-B	Hot	Aw	1	1		0	L	1	2	•
	Tenetehara	3S	46W	0	MB-F	Hot	Am	2	2	•	•	L	2	••	••
	Timbira	7S	45W	0	MBF	Hot	Aw	1	1		0	L	2	0	2

Note: In all cases ( ) indicate an assumed rating; a : indicates that the variable has not yet been researched, and a . indicates that from available data the variable is not ascertainable. For further details, see text.

DOCUMENTARY SUPPORT FOR TABLE 9

Ab Thonga
Ethnographic Atlas (1962) postpartum sex taboo (2) changed to 4:
"After the birth . . . sexual intercourse is prohibited till the rite of tying the cotton string . . . has taken place. It is then allowed, but conception must be avoided until weaning, when relations are resumed in the normal way . . ." [Junod 1927:188].

Venda
"The usual time for weaning . . . is when the child is 3 or 4 years old, and until that time the mother may not have another child" [Stayt 1931:94].

Ac Bemba
Ethnographic Atlas (1962) postpartum sex taboo (2) changed to 5:
"There is a strong taboo observed by all except urbanized natives on the conception of a new child before the weaning of the last. When the child is four months old, a special rite . . . is performed . . . and after this ceremony, *coitus interruptus,* may be allowed . . . but it is considered very dangerous for the mother to become pregnant before her first baby has been successfully weaned" [Richards 1939:67].

Ila
Ethnographic Atlas (1962) rating for circumcision (0) has been changed to 5:
"The passage from childhood to adolescence lies through the initiation ceremonies. . . ."
"Also they take away the *fraenum.* They tie tightly the hair of a wildebeest, and after a whole day and night it cuts through" [Smith and Dale 1920:12, 31].

Ad Chagga
Ethnographic Atlas (1962) postpartum sex taboo (2) changed to 5:
"Theoretically, intercourse is debarred dur-

ing lactation, but in practice *coitus interruptus* is resorted to among pagans" [Raum 1940:88].

Nyakyusa

"*Coitus interruptus* is practiced until the mother is ready to conceive again. 'Formerly it was taboo to make a woman pregnant before her previous child was four or five years old. . . .' Now she becomes pregnant again when the elder is two" [Wilson 1957: 131].

Af Dahomeans

Ethnographic Atlas (1962) postpartum sex taboo (3) changed to 5:
"Throughout the period of lactation, which lasts two years or longer, she [the mother] abstains from sexual intercourse" [Murdock 1934:579].

Yoruba

Postpartum sex taboo coincides with weaning (Whiting 1962).

Ag Bambara

Ethnographic Atlas (1962) postpartum sex taboo (2) changed to 5:
"They do not, and cannot, conceive but every two or three years . . . since every mother nurses her child for at least two whole years, and quite often three, and during all that time she may not conceive" [Henry 1910:188].

Mossi

Ethnographic Atlas (1962) postpartum sex taboo (3) changed to 5:
"The under-nourished natives must rely on the mother's milk to feed their babies and must therefore wait two or even three years before resuming sexual relations with a wife who is a nursing mother" [Delobsom 1932: 86].

Cb Songhai

It is not unusual for the wife to deny the husband intercourse for long periods of time following the birth of a child. Thus the husband must be contented with intercourse once every two weeks (after 40 days impurity) (Miner 1953:214).

Ch Serbs "All mothers nurse their babies, sometimes for as long as three years if another child does not come along. . . . The usual period for weaning is from 12 to 14 months" [Halpern 1958:172].

Cj Rwala "During her monthly period . . . the man must not touch the woman for from three to five days, and not for forty days after the birth of a child" [Musil 1926:231].

Ed Japanese "Haiki . . . represents the end of the birth period [30 days]. Before this time . . . theoretically the mother has had no sexual intercourse with her husband" [Embree 1939:183].

Ee Burusho "As soon as a woman is aware that she has conceived, she quits her husband's side . . . and not until their child is weaned will the couple mate again" [Lorimer 1939:189].

Eg Bhuiya Postpartum sex taboo coincides with weaning (Ethnographic Atlas 1962:542).

Toda "On the morning after the child has been born, the mother is removed to a shed. . . . There she remains till the next new moon. . . . For a month after her return home, she appears to have the house to herself: her husband remaining indebted to friends for shelter meanwhile" [Marshall 1873:69–70].

Eh Andamanese "It not infrequently happens that the two youngest children are seen together at their mother's breast" [Man 1932:13].

	Vedda	"Connection is not avoided during pregnancy, or for any considerable period after childbirth . . ." [Seligman 1911:102].
Ei	Lakher	"A child is suckled by its mother until such time as another child is born . . ." [Parry 1932:387].
Ej	Semang	"On the sixth day after giving birth the mother can return to her normal work. . . . The mother is given a decoction to drink by the midwife, apparently to prevent her conceiving again too rapidly" [Evans 1937: 245].
Ie	Wogeo	Ethnographic Atlas (1962) circumcision rating (0) changed to 6: "Initiation is carried out by means of a protracted series of rites, but of these the most important is the cutting of the boys' tongues. . . . This operation is performed when the boy is about fourteen years of age. He is not taught to incise his penis until several more years have elapsed . . . [Hogbin 1935:332].
If	Trukese	"Intercourse is not resumed until the child can move around a little; ideally this should not take place until the child is weaned or at least can walk . . ." [Gladwin and Sarason 1953:136].
	Yapese	Ethnographic Atlas (1962) postpartum sex taboo (3) changed to 5 (84 months) (Schneider 1957).
Ig	Lesu	Ethnographic Atlas (1962) circumcision rating (0) changed to 4: "The fact that the boys of a village are circumcised together when they are about eight or ten years of age, that they spend several months excluded from all females, that after

this they sleep in the men's house, must help set this pattern of age grouping among them" [Powdermaker 1933:87].

Ii Ontong-Java   "Until the baby is 6 or 7 months old, the men folk are very rarely permitted to hold it. If it is the first born, the father is secluded from both it and the mother for up to 12 months" [Hogbin 1931:603].

Ij Marquesans   "All the circumcisions . . . appear to have been performed at a single site. . . . The boys were circumcised in groups at the same time as the sons of chiefs. The age varied . . . ranging from seven to twelve years, but the operation was always performed before tattooing and apparently before puberty" [Handy 1923:96].

Nb Kwakiutl   Ideal postpartum sex taboo is over two years (Ethnographic Atlas 1962:283).

    Yurok   "Furthermore, there is an especial premium on the baby's early having strong legs and being eager to creep, for it is in the period between his birth and his first energetic creeping that the parents are forbidden sexual intercourse" [Erikson 1943:285].

Nc Yokuts   Postpartum sex taboo assumed to coincide with the cleansing ritual at three months after birth (Gayton 1948:233b).

Ne Cheyenne   "It was long the custom that a woman should not have a second child until her first child was about ten years of age." "To attain this goal contraception was definitely not used. . . . The Cheyenne technique was rigid sex abstinence fortified by a holy vow" [Llewellyn and Hoebel 1941:141–42].

Nf Ojibwa   " 'It was considered a disgrace to have children like steps and stairs.' 'If a man had sense he didn't bother his wife while a child was young.' 'Some had many children, but none had them like steps and stairs; the men and women kept away from each other.' 'I didn't live with my man as husband until the baby was able to walk'" [Hilger 1951: 4].

Pawnee

"On the first indication of labor the husband left the lodge and did not return to his wife for four days. . . ." "Should a woman die in childbirth or shortly thereafter, the death was generally ascribed to the violation on the woman's part of one of the taboos, especially the drinking of water, which was prohibited . . . until four days after delivery" [Dorsey and Murie 1940:39, 41].

Ng Delaware

"While nursing the child, the mother must refrain from intercourse with any man other than her husband . . ." [Tantaquidgeon 1942:37].

Ni Papago

". . . apparently most women take no contraceptive measures, and the taboo on intercourse for one month after childbirth no longer prevails" [Joseph et al. 1949:116].

Sa Cuna

"Sexual relations are taboo during pregnancy and menstruation. . . ." A number of postnatal taboos mentioned, but no taboo on sex mentioned (Stout 1947:39).

Sb Cagaba

Postpartum sex taboo until baptism; several weeks to several months (Reichel-Dolmatoff 1949–50:174, 177).

Callinago

"When the wives are delivered of child, the husbands separate from them and they do not sleep together for five or six months" [Breton and De la Paix 1929:13].

Sc Yaruro

"The food taboos continue in effect for the full month for both husband and wife. Strict continence is practiced by the husband. When the month is over the family is reunited" [Petrullo 1939:224].

Se Tucuna

"After the birth of a child, the husband avoids his wife for one year, more or less" [Nimuendaju 1952:70].

Sf Aymara

"Birth control techniques are not practiced . . . ." "The mother is confined to the house for a week after birth, during which her diet is restricted . . ." [Tschopik 1946:548].

Sg Ona

"After the delivery there was no prescribed bath in the sea or stream. . . . After delivery she abstained for about a month from certain foods, while the father ate lightly; but there was no couvade" [Cooper 1946: 120].

Sh Mataco

"You must not sleep with a woman whose child has not yet cut any teeth for the woman will lose her mind and as the child cannot eat alone he will die" [Métraux 1939:113].

Si Nambicuara

"Sexual relations are also, at least theoretically, forbidden between husband and wife from the birth of the child to the time when he can walk" [Lévi-Strauss 1948:73].

Trumai

"Part of the father's anxiety was doubtless due to the taboos which restricted his activity until his child had learned to walk. The most important of these was a ban on sexual intercourse" [Murphy and Quain 1955:79].

ETHNOGRAPHIC BIBLIOGRAPHY

Breton, R., and A. de la Paix
  1929 "Relation de l'Ile de la Guadeloupe," in J. Rennard (ed.), *Les Caraibes, La Guadeloupe, 1635–56. Histoire Coloniale,* Vol. 1. Paris: Librairie General et Internationale, p. 13.
Cooper, J. M.
  1946 "The Ona," in J. H. Steward (ed.), *Handbook of South American Indians,* Vol. 1. Washington: Smithsonian Institution, p. 120.
Delobsom, A. A. Dim
  1932 *L'Empire du Mogho-Naba: Coutoumes des Mossi de la Haute-Volta.* Institut de Droit Comparé, Études de Sociologie et d'Ethnologie Juridiques, Vol. 2. Paris: Les Editions Domat-Montchrestien, p. 86.
Dorsey, G. A., and J. R. Murie
  1940 *Notes on Skidi Pawnee Society.* Field Museum of Natural History, Anthropological Series, Vol. 27, No. 2, pp. 39, 41.
Embree, J. F.
  1939 *Suye Mura: A Japanese Village.* Chicago: The University of Chicago Press, p. 183.
Erikson, E. H.
  1943 *Observations on the Yurok: Childhood and World Image.* University of California Publications in American Archeology and Ethnology, Vol. 35, No. 10, p. 285.
Evans, I. H. N.
  1937 *The Negritos of Malaya.* New York: Cambridge University Press, p. 245.
Gayton, Anna H.
  1948 *Yokuts and Western Mono Ethnography,* Vol. 2. University of California Anthropological Records, Vol. 10, Berkeley: University of California Press, p. 233b.
Gladwin, T., and S. Sarason
  1953 *Truk: Man in Paradise.* Viking Fund Publications in Anthropology, No. 20. New York: Wenner-Gren Foundation, p. 136.
Halpern, J. M.
  1958 *A Serbian Village.* New York: Columbia University Press, p. 172.

Handy, E. S. C.
  1923 *The Native Culture in the Marquesas.* Honolulu: Bernice P. Bishop Museum Bulletin No. 9.
Henry, J.
  1910 "L'Ame d'un peuple Africaine. Les Bambara: Leur vie psychique, ethique, sociale, religieuse." *Bibliotheque-Anthropos,* Vol. 1, Fasc. 2, p. 188.
Hilger, M. Inez
  1951 *Chippewa Child Life and Its Cultural Background.* Bureau of American Ethnology, Bulletin 146, p. 4.
Hogbin, H. I.
  1931 "Education at Ontong Java, Solomon Islands." *American Anthropologist,* 33: 603.
  1935 "Native Culture of Wogeo: Report of Field Work in New Guinea." *Oceania,* 5: 308–37.
Joseph, Alice, Rosamond B. Spicer, and Jane Chesky
  1949 *The Desert People: A Study of the Papago Indians.* Chicago: The University of Chicago Press, p. 116.
Junod, H. A.
  1927 *The Life of a South African Tribe,* Vol. 1. New York: Macmillan, p. 188.
Lévi-Strauss, C.
  1948 *La Vie familiale et sociale des Indiens Nambicuara.* Paris: Société des Americanistes, p. 73.
Llewellyn, K. N., and E. A. Hoebel
  1941 *The Cheyenne Way.* Norman: University of Oklahoma Press, pp. 141–42.
Lorimer, Emily O.
  1939 *Language Hunting in the Karakoram.* London: Allen & Unwin, p. 189.
Man, E. H.
  1932 *On the Aboriginal Inhabitants of the Andaman Islands.* London: Royal Anthropological Institute, p. 13.
Marshall, W. E.
  1873 *A Phrenologist amongst the Todas.* London: Longmans, pp. 69–70.
Métraux, A.
  1939 *Myths and Tales of the Matako Indians (The Gran Chaco, Argentina).* Ethnological Studies, Vol. 9. Gothenberg, Sweden: Walter Kaudern, p. 113.
Miner, H.
  1953 *The Primitive City of Timbuctoo.* Princeton: Princeton University Press, p. 214.
Murdock, G. P.
  1934 *Our Primitive Contemporaries.* New York: Macmillan, p. 579.
Murdock, G. P., et al.
  1962 Ethnographic Atlas. *Ethnology,* 1: 288, 542.

Murphy, R. F., and B. Quain
  1955 *The Trumai Indians of Central Brazil.* Monograph of the American Ethnological Society, No. 24, p. 79.
Musil, A.
  1926 *The Manners and Customs of the Rwala Bedouins.* The American Geographical Society, Oriental Explorations and Studies, No. 6, p. 231.
Nimuendaju, C.
  1952 *The Tukuna.* University of California Publications in American Archeology and Ethnology, Vol. 45, p. 70.
Parry, N. E.
  1932 *The Lakhers.* London: Macmillan.
Petrullo, V.
  1939 *The Yaruros of the Capanaparo River, Venezuela.* Anthropological Papers No. 11, Bureau of American Ethnology, Bulletin 123, p. 224.
Powdermaker, Hortense
  1933 *Life in Lesu: the Study of a Melanesian Society in New Ireland.* New York: Norton.
Raum, O. F.
  1940 *Chaga Childhood: A Description of the Indigenous Education in an East African Tribe.* Fair Lawn, N.J.: Pub. by the Oxford University Press for the International Institute of African Languages and Cultures, p. 88.
Reichel-Dolmatoff, G.
  1949–50 "Los Kogi." *Revista del Instituto Ethnologico National.* Bogotá, No. 4, pp. 174, 177.
Richards, Audrey I.
  1939 *Land, Labour and Diet in Northern Rhodesia: An Economic Study of the Bemba Tribe.* Fair Lawn, N.J.: Pub. by the Oxford University Press for the International Institute of African Languages and Cultures, p. 67.
Schneider, David M.
  1957 Personal communication.
Seligman, C. G., and Brenda Z. Seligman
  1911 *The Veddas.* New York: Cambridge University Press, p. 102.
Smith, E. W., and A. M. Dale
  1920 *The Ila Speaking Peoples of Northern Rhodesia,* Vol. 2. London: Macmillan.
Stayt, H. A.
  1931 *The Bavenda.* Fair Lawn, N.J.: Oxford University Press, p. 94.
Stout, D. B.
  1947 *San Blas Cuna Acculturation: An Introduction.* Viking Fund Publications in Anthropology, No 9. New York: Wenner-Gren Foundation, p. 39.
Tantaquidgeon, Gladys
  1942 *A Study of Delaware Indian Medicine Practice and Folk Beliefs.* Harrisburg: Pennsylvania Historical Commission, p. 37.

Tschopik, H., Jr.
    1946 *The Aymara.* Bureau of American Ethnology, Bulletin No. 143, Vol 2, p. 548.
Whiting, Beatrice B.
    1962 Unpublished field notes, summer.
Wilson, Monica H.
    1957 *Rituals of Kinship among the Nyakyusa.* Fair Lawn, N.J.: Pub. by the Oxford University Press for the International Institute of African Languages and Cultures.

The following bibliography includes only those works specifically referred to in the text. For those judgments made at the Laboratory of Human Development from ethnographic sources, either the Human Relations Area Files have been used or, if the society has not been processed for the files, the sources listed in the Ethnographic Atlas have been consulted. In a few instances societies fulfilling neither of these qualifications have been included. In these cases the standard works have been used.

BIBLIOGRAPHY

Ashdhir, S.
    1962 "Human Milk Studies: Chemical Composition of Human Milk at Three Different Stages." *Indian Journal of Pediatrics,* 29: 99–109.
Autret, M., and M. Béhar
    1954 *Sindrome policarencial infantil (Kwashiorkor) and Its Prevention in Central America.* Rome: Food and Agriculture Organization of the United Nations, FAO Report No. 13.
Brock, J. F., and M. Autret
    1952 *Kwashiorkor in Africa.* Rome: FAO Nutritional Studies, No. 8.
Burton, R. V., and J. W. M. Whiting
    1961 "The Absent Father and Cross-sex Identity." *Merrill-Palmer Quarterly of Behavior and Development,* 7: 85–95.
Chatfield, Charlotte
    1954 *Food Composition Tables—Minerals and Vitamins.* Rome: FAO Nutritional Studies, No. 11.
Devereux, George
    1955 *A Study of Abortion in Primitive Societies.* New York: Julian Press.
Espenshade, E. B. (ed.)
    1957 *Goode's World Atlas,* 10th ed. Chicago: Rand McNally.
FAO [Food and Agriculture Organizations of the United Nations]
    1953 *Maize and Maize Diets: A Nutritional Survey.* Rome: FAO Report No. 9.

Finch, V. C., et al.
  1957 *Physical Elements of Geography.* New York: McGraw-Hill.
Gusinde, M.
  1937 *Die Yamana: von Leben und Denken der Wassernomaden am Kap Hoorn. Die Feuerland-Indianer,* Vol. 2, *Expeditions,* Serie 2. Müdling bei Wien: Anthropos, Bibliothek.
Murdock, G. P.
  1949 *Social Structure.* New York: Macmillan.
  1957 World Ethnographic Sample. *American Anthropologist,* 59: 664–87.
Murdock, G. P., et al.
  1962 Ethnographic Atlas. *Ethnology,* Vol. 1, Nos. 1–4.
Scrimshaw, N. S., and M. Béhar
  1961 "Protein Malnutrition in Young Children." *Science,* 133: 2039–47.
Smith, Mary F.
  1954 *Baba of Karo: A Woman of the Muslim Hausa.* London: Faber.
Waterlow, J., and A. Vergara
  1956 *Protein Malnutrition in Brazil.* Rome: FAO Nutritional Studies, No. 14.
Whiting, J. W. M., R. Kluckhohn, and A. S. Anthony
  1958 "The Function of Male Initiation Ceremonies at Puberty," in E. E. Maccoby, T. Newcomb, and E. Hartley (eds.), *Readings in Social Psychology.* New York: Holt, pp. 359–70.
Whiting, Marjorie G.
  1958 "A Cross-Cultural Nutrition Survey of 118 Societies Representing the Major Culture Areas of the World." Unpublished Ph.D. Thesis, Harvard School of Public Health.
Young, F. W.
  1962 "The Function of Male Initiation Ceremonies: A Cross-Cultural Test of an Alternative Hypothesis." *American Journal of Sociology,* 67: 379–96.

23 THE ECOSYSTEM CONCEPT AND THE PROBLEM OF AIR POLLUTION

Otis Dudley Duncan

LEVELS AND SYSTEMS

Aᴌᴌ ꜱᴄɪᴇɴᴄᴇ proceeds by a selective ordering of data by means of conceptual schemes. Although the formulation and application of conceptual schemes are recognized to entail, at some stage of inquiry, more or less arbitrary choices on the part of the theorist or investigator, we all acknowledge, or at least feel, that the nature of the "real world" exercises strong constraints on the development of schemes in science. Some schemes, used fruitfully over long periods of time, come to seem so natural that we find it difficult to imagine their being superseded. One type of scheme is deeply ingrained by our training as social scientists, to wit, the organization of data by *levels.* Kroeber (1952:66–67) is only voicing the consensus of a majority of scientists when he writes:

> The subjects or materials of science . . . fall into four main classes or levels: the inorganic, organic, psychic, and sociocultural. . . . There is no intention to assert that the levels are absolutely separate, or separable by unassailable definitions. They are substantially distinct in the experience of the totality of science, and that is enough.

MacIver gives substantially the same classification, but instead of using the relatively colorless term "levels," he chooses to segregate

Reprinted from "From Social System to Ecosystem," *Sociological Inquiry*, Vol. 31 (1961), pp. 140–49, by permission of the author and publisher. The first two paragraphs and the last sentence of the original article have been omitted.

the several "nexus of causation" into "great dynamic realms," (1942:271–72).

It is significant that scientists, insofar as they do accept the doctrine of levels, tend to work *within* a level, not *with* it. The scheme of levels does not itself produce hypotheses; it can scarcely even be said to be heuristic. Its major contribution to the history of ideas has been to confer legitimacy upon the newer scientific approaches to the empirical world that, when they were emerging, had good use for any kind of ideological support.

Quite another type of conceptual scheme, the notion of *system,* is employed by the scientist in his day-to-day work. Conceptions of interdependent variation, of cause and effect, or even of mere patterning of sequence, derive from the idea that nature (using the term broadly for whatever can be studied naturalistically) manifests itself in collections of elements with more than nominal properties of unity.

No doubt there are many kinds of system, reflecting the kinds of elements comprising them and the modes of relationship conceived to hold among these elements. The point about this diversity that is critical to my argument is this. When we elect, wittingly or unwittingly, to work *within* a level (as this term was illustrated above) we tend to discern or construct—whichever emphasis you prefer—only those kinds of system whose elements are confined to that level. From this standpoint, the doctrine of levels may not only fail to be heuristic, it may actually become anti-heuristic, if it blinds us to fruitful results obtainable by recognizing *systems that cut across levels.*

One such system, probably because it is virtually a datum of immediate experience, is rather readily accepted by social scientists: personality. Manifestly and phenomenologically an integration of nonrandomly selected genetic, physiologic, social, and psycho-cultural elements, personality has a kind of hard reality that coerces recognition, even when it can be related to other systems only with difficulty or embarrassment. If I am not mistaken, however, the concept of personality system enjoys a sort of privileged status. We do not so readily accede to the introduction into scientific discourse of other sorts of system concept entailing integration of elements from diverse levels. The resistance to such concepts is likely to be disguised in charges of "environmental determinism" or "reductionism." An example:

The working assumption of some human ecologists that the human community is, among other things, an organization of activities in physical space is criticized (though hardly refuted!) by the contention that such a conceptual scheme is contrary to "essentially and profoundly social" facts, i.e., "conscious choice of actors who vary in their ends and values" (Feldman and Tilly 1960:878). We must resist the temptation to comment here on the curious assumption that the "essentially and profoundly social" has to do with such personal and subjective states as "ends and values," rather than with objective relations among interdependent living units. (Surely the latter is the prior significance of the "social," in an evolutionary if not an etymological sense.) The point to emphasize at present is, rather, that such a reaction to ecological formulations is tantamount to a denial of the crucial possibility that one can at least conceive of systems encompassing both human and physical elements. The "dynamic realm" of the psycho-social has indeed become a "realm," one ruled by an intellectual tyrant, when this possibility is willfully neglected or denied.

THE ECOSYSTEM

Acknowledged dangers of premature synthesis and superficial generalization notwithstanding, ecologists have been forced by the complexity of relationships manifested in their data to devise quite embracing conceptual schemes. The concept of ecosystem, a case in point, has become increasingly prominent in ecological study since the introduction of the term a quarter-century ago by the botanist, A. G. Tansley. "The *ecosystem,*" according to Allee and collaborators, "may be defined as the interacting environmental and biotic system" (Allee et al. 1949:695) Odum (1953:9) characterizes the ecosystem as a "natural unit . . . in which the exchange of materials between the living and non-living parts follows circular paths." The first quotation comes from an enlightening synthesis of information now available on the evolution of ecosystems; the second prefaces an exposition of principles concerning the operation of "biogeochemical cycles" in ecosystems. Social scientists whose acquaintance with general ecology is limited to gleanings from the essays of Park (1952) or the polemic by Alihan (1938) might do well to inform themselves concerning current developments in ecological theory by consulting such sources as these. Even more readily accessible is the statement of Dice (1955:2–3):

> Ecologists use the term ecosystem to refer to a community together with its habitat. An ecosystem, then, is an aggregation of associated species of plants and animals, together with the physical features of their habitat. Ecosystems . . . can be of any size or ecologic rank. . . . At the extreme, the whole earth and all its plant and animal inhabitants together constitute a world ecosystem.

Later in his text (ch. xv) the same author undertakes a classification of "human ecosystems." This classification presents in elementary fashion much material familiar to social scientists; but it also conveys an unaccustomed emphasis on the "diverse relationships" of human societies "to their associated species of plants and animals, their physical habitats, and other human societies" (Dice 1955:252–53).

Popularization of the ecosystem concept is threatened by the felicitous exposition by the economist, K. E. Boulding (1958:14–16), of "society as an ecosystem." The word "threatened" is well advised, for Boulding uses "ecosystem" only as an analogy, illustrating how human society is "something like" an ecosystem. His ecosystem analogy is, to be sure, quite an improvement over the old organismic analogy. But ecosystem is much too valuable a conceptual scheme to be sacrificed on the altar of metaphor. Human ecology has already inspired a generation of critics too easily irritated by figures of speech.

If the foregoing remarks suggest that general ecologists have come up with cogent principles concerning the role of human society in the ecosystem, then the discussion has been misleading. Actually, the writing of Dice is exception as a responsible attempt to extend general ecology into the human field. Most biological scientists would probably still hold with the caution of Clements and Shelford (1939:1), that "ecology will come to be applied to the fields that touch man immediately only as the feeling for synthesis grows" (cf. Darling 1955a). There is abundant evidence in their own writing of the inadvisability of leaving to biological scientists the whole task of investigating the ecosystem and its human phases in particular. As a discipline, they clearly have not heeded the plea of the pioneer ecologist, S. A. Forbes (1922:90), for a "humanized ecology":

> I would humanize ecology . . . first by taking the actions and relations of civilized man as fully into account in its definitions, divisions, and coordinations as those of any other kind of organism. The ecological system of the existing twentieth-century world must include the twentieth-century man as its dominant species— dominant, that is, in the sense of dynamic ecology as the most influential, the controlling member of his associate group.

Symptomatically, even when discussing the "ecology of man," the biologist's tendency is to deplore and to exhort, not to analyze and explain. The shibboleths include such phrasings as "disruption," "tampering," "interference," "damage," and "blunder," applied to the transformations of ecosystems wrought by human activities. Such authorities as Elton (1958), Darling (1955b), and Sears (1957) state very well some of the dilemmas and problems of human life in the ecosystem (see also Darling 1955–56; Chapp 1955). They evidently need the help of social scientists in order to make intelligible those human behaviors that seem from an Olympian vantage point to be merely irrational and shortsighted. Insofar as they recommend reforms—and surely some of their suggestions should be heeded—they need to be instructed, if indeed social science now or ultimately can instruct them, in "The Unanticipated Consequences of Purposive Social Action."[1] If social science falls down on its job, a statement like the following will remain empty rhetoric: "Humanity now has, as never before, the means of knowing the consequences of its actions and the dreadful responsibility for those consequences" (Sears 1957:50).

ILLUSTRATION

Now, it is all very well to assert the possibility of conceptual schemes, like ecosystem, ascribing system properties to associa-

---

[1] Title of an early essay by Merton (1936); a recent statement, pertinent to ecology, is Firey's (1960).

tions of physical, biological, and social elements. But can such a scheme lead to anything more than a disorderly collection of arbitrarily concatenated data? I think the proof of the ecosystem concept could be exemplified by a number of studies, ranging from particularistic to global scope, in which some such scheme, if implicit, is nevertheless essential to the analysis.[2] Instead of reviewing a sample of these studies, however, I would like to sketch a problematic situation that has yet to be analyzed adequately in ecosystem terms. This example, since it is deliberately "open-ended," will, I hope, convey the challenge of the concept.

The framework for the discussion is the set of categories suggested elsewhere (Duncan 1959) under the heading, "the ecological complex." These categories, population, organization, environment, and technology (P, O, E, T), provide a somewhat arbitrarily simplified way of identifying clusters of relationships in a preliminary description of ecosystem processes. The description is, by design, so biased as to indicate how the human elements in the ecosystem appear as foci of these processes. Such an anthropo-centric description, though perfectly appropriate for a *human* ecology, has no intrinsic scientific priority over any other useful strategy for initiating study of an ecosystem.

The example is the problem of air pollution, more particularly that of "smog," as experienced during the last two decades in the community of Los Angeles. Southern California has no monopoly on this problem, as other communities are learning to their chagrin. But the somewhat special situation there seems to present a configuration in which the role of each of the four aspects of the ecological complex, including its relation to the others, is salient. I have made no technical investigation of the Los Angeles situation and have at hand only a haphazard collection of materials dealing with it, most of them designed for popular rather than scientific consumption. (The personal experience of living through a summer of Los Angeles smog is of value here only in that it permits sincere testimony to the effect that the problem is real.) The merit of the illustration, however, is that ramifying influences like those postulated by the ecosystem concept are superficially evident even when their nature is poorly understood

---

[2] The following are merely illustrative: Hallowell (1949); Thompson (1949); Anderson (1952); Cottrell (1955); Brown (1954).

and inadequately described. I am quite prepared to be corrected on the facts of the case, many of which have yet to come to light. I shall be greatly surprised, however, if anyone is able to produce an account of the smog problem in terms of a conceptual scheme materially *less* elaborate than the ecological complex.

During World War II residents of Los Angeles began to experience episodes of a bluish-gray haze in the atmosphere that reduced visibility and produced irritation of the eyes and respiratory tract (E→P); it was also found to damage growing plants (E→E), including some of considerable economic importance, and to crack rubber, accelerating the rate of deterioration of automobile tires, for example (E→T). In response to the episodes of smog, various civic movements were launched, abatement officers were designated in the city and county health departments, and a model control ordinance was promulgated (E→O). All these measures were without noticeable effect on the smog. At the time, little was known about the sources of pollution, although various industrial operations were suspected. By 1947, a comprehensive authority, the Los Angeles County Air Pollution Control District, was established by action of the California State Assembly and authorized to conduct research and to exercise broad powers of regulation. Various known and newly developed abatement devices were installed in industrial plants at the instance of the APCD, at a cost of millions of dollars (O→T).

Meanwhile, research by chemists and engineers was developing and confirming the "factory in the sky" theory of smog formation. Combustion and certain other processes release unburned hydrocarbons and oxides of nitrogen into the atmosphere (T→E). As these reach a sufficiently high concentration and are subjected to strong sunlight, chemical reactions occur that liberate large amounts of ozone and form smog. In particular, it was discovered that automobile exhaust contains the essential ingredients in nearly ideal proportions and that this exhaust is the major sources of the contaminants implicated in smog formation. It became all the more important as a source when industrial control measures and the prohibition of household open incinerators (O→T) reduced these sources (T→E). Also implicated in the problem was the meteorological situation of the Los Angeles Basin. Ringed by mountains and enjoying only a very low average wind velocity, the basin frequently is blanketed by a layer of warm air moving in from the Pacific. This temperature inversion prevents the polluted air from rising very far above ground level; the still air hovering over the area is then subject to the afore-mentioned smog-inducing action of Southern California's famous sunshine (E→E).

The problem, severe enough at onset, was hardly alleviated by the rapid growth of population in the Los Angeles area, spread-ing out as it did over a wide territory (P→E), and thereby heightening its dependence on the already ubiquitous automobile as the primary means of local movement (T↔O). Where could one find a more poignant instance of the principle of circular causation, so central to ecological theory, than that of the Los Angelenos speeding down their freeways, in a rush to escape the smog produced by emissions from the very vehicles conveying them?

A number of diverse organizational responses (E→O) to the smog problem have occurred. In 1953 a "nonprofit, privately supported, scientific research organization, dedicated to the solu-tion of the smog problem," the Air Pollution Foundation, was set up under the sponsorship of some 200 business enterprises, many of them in industries subject to actual or prospective regulatory measures. The complex interplay of interests and pressures among such private organizations and the several levels and branches of government that were involved (O→O) has not, to my knowl-edge, been the subject of an adequate investigation by a student of the political process. Two noteworthy outcomes of this process merit attention in particular. The first is the development of large-scale programs of public health research and action (O→P, E) concerned with air pollution effects (E→P). Comparatively little is known in this field of epidemiology (or as some research workers would say nowadays, medical ecology), but major pro-grams have been set up within the last five years in the U. S. Public Health Service (whose interest, of course, is not con-fined to Los Angeles) as well as such agencies as the California State Department of Public Health. Here is a striking instance of interrelations between medical ecology and the ecology of medicine illustrating not merely "organizational growth," as studied in conventional sociology, but also an organizational re-sponse to environmental-demographic changes. Second, there has been a channeling of both public and private research effort into the search for a "workable device," such as an automatic fuel cutoff, a catalytic muffler, or an afterburner, which will eliminate or reduce the noxious properties of automobile exhaust. California now has on its statute books a law requiring manufacturers to equip automobiles with such a device if and when its workability is demonstrated ($O \rightarrow T$).

Some engineers are confident that workable devices will soon be forthcoming. The Air Pollution Foundation has gone so far as to declare that the day is "near when Los Angeles' smog will be only a memory." Should the problem be thus happily resolved, with reduction of pollution to tolerable levels, the resolution will surely have to be intercepted as the net result of an intricate interaction of factors in the ecological complex ($P, O, T \rightarrow E$). But if the condition is only partially alleviated, how much more growth of population and increase in automobile use will have to occur before even more drastic technological and organizational changes will be required: redevelopment of mass transit, introduction of private electric automobiles, rationing of travel, limitation of population expansion, or whatever they may be? What will be the outcome of experience with increasing air pollution in other communities, whose problems differ in various ways from that of Los Angeles? And the question of questions—Is the convulsion of the ecosystem occasioned by smog merely a small-scale prototype of what we must expect in a world seemingly destined to become ever more dependent upon nuclear energy and subject to its hazards of ionizing radiation?

CONCLUSION

I must assume that the reader will be kind enough to pass lightly over the defects of the foregoing exposition. In particular, he must credit the author with being aware of the many complications concealed by the use of arrows linking the broad and heterogeneous categories of the ecological complex. The arrows are meant only to suggest the existence of problems for research concerning the mechanisms of cause, influence, or response at work in the situation so sketchily portrayed. Even the barest account of that situation, however, can leave no doubt that social change and environmental modification occurred in the closest interdependence—so close, in fact, that the two "levels" of change were *systematically* interrelated. Change on either level can be comprehended only by application of a conceptual scheme at least as encompassing as that of ecosystem.

The reader's imagination, again, must substitute for documentation of the point that smog, though a spectacular case and full of human interest, is no isolated example of how problems of human collective existence require an ecosystem framework for adequate conceptualization. I do not intend to argue, of course, that sociologists must somehow shoulder the entire burden of research suggested by such a conceptualization. Science, after all, is one of our finest examples of the advantages of a division of labor. But labor can be effectively divided only if there is articulation of the several sub-tasks; in scientific work, such articulation is achieved by employment of a common conceptual framework.

Sociologists may or may not—I am not especially optimistic on this score—take up the challenge to investigate the social life of man as a phase of the ecosystem, with all the revisions in their thought patterns that this kind of formulation will demand. If they shirk this responsibility, however, other disciplines are not unprepared to take the leadership. Anthropology of late has demonstrated its hospitality to ecological concepts (Bates 1953; Clark 1952; Steward 1955). Geography, for its part, cannot forget that it laid claim to human ecology as early as did sociology (Barrows 1923; Thomas 1956).

Of even greater ultimate significance may be the impending reorientation of much of what we now call social science to such concepts as welfare, level of living, and public health. Programs to achieve such "national goals" (to use the former President's language), like the studies on which such programs are based, are finding and will find two things: first, each of these concepts is capable of almost indefinite expansion to comprehend virtually any problem of human collective life; and, second, measures or indicators of status or progress in respect to them must be multifaceted and relational. Public health, to take that example, is surely some sort of function of all elements in the ecological complex; it is observable in any sufficiently comprehensive sense only in terms of interrelations of variables located at all levels of the ecosystem. Extrapolation of current trends over even a short projection period is sufficient to suggest the future preoccupation of the sciences touching on man with much more macroscopic problems than they now dare to set for themselves. It is perhaps symptomatic that spokesmen for the nation's health programs now declare that the "science of health is a branch of the wider science of human ecology" (President's Commission on the Health Needs of the Nation 1953:13), and that expositions of the problem of economic development have come to emphasize the necessary shift "From Political Economy to Political Ecology."[3] Even the literati proclaim that the "fundamental human problem is ecological" (Huxley 1959:302). (Cf. the similar remark of Kenneth Burke [1937:192]: "Among the sciences, there is one little fellow named Ecology, and in time we shall pay him more attention.") If one holds with Durkheim that the basic categories of science, as well as the interpretive schemes of everyday life, arise from the nature and exigencies of human collective existence, it cannot be long before we are forced to conjure with some version of the ecosystem concept.

---

[3] Title of an essay by de Jouvenel (1957).

Alihan, Milla Aissa
  1938 *Social Ecology: A Critical Analysis.* New York: Columbia University Press.
Allee, W. C., Alfred E. Emerson. Orlando Park, and Karl P. Schmidt
  1949 *Principles of Animal Ecology.* Philadelphia: Saunders.
Anderson, Edgar
  1952 *Plants, Man, and Life.* Boston: Little, Brown.
Barrows, H. H.
  1923 "Geography as Human Ecology." *Annals of the Association of American Geographers,* 13: 1–14.
Bates, Marston
  1953 "Human Ecology," in A. L. Kroeber (ed.), *Anthropology Today.* Chicago: University of Chicago Press.
Boulding, Kenneth E.
  1958 *Principles of Economic Policy.* Englewood Cliffs, N.J.: Prentice-Hall.
Brown, Harrison
  1954 *The Challenge of Man's Future.* New York: Viking Press.
Burke, Kenneth
  1937 *Attitudes Toward History,* Vol. 1. New York: New Republic.
Chapp, Donald F.
  1955 "Ecology—A Science Going to Waste." *Chicago Review,* 9: 15–20.
Clark, J. G. D.
  1952 *Prehistoric Europe: The Economic Basis.* New York: Philosophical Library.
Clements, Frederick E., and Victor E. Shelford
  1939 *Bio-ecology.* New York: John Wiley.
Cottrell, Fred
  1955 *Energy and Society.* New York: McGraw-Hill.
Darling, F. Fraser
  1955a "Pastoralism in Relation to Populations of Men and Animals," in J. B. Cragg and N. W. Pirie (eds.), *The Numbers of Men and Animals.* Edinburgh: Oliver and Boyd.

Darling, F. Fraser
1955b *West Highland Survey: An Essay in Human Ecology.* Oxford: Oxford University Press.
1955–56 "The Ecology of Man." *American Scholar,* 25: 38–46.

De Jouvenel, Bertrand
1957 "From Political Economy to Political Ecology." *Bulletin of the Atomic Scientists,* 8: 287–91.

Dice, Lee R.
1955 *Man's Nature and Nature's Man: The Ecology of Human Communities.* Ann Arbor: University of Michigan Press.

Duncan, Otis Dudley
1959 "Human Ecology and Population Studies," in Philip M. Hauser and Otis Dudley Duncan (eds.), *The Study of Population.* Chicago: University of Chicago Press.

Elton, Charles S.
1958 *The Ecology of Invasions by Animals and Plants.* London: Methuen.

Feldman, Arnold S., and Charles Tilly
1960 "The Interaction of Social and Physical Space." *American Sociological Review,* 25: 877–84.

Firey, Walter
1960 *Man, Mind and Land: A Theory of Resource Use.* Glencoe, Ill: The Free Press.

Forbes, Stephen A.
1922 "The Humanizing of Ecology." *Ecology,* 3: 89–92.

Hallowell, A. Irving
1949 "The Size of Algonkian Hunting Territories: A Function of Ecological Adjustment." *American Anthropologist,* 51: 34–45.

Huxley, Aldous
1959 *The Devils of Loudon,* Torchbook Edition. New York: Harper.

Kroeber, Alfred L.
1952 "So-Called Social Science," in Alfred L. Kroeber, *The Nature of Culture.* Chicago: University of Chicago Press.

MacIver, R. M.
1942 *Social Causation.* Boston: Ginn.

Merton, Robert K.
1936 "The Unanticipated Consequences of Purposive Social Action." *Amercian Sociological Review,* 1: 894–904.

Odum, Eugene P.
1953 *Fundamentals of Ecology.* Philadelphia: Saunders.

Park, Robert E.
1952 *Human Communities: The City and Human Ecology.* Glencoe, Ill: The Free Press.

President's Commission on the Health Needs of the Nation.
1953 *America's Health Status, Needs, and Resources. Building America's Health.* Vol. 2. Washington: Government Printing Office.

Sears, Paul B.
1957 *The Ecology of Man.* Condon Lectures. Eugene: Oregon State System of Higher Education.

Steward, Julian H.
  1955 *Theory of Culture Change.* Urbana: University of Illinois Press.
Thomas, William L., Jr. (ed.)
  1956 *Man's Role in Changing the Face of the Earth.* Chicago: University of Chicago Press.
Thompson, Laura
  1949 "The Relations of Men, Animals, and Plants in an Island Community (Fiji)." *American Anthropologist,* 51: 253–76.